I don't expect recognition while I live but if I thought I could write something that would go on living after I'm gone, I'd be satisfied with an attic and a crust all my life.

First photograph of Robinson to appear with a review of his poems, in the Critic, *March 1903, page 234. Ironically, it was captioned: Mr. Edward A. Robinson.*

COPYRIGHT 1974

by

COLBY COLLEGE PRESS

EARLY RECEPTION OF EDWIN ARLINGTON ROBINSON: THE FIRST TWENTY YEARS

RICHARD CARY

COLBY COLLEGE PRESS
WATERVILLE, MAINE
1974

PS
3535
.O25
Z618

CONTENTS

EDITORIAL MEMORANDA	1
PRELIMINARY VISTAS	3
GENESIS OF A POET	19

THE TORRENT AND THE NIGHT BEFORE (1896)

Introduction	23
Title Page	29
Contents	30
REVIEWS:	
Joseph E. Chamberlin, BOSTON EVENING TRANSCRIPT	31
INDEPENDENT	32
A Booktaster, TIME AND THE HOUR	34
NEW ORLEANS DAILY PICAYUNE	35
Nathan Haskell Dole, BOOKSELLER, NEWSDEALER AND STATIONER	36
GARDINER DAILY REPORTER-JOURNAL	38
R.H.B., DENVER TIMES	39
CHRISTIAN REGISTER	43
CHICAGO RECORD	44
CLEVELAND LEADER	45
Robert Steed Dunn, HARVARD MONTHLY	47
Harry Thurston Peck, BOOKMAN	49
William Morton Payne, DIAL	50
Edward Eggleston, OUTLOOK	52
BANGOR DAILY COMMERCIAL	53
William Peterfield Trent, SEWANEE REVIEW	54
Helen Archibald Clarke, POET-LORE	59
Edward Abbott, LITERARY WORLD	60
William Henry Thorne, GLOBE	61

THE CHILDREN OF THE NIGHT (1897)

Introduction	65
Title Page	70
Contents	71
REVIEWS:	
DAILY KENNEBEC JOURNAL	73
BOSTON EVENING TRANSCRIPT	73
LEWISTON SATURDAY JOURNAL	76
TIME AND THE HOUR	78
NEW YORK DAILY TRIBUNE	78
Edith Brower, WILKES-BARRE TIMES	79
CHRISTIAN REGISTER	86
John Hays Gardiner, BOSTON EVENING TRANSCRIPT	87
OUTLOOK	91
DENVER REPUBLICAN	92
NEW ORLEANS DAILY PICAYUNE	93
HARTFORD POST	93
CHAP-BOOK	93
William Morton Payne, DIAL	95
William Henry Thorne, GLOBE	96
William Peterfield Trent, SEWANEE REVIEW	100
Thomas Wentworth Higginson, NATION	100
ACADEMY	102
Vance Thompson, MUSICAL COURIER	102
Helen Archibald Clarke, POET-LORE	104
Edward Abbott, LITERARY WORLD	105

CAPTAIN CRAIG (1902)

Introduction	107
Title Page	114
Contents	115
REVIEWS:	
Horace Traubel, CONSERVATOR	116
NEW YORK EVENING SUN	117
BOSTON DAILY ADVERTISER	118
John A. Macy, CHICAGO EVENING POST	119
NEW YORK MAIL AND EXPRESS	122
BOSTON EVENING TRANSCRIPT	123
NEW YORK TRIBUNE	128
M.L.B.W., PORTLAND DAILY PRESS	129
LEWISTON JOURNAL	129
Frank Dempster Sherman, BOOK BUYER	131
Bliss Carman, READER	132
CHICAGO EVENING POST	134

GARDINER DAILY REPORTER-JOURNAL	135
Thomas Wentworth Higginson, NATION	139
BOSTON JOURNAL	140
William Morton Payne, DIAL	141
ARGONAUT	143
UNIDENTIFIED NEWSPAPER	144
CHICAGO TRIBUNE	144
INDEPENDENT	145
Clinton Scollard, CRITIC	148

Title Page: Captain Craig (1903) 151
  H.W. Boynton, ATLANTIC MONTHLY 152
  J.B. Kerfoot, LIFE 153
  NEWARK NEWS 154
  Trumbull Stickney, HARVARD MONTHLY 154
  Joseph Lewis French, NEW YORK WORLD 158

THE CHILDREN OF THE NIGHT (1905)

Introduction 165

Contents 168

Title Page 169

REVIEWS:
  Theodore Roosevelt, OUTLOOK 170
  BANGOR DAILY COMMERCIAL 173
  NEW YORK EVENING POST 174
  NEW YORK TIMES SATURDAY REVIEW OF BOOKS 177
  LEWISTON JOURNAL 178
  A.G. Chase, BOSTON SUNDAY GLOBE 180
  LITERARY DIGEST 182
  CURRENT LITERATURE 183
  UNIDENTIFIED PERIODICAL 183
  BOOKMAN 184
  Robert V. Hardon, BOSTON EVENING TRANSCRIPT 186
  BOSTON HERALD 187
  DIAL 187
  BOSTON EVENING TRANSCRIPT 188
  NEW YORK TIMES SATURDAY REVIEW OF BOOKS 189
  NEW YORK TRIBUNE 190
  BOOK BUYER 190
  CRITIC 191
  Joseph Lewis French, NEW ENGLAND MAGAZINE 191
  Mowry Saben, DENVER REPUBLICAN 193
  LOUISVILLE COURIER-JOURNAL 197
  MILWAUKEE EVENING WISCONSIN 197
  ARGONAUT 198
  Ferris Greenslet, NATION 198
  DETROIT FREE PRESS 199

John B. Henneman, SEWANEE REVIEW	199
Lillian Kendrick Byrn, BOB TAYLOR'S MAGAZINE	200
May Sinclair, ATLANTIC MONTHLY	201
T.P. O'Connor, T.P.'S WEEKLY	204
Edwin Markham, NEW YORK AMERICAN	206

THE TOWN DOWN THE RIVER (1910)

Introduction	208
Title Page	212
Contents	213
REVIEWS:	
BOOK BUYER	214
BOSTON DAILY ADVERTISER	214
William Stanley Braithwaite, BOSTON EVENING TRANSCRIPT	215
BOOK BUYER	219
POET-LORE	221
DENVER REPUBLICAN	221
CURRENT LITERATURE	222
BROOKLYN DAILY EAGLE	222
UNIDENTIFIED PERIODICAL	223
BANGOR DAILY COMMERCIAL	224
Richard LeGallienne, FORUM	225
NATION	229
NEW YORK TIMES REVIEW OF BOOKS	230
William Morton Payne, DIAL	231
INDEPENDENT	233
LITERARY DIGEST	234
OUTLOOK	235
Joyce Kilmer, NEW YORK TIMES REVIEW OF BOOKS	236
Louis V. Ledoux, NEW YORK TIMES REVIEW OF BOOKS	240
Harriet Monroe, POETRY REVIEW	243
Louis V. Ledoux, MINNEAPOLIS JOURNAL	244
Hermann Hagedorn, NEW YORK TIMES REVIEW OF BOOKS	246
Fred W. Thompson, BOSTON SUNDAY POST	247
Edwin Carty Ranck, BOSTON EVENING TRANSCRIPT	248
William Stanley Braithwaite, BOSTON EVENING TRANSCRIPT	251
BOSTON POST	256
Harold Trowbridge Pulsifer, OUTLOOK	261
Otto Frederick Theis, FORUM	262
LITERARY DIGEST	269

CAPTAIN CRAIG (1915)

Introduction	270
Title Page	274
Contents	275

Reviews:
    ROCHESTER HERALD   276
    BROOKLYN DAILY EAGLE   278
    Lincoln MacVeagh, NEW REPUBLIC   281
    NEW YORK EVENING SUN   284
    AMERICAN REVIEW OF REVIEWS   286
    Oscar W. Firkins, NATION   287
    Zoë Akins, REEDY'S MIRROR   288
    William Stanley Braithwaite, BOSTON EVENING TRANSCRIPT   289
    William Stanley Braithwaite, BOSTON EVENING TRANSCRIPT   293
    Louis Untermeyer, CHICAGO EVENING POST   295

Title Page: *The Man Against the Sky* (*1916*)   297

EPILOGUE   298

    Alanson Tucker Schumann, BOSTON EVENING TRANSCRIPT   301
    Percy MacKaye, POEMS AND PLAYS   302
    Louis Untermeyer, "——— AND OTHER POETS"   303

NOTES   305

INDEX: GENERAL   312

INDEX: ROBINSON'S WRITINGS   319

EDITORIAL MEMORANDA

FROM *The Torrent and The Night Before* in November 1896 to the posthumous *King Jasper* in October 1935, Edwin Arlington Robinson produced a score of new volumes of poetry, interspersed by as many revised and variant editions, collections and selections. At first published and distributed gratis by himself, then printed successively by virtue of neighbors' subsidies and under presidential persuasion of unconvinced editors, finally his books were sought after and brought out with éclat by one of America's most distinguished houses. His reputation with readers of poetry ran a parallel course. Overlooked or underrated in the beginning, he approached notability by excruciating, slow degrees, then suddenly vaulted to a zenith of regard, where he stayed to the day he died.

The change from relative anonymity to international fame as a poet occurred at precise midpoint in Robinson's career, after nineteen years of publication and with nineteen years to go. Wholesale acclaim followed the appearance of *The Man Against the Sky* early in 1916, bearing faint overtones of a Byron awaking. From that date onward Robinson attuned himself to the metronomic pattern of turning out a book a year to the combined hosannas of critics and public. Eleven of his fifteen offerings in this latter period were book-length narratives through which most of his readers in the Twenties and Thirties came to know him. Conversely, not one of his books issued during the first phase consisted wholly of one poem, not even *Captain Craig* which he had originally cast as such.

The consensus of recent literary criticism leans to the view that Robinson's finer accomplishment lies in the shorter works of his first twenty years as a poet, and that the longer writings of his second vicennial are not wearing as well despite their stronger initial acceptance. It is out of this consequence that the present volume evolved. Questions persisted. Why, when he was putting out his best poems, was Robinson consistently rebuffed by editors, disdained by critics, and virtually ignored by the reading public? Were editors mired in the vacuous standards of the times? Were critics blindered by old notions of admissible forms and substance? Did both fail to rouse somnolent readers to the fact of a vital new song unheard amid the clamor of moribund echoes? Since the private strategies of selection favored by dead editors are forever moot, at least partial answers to the puzzle of Robinson's prolonged, traumatic obscurity can be abstracted from the recorded opinions of contemporary critics and the impact they ostensibly conveyed. What they said and what they implied must certainly have influenced Robinson's failure to rise as rapidly as the quality of his early poems merited.

To that end is gathered in this volume every known review, interview, and essay pertaining to Robinson which was published between 1896 and 1916, excluding appraisals of his two plays, *Van Zorn* (1914) and *The Porcupine* (1915). Some seventy items are listed in Charles Beecher Hogan's *A Bibliography of Edwin Arlington Robinson* (New Haven, 1936) and William White's *Edwin Arlington Robinson: A Supplementary Bibliography* (Kent, Ohio, 1971). Personal search of fourscore periodicals and newspapers by the present editor has uncovered approximately ninety additional entries. Others indubitably exist in unexplored places, but for the purpose of this inquiry the compilation herein may serve as definitive.

Seven books were issued under Robinson's name during this interval, providing occasion for literary evaluation and other acknowledgment of his unremitting commitment to poetry: *The Torrent and The Night Before* (1896), *The Children of the Night* (1897), *Captain Craig* (1902), second edition (1903), *The Children of the Night*, second edition (1905), *The Town Down the River* (1910), *Captain Craig,* revised edition (1915). Each title is accorded a separate chapter in this volume, comprising (1) a preface detailing its genetic ordeals and publishing history; (2) reproduction of every discovered press notice; (3) documentation of all references and allusions in the reviews; (4) Robinson's own opinions of the poems under consideration and his occasional reactions to the critiques.

Texts are transcribed as rendered in the original publication, save for silent correction of obvious typographical errors and small adjustments of punctuation in the interest of clarity. Obsolete hyphenations or spellings are not modernized, but current convention is observed in regard to italics for titles of volumes and quotation marks for single poems. Since the number of blunders in these newspaper and magazine reviews is inordinate, all citations from the poems are copied literatim from the book under discussion, hopefully to spare Robinson further indignities and to preclude future misquotation. (Poems quoted in full in these reviews are indicated only by title in this volume if they are included in Robinson's *Collected Poems* of 1937 and subsequent reprints.) Misstatements are corrected in the notes; misleading statements remarked. Extracts from other authors, introduced by the critics, are identified. Where the writer of an anonymous or initialed article has been reliably ascertained, the full name is affixed without special markings.

The principal editorial objective, however, was to annotate these commentaries exhaustively, to adduce Robinson's relation to the critic or his response to the uttered judgment, and to juxtapose Robinson's own dicta on specified subjects, drawn from his conversations and correspondence. Through this method of (usually invidious) comparison, a perceptible grammar of intent and interpretation emerges. Each reader may thereby define the syntax and determine to his own satisfaction the decisive factors in the long languishment of Edwin Arlington Robinson.

PRELIMINARY VISTAS

The Cultural Ambience

The advent on the American literary scene of Robinson's slim, unassuming blue booklet precipitated no untoward groundswell. In a year when William Dean Howells, already revered as editor, critic-pundit, travel writer, and novelist, chose to make his debut as a poet with *Stops of Various Quills;* when Lizette Woodworth Reese brought out another bouquet of her crisp pastoral lyrics; when Emily Dickinson's *Poems: Third Series* memorialized the tenth anniversary of her death; when Bliss Carman and Richard Hovey offered *More Songs From Vagabondia,* and Paul Laurence Dunbar combined the best of two earlier books in *Lyrics of Lowly Life;* when Madison Cawein, Sam Foss, Eugene Field, Clinton Scollard, and James Whitcomb Riley came to market with new titles; and when Kipling's *The Seven Seas,* Housman's *A Shropshire Lad,* and Yeats's *Poems* were being imported bright from overseas, it is no wonder that a neophyte with some disturbing propensities could not divert the public ear to his especial resonance.

The incessant chorus of established poets in the daily and periodical press provided distraction from yet another quarter. The major names of that era are at best barely recognized by any except encyclopedists of American poetry. At the forefront of popular esteem were Edwin Markham, Riley, and Field; in the next echelon, Thomas Bailey Aldrich, Richard Henry Stoddard, Edmund Clarence Stedman, Scollard, Henry Cuyler Bunner, Cawein, Henry Van Dyke, Richard Watson Gilder, William Vaughn Moody; in contiguous flanks, Louise Imogen Guiney, Henry Underwood Johnson, Celia Thaxter, Louise Chandler Moulton, Edith M. Thomas, Frank Dempster Sherman, John Bannister Tabb, Edna Dean Procter; beyond them a numberless, faceless legion of foot soldiers of song. It was a fearsome babel to contend against.

The likes of Whitman, Dickinson, Bierce, and Stephen Crane would have to wait for later generations to discern their worth. In this period the keynote was a distant temple bell, the vista an incandescent twilight, the goal a castle in the air. The poetic product was hollow, torpid, exuding an aroma of perfumed decay. Immersed in conservatism, the vast bulk of verse exhibited inert homogeneity of form, effete reorchestration of worn themes, and a parlous dearth of unglossed emotion. Elegance was preferred over strength, archaism and Arcady over candor and realism. Diction was too florid or too pallid, and symbology groaned under a borrowed freight. The art of poetry at this time in America shrank to the status of an occupation. Hence Robinson's tortured Apollonian cry: "Oh, for a poet . . . / To rift this changeless glimmer of dead gray."

It may be accepted as axiomatic that the lulled Victorian audience got precisely what it wanted — and deserved (*vide* Whitman's apposite epigram, and Richard LeGallienne's slash at "the bad taste and general ignorance of the so-called 'reading public' "). Snug in the barmy, ormolu culture, the largely female component of poetry readers sought confirmation of its own chosen orbit, not turmoil of sensibility, not challenge of morality. In their professional capacity, if not by personal predilection, editors of aspiring newspapers, magazines, and publishing houses to some extent reflected this inclination to quiescence and conformity. Willy-nilly, the immense majority displayed a cognate myopia toward individual expression or other untidy innovation.

Critics who reviewed Robinson's earliest books were mostly of middling stature, thus presumably as susceptive to the prevailing ethos as were editors. It was not a brave age; few had the courage to extol experiment or endorse iconoclasm. Reviewers set their sights by the communal norms, measured the volume at hand against them, rendered judgments on a vertical scale, and routinely dismissed or derided departures. Preoccupied with classification by canon, they were apt to pass over significant fresh modulations without a word. Because Robinson adhered to traditional forms and meters, his whole poetic work was inanely assessed as yet another mimicry of tradition and matched — often pejoratively — with recent reputable usages. His muted revolution against extravagant imagery, artificial attitudes, sentimentality, remoteness, and orotundity, his interjection of psychological portraiture, objectivity, compactness of line, and unconfected idealism made no appreciable imprint on the aggregate critical consciousness. He did not go unnoticed, but it may be said that he was repeatedly noticed for the wrong reasons.

Literary Analogues

It is in the nature of literary critics to find in the work being considered certain resemblances, for good or ill, to works previously read. The continuum of the humanities is thus elongated and sometimes embellished, though the potential for distortion hovers dangerously over every nexus of this sort. Authors of all grades have suffered this autocratic coupling, so frequently a sly peepshow of erudition on the reviewer's part. Robinson bore more than his share, not without irritation, indignation, or moments of amusement. At the outset he may have had nobody to blame so much as himself. On the title page of *The Torrent and The Night Before* he emblazoned François Coppée's provocative quip, *"Qui pourrais-je imiter pour être original?"* It was bound to ruffle some feathers, most smartly Robert Steed Dunn's, who used the quotation as a flog against the poor devil author and called up an austere brace of masters under whom Robinson had palpably served "a healthy pupilship."[1] If other critics did not overreact to what Dunn saw as a deliberate taunt, it at least disposed them to sweep the reaches of their memory for plausible antecedents.

The number of Robinson counterparts detected by critics during his first twenty years as a poet is as alarming as the range and disparity. Over the course of his enforced apprenticeship Robinson's name was linked in review after review with those of more than thirty writers of every conceivable persuasion. In respect to philosophy, form, subject matter, style, mood, and consecration Robinson was compared directly or by implication with Thomas Bailey Aldrich, Matthew Arnold, Robert Browning, William Cullen Bryant, George Crabbe, Gabriele D'Annunzio, Emily Dickinson, Ralph Waldo Emerson, Erasmus, Thomas Gordon Hake, William Ernest Henley, A.E. Housman, William Dean Howells, John Keats, Rudyard Kipling, Maurice Maeterlinck, Stéphane Mallarmé, Andrew Marvell, George Meredith, Thomas Paine, Walter Pater, Percy Bysshe Shelley, Laurence Sterne, Algernon Charles Swinburne, Alfred Lord Tennyson, Francis Thompson, Émile Verhaeren, François Villon, Walt Whitman, John Greenleaf Whittier, Owen Wister, William Wordsworth, William Butler Yeats and the early Irish literary school. For good measure Robinson was several times lumped with the classical Greeks for lucidity, use of nature, and simplicity.

Not always did Robinson come off the worse for comparison. Indeed William Henry Thorne maintained that some of the sonnets and octaves in his first two books were "equal to the best that Keats and Shelley wrote," while John Hays Gardiner, more soberly, saw in the sonnets "a kind of natural realism of method which reminds one of Wordsworth." But adverse or judicious, the net effect of this continual critical joinery was to create the impression that Robinson's mode was a not altogether unpleasant blend of older, acceptable conventions. His guileless protestation — "I've never been conscious of the influence of any particular poet"[2] — availed him nothing. He once asked himself if John Donne were not "my poetical grandfather"; another time admitted to "a sort of internal affinity" with Heine and morosely wondered why "no one else seems to have thought of it."[3] Some of the far-fetched homologues he disowned out of hand. The critics went on pairing him indiscriminately.

Browning, Browning, Browning

Among the elect, the names of Emerson, Kipling, Tennyson, and Wordsworth rose most readily, but Robinson's ubiquitous *bête noire* turned out to be Robert Browning. Despite patent differences in their world-view, psychology, tone, diction, and imagery, no less than a score of public notices in the first two decades professed to see root similarities in these two poets, whose only substantial likeness lay in their copious use of dramatic monologue and duologue. Here again, overt structural appearance was embraced by Robinson's critics as the token of a poem's total depth and ramification.

Robert Steed Dunn, first of the long line to dovetail the names of Browning and Robinson, was exceeded in petulance by the anonymous reviewer of the New York *Evening Sun* who saw suggestions of *Sordello* and *The Ring and the Book*. Besides upbraiding Robinson for stooping to "bad examples," he demanded querulously, "Why can't Mr. Robinson be himself?" Thomas Wentworth Higginson objected to Robinson's losing "himself and his readers in regions of abstract thought," and Bliss Carman found "Captain Craig" *worse* than Browning. Yet, the majority intended the consociation to be laudatory. William Peterfield Trent espied "Browning-like verve," H.W. Boynton his "mental ingenuity," William Morton Payne his dramatic quality and sardonic humor. Theodore Roosevelt vaguely invoked "Childe Roland to the Dark Tower Came," while William Stanley Braithwaite placed it alongside "The Return of Morgan and Fingal." May Sinclair rated Robinson's "The Night Before" with "A Soul's Tragedy" for "imaginative insight, subtlety, and emotional volume." In Louis V. Ledoux's eyes Robinson's philosophy resembled Rabbi Ben Ezra's, except that the latter had a more pronounced optimism. Harold T. Pulsifer liked both poets' capacity to batter down walls of complacency. Braithwaite formed an explicit parallel of Robinson's sonnet portraits and Browning's monologues "as a medium of spiritual psychology."

Several commentators fell between two stools, conjuring Browning but in the next breath asseverating Robinson's independence, their common emollient, "no imitation implied." Most arrant of this Janus-type diplomat was Richard LeGallienne, who puffed Robinson's "very marked individuality" then deflated him as "none the less . . . markedly influenced." The *Argonaut* and even the exemplary Braithwaite sang the same dichotomous tune. No one mounted a positive remonstrance, although Carty Ranck did characterize Robinson as "not the kind of optimist that opens his window and shouts to the passing throng that 'God's in his heaven; all's right with the world,' " and Louis Untermeyer did put down derisively "the tribe of ticketers and pigeon-hole experts [who] name him the 'Browning of America.' " Not seven months after release of *The Torrent* Robinson was squirming under the onus of clientage, self-doubt, and self-defense.

> I have had this thing happen too many times. Not that I dislike Browning, but cannot help feeling that my own little efforts must leave, with the intellectual reader, an impression at least of unconscious imitation. . . . [What] makes so many people say the same thing. Is the resemblance in the style or in the thought? If it is in the style, I'm afraid there is no hope for me; if it is in the thought, I can only say that I write what is in me and let it go for what it is.[4]

Years later, as his reputation and the affiliation grew, Robinson ceased wearily to deny the imposed relationship. When reminded that he was called "The American Browning," he replied after an attenuated pause, "Well, people are likely to call you anything."[5]

Originality

It is part of the paradox of Robinson's twenty-year recognition gap that the quality most abundantly publicized in his early poetry was its originality. Affidavits to that point clearly outnumbered the charges of imitation yet failed to countermand their effect. Until the emancipating year of 1916, in fact, the benefits accruing to Robinson were essentially invisible. If anything, his insistent individuality rendered him suspect, a threat rather than a boon to entrenched propriety. Critics annunciated his fresh approach with conviction ranging from the hesitant to the vociferous, without accelerating his arrival by as much as a season. It was the momentum of the great reformation of American poetry in 1912 that actually caught him up and swept him across the barrier. For all his purposive vision, Robinson, like many another prophet, had to be carried into the promised land.

Reviewers at the lowest rung of approbation relied upon the dubious device of negative distinction. Joseph E. Chamberlin assured his readers that Robinson "isn't measuring the world according to somebody else's system," the New York *Times Saturday Review of Books* assigned him "little tendency to echo poets of a larger gift," and the Boston *Evening Transcript* said he sang "without a thought of imitation." Trent took a step up by titling his review "A New Poetic Venture" but two steps down by detecting "the influence of other poets in his work." Boynton applied the adjective "original" to *Captain Craig* and instantly retracted by declaring it had "little or no poetry." The most reflective of these indeterminate verdicts is the *Independent's* "A New Poetry," which goes on: "He has a temperament, an outlook, a poetic nature which are his own, not because he is outside all influence, but because he has assimilated them directly from the medium in which he lives, as the plant draws its nutriment immediately from its own inorganic surroundings." Heroically kind. Nonetheless, Robinson came off with a stain of sublimated plagiary. All of these critics sensed the advent of a pulsating force and all of them wavered in its presence.

Three lions of the time — Edward Eggleston, Edmund Clarence Stedman, Theodore Roosevelt — raised their voices in celebration of Robinson's originality with as slight results. (The glare of Roosevelt's presidency proved in the end to be much more helpful.) The New York *Evening Post* granted *Captain Craig* a certain "amorphous originality," and the *Outlook* commended Robinson for escaping "the strain of a deliberate and painful effort to be original" while successfully steering clear of the commonplace. In the modality of a theme and variations, the Brooklyn *Daily Eagle* extolled him for "doing his own work in his own way"; Otto Frederick Theis for working out "his own way uncompromisingly"; and Ferris Greenslet for being so "securely himself." With unalloyed directness Pulsifer called Robinson "the most individual of American poets."

In his probationary stage Robinson had humbly expressed the ambition "to be tolerably original."[6] A triad of critics saw fit to boost the pitch and vigor of his actual accomplishment. Joseph Lewis French designated Robinson's originality "striking"; the *Book Buyer* singled him among younger poets as "conspicuous for originality of thought"; Braithwaite labeled him "one of the very few and distinctively original notes in modern American poetry." The *Argonaut* vaulted over everyone in directness and degree: "He has absolute originality." The peril implicit in this crescendo may well have been a major determinant of Robinson's deferred recognition. The vibrations it loosed, so unlike the tinkling cymbalry of the day, inspired ominous connotations of a tocsin in a *fin de siècle* society wary of change. Epithets such as Edith Brower's "bold," "brave," "unconventional," or the Boston *Journal's* "utmost daring," "a new landmark" were not calculated to soothe the fears of boaters by the shore, fears that must have been aggravated by innuendoes from a profounder existence, felt but caged. With limited signification, the New York *Times Review of Books* exposed the heterodoxy: "[*The Town Down the River*] is addressing itself rather to a special than an average experience of understanding of life. That is to say, the book reveals a distinctly individual point of view and manner of feeling — something expressive of a small group more than of humanity at large." John A. Macy did not assuage the timid by dubbing Robinson "a revolter against the remote literary phrasing that has become so much a convention"; nor did the Chicago *Record's* report that he was "shattering many venerable and hitherto respected laws of versification."

As late as 1912, a rubric year for revelations in American poetry, Ledoux pondered the riddle of Robinson's delayed ascent. "In these days, when we are so prone to rush into the literary wilderness after some new thing, it is curious that work as strikingly original as Mr. Robinson's should not yet have become more widely known." The following spring Ranck, another estimable if volatile friend, also fretted over Robinson's plight the while testifying his uniqueness. "It has been a mystery to me why Mr. Robinson's work is not universally known. His poetry is ruggedly individual. There is nothing else like it now written in this country." It may therefore be accepted as unripe and ironic that in November 1912 the Minneapolis *Journal* should unveil a new trend in Robinson's role, "indications that his thoroughly original work may beget imitators." After the interminable allegations of undue "influence" on Robinson, how touching must have been this vindication of his faith. Poetic justice. He now had less than four years to wait before this foresight would emerge as fact.

Obscurity

When Harry DeForest Smith asked what one of his poems meant, Robinson ejaculated, "That's a hell of a question to ask a poet," and vouchsafed no answer.[7] Anent *The Torrent*, he wrote Miss Brower: "It never occurred to me that the poems would be considered obscure, but obscurity seems to be the strong point of my critics."[8] From the vantage of wearisome experience he reckoned, in 1927, that "about one in 1,000 reads poetry with a fair intelligence."[9] Robinson may be forgiven his cynicism in view of the massive miscomprehension his work encountered from the start. Only once in his first nineteen years as a published poet was he unprovisionally absolved from the accusation of obscurity: the Lewiston (Me.) *Journal* hailed "the clearness and elaboration of his thought" in *Captain Craig*. "He has a message and there is no groping in the light."

The next shading of judgment on this score came from critics who fundamentally denied the obscurity but, by their attendant diagnoses, affirmed its presence. Ledoux isolated the "cryptic quality . . . which has made Mr. Robinson a peculiarly difficult nut for the critical teeth to crack." Untermeyer deemed Robinson's poetic language "so over-chiseled at times that many, missing the long-familiar decorations, accused him of indirection and obscurity." Lincoln MacVeagh moved into subaqueous terrain: "his revelation, at the same time that it is complete, is so indirect and oblique that we may say he really never expresses himself, but rather symbolizes himself." John Gardiner attributed "the difficulty . . . to too great condensation [rather] than to any crudity and lack of pains in the expression."

A third grouping conceded the prevalence of obscurity but by way of abatement advanced an apologia. The *Argonaut* allowed, "True, he is obscure"; Theis, "the meaning is not always apparent at first glance"; and Higginson, "Obscure he may be and has a right to be." Respectively, they decreed that Robinson's "kernels of thought are worth earnest endeavor to find"; "The rich kernel is always there"; and "his thoughts are always worth consideration." Theodore Roosevelt beheld a certain nebulosity then quickly expounded, "it is not always necessary in order to enjoy a poem that one should be able to translate it into terms of mathematical accuracy."

Admitting the obscurity without clothing it in something like virtue, Pulsifer defined it as a fractional fault "which sometimes baffles even his most ardent admirers." The *Christian Register* hewed to the same line by first denouncing "The Torrent" as unclear after a fifth or sixth reading, then reneging — "But the poem is exceptional in this respect." Macy surmised that Robinson would "rid his work of obscurity" when he came "to the full power of plain speech." Two were less charitable in their modifications: Frank Dempster Sherman found that "some" of the poems would "baffle the most patient reader"; the *Literary Digest,* that "occasionally the meaning dives into complete obscurity."

The starched, academic mind of Oscar W. Firkins boggled at Captain Craig's "expansive introspective discourses." Firkins was simply "unable to follow [them] with any consecutive intelligence." To this kind of unregeneracy Robinson was particularly vulnerable. In naive bewilderment he had written to Miss Brower in December 1897: "To be honest, I must say that I was completely dazed when I was compelled to see that that blue book of mine was generally misinterpreted, for I thought it was as plain as daylight."[10]

Pessimism

The period 1890-1910 was one of constantly rising expectations in American economics and, according to Henry Miller, "an era . . . of cowlike bliss for the bourgeoisie." Pessimism, expressed in prose or verse, was not a popular philosophic stance. *Candide* was read as an amusing little fable, while Schopenhauer's grim picture of a world of unsatisfied wants had impact only on the minute intelligentsia. Revelations by Lombroso and Nordau of inhering human degeneracies achieved broad circulation, but they too failed to shake the beamish cast of mind of the times. The attribute "pessimism" applied to the work of a young writer could well deflect a substantial audience to less distressing fare.

While still a Harvard freshman Robinson had verbalized his essential vision of mankind's bent. "I used to think that I was a kind of pessimist, but I have outgrown that idea. The world as a whole is surely growing better and better, but there is yet an enormous field for improvement."[11] Within the same decade he spoke of "my incurable optimism" and described himself "a chronic optimist."[12] Any alert reading of *The Torrent* will endorse this overall conception. Nevertheless, the very second review of the book smeared it with dark pigment. Not alone did the *Independent* critic find Robinson's poems "all admirable illustrations of the modern order of pessimistic verse," he also implied the damnation of a stealthy, unhealthy trend. Following swiftly on the tracks of this impeachment came Harry Thurston Peck's famed thrust at Robinson's world as "a prison-house," which metaphor the poet vainly disowned in the next issue of the *Bookman*. And although Thorne of the *Globe* did not use the term "pessimism" in respect to *The Children of the Night,* he did wildly flail Robinson for lack of faith, hope, and love of God.

The first misreading of Robinson's *Weltanschauung* was promptly qualified within two weeks, Nathan Haskell Dole asserting the sonnets to be "full of strength and passion and — well, yes, perhaps pessimism, though they are too healthy to be really pessimistic." By way of completer repudiation, Edith Brower took Peck to task for his facile demarcation of *The Torrent*: "The most prominent of these notices dismissed Mr. Robinson as a pessimist; but the critic (?) must have had a curious idea of pessimism, or else he read superficially." In positive vein, the Boston *Evening Transcript* lauded Robinson's "hopeful aspiration," as did John Gardiner his "fine spirit of indomitable and determined cheerfulness" which "has little to do with the playing at pessimism and atheism" affected by "so many young poets of late." A.G. Chase could locate "not an element of morbidism" in *The Children of the Night* and "nothing but the brightest optimism and deepest faith" in the sonnet "When we can all so excellently give." The Milwaukee *Evening Wisconsin* in 1905 adopted the reasonable balance, hearing "a pessimistic strain for the most part, although here and there . . . the faith and hope which must sustain every man who fights the battle of life."

By 1912 any remaining uncertainties about Robinson's "pessimism" were effectively laid. After calling attention to the poet's bitter attitude and acrid expression, Payne conceded "his vision is transfigured with gleams of idealism"; Louis Ledoux reiterated Robinson's own boast of "incurable optimism" and cited his undertone of "hope in apparent hopelessness"; the Minneapolis *Journal* hooted "several foolishly superficial critics" who had misconceived Robinson's obviously "invincible optimism." Only Firkins continued in the perverse view, imputing a bogus streak to Robinson's upwardness. He condemned "these dismal incitements to cheerfulness" in "Captain Craig" (1915), and made sour epigram over "Isaac and Archibald": "Relieved of his optimism, Mr. Robinson becomes actually cheerful." Eighteen months earlier Robinson had summed up his egregious situation to Braithwaite: "I've been called a fatalist, a pessimist and an optimist so many times that I am beginning to believe that I must be all three." And in December of 1913 he delivered what he undoubtedly hoped might be the last words on the subject: "As a matter of fact, I suppose I'm the damnedest optimist that ever lived."[13]

Prospects and Prescience

Taken in a larger, rhetorical sense than was intended, the question posed by Robinson's inaugural reviewer was *the* most momentous for an outsetting poet. Less than two weeks after Robinson had propelled the first copies of *The Torrent* into the world outside Gardiner, Joseph E. Chamberlin of Boston asked: "Can this man do it?" The next nineteen years witnessed an ascending graph of response, not without indemnifying dips and wavers, yet surprisingly stable. Roughly 35% of the critiques during this period proclaimed Robinson's present or impending greatness. It would seem odd that the quantitative impact of these affirmations did not carry with it concomitant recognition for Robinson. But it must be remembered that the first truly unconditional certification from a notable source (the Boston *Journal*) did not come until the end of 1902 and that the bulk of these date from 1910 forward, when Robinson's hallmark had been set and he had behind him the tandem force of Roosevelt's favor and the bestirring wind of change in American poetry.

Before 1898 was out, Robinson's two books had elicited eight testimonials to his auspicious future, no fewer than four bandying the umbrageous term "promise." Helen Clarke, for instance, foresaw "plenty of promise" of future mastery, and the *Chap-Book* brightly titled its review "The Promise of Fame." The Boston *Evening Transcript* was "sure" that Robinson would "win his place and keep it among the true singers." John Gardiner had no doubt either, *when* Robinson "enlarges his experience and the scope of his effort"; Trent, *if* Robinson "goes on steadily devoting himself to his work." This corps of cautious believers was joined in 1902 by Bliss Carman, who felt that Robinson "will come to better things when he changes his purpose a little"; and by Higginson, as soon as Robinson would "follow his muse for a time, not direct it." Theodore Roosevelt undeniably inflated Robinson's public currency through the August 1905 *Outlook* article but, for all his ebullience, bowed out with faint heart: "Whether [Robinson] has the power of sustained flight remains to be seen." In this year and the following Joseph Lewis French and May Sinclair persevered in prognosticating "greater profundity of utterance" and a potential "great human drama" from this promising poet.

There were those in the first six years who examined Robinson's yield and beheld more than mere promise, though less than achieved primacy. Advance guard of this viewpoint, R.H.B. of the Denver *Times* placed *The Torrent* among the best of its kind for the year and declared Robinson "not only a young man of much promise, but a young man of great accomplishment." All in 1902, John Macy pronounced Robinson "worth watching" if still short of his "full power"; the Boston *Evening Transcript* reported fulfillment of his promise and evidence in "Captain Craig" that he could "handle large subjects" with "sure and steady hand"; and Horace Traubel abridged all the opinions that Robinson was on the verge of mastery. "Robinson," he blared, "you are almost arrived. But you have not arrived." A disciple of Whitman, Traubel blamed Robinson's retardation on the tautness and regulation of his prosody.

To a Maine newspaper, pardonably chauvinistic, must go the credit for first hailing Robinson — without ifs, buts or whens — as an enduring poet. In February 1897 the anonymous critic of the Bangor *Daily Commercial* stated unequivocally that the young author was "destined to more than passing fame." Nearly six years passed before the Boston *Journal* greeted him as "a new landmark in the world of books," and still another before Trumbull Stickney exulted: "So we have one poet more, one more of those men like us but more than we." French may be allowed on the perimeter of this elite company. In December 1905 he descried "flawless authority" and a "bid for immortality" in Robinson's work, but he diluted the heady draft with interjections of "perhaps" and "seems," and delimited the number of eligible poems.

From 1910 through 1915 a host of new-sprung prophets foregathered to trumpet Robinson's magnitude, but they were now of course only duplicating the wild surmise of their lonely predecessors upon that peak in Darien. Braithwaite preeminently, Ledoux, Hagedorn, Ranck, Pulsifer, Theis, and Untermeyer, as well as the unnamed reviewers in *Poet-Lore*, the Minneapolis *Journal*, the Brooklyn *Daily Eagle*, and the Rochester *Herald* bruited Robinson with unadulterated zeal as having "more than fulfilled the promise," as "one of the most distinctive and original notes in American poetry," as "one of the three or four foremost American poets," as "the most noteworthy living American poet," as "a truly great poet," as "destined to become a classic," as "to the manner born of the great lineage" of Shakespeare, Milton, and Wordsworth. At the end of 1912 Hagedorn glimpsed the beginnings of a rift in Robinson's beclouded status — "at last due recognition may come." He called Robinson "a very important figure in American literature" and advised Americans archly that "It might be excellent . . . if they found it out." In August 1915 Untermeyer, too, spotted Robinson "at last coming into his own . . . in a popular sense." It remained for Braithwaite to call the turn precisely. Six months before publication of *The Man Against the Sky,* he wrote: "I look forward confidently when his next book appears . . . to a general and popular acclamation of this great poet." And so it came to pass.

Before quitting the field of prevision, forethoughts on two minor matters are here convoked, the first because so right, the second because so wrong. Contemplating the fragile format of *The Torrent and The Night Before*, Nathan Haskell Dole was drawn to speculate about its extrinsic value: "I should not wonder if curiosity seekers should in future times pay high prices for the little treasure." Similarly the Bangor *Daily Commercial:*

"May not the copies of this 'little blue pamphlet' some day be as rare and sell for as high a price as Poe's *Tamerlane?*" It is a fact in the world of rare books today that Robinson's first, self-defrayed volume is as eagerly sought as Poe's first, self-defrayed volume, although the severer scarcity of the latter lends itself to proportionately steeper prices.

At the obverse angle of premonition, the Minneapolis *Journal* cited Robinson's "blending of pathos and humor" as "a quality that should make him eminently successful in the drama, should he yield to the easy temptation of that form as his genius for characterization by swift, subtle touches would lead one to suppose that he might." Unknown to the *Journal*, Robinson at this time (November 1912) had already drudged some six years at the composition of several plays, two of which were eventually published by Macmillan for reasons other than their qualifications as drama. Both were eminently *un*successful, *The Porcupine* never produced, *Van Zorn* given a week's performance at a Brooklyn Y.M.C.A.

Humor

No scholar has yet seen fit to isolate the styles and analyze the sensibility of humor employed by Robinson in the course of more than fifteen hundred pages of published poetry. It is a phenomenon of stolidity or astigmatism in his reviewers of the first twenty years that only three — Gardiner, Boynton, and Ledoux — took commensurate note of this quality of Robinson's mind and its effect on the totality of his art. Seventeen others gave it passing mention, providing little beyond mere habitation and a name.

The Torrent and The Night Before, admittedly rather somber, extracted two comments, both negative. The Denver *Times* scolded Robinson for excess of earnestness, unrelieved anywhere by "bright gleams of either laughter or joy." Peck's concept of Robinson's world as prison-house was barred at one end by "His humour is of a grim sort," and at the other by, "In the night-time there is weeping and sorrow, and joy does not come in the morning." *The Children of the Night,* with its increment of "Two Men," "Richard Cory," and "Cliff Klingenhagen," fared slightly better. The Lewiston (Me.) *Saturday Journal* suspired wistfully, "we would that he liked to make us laugh oftener." John Gardiner, first to sense a context, defined the book as "not without its note of fun, though the fun is of a subdued sort, rather quizzical than gay." He commended "Two Men" for its "gleam of sober amusement," and thought it a pity that Robinson did not reprint "A Poem for Max Nordau," for "It was a piece of most excellent fooling, and it bore more testimony to the sanity and wholesomeness of Mr. Robinson's talent."

The manifest comedy in the title poem of *Captain Craig* and its sequent piece, "Isaac and Archibald," induced the most voluminous reaction. Simple dictum or platitude imbues all except Boynton's. The Boston *Evening Transcript* talked of "a fine, large sense of humor"; the Chicago *Evening Post* sighted "flashes of characteristic humor" (but what is characteristic?); the Boston *Journal* rated the old Captain's wit and irony "remarkable"; Payne ascribed the "sardonic humor" to Browning's example; the *Argonaut* coupled Robinson's "rare, quaint humor" with pathos, as did Stickney and others; the Chicago *Tribune* turned up "a curious form of shrewd, if at times wearisome, humor" without staying to explain; and the *Independent* likened Craig to Falstaff, "with a glimpse of cosmic humor." Boynton strove honorably to encompass Robinson's "method," yet one is not confident that he made a clear point in holding up "humor in the pure sense" as a "valid distinction between verse and poetry." He too lugs in Browning, then shuffles off into paradox.

Between 1904 and 1912 reference to Robinson's humor was negligible; reviews of *The Children of the Night* reprint bore strongly on Roosevelt's audacity as a literary critic. In September 1912 Ledoux counted humor among Robinson's "most conspicuous" characteristics, at the same time calling it elusive, "a pervading essence seldom embodied in any concrete form." Like "the deity of the Pantheists: it cannot be proved, but may be observed anywhere." Robinson, he contended, "never has written a humorous poem" despite the inkling of humor in "nearly every one." A close friend, Ledoux knew by heart Robinson's bias for sympathy rather than ridicule in surveying the human condition. The Minneapolis *Journal* mulled over Robinson being "hailed by some as the prophet of a new humor," fell back upon the blend "of pathos and humor," and judged him capable of producing "some day a new 'Snowbound' of infinitely subtle humor. In 1915 the Rochester *Herald* spoke unexceptionally of his "exquisite humor" and Braithwaite's "Gentle Poet" rhetoricized Robinson's "soul of humor." The field for a definitive study of Robinson's modes and tones of humor is still invitingly open.

Nomen Est Omen

Robinson's fondness for conferring eye- and ear-catching names upon his poetic characters has received more attention these days than the versatility and subtlety of his humor. Numerous short studies in academic journals and select passages in longer works have probed the cultural and etymological derivations of Robinson's appellatives. It is strange, therefore, that these pointedly arresting names drew barely a baker's half dozen comments in the first segment of Robinson's career. The simplicity, indeed the naivete with which they were greeted is even stranger.

In December 1897 the Boston *Evening Transcript* was first and typical of the rest in holding up Robinson's "fancy for curious names," giving as examples Cliff Klingenhagen and Aaron Stark, and closing the matter with an offhand "they suit the owners well enough." The New York *Daily Tribune* added John Evereldown, Luke Havergal, Richard Cory, and Fleming Helpenstine to the roster, treating them as quirks, and suggesting only obliquely that they "attempt to hit off some salient trait." The *Chap-Book* (appending Reuben Bright and James Wetherell) was more resourceful, applying three dimensions to each name: its inherent "music," "its general poetic value," and its fitting the character "like a glove." However, the perspicacious edge was blunted by asserting Helphenstine "a mere misspelling of the German helfenstein, or stone of succor." The palpitating next layer was never exposed.

After adducing Browning, the scribe in the *Book Buyer* said Robinson "dramatizes and, to a certain extent, visualizes his philosophy" through usage of characterizing names. One of Robinson's superior critics, Ferris Greenslet, rose to the shoulder of the occasion, reading each of the "musical and suggestive names" as "a perfect symbol and almost a poem in itself, and they cling potently to the memory." Two others acquitted themselves less well. Theis simply concurred that the "oddish proper names . . . cling in the memory," and Joyce Kilmer made absolutely nothing of Robinson's "brief sketches in verse, labeled in most part with unusual proper names, such as Cliff Klingenhagen, Leffingwell, and Miniver Cheevy." The day of New Criticism was not yet.

Under this heading of signal nomenclature it does not seem amiss to consider the radius of Robinson's own name. The profuse distortions it suffered at the hands of careless critics and/or compositors in these reviews is such that cannot be ignored.

Because of his mother's ill health following his birth, Robinson remained unnamed for some six months. While she was recuperating at a resort in South Harpswell, Maine, the female vacationers there convinced her to accept the name which should be drawn from among several slips of paper placed in a hat. The one thus selected at random was Edwin; the home town of the lady who proposed the lottery was Arlington (Massachusetts), hence his middle name. Robinson's ingrained modesty rebelled against the archducal sonority of these polysyllables. He referred to them with jocular distaste, not unaware that they emitted as much connotation as the names he invented for his poetical personae. Once "he remarked that his name sounded like a tin pan rolling down hill! 'And why shouldn't it? Aren't my name's initials E.A.R., wholly concerned with *sound?*' "[14] Outside of title pages, he rarely used his full name, contenting himself with two initials and cognomen. To family and intimates he was "Win"; to friends "E.A." The familiar diminutive irked him. "You may call me anything you like — anything but Eddie," he told Edith Brower.[15]

The most frequently encountered misuse of his name is the seemingly unavoidable substitution of Edward for Edwin. Until he became inured, it cost him numberless qualms of annoyance. Among the more prominent applications of this misnomer: the second of his three Pulitzer Prize diplomas, a quartet of his poems set to music, an entry in the index of dissertation abstracts, divers volumes inscribed to him by grateful authors, and, saddest to relate, the headline over the obituary notice in his home-town newspaper. Tracing the full circle of transpositional irony, one biographical account dubbed him Edward, son of Edwin. Almost a fifth of the reviewers in this book misrepresent him as Edward,[16] including his glittering impresario Theodore Roosevelt. What is believed to be the first public photograph of Robinson, ornamenting Scollard's script, introduced him similarly. The caption of Miss Brower's essay misnamed him, though rectified in the text, so the fault may have been the typographer's, whose counterparts may also have been responsible for Payne's E.H. Robinson and for Thorne's Edwin Alington Robinson.[17] Who may say for sure? Moreover, how explain the idiosyncrasy of the New York *Times Saturday Review of Books,* which cropped him to merely Arlington Robinson in a subheading and on the Contents page of its November 25, 1905 issue? For a final fillip, and perhaps a token that Edwin by any other name would smell as sweet, one newspaper of unascertained place and date ran a copy of "Neighbors" under the mutation Edgar.

Vaulting The Torrent

During the first nineteen years of its existence *The Torrent and The Night Before* was expunged from the Robinson canon by at least a dozen subsequent reviewers. Through flat misstatement or inferential omission, they signified that his maiden effort as a book was *The Children of the Night.* Given Robinson's amateur formula for distribution, it may not seem astonishing that so many remained unaware of *The Torrent.* On the other hand, the volume did receive notice in large-circulation metropolitan dailies in Boston, Denver, Chicago, and Cleveland; in prestigious magazines like the *Independent, Bookman, Dial, Outlook, Sewanee Review, Poet-Lore,* and *Literary World*; and by such worthies as Dole, Peck, Payne, Eggleston, and Trent. Three reasonable explanations: 1) Samuel Johnson's "Ignorance, Madam, pure ignorance"; 2) critics at the turn of the century did not read one another as sedulously as do those in today's inbred fraternity; 3) in two or three indefinite cases *The Torrent* may have been passed over as wholly assimilated in *The Children.*

Vance Thompson and John Macy said with uncompromising inaccuracy that *The Children* was Robinson's first book. Thompson may well be pardoned, for his thought and labor was focused on the European scene. Macy, *au contraire*, was in training to become one of the principal harbingers of American writing as reputable literature. Frank Dempster Sherman, Bliss Carman, and the Minneapolis *Journal* plowed the same furrow, as did May Sinclair who, with formidable positivity, managed to surpass all of these. *Captain Craig,* she noted, was "Mr. Robinson's first volume, first published in 1903." Compounding her culpability was the fact that she had enjoyed unprecedented affinity with the poet during his Judson Hotel period. Three of Braithwaite's critiques demonstrate that *The Torrent* was also a cipher to him. In 1910 he revealed that his first acquaintance with Robinson came from *The Children,* which could mean that he had heard of *The Torrent* but had never read it. However, in 1913 he wrongheadedly wrote that Robinson "had published two books up to that time: *The Children of the Night,* 1896, and *Captain Craig,* 1902." (Could 1896 be a psychic slip?) In 1915, now full-fledged as an anthologist of American poetry, he accredited only *The Children of the Night, Captain Craig,* and *The Town Down the River* to Robinson. A year earlier Theis had made the same blunder.

The Boston *Evening Transcript* and the Lewiston (Me.) *Journal* each in its way left the impression that *The Children* was Robinson's initial offshoot, especially curious in that the very first review of *The Torrent* had appeared in the *Transcript*. In the *Dial* notice of *Captain Craig* Payne recalled only "A slender volume of verse . . . put forth several years ago." Since he had reviewed both *The Torrent* and *The Children* for the same magazine it is difficult to tell which one he effaced here. He did observe on January 16, 1898 that *The Children* was "not strictly the same volume" as *The Torrent*, but in the passage of time he may have come to consider it a synthesis of both. Carty Ranck, who let it be known he was preparing a massive biography of Robinson, had evidently failed to check before 1897 for his notes on the works. Ascribing "three volumes" to the poet by 1913, Ranck named only *The Children,* quoted from *The Town Down the River,* and had in mind, assumptively, *Captain Craig* as the third.

Olla Podrida

To bring these Vistas to a close, an odd lot of ancillary views are mustered under this head. None are exigent to an understanding of Robinson as poet; none are without interest to students of his uphill journey.

Without authentication by machine statistics, it may be safely stated that the most recurrent adjective applied to Robinson's work in these early critiques is *remarkable*. Manifest in the first sentence of the first review, it thereafter speckles the text as late as August 1915. Whatever their overall verdict, most of the sounder critics perceived that they had a marvel by the hand. Pity it took so long to filter outward.

Robinson's gift of *compression* runs next in order of recognition. In the efflorescent wordscape of contemporary verse, tautness caught the eye. The Boston *Evening Transcript* claimed that there was "more stuff" in Robinson's terse portraits of Tilbury Towners "than in the average three-volume novel." This sentiment Higginson grasped and refined, granting Robinson's "power of putting a whole life, or a whole generation of lives" into the "narrow compass of fourteen lines." Others in close verbal and ideational accord were the *Book Buyer* in 1910 — "each one of these striking poems suggests a whole life-story" — and the Minneapolis *Journal* in 1912, insisting that Miniver Cheevy could not have been more fully depicted in "a two-volume novel." May Sinclair and Braithwaite virtually italicized Higginson's dictum, and Hagedorn went along, though dragging his feet somewhat. Ranck intensified the scope to "*a volume*" and the count of lines to "half a dozen." Pulsifer calculated "a dozen lines" sufficient for Robinson "to sum up the tragedy of a whole life."

In an era outstanding for lack of *restraint* and *concreteness,* Robinson's abundant lode of both merits could hardly go unnoticed, and did not.

Finally, one is afflicted by the wholesale carelessness of not only the daily newspapers but also the more authoritative literary journals in such matters as quotation and biographical data. As regards erratic transcription of Robinson's verses, none excelled the *Independent* of March 2, 1911 or Richard LeGallienne, who breached the limits by substituting a word of his own for one possibly offensive to him. French and Chase vie wanly for the nadir of imprecision concerning events in Robinson's life. Even the simple collation of content changes from *The Torrent* to *The Children* proved unmanageable for the *Chap-Book* (*two* poems from *The Torrent* were excluded from *The Children*), for Thorne (there were no octaves in *The Torrent*), and for Helen Clarke, who welcomed *The Children* as an attractive reissue of *The Torrent*.

GENESIS OF A POET

About the time he reached twenty Edwin Arlington Robinson once and for all articulated to himself the conviction that "I was doomed, or elected, or sentenced for life to the writing of poetry."[1] He adds that his father never suspected it and that his mother died before she saw printed evidence of it. There were practical reasons enough why he would prefer not to broadcast "the grisly secret" in Gardiner Maine, prototype of his mercantile-minded Tilbury Town. His father's contempt for unproductive intellectual pursuits was outspoken; his mother often suffered the often silent queries about what was Win going to *do* now that he was out of school. Opposed or abashed, his parents nonetheless constituted the first forces to help clear the boy's route to his ultimate destination.[2]

On the maternal side, one must first assay the tenuous nexus of heredity: Mary Palmer Robinson descended in the line of Anne Bradstreet, America's self-styled Tenth Muse. Beyond that, Mrs. Robinson read with avidity verses printed or reprinted in newspapers and magazines, frequently clipped those which appealed to her and transferred them to a set of swelling scrapbooks. She was also known to compose verses of her own, though never with a thought of publication. Robinson's village neighbor, Laura E. Richards, attests that "His first memory of an interest in poetry is of reciting 'Lochiel's Warning' to his mother" and "At five, read 'The Raven'" to her.[3] Forty-five years later he mused that the latter poem "may have come as near as anything to determining my unfortunate career."[4]

Much has been made of the fact that Edward Robinson, disciple of commerce and skeptic of higher education, owned a prized *Works* of Shakespeare which he read regularly and enthusiastically for his own and his youngest son's delectation. Less has been said about the numerous other volumes of travel, history, fiction, and poetry available to the growing boy on the bookshelves in the Gardiner home.[5] Among the writers of prose fiction who seem to have stirred Robinson most deeply were Dickens, in a set of fifteen volumes, and Thackeray, in eleven, both (as was the Shakespeare) autographed by his father. Of all the categories, however, the last attracted Robinson the most. "There were many books of poetry in the house and I must have read nearly all of them," he recalled, "with the exception of Mrs. Hemans, for whom I had an ungallant and unconquerable aversion."[6]

The cardinal volume that "He and his father never tired of poring together over"[7] was William Cullen Bryant's *A Library of Poetry and Song* (1873), a loamy commingling of excellence and bromide. Within its pages are extracts from the work of at least twenty-five poets with whose names critics have yoked Robinson's at one time or another over the years, among them: Matthew Arnold, Browning, Bryant, Byron, Coleridge, Cowper, Crabbe, Dryden, Emerson, Hood, Keats, Milton, Thomas Moore, Poe, Dante Rossetti, Scott, Shelley, Spenser, Swinburne, Tennyson, Whittier, Wordsworth, Edward Young; also one which only Robinson himself acknowledged, Heine. Of these, Arnold, Browning, Byron, Coleridge, Crabbe, Dryden, Emerson, Heine, Hood, Keats, Milton, Moore, Poe, Rossetti, Scott, Shelley, Spenser, Whittier, Wordsworth, and Young were additionally represented by their books in the Gardiner collection. In his first years Robinson published poems about Arnold, Crabbe, Emerson, Hood, and Poe. (He paid homage to Whitman, Verlaine, and Hardy in like manner. There is a volume of Whitman in the Robinson library, none of Verlaine, but both were beyond the pale for Bryant. Hardy, whose novels Robinson read intently, had not yet abandoned prose for verse.)

To dissipate the accruing impression that Robinson was insufferably sobersided as a youth, one need only mark his protestation to Mrs. Richards: "When I was young I read mostly Dickens, dime novels (which cost five cents), Elijah Kellogg, Harry Castlemon, Oliver Optic, Horatio Alger, Bulwer Lytton, Thackeray, and Bryant's *Library of Poetry and Song*."[8] Other favorites were Jules Verne, the Nick Carter detective series, and Captain Marryat's unfailing thrillers of the sea.

Hermann Hagedorn declares that Robinson began writing verses at the age of eleven, "Surreptitiously, in the hayloft, or sitting in the old family sleigh, or at the oat-bin for a desk in the harness-room,"[9] mostly short poems and sonnets. Mrs. Richards agrees on the date and Mark Van Doren corroborates the locale.[10] Robinson's self-minimizing temperament is responsible for the abrupt extinction of this juvenilia. One day, in the cellar of the high school, he "pulled a sheaf of verses from his pocket, read them aloud, and asked the other boys what they thought of them. . . . They thought nothing of the verses, and said so frankly; whereupon the author thrust the papers into the furnace."[11] This was of a piece with his growing meticulosity. "In those days," he said later, "time had no special significance for a certain juvenile and incorrigible fisher of words who thought nothing of fishing for two weeks to catch a stanza, or even a line, that he would not throw back into a squirming sea of language where there was every word but the one he wanted."[12]

Two propelling events occurred while Robinson was still in high school. During his third year he "became violently excited over the structure and music of English blank verse" and set for himself the task of transfiguring Cicero's first oration against Catiline into "impeccable pentameters." This he "followed by a similar treatment of long passages from Virgil," emerging satisfied that he knew "a great deal more about the articulation and anatomy of English blank verse than I had known before."[13] This first real trial of strength by the poet-apprentice coincided happily with the interest he aroused in Alanson Tucker Schumann, a neighboring poet-homeopath adept in the intricacies of French prosody. Before long, Robinson was the extremely youngest member of a quartet which met weekly at the house of Caroline Davenport Swan, teacher and linguist, to discuss the craft of poetry, read their own recent fabrications, and eat apples. The fourth constituent was Henry Sewall Webster, a judge of probate. The value of Robinson's exposure in his crucial late teens to these adults, each of whom wrote with depth and skill enough to attain publication, cannot be understated.

Robinson's first emergence in print was a prose essay, "Bores," one of fifteen in *The Amateur,* published by the Class of '88 of Gardiner High School shortly before July 1, 1887. A two-page historical survey of the more prevalent types of mortal bores, it is stylistically indistinctive except for an undercurrent of amenable irony and a precursive Arthurian allusion. Portentous, too, is young Robinson's complaint that "At present day the world is overflowing with a light class of literature, much of which in material has the same ideas and ends, usually spun to a tiresome length" — for the best of his early poems were to be uncommonly stringent, probing new means toward a new idiom. For graduation day he was delegated to write the class ode, which he read to the rhythm of rain on the roof at the commencement exercises. Listed alongside his name on the programme, *"Mulieria,* A Metrical Discourse" recounts satirically the predicament of a solitary male who strays into a town totally inhabited by women and barely makes his escape by playing on their mental vacuity.

At this juncture, not having taken the college preparatory course and acutely disinclined "To fill the frittered minutes of a day" at some obnoxious, clockbound clerical job, Robinson reclined into a mood of introverted stasis. He re-entered high school for a postgraduate year of courses in Horace and Milton, read voraciously in English romantic poetry and German philosophical idealism. Concurrently, he multiplied his output of sonnets, poems in French forms, and metric translations of Latin eclogues and epic. Now, more than ever, he looked to Schumann as companion and confidant, and it was the doctor who unfurled the prophecy, "I guess you will have to write poetry or starve."[14] Nine months after Robinson completed the extra stint at school the Gardiner *Reporter Monthly* published his first poem, "Thalia," a sonnet fraught with alliteration, personification, and classical reference. Two months later "The Galley Race," translated in blank verse from Book V, lines 104-285 of the *Aeneid,* appeared in the same journal.[15]

The public poet was irreversibly launched. However, calm seas and prosperous voyage were still very distant prospects. For two years at home in Gardiner it devolved upon Edwin to care for his ailing mother, his aging father, and his addicted brother Horace. He tended the house and the garden, tried fecklessly to learn stenography, took temporary jobs with the River Survey and the ice company, turned down others. Necrosis of the inner ear necessitated his going to Boston for treatment, and intercession by brother Herman persuaded their father to permit Edwin to attend Harvard College. In September 1891 he was admitted as a nonmatriculating student, and the first buoyant era in the chronology of his maturation as a poet unfolded.

Despite the felt obloquy of his footing as a special student and his repudiation by the elitist editors of the *Harvard Monthly,* Robinson savored eagerly the stimulating intellectual atmosphere of the Yard and the cultural possibilities of its larger ambience, Boston. The fascination was illimitable. "I feel as though I had always been here, and as if I should always like to stay here," he wrote to Arthur R. Gledhill[16] after a month in residence. Freed from former constrictions of spirit, he mixed more easily with likeminded associates, at least ten of whom he corresponded or consorted with the rest of his life. And he composed poems with daemonic abandon, even joking about the amount of "Hell business" they contained. The *Monthly* coolly turned down "Thomas Hood," published five years later in the *Globe,* but the *Harvard Advocate* proved more receptive, printing five of his contributions between October 1891 and June 1892.[17] Three are in the French mode of ballade, villanelle, and rondeau; the fourth, a dramatic sonnet with classical garb and Petrarchan base; the fifth, "Supremacy," another Petrarchan sonnet strait in form yet symptomatic in tone, phrase, and imagery of a unique, assertive individualist.

In the last week of June 1893 Robinson left Cambridge, "my life . . . infinitely larger for my going there."[18] If ever he had wavered about the direction his talent would take, the entrancing panorama glimpsed here and the heady encouragement of publication left him no other course to pursue. As unswervable as Captain Ahab on his grim ride toward the White Whale, Robinson was now doomed — or dedicated — to confront his destiny as an artificer of words and visions.

THE TORRENT AND THE NIGHT BEFORE (1896)

Robinson's circumstance in Gardiner, after the two years at Harvard, had conspicuously worsened. His father had died in 1892, Horace's health was more precarious, and Herman's investment of the family's patrimony in disastrous shape. These pressures on Edwin to take up some lucrative employment were intensified by the extreme economic pinch in 1893, a year of financial panic. He remained immutable in his purpose, deliberately deaf to the needs about him. "This itch for authorship is worse than the devil and about spoils a man for anything else," he wrote Gledhill in October 1893. "I will make a clean confession and say that writing has been my dream ever since I was old enough to lay a plan for an air castle. Now for the first time I seem to have something like a favorable opportunity and this winter I shall make a beginning."[1] The townspeople of Gardiner put him down as an odd, impecunious prodigal, and he himself had some twinges about one day becoming "respectable." His only immediate consolation derived from a sympathetic few: his compatriots in The Quadruped, a club comprising Arthur Blair, Seth Ellis Pope, and Linville Robbins; also Dr. Schumann, Mrs. Richards, Kate Vannah, Harry DeForest Smith, and a Christian Scientist named Jones. To the rest, Robinson addressed the sonnet "Dear Friends," wryly entreating them not to pity his foolish bubble-work, since "The shame I win for singing is all mine, / The gold I miss for dreaming is all yours."

Robinson did not at this time envisage himself exclusively a poet but as a *"prospectus literatus."* This may have been a subconscious hedge against monolithic failure. At any rate, his first concerted work upon return was a series of prose sketches and tales, some fifteen of which he swore to see published under the title *Scattered Lives* "even though it be printed on toilet paper with a one-hand printing press."[2] All his travail on this project came to naught. Not a single word ever reached print. In between stories he persisted at poetry, turning numerous sonnets, eulogizing his literary gods, and brushing off a pigeonholed tragic monologue, "The Night Before." In February 1894 he proposed that Harry Smith write out "a correct prose version" of Sophocles' *Antigone* in English, which Robinson would remold into sonorous, picturesque, mainly unrhymed metrics, and which they would publish as joint authors. Although for more than three years Robinson labored, first diligently, then desultorily at the provided text, it too died aborted.[3]

Less grandiose efforts were begetting no better results. Poems submitted to the *Atlantic Monthly, Harper's, Century, Dial, Lippincott's, Scribner's, Chap-Book, Cosmopolitan,* and even *Youth's Companion* came back with relentless regularity. "My rejection slips," he mourned, "must have been one of the largest and most comprehensive in literary history, with innumerable duplicates."[4] Yet, a modicum found haven, enough to keep him going. After two years and two months of absolute blackout, "The House on the Hill" and "The Miracle" came to light in the pages of the *Globe,* a cultist New York magazine which offered no remuneration for the verses. Shortly thereafter the *Critic,* a literary journal of far wider circulation and influence, printed his sonnet "Oh, for a poet," and similarly deigned not "to pay for my shoes."[5] "For a Copy of Poe's Poems," rebuffed by the *Dial,* was accepted by *Lippincott's* which sent a check for $7.00 but put off publication of the poem for eleven and a half years.

Robinson's first public approbation as a poet came in the same issue of the *Globe* that carried his two poems. As a postscript to his excoriation of the "general dilettante dullness" of modern New England writing, editor W.H. Thorne commended the Gardiner group (Caroline Swan, Alanson Schumann, and Henry Webster were also represented in the number) as exceptions. Schumann came in for the heartiest praise, albeit "Mr. Robinson — a much younger person — bids fair to outshine all competitors in his native state."[6] Austerely brief and comparatively modest by Thorne standards, this pronouncement nevertheless radiated the reassurance Robinson craved.

Hopefully, he stepped up his production of poems and submitted them in greater quantities to unresponsive editors. During the entire year of 1895 he succeeded in placing only two, both in old places, the *Globe* and the *Critic.* By November, thoroughly frustrated, he decided to circumvent the closed portals of the periodical press and make a book of his accumulating manuscripts.[7] Looking back thirty-five years later he conjectured that the spark which "started and set going some new wheels in my emotional machinery" was probably the capricious way Paul Dana of the New York *Sun* had chosen to remand "The Clerks," a sonnet which had wearily gone the rounds. At this point "I made a selection of about forty poems from everything that I had written during the past six or seven years." The resultant packet came back to him "with a speed that would be remarkable with even our present aerial facilities." "With no feeling of humiliation or surrender" he resolved "to print the unwelcome little volume at my own expense."[8] As may be surmised, the actual process was neither so simple, swift, or unscathing as his memory was pleased to present it long after the fact.

A fortnight after Robinson determined to assemble an acceptable array of his poems, the agony began to show through. He described to Smith "the hard pull my poems are giving me. If that little book ever goes out, I am half afraid that I shall go with it. I never had such a damned time in life with anything as with some of those verses which ought to go like bees and things and which want to go like camels. It is hunting for hours after one word and then not getting it that plays the devil with a man's gray matter and makes him half ready to doubt the kindness of the Scheme."[9] Early in October 1894 he had commenced writing a set of Tavern Songs into which he endeavored "to put a little mysticism . . . and make them worth while as literature; at the same time trying to make them musical enough in themselves to be songs first and poems after."[10] Now in December 1895 he was finding them "villainously hard to make" yet ineradicably a part of the book he hoped "will be pretty well shaken out by the first of February" and "sent off."[11]

The next three months proved to be "a grind" and "probably . . . all for nothing." February 1 came and was gone before he could fulfill his design; by the 19th it was "fast nearing completion" and he expected to "pack it off sometime this month." Although he had "not lost any faith in the stuff" he began to entertain the idea that he might have to print the book himself "and then give it away — if I can." As of March 7 he had "finished up my poems and sent them away." Emotionally drained, he was doing "nothing but exist and read postage-stamp catalogues."[12]

The manuscript Robinson mailed out would embody a book of "something like a hundred pages and will be called *The Tavern and The Night Before*." Caught up in the moil of an initiatory experience, he added with perhaps a shade too much euphoria: "if the publishers, and then the public, are as well satisfied with the contents as I am with the title, there will be no further trouble with this first venture." A month of utter silence elapsed and his spirit faltered. "When I sent my book away . . . I thought that I should think it a small matter when it came back; but I may as well confess that I am in no mood now for such a thing to happen. . . . Its return will hurt a little, considerable, I fancy," but he would absorb the blow "with a kind of optimistic desperation." On April 8 he reported bleakly: "No news from *The Tavern*." By May 13 his worst misgivings were realized. "My first venture with the book has proved a fizzle, as I knew it would. I was so thoroughly satisfied that the stuff would be rejected that the information hardly touched me." He was merely whistling at an amorphous, hairy creature in the dark. Inserting "Verlaine" and "The Dead Village" (written in the interim) into the manuscript, he posted it once more. June 7: "I don't hear anything from my book." On this day he definitely resolved to "print it on my own hook." After the second rejection he jettisoned the group of Tavern Songs, did a yeoman job of revision and rearrangement on the remainder, and changed his once adored title to *The Torrent and The Night Before*. The rage to publish was ungovernable. "It's a good deal like rum, only a little worse, if anything."[13]

Setting aside any lingering qualms about whether "that confounded little book of mine" was worth printing, on September 12 Robinson dispatched it to the Riverside Press in Cambridge. Now consisting of forty-six individual poems on forty compact pages, the book was undertaken by the Press in the midst of a crowded "holiday and educational work" schedule "only through the friendly intercession" of his uncle Edward Proby Fox, who worked there. Titillated again by his imminent baptism, Robinson regaled Smith with the quality of *The Torrent's* "typographical art" — "it will be about the best piece of work the Riverside Press ever produced," cautiously appending, "which is not saying very much."[14] To Gledhill, Robinson unwound himself about the book's content and his general poetic principle.

> You won't find much in the way of natural description. There is very little tinkling water, and there is not a red-bellied robin in the whole collection. When it comes to "nightingales and roses" I am not "in it" nor have I the smallest desire to be. I sing, in my own particular manner, of heaven & hell and now and then of natural things (supposing they exist) of a more prosy connotation than those generally admitted into the domain of metre. In short I write whatever I think is appropriate to the subject and let tradition go to the deuce.[15]

"This book will probably mark the end of my poetical career," he concluded gloomily.

Robinson's distress over the unwonted arrest of his first book was somewhat alleviated by a felicitous rise in acceptances of his poems by the *Globe*, the *Critic*, and a brand new outlet the Boston *Evening Transcript*. Between January and October 1896 seven of his poems appeared in their pages, and of these six found place in the final draft of *The Torrent*.[16]

In the first days of November he was chafing, understandably yet unreasonably. "That devilish book of mine . . . has been put on the shelf for a while on account of the great rush," he said to Smith, and supposed it would not be until the early part of December before it would materialize.[17] He "received in due time three hundred copies of an inconspicuous blue-covered little pamphlet, which I had named, rather arbitrarily, from the first and the last poem: *The Torrent and The Night Before*. The entire edition cost me fifty-two dollars."[18]

As near as can be calculated, the shipment arrived on the last day of November or the first two in December. Robinson's mixed reaction to this incarnation of his long-suppressed daydreams was further complicated by the recent (November 22) death of his mother, whom he had intended to surprise with his triumph. The syndrome he described to Smith on December 7 is not unlike the instant repugnance felt by most artists for a finished work revisited and the gradual supersession of pride in the offspring. Robinson reported receiving the books "the other morning, but did not take enough interest in them to open the package until evening. In fact, I feel as if I should like to kick them from here to Augusta and never see them again. They looked so small and so devilish blue to me that they made me sick; but now I am feeling better and am beginning to foster my same old ridiculous notion that they may amount to something some day."[19]

In retrospect of thirty-four years, however, Robinson recalled only unilateral joy in the event. "When my three hundred copies arrived (or three hundred and twelve, to be exact) I knew that something important had happened to me. It never occurred to my confident enthusiasm that their arrival, or their existence, might not be important to anybody else, and it was therefore with an untroubled zeal that I began to send them out into the world — most of them to periodicals for possible critical notice, and to strangers who were known to me only by reputation. Perhaps thirty or forty of them went to friends and acquaintances, but most of them went, as they were intended to go, unsolicited and unannounced into the unknown."[20] He explained this seeming temerity to Rollo Brown, a neighbor in the MacDowell Colony: "I wanted a hearing . . . and that seemed to be about the only way to get it." He subjoined, as if in appeasement, "I can't say that the volume exactly set the world on fire."[21]

On December 3 Robinson began inscribing and projecting these hieroglyphs of his spirit beyond the occlusive walls of Gardiner, Maine. Three days before Christmas he wrote with relief to Smith in Germany, "The books are all gone now and I am glad of it."[22] He kept no record of the recipients, approximately half of whom have been identified through surviving copies, press reviews, and references in letters.[23] The other copies, Robinson speculated, "may have been lost or destroyed." Two instances tend to corroborate. Laura Richards remembers "his little nieces found that they made enchanting dollhouses — blue walls — blue roofs. They served this purpose for a time, and then, 'as rare things will, they vanished.'"[24] Leonard M. Barnard, a Gardiner friend, recounts the doleful fate of his presentation copy: "Unguarded upon the center-table, its title page and cover furnished a meal for one of my children."[25]

The known periodicals, newspapers, and critics to whom Robinson distributed *The Torrent* may be ascertained from the Contents table in this volume. Other literary figures, critics or editors who did not publicly notice the book included: Thomas Bailey Aldrich, George Pierce Baker, Robert Bridges, Witter Bynner, Bliss Carman, John Vance Cheney, George Wharton Edwards, Edgar Fawcett, Richard Watson Gilder, Edmund Gosse, Thomas Hardy, Thomas R. Lounsbury, Edward S. Martin, S. Weir Mitchell, William Vaughn Moody, Louise Chandler Moulton, Charles Eliot Norton, Laura E. Richards, Charles G.D. Roberts, Clinton Scollard, Horace E. Scudder, Edmund Clarence Stedman, Frederic J. Stimson, Algernon Charles Swinburne, Horace L. Traubel, and Barrett Wendell. Some of the booklets never reached their destination. Edith Brower's, for example, was originally inscribed to a person not located by the postman, was returned, reinscribed, and sent to her instead. Scores of others were laid aside unread; Swinburne's was uncut.

For "A book of untried stuff, more or less poetical,"[26] thin and tentative-looking, bylined by an unknown, and without the imprimatur of a recognized publisher, *The Torrent* garnered more than its warrantable share of attention. Hagedorn, while correctly stating that "The reviews were scanty and, with a few exceptions, unperceptive rather than hostile,"[27] tends to minimize the response. Robinson, on his part, experienced a lift of heart. "Only a few of them — possibly ten or twelve — failed in drawing from its recipient some sort of response. Considering its unimpressive appearance as a publication and the complete obscurity of its origin, it was received generally with a respect and enthusiasm that was gratifying, and was all that I needed to keep me going through the years of obscurity and material uncertainty that were so definitely before me."[28] To Edith

Brower, a lifelong devotee after she accidentally encountered *The Torrent,* he said on January 13, 1897: "The fact, however, that certain people can read it and take the trouble to write about it, gives me a little courage to think it something else than absolute drivel"; and less than two weeks later, his confidence still on the rise: "At first I was rather sorry for the poems and for myself; but since they have met the approbation of almost everyone who has read them (publishers excepted) . . . "[29] Early in February his expectations leveled off. "But a little time will settle the whole difficulty and perhaps dispose of the whole book by consigning it to that untroubled region where, as A. Lang once said, 'the old moons go.' "[30] And by April 10 his tone turned desponding. "I don't feel that I have done very much as it is, and I doubt very much, sometimes if ever I shall do anything better,"[31] he wrote Miss Brower, now the receptacle of his literary hopes and fears.

Deep inside, though, Robinson clenched a stark, unshakeable faith in himself for the long run. With mantic assurance he declared: "I was unable to foresee oblivion for the poems, though I could foresee too surely a long and obscure journey for them before they should have more than a small number of friends."[32] And peering ahead to the time when he would have traversed his "drear and lonely tract of hell," Robinson remarked to schoolmate Will Gay, "Some day that's going to be worth something," as he handed him a copy of *The Torrent and The Night Before.*[33]

. . / / . .

THE TORRENT AND THE NIGHT BEFORE. The quotation on the title page, here reproduced, is from the close of François Coppée's Scene III in *Le Trésor* (Paris, 1879), p. 23. At middle, verso of title page: statement of copyright by Robinson, dated 1896; at bottom, verso: The Riverside Press, Cambridge, Mass., U.S.A. / Printed by H.O. Houghton and Company. On facing page: *This book is dedicated to any man, / woman, or critic who will cut the / edges of it. — I have done the top.* No table of contents. Bound in light blue wrappers, title printed on front cover; top edge trimmed, front and bottom edges untrimmed; leaves measure 17.1 by 11 centimeters; 312 copies, distributed gratis.

THE TORRENT
AND THE NIGHT BEFORE
BY EDWIN ARLINGTON
ROBINSON, GARDINER
MAINE, 1889-1896

Qui pourrais-je imiter pour être original?
          Coppée

PRINTED FOR THE AUTHOR
MDCCCXCVI

THE TORRENT AND THE NIGHT BEFORE

Contents

The Torrent	[5]
Aaron Stark	[5]
The Dead Village	6
Ballade of a Ship	6
Dear Friends	7
Sonnet (When we can all)	8
Her Eyes	8
Sonnet (The master and the slave)	9
Zola	10
Ballade (In dreams I crossed)	10
For Some Poems by Matthew Arnold	11
George Crabbe	11
Sonnet (Oh, for a poet)	12
The Altar	12
The House on the Hill	13
The Wilderness	13
Luke Havergal	15
The Chorus of Old Men in "Ægeus"	16
The Miracle	18
Horace to Leuconoe	18
The Ballade of Dead Friends	18
Villanelle of Change	19
Thomas Hood	20
For a Book by Thomas Hardy	20
Supremacy	21
Three Quatrains	
I (As long as Fame's)	21
II (Drink to the splendor)	22
III (We cannot crown ourselves)	22
For Calderon	22
John Evereldown	24
The World	25
Credo	26
The Children of the Night	26
The Clerks	28
A Ballade by the Fire	28
On the Night of a Friend's Wedding	29
Verlaine	29
The Garden	30
Two Sonnets	
I (Just as I wonder)	30
II (Never until our souls)	31
Walt Whitman	31
Kosmos	32
An Old Story	32
A Poem for Max Nordau	33
Boston	33
The Night Before	34

Can this man do it?

THE TORRENT AND THE NIGHT BEFORE
Joseph E. Chamberlin

Speaking of personal expressions, a remarkable thing of that sort has come to the Listener in the form of a very little unbound book of verse by Edwin A. Robinson of Maine. His personal expression [is] carried almost to the point of literary pamphleteering. But pamphleteering or what not, is it not a pleasure to get hold of a man who knows something on his own account, and isn't measuring the world according to somebody else's system? One who can praise and see into the very heart of and reason for George Crabbe[1] and Paul Verlaine,[2] Matthew Arnold[3] and Emile Zola,[4] getting at the kernel of real thought that makes each one of these a force, is not an ordinary echoer of others and judge of things according to pedantic systems. But it is desirable that one who puts out verses, even at his own expense, should be able to write verse. Can this man do it? The Listener is not a critic of poetry, but he rather likes things like this, about one Aaron Stark[5]; ["Aaron Stark" follows.]

From "The Listener," Boston *Evening Transcript* (December 16, 1896), 5.

Joseph Edgar Chamberlin (1851-1935), editor and author, conducted a column, "The Listener," in the Boston *Evening Transcript* for many years, ranging widely in his choice of subjects. Among his books: *The Listener in the Country* (1896), *John Brown* (1899), *The Ifs of History* (1907), and a history of the newspaper.

Robinson said: "The only newspaper notice that amounts to anything was written by Mr. Chamberlin, the 'Listener,' in the Boston *Transcript*." (Denham Sutcliffe, editor, *Untriangulated Stars: Letters of Edwin Arlington Robinson to Harry DeForest Smith 1890-1905* [Cambridge, Mass., 1947], p. 267.) Chamberlin invited Robinson "to go to the St. Botolph club with him and meet some 'bright men,'" and told him, "A man who can do the things you have done in *The Torrent* does not need the small praise of a small man like me. . . . The world may not have it, but go on doing it just the same." (Sutcliffe, pp. 270, 272.)

Chamberlin's review was reprinted verbatim in "Some Current Book-Talk," Lewiston (Me.) *Saturday Journal* (December 19, 1896), 10, evidently the first on Robinson's book in his home state of Maine. It was also reproduced in full by his home town paper, the Gardiner (Me.) *Daily Reporter-Journal* (January 13, 1897), [3], under the caption "Complimentary Words," and the introduction, "The following complimentary words on the work of a Gardiner author appeared in a recent number of the Boston *Transcript*." It was repeated in the Friday weekly edition of the *Reporter-Journal* on January 15.

1 At Harvard (1891-1893) "Robinson's literary tastes were already formed. He had discovered Crabbe, and had much to say of him." (George W. Latham, "Robinson at Harvard," *Mark Twain Quarterly*, II [Spring 1938], 19.)

Around 1900 Robinson "asked me if I had read George Crabbe. . . . if the reader will read Crabbe he will know more of the mind and art of Robinson." (Fullerton Waldo, "The Earlier E.A.R. Some Memories of a Poet in the Making," *Outlook*, CXXIX [November 30, 1921], 552.)

"I have a set of Crabbe," [Robinson] said. "Somebody thought I was crazy about him because I wrote a sonnet about him, and gave me a set. . . . There are some good things in him." (Winfield Townley Scott, *Exiles and Fabrications* [New York, 1961], p. 167.) The set was given him by first cousin Fanny M. Robinson, a schoolteacher, and is now in Colby College Library.

Robinson to H. Bacon Collamore, January 22, 1929: "please don't send the Crabbe volumes — as I had five large volumes of that good man's work given me last winter. I used to like him, but somehow there isn't time for him now." (Colby College Library)

2 While still in high school Robinson attended gatherings in the house of Caroline D. Swan, with A.T. Schumann and Henry S. Webster, and would hear "some bit of Ronsard or Villon or Verlaine which Miss Swan would read in the original and translate line for line." (Hermann Hagedorn, *Edwin Arlington Robinson: A Biography* [New York, 1938], p. 36.) "Yet he became an enthusiast over the poetry of Paul Verlaine. Much, he concluded, must be forgiven genius." (p. 74.)

See also Edwin S. Fussell, *Edwin Arlington Robinson: The Literary Background of a Traditional Poet* (Berkeley, 1954), p. 198, notes 3, 4.

3 "He admired Arnold's poetry. I recall his saying once that the average level of Arnold's poetry was higher than that of any of the other Victorians." (Latham, p. 20.)

"Arnold he liked best of all and from him he most frequently read aloud, usually selecting a short poem or sonnet. He liked 'Sohrab and Rustum' and was interested in the Arthurean legends. . . . He read aloud, if I remember right, 'Calais Sands' with admiration." (James L. Tryon, *Harvard Days With Edwin Arlington Robinson* [Waterville, Maine, 1941], p. 11.)

"Once in impatience he took down his Matthew Arnold and read 'Pis-Aller,' which tells the man who sees no moral plan, nothing but darkness outside his creed, to go forthwith and believe it then. A poem of Matthew Arnold's which Robinson read to me as one of his favorites is entitled 'Second Best.' It is the expression of a self-controlled person who, in a confused world, finds it necessary to discriminate, and, pushing aside what is irrelevant, concentrates upon that which means most to him." (Tryon, p. 13.)

While rereading Arnold's *Culture and Anarchy,* Robinson said: "His 'mission' stopped his poetry and I have always regretted it." (Sutcliffe, pp. 123-124.)

4 Robinson nevertheless wrote to Laura E. Richards, June 1929: "You are entirely wrong about my being steeped in Zola and Hardy when I was young. . . . When I wrote that rather pinfeatherish Zola sonnet, I had read only *L'Assommoir,* and I have read only one of his books since then." (Laura E. Richards, *E.A.R.* [Cambridge, Mass., 1936], p. 14.)

"Zola is the greatest worker in the objective that the world has ever seen, and someday he will be recognized for what he is," said Robinson to Harry Smith while reading the novel in April 1897, and considering it "the most astonishing example of cumulative power that I have ever met with." (Sutcliffe, p. 282.)

5 Hagedorn (p. 52) implies that "Southwest" Tarbox, town miser of Gardiner, was the original of this character. However, Robinson wrote a wholesale repudiation to Laura E. Richards, March 9, 1902: "Aaron Stark, on the contrary, has nothing whatever to do with the late N.M. Whitmore, or with anyone else." (Ridgely Torrence, editor, *Selected Letters of Edwin Arlington Robinson* [New York, 1940], p. 51.)

In later years he could be less defensive. "Asked whether he had had actual originals in mind for Captain Craig or Miniver Cheevy or Uncle Ananias or Richard Cory or John Evereldown or Leffingwell or Clavering or Tasker Norcross, he would answer frankly enough, and even mention names." (Carl Van Doren, "Post-War: The Literary Twenties," *Harper's,* CLXXIII [July 1936], 155.)

. . / / . .

The modern order of pessimistic verse

THE TORRENT AND THE NIGHT BEFORE

A small pamphlet, about as large as one of Mr. Mosher's *Bibelots*,[1] has been issued by Edwin Arlington Robinson, of Gardiner, Me. *The Torrent and The Night Before* is the name of the little book, which is filled with poems, ballades, quatrains and sonnets, all admirable illustrations of the modern order of pessimistic verse.[2] Its clever dedication reads as follows: "This book is dedicated to any man, woman, or critic who will cut the edges of it. — I have done the top."[3] The poor critics evidently in this author's mind are classified with Poe's[4] awesome creatures, who are "neither man nor woman."

From "Literary Notes," *Independent*, XLVIII (December 17, 1896), 25.

---

1   Thomas Bird Mosher (1852-1923), Maine publisher of inexpensive though attractive editions of literature little known in the United States, also issued this monthly magazine of similar selections between 1895-1914. Bound in blue-grey wrappers, averaging 20-30 pages per issue, and measuring 4½ by 6¼ inches, it did resemble *The Torrent* with blue wrapper, 44 pages, measuring 4¼ by 6¾ inches.
   For Robinson's reaction to *The Bibelot* see Sutcliffe, p. 213.

2   See the section *Pessimism* in the chapter "Preliminary Vistas" of this volume.
   Even before his first book appeared Robinson began to reject this perfunctory label. He wrote to his friend Arthur R. Gledhill on April 2, 1895: "You may be tempted to think that I am getting to be a pessimist, but I am not — nothing of the kind. The universe is a great thing and the power of evil never put it together. Of that I am certain and I am just as certain that this life is but one little scene in the big show. I may be something of a fatalist but I cannot help that." (Harvard College.)
   Worn down over the years by the relentless misapplication of this epithet, Robinson persistently albeit wearily warded it off. "As a matter of fact," he said to Hermann Hagedorn in 1913, "I suppose I'm the damndest optimist that ever lived." (Torrence, pp. 80-81.)
   In *Harvard College Class of 1895, Fifth Report* (Cambridge, 1915), pp. 272-273, he protested: ". . . certain superficial critics who have called me a pessimist have been entirely wrong in their diagnosis. In point of fact, one has only to read my books to wish that half the world might have half my optimism."
   "When people call me a pessimist I can only wonder what they mean by pessimism." (Herbert S. Gorman, "Edwin Arlington Robinson, and a Talk With Him," New York *Sun* [January 4, 1920], 7.)
   "In point of fact . . . I recommend a careful reading of my books to anyone who wishes to become an incurable optimist." (Mark Van Doren, *Edwin Arlington Robinson* [New York, 1927], p. 30.)
   "As I see it, my poetry is not pessimistic, nothing of an infinite nature can be proven or disproven in finite terms — meaning words — and the rest is probably a matter of one's individual ways of seeing and feeling things. There is no sense in saying that this world is not a pretty difficult place, but that isn't pessimism. The real pessimist sees too much of one thing, and the optimist is too likely to see only what he wishes to see." (Letter to Bess Dworsky, December 7, 1931, Torrence, pp. 165-166.)
   "Mr. Robinson said he was a pessimist only in so far as this world was concerned, that he did not see how any thinking man could refuse to admit that there was more grief and suffering than anything else, but that he looked to other existences to answer the problem." (Esther Willard Bates, *Edwin Arlington Robinson and His Manuscripts* [Waterville, Maine, 1944], pp. 13-14.)
   "As a citizen of Infinity I cannot be a pessimist, but I wouldn't give much for this world during the next hundred years." (Letter, November 16, 1919, in Virginia Harlow, *Thomas Sergeant Perry: A Biography* [Durham, N.C., 1950], p. 352.)

3   "I wouldn't mind if you could forget that dedication. It was a cocky thing to do. I must have been conceited and still a little bit mad. Maybe it attracted some attention. Anyhow, the edges on some of them were cut in the course of time." (M.K.

Wisehart, " 'By Jove' Said Roosevelt 'It Reads Like the Real Thing!' " *American Magazine,* CV [April 1928], 76.)

4   At five years of age Robinson is said to have read "The Raven" to his mother while she sat sewing, and he kept a portrait of Poe hanging opposite the foot of his bed in the Gardiner homestead.

He sold a sonnet, "For a Copy of Poe's Poems," to *Lippincott's* in 1895, which they did not publish until August 1906. He wrote to Arthur R. Gledhill, April 2, 1895: "I could no more help making it than I can help feeling nervous in my hair when any one mentions the subject in my presence." (Fussell, p. 17.) As the months rolled by with no sign of it in print, Robinson grew more and more disillusioned. "Two years ago its appearance would have tickled me, but I have grown old since then and would not give five cents to see it now. In fact, I am not entirely sure that I would not rather have him [the editor] keep it pigeonholed for good; there are places in it that don't suit me at all, though I fancy the sestet is tolerable." (Richard Cary, editor, *Edwin Arlington Robinson's Letters to Edith Brower* [Cambridge, Mass., 1968], p. 48.) By the time it finally appeared, eleven years after submission, he undoubtedly viewed it as a youthful indiscretion. He never included it in any of his books.

"Poe, he thought, had achieved a music no one else ever had, 'without jingle, too. But I have never read a poem of his in which something didn't strike me wrong.' " (Scott, p. 167.)

The quotation is from stanza 4, line 86 of Poe's "The Bells."

. . / / . .

A good thing, albeit a little one

THE TORRENT AND THE NIGHT BEFORE
A Booktaster

From Gardiner, Maine, there comes a good thing, albeit a little one, — even a pamphlet of forty-four pages of poems[1]; and though no publisher has discovered the poet who is self-revealed by a booklet "printed for the author," Mr. Edward[2] Arlington Robinson has the heart and a good deal of music of the true singer. This is his "Credo": [The poem follows.]

From *Time and the Hour,* IV (December 26, 1896), 10-11.

The pseudonymous author of this review is probably Edwin Munroe Bacon (1844-1916), one-time managing editor of the New York *Times,* then chief editor in turn of the Boston *Globe, Advertiser,* and *Post.* He retired in 1891, engaging himself thereafter in writing half a dozen literary-historical books on Boston and New England, and editing this Boston periodical from 1896-1900.

1   As Joseph E. Chamberlin misleads in describing *The Torrent* as "unbound" — meaning not hard covers but paperbound — so does this statement. The pagination reaches to number 44 but there are actually only 40 pages of poems, the first one starting on unpaged number [5].

2   See the section *Nomen Est Omen* in the chapter "Preliminary Vistas" of this volume.

Robinson's name was so often maltreated in print that he became philosophically rueful about it, as already noted. Because of the extraordinary frequency of oversight, which ultimately says something about the reviewer or the publication, errors in the rendition of his name are deliberately retained in the reviews transcribed for this volume.

In *The Friends* (Muscatine, Iowa, 1939), p. 25, James Norman Hall agilely sums up Robinson's intermittent remarks on the topic:
>Once he said that 'Edwin Arlington'
>With 'Robinson' attached, was such a load
>As few beside himself had had to hoist
>And stagger under toward a distant grave.
>Eight syllables, and one of them a 'ton',
>Was much too much for any Robin's son.
>The lot, spilled out at once, reminded him
>He said, of just so many empty cans
>Thumping down three times as many steps.

. . / / . .

Highly dramatic piece

THE TORRENT AND THE NIGHT BEFORE

The *Picayune* has received a little paper book, containing a series of poems, called *The Torrent,* and a longer and highly dramatic piece, called "The Night Before."[1] It is the work of E.A. Robinson, of Gardiner, Me., who is also the publisher.

From "Recent Publications," New Orleans *Daily Picayune* (December 27, 1896), 6.

This notice and Robinson's note on the opinion of "a man in Oregon" (Sutcliffe, p. 269) indicate his ambitious geographical coverage of the United States in self-distributing *The Torrent.*

"Recent Publications" was a Sunday book review section in the *Picayune*, usually two to four columns, covering anonymously a score or more books. This was followed by a digest of the contents in current magazines. This capsule notice is tucked in at the end of those items, but Robinson thought highly enough of it to quote a snatch to his confidant Harry DeForest Smith. (Sutcliffe, p. 272.)

1 In *Where the Light Falls: A Portrait of Edwin Arlington Robinson* (New York, 1965), p. 102, Chard Powers Smith reports a "first draft" of this poem presumably begun February 12, 1890, the night Robinson's brother Herman married Emma Shepherd.
Robinson first mentions the poem to Harry Smith on May 27, 1894, giving no intimation of a previous draft: "I have been too much occupied of late to do any writing except two sonnets and some ninety lines of a queer poem called 'The Night Before'. . . . It is a tragic monologue written in unrhymed tetrameters — that is, like *Evangeline*, with two feet left out. . . . Yesterday I did fifty-five lines." (Sutcliffe, pp. 158-159.) On June 3: "I have written 225 lines of 'The Night Before,' and am getting rather enthusiastic over the thing. . . . Fifteen lines an hour is good work and I feel better after I have done them. The story is unpleasant, founded upon my system of 'opposites' that is, creating a fictitious life in direct opposition to a real life which I know." (p. 161.) Then: "this story, which by the way, comes dangerously near to being what the world calls 'hot stuff' is doing me a good service in working off my general discontent. It reflects, in a measure, my present mood in the narration of things of which I know nothing except my instinctive fancy." (p. 161.) And: "The main purpose of the thing is to show that men and women are individuals; and there is a minor injunction running through it not to thump a man too hard when he is down. This, however, is hidden, and would probably not be noticed by one reader in a hundred. If the poem is a little fatalistic, you must excuse me. I write it because I

cannot help it, and this is also true of the way in which I do it." (p. 162.) Eighteen months later comes his only observation about revision: "I have spent the last three weeks mostly in rewriting that story of mine, 'The Night Before.'" (p. 238.)

Robinson complained to Harry Smith about the "conflicting" opinions roused by the poem, though he was himself no less contradictory. On October 28, 1896 he wrote to Arthur R. Gledhill: "'The Night Before' is an attempt to be absolutely impersonal which, of course, is an impossibility." (Torrence, p. 13). Yet, to Smith on February 3 of the following year: "Of course 'The Night Before' is purely objective, and may be called anything from pessimism to rot. I must confess that I haven't the slightest idea whether it is good for anything or not." (Sutcliffe, p. 273.)

. . / / . .

Too healthy to be really pessimistic

THE TORRENT AND THE NIGHT BEFORE
Nathan Haskell Dole

Boston
December 23, 1896

To the Editor:

It would seem as if a Keats or a Chatterton would have little chance of dying in poverty and neglect these days, when the literary searchlight of so many explorers is directed into every nook and corner of the wide, wide field. It was the keen eye of Thomas Mosher of Portland who discovered the merits of the wonderful poems of the Dublin genius, "A.E.,"[1] and who brought them out in the most artistic and attractive form. And now the attention of lovers of striking verse is arrested by a little blue-bound pamphlet emanating from Gardiner, Maine, and entitled *The Torrent and The Night Before*. The author is Mr. Edwin Arlington Robinson, and the book "is dedicated to any man, woman, or critic who will cut the edges of it." Here is his call for a poet: ["Sonnet" (Oh, for a poet) follows.][2]

And here is his sonnet on Zola: ["Zola" follows.]

There are sonnets to Max Nordau,[3] to Matthew Arnold, Thomas Hood, and others, full of strength and passion and — well, yes, perhaps pessimism, though they are too healthy to be really pessimistic.[4] They are vital, virile expressions of a wholly modern spirit, but he can sing tenderly also, as witness this melodious little song: ["An Old Story" follows.]

But for vehemence and strong portraiture read this: ["Aaron Stark" follows.]

This little volume has only forty-four pages, but I should not wonder if curiosity seekers should in future times pay high prices for the little treasure,[5] especially if Mr. Robinson goes on in the same free, bold course.

From "Correspondence," *Bookseller, Newsdealer and Stationer*, V (January 1, 1897), 491.

This semimonthly magazine was published in New York by the American News Company, 1894-1923.

Nathan Haskell Dole (1852-1935), a prolific Massachusetts poet, essayist, editor, and novelist, was esteemed for his translations of Tolstoy and Daudet. A fortnight before this review appeared, Dole wrote Robinson: "I should like to know you. When you come to Boston, please let me shake hands with you and thank you by word of mouth for your book which I have read with unconditional delight." (Sutcliffe, p. 268.) Dole was the first editor of John Bartlett's *Familiar Quotations* to admit Robinson. On page 851 of the revised and enlarged Tenth Edition (1914), he included four quotations from *Captain Craig*. Robinson's appreciation was long-lived. In 1928 he told Dole, "I should always be grateful to you as one of the first to find something in my work." (Torrence, p. 155.)

1   This is the second comparison of Mosher imprints with *The Torrent*. See *Independent*, December 17, 1896, in this volume.
"A.E." is the pen name of George William Russell (1867-1935), Irish poet, playwright, artist, editor, and agrarian reformer. Mosher had published his *Homeward Songs by the Way* in March 1895, with designs by Bruce Rogers.

2   A possible source of the poem: "In *Questions at Issue*, published in 1893, Edmund Gosse, the British critic, attempted to answer some important literary questions that were being discussed on both sides of the Atlantic. One of these questions was 'Has America Produced a Poet?' His answer was doubtful, if not negative, although he paid his respects to Longfellow, Emerson, Bryant and Poe, none of whom in his opinion could be classed with the truly great poets of Britain. It was a time of transition. Robinson knew it and expressed the longing of the American heart." (Tryon, p. 16.)
Robinson did not go entirely without compensation for this poem. "The *Critic* has seen fit to accept one of my sonnets, but it positively refuses to pay for my shoes. I have the consolation of a year's subscription, however, which is quite as good." (Sutcliffe, pp. 165-166.)
Within five months of this reprint of the poem, Robinson wrote: "I'm getting . . . very sick of the sight of 'Oh! for a Poet.' If that is the best thing I have done, the sooner I stop the better. When I put the book together I had half a mind to throw it out." (Cary, p. 43.)

3   "A Poem for Max Nordau" is not a sonnet; it consists of three stanzas of irregular hexameter rhymed abba abab abbaa. Robinson's heavy lather of alliteration and assonance clearly indicated a spoof of the Symbolist school of poets (Baudelaire, Mallarmé, Valéry, Swinburne, early Yeats, *et al.*, trailing Poe's resonant footfalls). In his book, *Degeneration*, translated into English in 1895, Nordau considers "echolalia" and "predilection for refrain" as signs of degeneracy. (See Sutcliffe, pp. 229, 233.)

4   This coincides with Robinson's basic attitude, as expressed in a newspaper interview. "Well, I can only say that while I have a fairly well developed sense of humor, life has always seemed to me a pretty serious business. I haven't much to complain of in my own experience, but my observation of what others have had to endure has not encouraged me to sing the joy of living quite so loudly or so confidently as might be wished." (Gorman, p. 7.)

5   An acute prognostication at this early date. See closing sentence of review in the Bangor *Daily Commercial*, February 13, 1897, and note 7, in this volume.

. . / / . .

Under "Publications Received" in its issue of January 9, 1897, p. 33, the *Critic* listed *The Torrent and The Night Before* but no review of it subsequently appeared. Two of the poems in the book had first been published in the *Critic*: "Sonnet" (Oh, for a poet) on November 24, 1894, and "For a Book by Thomas Hardy" on November 23, 1895. To the latter, the editors cautiously appended this note: "Written before the appearance of

'Hearts Insurgent' " — the serial title of *Jude the Obscure*, which caused such a public ruckus that Hardy never wrote another novel.

. . / / . .

Letters from critics, congratulations from friends

THE TORRENT AND THE NIGHT BEFORE

The Gardiner reporter of the Kennebec *Journal* says that Edward [*sic*] A. Robinson of this city has written a book of sonnets and ballads. The first edition of 300 copies[1] has been exhausted and Mr. Robinson has received letters from many literary critics commending his work, including one from Prof. Norton of Harvard, one of the best critics of the English language in America, praising his work in the highest degree.[2] Mr. Robinson has received many congratulations from friends on his work and is the recipient of over 50 letters from persons who have read this book.[3] Some of the sonnets appeared in the *Harvard Crimson*[4] but the others are given to the public in this collection for the first time.

From "Local Gleanings," Gardiner *Daily Reporter-Journal* (January 2, 1897), [3].

Robinson's home town newspaper cannot be charged with ignoring his book publications, even if its slight notices were transmitted at secondhand. Five times in this early period it borrowed from other sources, extending an original, full-scale review only to the 1902 edition of *Captain Craig*. A greater irritant to Robinson, who did not in any case expect much in the way of esthetic appreciation from Gardiner, must have been the persistence with which the *Reporter-Journal* alluded to him by his father's name Edward, not once Edwin in these first twenty years of looking at his title pages.

1   The edition totaled 312. Of the forty-six poems in this book, twenty-five are sonnets, four ballades.

2   Charles Eliot Norton (1827-1908), professor of literature and the history of fine arts at Harvard, translated Dante's *Divine Comedy* into English prose, was co-editor of the *North American Review* and the *Nation,* and author of numerous biographies and scholarly studies. While at Harvard Robinson took Norton's course in Ancient Art, which was rated by students as a "snap" but which Robinson found "simply magnificent," and he enjoyed attending receptions at Shady Hill, Norton's Cambridge residence.
   The letter in question (now in Colby College Library) was written by Norton on December 14, 1896: "Dear Sir: I beg you to accept my thanks for your gift to me of a copy of your little blue book. I have read enough in it to recognize the debt of gratitude which you owe to the Muse for the gift with which she has enriched your life." On December 10 Robinson had sent him an inscribed copy "with compliments (and apologies)."

3   See Sutcliffe, pp. 267-272, 275-276.

4   None of Robinson's poems appeared in the *Crimson*. While a special student at the college Robinson did publish "Ballade of the White Ship," "Villanelle of Change," "In Harvard 5," "Menoetes," and "Supremacy" in the *Harvard Advocate*, 1891-1892. The last two are sonnets; only the first, second, and fifth were collected in *The Torrent*.

. . / / . .

Willingness to cry "Kismet!"

THE TORRENT AND THE NIGHT BEFORE
R.H.B.

A modest little volume of some forty pages, soberly clad in paper covers, is *The Torrent and The Night Before*, a collection of poems by Edwin Arlington Robinson, published for the author at the University Press.[1] There are forty-three poems,[2] varying greatly in form, subject and merit, but all pervaded by a certain sober dignity that before long impresses the reader with its almost monotonous earnestness. There are no bright gleams of either laughter or joy — what smiles there are bring the tears close behind them, and the joy is a gray sort of happiness at best.[3] The queer, uncanny poem, entitled "Luke Havergal,"[4] will illustrate the somberness of them all:

> Go to the western gate, Luke Havergal, —
> There where the vines cling crimson on the wall, —
> And in the twilight wait for what will come.
> The wind will moan, the leaves will whisper some —
> Whisper of her, and strike you as they fall;
> But go, and if you trust her she will call, —
> Go to the western gate, Luke Havergal, —
> Luke Havergal.

There is a helplessness, a hopelessness in all the poet's lines that touches a responsive chord in the heart and arouses a sympathy which, upon investigation, we find is not asked. For the helplessness is a helplessness against the inevitable, not against the ordinary ills and sorrows of life. With this same yielding helplessness is a fine, firm strength, borrowed, perhaps, from the cold, hard winter nights and days that are the greatest charm of the northland where the book was born. The author is greatly in earnest, there can be no doubt of that. He believes implicitly in the all-wisdom of the principle that governs our lives and is evidently a disciple of the theory of preordination; nevertheless his willingness to cry "kismet!" as exhibited in his verses, brings him, apparently, no comfort.

To our mind the poem of "The House on the Hill"[5] is the finest in the volume, although we are ready to believe that few will agree with us. It is modest in form, a villanelle, and more modest in subject, yet it is like a little bit of a human heart spread out in paper and print, and is one of the most characteristic poems in the volume, with its little rune of sorrow and lament creeping along amidst the lines: ["The House on the Hill" follows.]

Mr. Robinson displays a fondness for unrhymed verse and, it must be acknowledged, a real skill in fashioning it. As an example we quote a stanza and refrain from "The Wilderness"[6]:

> Come away! come away! — there's a frost along the marshes,
> And a frozen wind that skims the shoal where it shakes the dead black water;
> There's a moan across the lowland and a wailing through the woodland
> Of a dirge that sings to send us back to the arms of those that love us.

> There is nothing left but ashes now where the crimson chills of autumn
> Put off the summer's languor with a touch that made us glad
> For the glory that is gone from us, with a flight we cannot follow,
> To the slopes of other valleys and the sounds of other shores.
>
> *Come away! come away! — you can hear them calling, calling,*
> *Calling us to come to them, and roam no more.*
> *Over there beyond the ridges and the land that lies between us,*
> *There's an old song calling to come!*

An excellent bit is "The Ballade of Dead Friends," with its reckless swing and hurry, and sounding like Villon[7] at his best:

> As we the withered ferns
> By the roadway lying,
> Time, the jester, spurns
> All our prayers and prying, —
> All our tears and sighing,
> Sorrow, change, and woe, —
> All our where-and-whying
> For friends that come and go.
>
> Life awakes and burns,
> Age and death defying,
> Till at last it learns
> All but Love is dying; —
> Love's the trade we're plying,
> God has willed it so;
> Shrouds are what we're buying
> For friends that come and go.
>
> . . . .
>
> And thus we all are nighing
> The truth we fear to know:
> Death will end our crying
> For friends that come and go.

A sonnet that is both simple and sweet, and, by comparison with the rest, almost cheerful in tone, is "The Miracle"[8]:

> "Dear brother, dearest friend, when I am dead,
> And you shall see no more this face of mine,
> Let nothing but red roses be the sign
> Of the white life I lost for him," she said;
> "No, do not curse him, — pity him instead;
> Forgive him! — forgive me! . . . God's anodyne
> For human hate is pity; and the wine
> That makes men wise, forgiveness. I have read
> Love's message in love's murder, and I die."
> And so they laid her just where she would lie, —
> Under red roses. Red they bloomed and fell;
> But when flushed autumn and the snows went by
> And spring came, — lo, from every bud's green shell
> Burst a white blossom. — Can love reason why?

Mr. Robinson often says things in his verses that startle with their vividness of truth. For instance, a verse or two of "The Children of the Night"[9]:

THE TORRENT AND THE NIGHT BEFORE (1896)   41

> And if God be God, He is Love; —
> And though the Dawn be still so dim,
> It shows us we have played enough
> With creeds that make a fiend of Him.
>
> There is one creed, and only one,
> That glorifies God's excellence; —
> So cherish, that His will be done,
> The common creed of common sense.
>
> . . . .
>
> Let us, the Children of the Night,
> Put off the cloak that hides the scar! —
> Let us be Children of the Light,
> And tell the ages what we are!

There are a few commonplace verses in the little volume, such as "A Poem for Max Nordau," "The Night Before," and "For Calderon," but it is unjust to judge a man by his worst traits or a writer by his poorest work.[10] Mr. Robinson's best work is very good work, indeed, so fine that this little book of his is one of the books of poetry of the year; not for its binding or printing, but for what is inside of it. Mr. Robinson is, we believe, a young man yet; if so, he is not only a young man of much promise, but a young man of great accomplishment, for to write verse on a plane with his is a task beyond all, save some half dozen of our poets. And perhaps that is a too liberal estimate; just at present we can't recall that number to mind. Much of Mr. Robinson's seriousness may be only that of youth, for youth is ever prone to take itself and its friends and life much too gravely. It is a fault, if fault it is, that wears off with increasing age.

Technically Mr. Robinson's verses are well done: he neither struggles to preserve rhyme at the cost of reason, nor abandons his purpose for the want of a perfect rhyme. He can be unconventional without becoming undignified; he is often mystical but never absurd.[11] (The attention of Mr. Bliss Carman is respectfully requested.)[12]

The author dedicates his book "to any man, woman, or critic who will cut the edges of it. — I have done the top." And men, women, and critics can do many less advantageous things than read Mr. Robinson's poems; and cutting the leaves of his volume is a labor well repaid by the pleasure that follows.

From "Some New Things in the Book World," Denver *Times* (January 16, 1897), 11.

---

1 The formal listing of the book at the end of this review correctly cites the Riverside Press of H.O. Houghton and Company as the printer. The University Press, another printing establishment in Cambridge, Mass., which turned out much work for Ticknor & Fields and Little, Brown & Company, did print Robinson's next book.

2 If "Three Quatrains" and "Two Sonnets" are each considered one poem, this count may be accepted. However, it is equally accurate to count each of the poems under these covering titles as a unit and render the total as forty-six.

3 Of this critique Robinson said to Harry Smith, February 3, 1897: "There is a man in Denver who has a kind of unconscious numerical sympathy with you in your esti-

mate of my importance, but it is very clear to me that you are both all wrong. . . . The same man in Denver, Colorado, thinks I have blue devils, but I assure you I have not." (Sutcliffe, p. 273.)

On this subject to Laura E. Richards, January 18, 1902: "I have my own paint-pots to dabble with. Blacks and grays and browns and blues for the most part — but also a trick, I hope, of letting the white come through in places." (Torrence, p. 49.) And "during one of his last summers at the MacDowell Colony, . . . to some young colonists who spoke of his work as done in blacks and grays: 'Those are the colors that last.'" (p. 186.)

4 Robinson intended to include a group of "Tavern Songs" in *The Torrent*. He was going to try "to put a little mysticism in them, and make them worth while as literature; at the same time trying to make them musical enough in themselves to be songs first and poems after." (Sutcliffe, p. 170.) "Luke Havergal," completed in December 1895, was initially one of the "Tavern Songs." "I also have a piece of deliberate degeneration called 'Luke Havergal,' which is not at all funny," he wrote Smith. (p. 238.)

Robinson to Edith Brower, April 21, 1897: "In a thing like 'Luke Havergal,' of course the meaning is all suggested, and is not capable of a definite working-out by anyone who doesn't happen to sympathize with the writer's fancy." (Cary, p. 39.) On April 28, 1901: "'Luke Havergal' is the most rural of all the things I have done — not excluding 'Isaac and Archibald.'" (p. 141.)

"He called 'Luke Havergal' and 'John Evereldown,' written when he was 23, 'young poems.' 'I don't know where they came from. They just came, out of the air.'" (Karl Schriftgiesser, "An American Poet Speaks His Mind," Boston *Evening Transcript Book Section* [November 4, 1933], 2.)

5 Robinson wrote this poem on February 25, 1894, describing it to Smith as "a little mystical perhaps" and "an attempt to show the poetry of the commonplace." "These old French forms always had a fascination for me which I never expect to outgrow. I don't know that I care to outgrow it, but still it interferes with my more serious work to an unpleasant extent. When one of the things begins to run in my mind there is little rest for me until it is out. Fortunately this one was made very quickly (in about twenty minutes)." Sutcliffe, pp. 132, 133.) And comparing an unpublished poem of his with "The House on the Hill," Robinson said to Smith on April 22: "As for myself, I think I prefer the villanelle. I have a weakness for the suggestiveness of those artificial forms — that is, when they treat of something besides bride-roses and ball-rooms. *Vers de société* pure and simple, has little charm for me." (p. 146.)

"Oaklands," the home of the Gardiner family was often identified as the inspiration for this poem. Robinson specifically denied this in a letter to Laura E. Richards: "'The House on the Hill' is no house that ever was, and least of all a stone house still in good order. I don't know why people will say such foolish things." (Richards, p. 53.) Another repudiation to Henry E. Dunnack, December 22, 1929: "'The House on the Hill' does not refer to any particular house that is or ever was. . . . People who insist on identifying things or people in my poems are likely to go far astray." (C. Lennart Carlson, "Robinsoniana," *Colby Mercury*, VI [December 1939], 283.)

6 Robinson to Smith, January 17, 1897: "There is a man in Oregon who thinks 'The Wilderness' is the best thing in the book. I was very glad to hear from him, as I had begun to fear the poem was 'no good.'" (Sutcliffe, p. 269.)

7 Robinson heard bits of Villon in French and line by line translation in the house of Caroline D. Swan. (Hagedorn, p. 36.) He evidently never outgrew his enthusiasm for French forms (see note 5, above). In 1926 his friend Arthur Davis Variell presented him with a three-volume edition of François Villon's *Oeuvres*, now in Colby College Library.

8 On October 6, 1895 Robinson mentioned "my 'Miracle' business" and characterized "Kosmos" as "crazier than that." (Sutcliffe, p. 234.)

9 Hagedorn (p. 101) reports Robinson telling Smith about this poem: "I was painting the front fence when the thing came so fast that I had to go into the house and write it down."

Mrs. Richards was "surprised and distressed" not to find this poem in Robinson's

Collected Poems and wrote to him, protesting. "He replied that he thought he had said practically the same thing, and said it better in 'The Man Against the Sky.'" (Laura E. Richards, "A Book and Its Author," *Yankee*, II [June 1936], 28.)

10 There is noteworthy affinity of taste between R.H.B. and E.A.R. in this matter. After *The Torrent*, Robinson never reprinted "A Poem for Max Nordau" or "For Calderon." "His reason for rejecting ["Nordau"] was that it was meant to be funny, and he was afraid people might not realize this." (Richards, *E.A.R.*, pp. 57-58.) Robinson repeated "The Night Before" in his second volume, *The Children of the Night* (1897), but dropped it thereafter. "I am afraid it is one of those unfortunate narrative pieces which require a second reading before it amounts to anything at all." (Sutcliffe, pp. 273-274.)

11 Robinson to Helen Grace Adams, January 1, 1930: "There is no 'philosophy' in my poetry beyond an implication of an ordered universe and a sort of deterministic negation of the general futility that appears to be the basis of 'rational' thought. So I suppose you will have to put me down as a mystic, if that means a man who cannot prove all his convictions to be true." (Torrence, p. 160.)

12 Bliss Carman (1861-1929), Canadian romantic poet who collaborated with Richard Hovey on *Songs from Vagabondia* (1894) and *More Songs from Vagabondia* (1896), does not seem to have publicly responded to this jibe or the one by Robert Steed Dunn (see his *Harvard Monthly* review, February 1897, in this volume). Carman reviewed Robinson's *Captain Craig* in the *Reader*, December 1902.

Robinson did not share the scorn of these two critics. On May 5, 1895 he attributed "an unquestionable touch of greatness" to Carman's "Little Lyrics of Joy—V" in the *Chap-Book* of May 1, 1895. (Sutcliffe, p. 222.)

. . / / . .

In his letter of January 17, 1897 to Harry Smith (Sutcliffe, p. 271), Robinson quotes from "a few more notices" of *The Torrent*. This one — ". . . There are poems in this little book that exhibit the finest taste in their making and whose standard is far above that of ordinary verse." — he attributes datelessly to the Boston *Courier*. Search of all available editions between issuance of the book and Robinson's letter did not yield up the full review.

. . / / . .

Poetry which is poetry indeed

THE TORRENT AND THE NIGHT BEFORE

Very beautiful and rare is such modesty as that of Edwin Arlington Robinson of Gardiner, Me., who has printed, but not published,[1] forty-four pages of poetry which is poetry indeed. Many are the poets who rush into publication with things far inferior to this. The first and last poems name the book, — "The Torrent" and "The Night Before." Either we are dull of comprehension, or "The Torrent," which begins grandly in the octave (it is a sonnet) does not run itself clear in the sestette. A fifth or sixth reading does not make the meaning clear.[2] But the poem is exceptional in this respect.

From "Miscellaneous," *Christian Register*, LXXVI (January 21, 1897), 43.

In the adjoining column, under the caption "Charming Books for Winter Reading," are listed twenty current favorites against which Robinson's obscure booklet was unsuccessfully competing for public attention, among them: Thoreau's *Cape Cod*, "beautifully illustrated," in two volumes for $5.00; Sarah Orne Jewett's *magnum opus* of Maine life, *The Country of the Pointed Firs*; Thomas Bailey Aldrich's *Judith and Holofernes*; Kate Douglas Wiggin's *Nine Love Songs and a Carol*; John Burroughs' biography of Walt Whitman; John Morse's life of Holmes; three of Elizabeth Stuart Phelps Ward's chronic bestsellers; the fashionable F. Hopkinson Smith's *Tom Grogan*; and yet another version of the Joan of Arc legend.

1 An allusion to the fact that Robinson had brought out the book under his own auspices and had paid for it himself. Standing unabashed, on the title page, in capitals: PRINTED FOR THE AUTHOR.

2 What disappointed Robinson most about his first book was "the total inability of almost everybody who reads the book to find out what I mean by the last two lines of 'The Torrent.'" (Cary, p. 39.) Eight months later he was still writing querulously to Edith Brower on this score. "[Titus Munson Coan] did not find much fault, however, with anything but the last two lines in 'The Torrent,' which are getting to be a subject over which I can no longer talk with much enthusiasm. I feel that they are as good as I can do them." (p. 67.) His insistence upon keeping them exactly as they were — they remained unaltered through eight of his books from 1896 to 1929 and in the final *Collected Poems* — prevented him from selling the poem to a periodical. The editor to whom it was submitted rejected it because Robinson refused to revise them.

Robinson to L.N. Chase, July 11, 1917: "I suppose that I have always depended rather more on context than on vocabulary for my poetical effects, and this offense has laid me open to the charge of over-subtlety on the part of the initiated and of dullness on the part of the dull." (Torrence, p. 102.)

. . / / . .

Shattering venerable laws of versification

THE TORRENT AND THE NIGHT BEFORE

"This book is dedicated to any man, woman, or critic who will cut the edges of it. — I have done the top." With this modest foreword one's interest is stirred to effort; opinions may differ according to mood whether it is worth the while. In this day there are so many oddities in versification that one hesitates over his own conviction and is at a loss to know whether the fault is his or the poet's.

This is Mr. Robinson's picture of "The Torrent"[1]: [The poem follows.]

In very limited space Mr. Robinson succeeds in shattering many venerable and hitherto respected laws of versification.[2]

From "Books and Authors," Chicago *Record* (January 23, 1897), 11.

1 Despite Robinson's intransigence concerning the final couplet of this poem (see note 2, preceding review) he was instantly amenable to Miss Brower's suggestion for the second part of line 8, "But a gladness now and then." On June 6, 1897 he wrote her: "I like your change of *but* to *yet*." (Cary, p. 48.) Good as his word, he effected the change in *The Children of the Night* (1897) and retained it in every subsequent reprinting.

2 James L. Tryon (pp. 12-13) reveals the following from his Harvard days. "There were certain books relating more particularly to Robinson's craft as poet which he recommended to me to read:

William Matthews: *Words: Their Use and Abuse*
Hours With Men and Books
Andrew Lang: *Letters to Dead Authors*
Letters on Literature
Essays in Little
Edmund Gosse: *Questions at Issue*
On Viol and Flute
Wilfred S. Blunt: *Love Sonnets of Proteus*
Alfred Austin: *Sonnets*
Austin Dobson: *Old World Idyls*
W.S. Landor: *Poems*
Pericles and Aspasia
William Sharp: *Sonnets of the Nineteenth Century*
François Coppée: *Ten Tales* (Learned)
W.E. Henley: *Views and Reviews*
Arthur Symons: 'The Decadent Movement in Literature,' in *Harper's Magazine* for November 1893."

Over the years Robinson made a number of inevitably offsetting statements about methodology in verse:

To Arthur R. Gledhill, October 28, 1896: "I sing, in my own particular manner . . . of a more prosy connotation than those generally admitted into the domain of metre. In short, I write whatever I think is appropriate to the subject and let tradition go to the deuce." (Torrence, p. 13.)

To Amy Lowell, March 18, 1916: "I don't care a pinfeather what form a poem is written in so long as it makes me sit up." (Torrence, p. 93.)

"I know that many of the new writers insist that it is harder to write good *vers libre* than to write good rhymed poetry. And judging from some of their results, I am inclined to agree with them." (Joyce Kilmer, "Edwin Arlington Robinson Defines Poetry," New York *Times Magazine Section* [April 9, 1916], 12.)

"I am essentially a classicist in poetic composition, and I believe that the accepted media for the masters of the past will continue to be used in the future. There is, of course, room for infinite variety, manipulation and invention within the limits of traditional forms and meters, but any violent deviation from the classic mean may be a confession of inability to do the real thing, poetically speaking." (Lucius Beebe, "Robinson Sees Romantic Strain in Future Verse," New York *Herald Tribune* [December 22, 1929], I, 19.)

"'Poetry must be music,' he said, 'not that it must jingle, but it *must be music*. And that is the defect of free verse. Maybe it's not memorable either. I cannot recall a single poem written in free verse, can you?'" (Nancy Evans, "Edwin Arlington Robinson," *Bookman*, LXXV [November 1932], 676-677.)

"One writes as one paints. There really is no method." (Schriftgiesser, p. 1.)

"Do you write free verse?" "'No, I write badly enough as it is.'" (Malcolm Cowley, "Edwin Arlington Robinson," in Malcolm Cowley, editor, *After the Genteel Tradition: American Writers 1910-1930* [Carbondale, Illinois, 1964], p. 33.)

See also Robinson's observations in Gorman, p. 7.

. . / / . .

A large degree of merit

THE TORRENT

In spite of the modest appearance of *The Torrent and The Night Before*, and that it was printed for the author, and its too simple dedication, one finds in Edwin Arlington Robinson's paper-bound volume of poems a large degree of merit. Our method of printing it may not be sufficiently intelligible, so it may be explained that the author combines those of the first and last poems of the book to produce his title. There is a remarkably striking resemblance in the story of "The Night Before" to D'Annunzio's *Episcopo & Co.*,[1] the death-bed confession of a murderer who is to suffer for his crime in a few hours, but it is entirely permissible for poets to choose their subjects from prose works, and whether it was intentional or not does not detract from the commendable character of the blank verse production of Mr. Robinson.[2] One does not have to read far in "The Night Before" to discover its merit:

> Look you, Domine; look you, and listen.
> Look in my face, first: search every line there;
> Mark every feature, — chin, lip, and forehead.
> Look in my eyes, and tell me the lesson
> You read there; — measure my nose, and tell me
> Where I am wanting. A man's nose, Domine,
> Is often the cast of his inward spirit; —
> So mark mine well.... But why do you smile so? —
> Pity, or what? — Is it written all over,
> This face of mine, with a brute's confession? —
> Nothing but sin there? nothing but hell-scars? —
> Or is it because there is something better —
> A glmmer of good, maybe, — or a shadow
> Of something that's followed me down from childhood —
> Followed me all these years and kept me,
> Spite of my slips and sins and follies —
> Spite of my last red sin, my murder, —
> Just out of hell? — Yes? — something of that kind?
> And you smile for that? ... You're a good man, Domine. —
> The one good man in the world who knows me —
> My one good friend in a world that mocks me,
> Here in this hard stone cage.... But I leave it
> To-morrow.... To-morrow! — My God; am I crying? —
> Are these things tears? — Tears! — What! am I
>   frightened? —
> I who swore I should go to the scaffold
> With big strong steps, and... No more, — I thank you,
> But no.... I am all right now! ... No! — listen!

A few lines more are necessary to show the purity of the verse:

> I loved that woman! —
> Not for her face, but for something fairer —
> Something diviner — I thought — than beauty:
> I loved the spirit — the human something
> That seemed to chime with my own condition,
> And make soul-music when we were together; —
> And we were never apart from the moment
> My eyes flashed into her eyes the message
> That swept itself in a quivering answer
> Back through my strange lost being. My pulses
> Leapt with an aching speed; and the measure
> Of this great world grew small and smaller,
> Till it seemed the sky and the land and the ocean
> Closed at last in a mist all golden
> Around us two. — And we stood for a season
> Like gods outflung from chaos, dreaming
> That we were the king and the queen of the fire
> That reddened the clouds of love that held us
> Blind to the new world soon to be ours —

Ours to seize and sway. The passion
Of that great love was a nameless passion —
Bright as the blaze of the sun at noonday,
Wild as the flames of hell; but, mark you,
Never a whit less pure for its fervor.
The baseness in me (for I was human)
Burned like a worm, and perished; and nothing
Was left me then but a soul that mingled
Itself with hers, and swayed and shuddered
In fearful triumph. — When I consider
That helpless love and the cursed folly
That wrecked my life for the sake of a woman,
Who broke with a laugh the chains of her marriage
(Whatever the word may mean) I wonder
If all the woe was her sin, or whether
The chains themselves were enough to lead her
In love's despite to break them. . . . Sinners
And saints — I say — are rocked in the cradle,
But never are known till the will within them
Speaks in its own good time. . . .

From "The Book World," Cleveland *Leader* (January 31, 1897), 21.

1   Gabriele D'Annunzio (1863-1938), histrionic Italian poet, dramatist, novelist, World War I hero, fascist, published *Giovanni Episcopo* in 1892. It was translated by Myrta Leonora Jones as *Episcopo and Company* and issued by Herbert S. Stone & Co., Chicago, in 1896. It was said to show the unmistakable influence of Dostoievski's *Marmeladof*; compared to Baudelaire, Flaubert, Gautier, Maupassant, Dante Rossetti; accused of flat plagiarism from Joséphin Péladan (1859-1918), French novelist, mystic, esthete, art and drama critic. Robinson's poem has the same staccato question and confession format as D'Annunzio's, and both lean toward the melodramatic. The latter engrosses a more complicated plot than Robinson's simple triangle, and the central figure undergoes greater degradation.

2   Robinson to Edith Brower, May 15, 1897: "If it is good for anything, it will stand; if it isn't, it won't." (Cary, p. 45.)

. . / / . .

Many opals; much clay

THE TORRENT AND THE NIGHT BEFORE
Robert Steed Dunn

What we want first to know after reading this little pamphlet of verse, — for outwardly it is hardly more, — is whether Mr. Robinson, by force of publisher's and other circumstances, had his little volume printed at his own expense, or whether he did so wishing to remain unidentified with our Bliss Carmans and Richard Hoveys. Our faith is in the latter judgment; at any rate, what lies between his plain blue paper covers is far too sincere and healthy to bear heralding in a book-stall by outrageous drawings (?) of purple meadows and green maidens. Mr. Robinson has struck out from the log-path of minor American poets of to-day, returning by a short cut to a healthy pupilship under disregarded volumes of Arnold and Browning.¹ He might have gone back further by thirty or forty years for his models, and drowned out some of the inanity of fag-end-of-the-century verse. The chief fault to pick is that he reflects too much the spirit of his patrons, he gives too little of an unadulterated self, except in the less noticeable poems. This is not happily ominous, for his chance of future success lies in the question whether, when he has demolished his scaffolding, he can stand by himself.

For a long time we have not seen verse which deserves greater praise in proportion to the obscurity which the manner of its birth is destined to give it. We grieve with Mr. Robinson that a smiling paragraph in a review of boasted circulation is a greater impetus to fame in these days than any amount of "true worth." Of course the auther has not always shown tact of selection; there are many opals; there is much clay, but the process of choice on the reader's part is worth the reward, and does not numb the mind for the vigor of the imagination that rings vividly through the best of the work, that is effective because it is sincere, that is poetic, because the man is — a poet. There are some rare examples of compression of phrase, notably the first stanza of "The Children of the Night." Mr. Robinson, however, does not seem quite to have mastered the mysteries of refrain. The repetition at the end of each stanza of "Luke Havergal" fails somehow, nay, mars, what is otherwise the most impressive composition in the little volume.

But that he is not original,² the author seems to know, and it is exasperating that the tone of the little quotation on the title-page sums up the faults of work we cannot help taking seriously, withal so flippantly. He says, quoting Coppée: "*Qui pourrais-je imiter pour etre original?*"³

From *Harvard Monthly*, XXIII (February 1897), 205-206.

Robert Steed Dunn (1877-1955), of Katonah, New York, was a junior at Harvard when he wrote this review. He became a newspaper correspondent, reporting the Russo-Japanese war and a world cruise of the U.S. Fleet in 1907. Author of six volumes, including a novel and a collection of poems, he served in naval intelligence, as high commissioner and naval attaché in Turkey.

1 See the section *Browning, Browning, Browning* in the chapter "Preliminary Vistas" of this volume.

From the very start Robinson was yoked to Browning despite the salient differences in major aspects of their poetry. He frequently disavowed the connection — in conversation, in correspondence, in interviews — in fact, expressed strong aversion to the bulk of the Englishman's works: "I care nothing for Browning outside of his lyrics. They are the greatest we have, to my mind, but the longer things I cannot read. . . . I gave up the plays long ago." (Cary, p. 71.) The latter were "so deadly dull that I have always found it next to impossible to read them." (Torrence, p. 47.) In 1930 he wrote Helen Grace Adams that he disliked "Rabbi Ben Ezra" so much that he hadn't read it "in something like thirty years." (Torrence, p. 160.) In his poem "Momus" (1910) he inquired slyly, "What's become of Browning?" And in 1916 he singled Browning out as "a great modern instance" of the tendency toward oddity and violence in poetry. (Kilmer, p. 12.)

Robinson's definitive repudiation of the ascribed influence is contained in his letter to Lewis N. Chase, July 11, 1917: "When I was younger, I was very much under the influence of Wordsworth and Kipling, but never at all, so far as I am aware, under that of Browning, as many seem to believe. As a matter of fact, I have never been able to understand the alleged resemblance unless it can be attributed to my use of rather more colloquial language than 'poetic diction' has usually sanctioned. I began the writing of verse long before I was old enough to know better, and I fancy that I am safe in saying that my style, such as it is, was pretty well formed by the time my first book was published, in 1896." (Torrence, p. 102.) Against this must be weighed the words of his Harvard contemporary, Mowry Saben, in a review of the Torrence edition of *Selected Letters*: "But I recall distinctly that, in letters to me written between forty and fifty years ago, he was revealed as a Browning enthusiast. He was almost obsessed at this time by 'Waring,' and he urged me to read *Prince Hohenstiel-Schwangau, Saviour of Society* with all the fervor of the true disciple. I do not know how long the fervor lasted, and am inclined to think that it was Browning's optimism that finally made the English poet indigestible, for there was nothing truly optimistic in Robinson's credo." (*Argonaut*, CXIX [March 29, 1940], 22.)

By 1917 Robinson had learned to shrug him off philosophically. "I suppose I shall have to be 'like Browning' to the end of my days," he told Edith Brower. (Cary, p. 169.) And in 1930 he exuded total indifference in this letter to Lilla Cabot Perry: "I don't know just what to say about Browning except that he don't give me any great pleasure." (Colby College Library.)

2 There is drastic variance of opinion on Robinson's originality in these early reviews. See the section *Originality* in the chapter "Prelminary Vistas" of this volume.

3 Closing line of Scene III, François Coppée, *Le Trésor* (Paris, 1879), p. 23, a comedy in eight scenes. Robinson omits the comma after *imiter*.

Between January and April in 1894 Robinson wrote of Coppée to Harry Smith several times, commending his "wholesome" tone and "healthy naturalism." (Sutcliffe, pp. 122, 124, 128, 143.)

. . / / . .

His world is a prison-house

THE TORRENT AND THE NIGHT BEFORE
Harry Thurston Peck

A little book of poetry containing some forty-four pages, and bound in a plain sky blue paper cover, called *The Torrent and The Night Before*, has come to our table during the past month. It is printed by Messrs. Houghton, Mifflin and Company for the author,[1] Mr. Edwin Arlington Robinson, whose address is Gardiner, Me., and is dedicated to "any man, woman, or critic who will cut the edges of it. — I have done the top." "The Torrent" begins,

> I found a torrent falling in a glen
> Where the sun's light shone silvered and leaf-split;
> The boom, the foam, and the mad flash of it
> All made a magic symphony; . . .

and those who read this and have any liking for poetry will read on to the end. Some of the verses we do not care for, especially the long poem at the end. There is true fire in his verse, and there are the swing and the singing of wind and wave and the passion of human emotion in his lines; but his limitations are vital. His humour is of a grim sort, and the world is not beautiful to him, but a prison-house.[2] In the night-time there is weeping and sorrow, and joy does not come in the morning. But here and there in a sonnet he lets himself go, and the cry of a yearning spirit[3] enters the lute of Orpheus and sounds a sweet and wondrous note. We quote one sonnet which is free and unstrained and spontaneous in its outburst, flinging itself into form with a natural *abandon* and full-blooded life: ["Sonnet" (Oh, for a poet) follows.]

From "Chronicle and Comment," *Bookman*, IV (February 1897), 509-510.

Harry Thurston Peck (1856-1914), writer of verses, biography, history, juvenilia, classical philology, and literary criticism, taught Latin language and literature at Columbia University for twenty-six years. He was editor in chief of *Bookman*, 1895-1902, during which period he wrote most of the commentary. Extra-marital difficulties led to collapse and suicide. Like William Henry Thorne and Vance Thompson who also reviewed Robinson's poems, Peck might quite as well have modeled for one of his offbeat characterizations. Harry Smith apparently commented on Peck's poem in the *Bookman* for March 1895, "The Other One," a sentimental bromide on the transience of babyhood. Robinson responded with as little admiration for Peck as he for Robinson's dismal vision. "I don't think I care over much for Prof. Peck's poetry. The thought was all that made it tolerable." (Sutcliffe, p. 223.)

1 The printing was done by H.O. Houghton & Company's Riverside Press, duly noted on verso of title page, not by the publishers Houghton, Mifflin & Company.

2 This statement elicited the now famous retort by Robinson in his letter to the *Bookman*, V (March 1897), 7. The entire item, printed in "Chronicle and Comment," reads: "Mr. E.A. Robinson writes thanking us for the 'unexpected notice' of his book of poems called *The Torrent and The Night Before* in these columns in the February *Bookman*. Mr. Robinson adds: 'I am sorry to learn that I have painted myself in such lugubrious colours. The world is not a prison house, but a kind of spiritual kindergarten, where millions of bewildered infants are trying to spell God with the wrong blocks.'" Years later he said with "a sort of fond disapproval" to Nancy Evans, "I was young then and it was a smart thing to say." (Evans, p. 680.) At the time, he exclaimed to Harry Smith, "The *Bookman* evidently takes me for a yelling pessimist, and that I must say that I am very much surprised.... Because I don't dance on [an] illuminated hilltop and sing about the bobolinks and bumble-bees, they tell me that my world is a 'prison house, etc.'" (Sutcliffe, p. 273.)

Robinson's prison-house trope undoubtedly owes something to Wordsworth's "Ode on Intimations of Immortality," stanza 5:

> Heaven lies about us in our infancy!
> Shades of the prison-house begin to close
> Upon the growing Boy,
> But he beholds the light...

On February 16, 1895 Robinson wrote to Harry Smith: "In my private opinion his 'Ode on the Intimations of Immortality' is worth all the rest of his work put together." (Sutcliffe, p. 207.)

3 This phrase was picked for use in an unidentified advertising circular, about which Robinson commented wryly, "I may be 'a yearning spirit' but I don't like to tell people so." (Cary, p. 60.)

. . / / . .

Note of austere restraint

THE TORRENT AND THE NIGHT BEFORE

William Morton Payne

"This book is dedicated to any man, woman, or critic who will cut the edges of it. — I have done the top." This notice introduces Mr. E.H. [*sic*]

Robinson's unpretentious pamphlet of verse, and we hasten to say, ignoring the implication that critics are epicene (a charge made once before by "Christopher North"), that we have not only cut the pages, but would cut many more of the sort, and be grateful to the writer for a number of reasons. One reason for instance, is that he has furnished an apt text for the reviewer of minor poetry.

> Oh, for a poet — for a beacon bright
> To rift this changeless glimmer of dead gray:
> To spirit back the Muses, long astray,
> And flush Parnassus with a newer light:
> To put these little sonnet-men to flight
> Who fashion, in a shrewd mechanic way,
> Songs without souls that flicker for a day
> To vanish in irrevocable night.

It would not be fair, at least relatively, to apply these verses to Mr. Robinson's own poems, which are far above the average in thought and expression. They strike many grateful notes, and particularly the note of austere restraint that is so rarely heard in contemporary song. A striking example of the writer's workmanship in the close of his sonnet to "Verlaine," surely the work of no "little sonnet-man."

> Song sloughs away the sin to find redress
> In art's complete remembrance: nothing clings
> For long but laurel to the stricken brow
> That felt the Muse's finger; nothing less
> Than hell's fulfilment of the end of things
> Can blot the star that shines on Paris now.

We are not quite prepared to say all this of Verlaine himself, but the doctrine is of wide application, and gives pause to the professional belittler of great and shining names.

From "Recent Poetry," *Dial*, XXII (February 1, 1897), 92-93.

William Morton Payne (1858-1919), accomplished in seven languages, was a noted translator, teacher, author, and literary critic along Arnoldian principles. He served as literary editor on two Chicago newspapers before assuming associate editorship of the *Dial*, 1892-1915. Robinson often disparaged him in letters to Harry Smith. May 13, 1894: "What do you think of William Morton Payne's wholesale reviewing of poetry and fiction? It seems to me that he does it a little too easily." (Sutcliffe, p. 153.) November 4, 1894: "Payne's criticism of *Lord Ormont* . . . seems to me almost an insult — not so much for what he says as for what he doesn't say." (p. 178.) May 12, 1895: "If possible, it is worse than the patronizing ease of Wm. Morton Payne in the *Dial*." (p. 225.) September 27, 1896: "When I say the *Dial*, of course I mean William Morton Payne — his name and all that goes with it." (p. 257.) And shortly following this review: "The *Dial*, by the way, was very kind," Robinson admitted, then referred to Payne, not without irony, as "our old friend," and proceeded to quote him generously. (p. 277.)

. . / / . .

Denham Sutcliffe (pp. 274-275) records the following sentence as one of the comments on *The Torrent* enclosed in Robinson's February 3, 1897 letter to Harry Smith: " '. . . The result will probably repay the expenditure of trouble, as Mr. Robinson has a respectable knack of versification.' — *Philadelphia Press*." Search of extant editions of this newspaper failed to turn up the item from which this quotation was extracted.

. . / / . .

A book that I cannot help reading

THE TORRENT AND THE NIGHT BEFORE
Edward Eggleston

... When I look into some modern novels, I say, "Here is a man who says, 'Go to, I will do something original.' " It reminds me of Coppée's saying, "Whom shall I imitate to be original?"

Which reminds me that a man in Gardiner, Maine, has written lately some delightfully original[1] little bits of poetry and printed them in a little blue pamphlet with this sentence from Coppée for a motto. He calls it *The Torrent and The Night Before*. His name is Edwin Arlington Robinson. I never heard of him till he sent me his booklet. They send me books of poetry until I cannot get around for them, but he has sent me a book that I cannot help reading.[2]

From "Edward Eggleston: An Interview," *Outlook*, LV (February 6, 1897), 436.

Edward Eggleston (1837-1902) was an Indiana Bible agent and circuit-riding Methodist preacher who turned to writing short stories, historical romances, biographies, satires, and juvenile fiction. *The Hoosier Schoolmaster* (1871) was his major work, a somewhat sentimentalized though authentic masterpiece in the realistic local color genre.

Eggleston was so impressed by *The Torrent* that, according to Hagedorn (p. 109), "He carried the book about in his pocket, thrust it under the eyes of friends whose judgment he trusted. 'Do you know this man?' They read the poems and shared his wonder that this phenomenon should be unknown."

Eggleston was the most prominent figure to have publicly recommended Robinson so far, almost to the latter's embarrassment. "Dr.[3] Eggleston stirred things up with his kind reference, in the *Outlook*, to my masterpieces, and I am getting more applications for non-existing copies of my book than please me." (Sutcliffe, p. 277.)

For the third time in respect to *The Torrent*, the Gardiner (Me.) *Daily Reporter-Journal* saw fit to import commentary rather than offer some of its own. Among "Local Gleanings" on February 6, 1897, p. [3], appeared this item: "Dr. Edward Eggleston in the *Outlook*, commenting on men and things, has the following complimentary words for a young Gardiner author:" [here quoting the last paragraph of his remarks]. The whole was repeated in the Friday weekly edition on February 12.

1 In his preceding remarks on recent poetry Eggleston lamented the tendency toward "more will than spontaneity," and held up Hardy and George Meredith as examples of poets who were "trying to do something unusual"

2 In a letter to Robinson on January 10, 1897 (which he unmindfully dated 1896), Eggleston elaborated on this declaration:
   My Dear Sir:
      I don't thank you for sending me a book for I get books of poetry until I haven't shelf-room for them. But you have given me a rare sensation! You have

sent me a book that I can read and for that I thank you. I am a very busy man but you have sent me a book I can not help reading, and for that I forgive you. I can not find anybody in my circle who knows you — I find friends of good judgment who on reading your poems wonder and wonder how it is that you are yet unknown. And so, in this world where are like men speaking to one another for cheer's sake in the dark, let a total stranger hail you with admiration, putting aside all flattering words of which you have no need, for which you have no desire.
               Yours with sincere emotion,
                    Edwd. Eggleston

To Edward [sic][4] Arlington Robinson
Gardiner, Maine.
   I have ventured to use some of the expressions in this letter in an interview to be published in February. If the passage should get into print you will kindly forgive the repetition.

3   Eggleston received an honorary D.D. from Indiana University in 1870 and an L.H.D. from Alleghany College in 1893.

4   Eggleston also addressed the envelope of this letter (now in Colby College Library) to Edward.

. . / / . .

Destined to more than passing fame

THE TORRENT AND THE NIGHT BEFORE

A new Maine author destined to more than passing fame has come into prominence of late as the writer of remarkable verse. He is Mr. Edwin Arlington Robinson of Gardiner who published a few months since an edition of 300 copies of a book of sonnets and ballads with the title *The Torrent and The Night Before*. Some of the sonnets in the little brochure originally appeared in the *Harvard Crimson* — Mr. Robinson is, we believe, a graduate of Harvard[1] — the others having been given to the public for the first time in the collection under the above named title.[2] Mr. Robinson has received letters from many literary critics commending his work, including one from Prof. Charles Eliot Norton, of Harvard, one of the best critics of the English language in America, praising it in the very highest degree. In the number of the *Outlook* for Feb. 6, there is a report of a long interview with Dr. Edward Eggleston, commenting upon men and books, in the course of which he says, "A man in Gardiner, Maine, has written lately some delightfully original little bits of poetry and printed them in a little blue pamphlet with this sentence from Coppée for a motto: "Whom shall I imitate to be original?" He calls it *The Torrent and The Night Before*. His name is Edwin Arlington Robinson. I never heard of him until he sent me his booklet. They send me books of poetry until I cannot get around for them, but he has sent me a book that I cannot help reading."[3] This is very high praise. May not the copies of this "little blue pamphlet" some day be as rare and sell for as high a price as Poe's *Tamerlane*?[4]

From Bangor *Daily Commercial* (February 13, 1897), 16.

The first half of this review has many phrases in common with the note in the Gardiner (Me.) *Daily Reporter-Journal* of January 2, 1897, reprinted in this volume. Two errors — 300 instead of 312 copies of *The Torrent*, and attribution to the *Harvard Crimson* instead of the *Harvard Advocate* — are also repeated

Robinson provides a sidelight to this review in his growingly typical self-deprecatory tone. On February 11, 1897 he wrote to Harry Smith: "Yesterday I received a very funny letter from Mr. S.J. Boardman of the Bangor *Commercial*. He wants my photograph and autobiography for publication. I appreciate his kindness, but I do not sympathize with his notions of human sanity." (Sutcliffe, p. 277.) No photograph accompanied the review.

1 Robinson entered Harvard in September 1891 and completed two years of study. He did not earn nor was ever granted a degree.

2 The reviewer is in error here too. Outside of those published in the *Harvard Advocate*, eleven poems were printed in other sources before inclusion in *The Torrent*.

3 Coppée's motto is interpolated here and one word is altered, otherwise Eggleston's comment is faithfully transcribed (see preceding review).

4 See the end of Nathan Haskell Dole's review for a similar prophecy. The odds on *The Torrent* ever becomng as rare numerically as *Tamerlane* are improbable; about 125 *Torrents* are currently known to have survived as against less than ten of the latter. As to monetary value, *The Torrent* is already notable as "easily the most costly unit of American verse of its generation," although a newly available *Tamerlane* would command a price fifty to a hundred times higher. See Robinson's "The First Seven Years," *Colophon*, Part IV (1930), n.p.; and Richard Cary, " 'Go Little Book': An Odyssey of Robinson's *The Torrent and The Night Before*," *Colby Library Quarterly*, VII (December 1967), 515, 525-527.

.. / / ..

That indefinable something called poetry

A NEW POETIC VENTURE
William Peterfield Trent

Mr. Edwin Arlington Robinson, of Gardiner, Maine, has sent us a tiny volume of verse privately printed for him at the Riverside Press. He names his booklet, from its first and last poems, *The Torrent and The Night Before*. There are only forty-four pages all told, but in his use of them Mr. Robinson shows that he possesses what so many poets lack — a modicum of common-sense. He utilizes his pages to the full by printing his verses straight along without wasting space by giving us what the printer calls "fat pages." This is so sensible a procedure, especially in a privately printed book, that we feel bound to commend it.[1] We wish we could praise as heartily the independence shown in the short dedication which runs as follows: "This book is dedicated to any man, woman, or critic who will cut the edges of it. — I have done the top." Independence is all very well — but Mr. Robinson's has an unnecessary note of flippancy about it.[2]

We have, however, made ourselves one of his dedicatees, for we have cut the edges of this book and we are glad to have done so. Mr. Robinson has one important quality of the poet — one that is a sufficient excuse for his having published his verses — to-wit, a knowledge of the technique of his art and an obvious love for it. We fancy that he is young, for we detect the influences of other poets in his work, and if he is, we have decided hopes of him — nay, we not only have hopes of him, which is what almost any kindly critic may say of any fledgling poet, but we have a positive desire to see his next volume. The maturity which years will bring and the love and respect for his art which he already has will surely enable him to take longer and higher flights away from the commonplace level of mere versifying around which so many contemporary poets keep hovering.[3]

Mr. Robinson has, of course, a good deal to learn in the coming years. He must learn that if he wishes to write "ballades" he must improve on those given on pages 6 and 10 of his book.[4] He must learn that the impressionist effect produced in "The House on the Hill" is not worth striving after, and that the chaotic effect produced in "A Poem for Max Nordau" is distinctly to be avoided.[5] He must learn to put a little more concreteness into such poems as "Her Eyes," and "An Old Story," if he wishes to be loved and "understood" of the people. But it is always easy enough to shower advice good or bad on a young poet, so let us rather give him some ungrudging praise.

We think that he handles the sonnet very well indeed — especially when he writes of his favorite authors. Take for example the close of one to Matthew Arnold: —

>   Still does a cry through sad Valhalla go
>   For Balder, pierced with Lok's unhappy spray —
>   For Balder, all but spared by Frea's charms;
>   And still does art's imperial vista show,
>   On the hushed sands of Oxus, far away,
>   Young Sohrab dying in his father's arms.[6]

Almost if not equally as good are the sonnets on Crabbe, Hood, Thomas Hardy, and Verlaine. The verses on Whitman are also excellent, although some may not agree with their note of praise.[7] But everyone will agree with the eloquent close of this sonnet which has no name: ["Sonnet" (Oh, for a poet) follows.]

If all our "sonnet-men" wrote sonnets like the above, Mr. Robinson would not be justified in calling them "little."[8]

But our poet does good work in those commoner measures, which, as Goethe remarked long since, go more swiftly to the heart than the elaborate verse-forms that find so much favor to-day. Here, for example, are some strong stanzas from a poem entitled "The Children of the Night":

>   And if there be no other life,
>   And if there be no other chance
>   To weigh their sorrow and their strife
>   Than in the scales of circumstance —
>
>   'Twere better, ere the sun go down
>   Upon the first day we embark,
>   In life's embittered sea to drown
>   Than sail forever in the dark.

. . . .

> If there be nothing, good or bad,
> But chaos for a soul to trust, —
> God counts it for a soul gone mad,
> And if God be God, He is just.
>
> . . . .
>
> There is one creed, and only one,
> That glorifies God's excellence; —
> So cherish, that His will be done,
> The common creed of common sense.

The thought expressed in the above verses is not new or profound, the feeling is and has been experienced as intensely by many men, but it is impossible to deny that Mr. Robinson has transmuted them into that indefinable something called poetry.[9]

There are other things to praise in Mr. Robinson's book, the Browning-like verve of the last poem,[10] the felicity of the "Horace to Leuconoë"[11] (though surely Mr. Robinson must feel that the sonnet form is a lame one in which to render Horace in spite of the example of a distinguished living poet), the homely patriotism of the sonnet in praise of Boston. There are also other things to condemn such as the lack of restraint in the poem entitled "The Wilderness."[12] Our space, however, is limited and we do not wish our readers to suspect us as posing as a "poet-finder." That is a dangerous and somewhat unnecessary thing to do. The true poet sooner or later finds his public and his public finds him — often without the intervention of the critic, sometimes in spite of the latter's denunciations. Our purpose is a more modest one — viz. to encourage Mr. Robinson with the thought that he has had at least one interesting reader. To have one such reader is better than nothing, although even so Mr. Robinson may be in a worse plight than an author of whom we have heard who went to his bookseller at the end of a year to inquire the fate of his volume of poems and found that exactly one copy had been bought. Perhaps Mr. Robinson has not had — or desired to have — even this success. Certainly the copy that found its way to our table was not bought — but we have bought many worse books.

From *Sewanee Review*, V (April 1897), 243-246.

William Peterfield Trent (1862-1939), professor of English at the University of the South currently and at Columbia University after 1900, founded the *Sewanee Review*. He published considerable criticism on American and English literature, and was an editor of *The Cambridge History of American Literature*.

Robinson to Edith Brower, May 9, 1897: "The . . . Professor's criticism was on the whole most friendly, however, and he won my lifelong affection by speaking a good word for 'The Night Before'. . . . most people give it the 'damnation of silence.'" Cary, p. 42.) Actually, Trent makes a transient, blind allusion to the poem, and it is surprising that Robinson did not grumble at the affiliation with Browning.

1 Robinson was a little proud, a little optimistic, and discreetly skeptical about the ultimate physical appearance of *The Torrent*. To Harry Smith he said: "You will like the typography, at any rate, and at the same time will have a chance to test my judgment in the matter of page arrangement and typographical art in general. If the book turns out, mechanically, as I think it will, it will be about the best piece of

work the Riverside Press ever produced, which is not saying very much." (Sutcliffe, p. 257.) The format of the booklet is, as a matter of fact, run of the mill.

2 Robert Steed Dunn (see his review in this volume) makes the same accusation of flippancy in regard to Robinson's use of Coppée's line as epigraph on the title page. It would be more in accordance with Robinson's temperament to have said he was being defensively ironic in both cases.

3 Robinson developed a definite theory about the proper moment for a poet's coming-out. To Helene Mullins, April 30, 1927: "My advice to young writers is not to publish a book of poems before they are thirty; and of course my advice is, naturally never taken." (Colby College Library.) To Harry Salpeter: "I always tell young people not to publish anything until they're thirty. If they'd wait they'd save themselves a lot of needless heartache. I try to dissuade them from publishing at all, but that's impossible." ("E.A. Robinson, Poet," New York *World* [May 15, 1927], 8M.) He similarly cautioned Malcolm Cowley, who sent him a copy of his *Blue Juniata* (1929) inscribed "from one who published a book while he was still thirty (and not before, on your advice) and wonders now — was he right!" (Colby College Library.) To Winfield Townley Scott: "Don't publish a book till you're thirty. Thirty's time enough." ("To See Robinson," *New Mexico Quarterly*, XXVI [Summer 1956], 170.) Robinson was just short of his twenty-seventh birthday when he brought out *The Torrent*.

4 "Ballade of a Ship," pp. 6-7, originally titled "Ballade of the White Ship," reprinted in *The Children of the Night* (1897) but in no edition of his *Collected Poems*. "Ballade" (In dreams I crossed a barren land), pp. 10-11, which he renamed "Ballade of Broken Flutes," dedicated it "To A.T. Schumann," and incorporated in successive editions of his *Collected Poems*. "Schumann stimulated the youth to compress thought and emotion within accepted confines, to sharpen his poetic teeth on the intricate French forms." (Hagedorn, p. 37.)

Robinson's copy of Gleeson White's *Ballades and Rondeaus, Chants Royal, Sestinas, Villanelles, &c* (London, 1887) is now in Colby College Library. He also read Thomas B. Mosher's *Old World Lyrics* (Portland, Maine, 1893), containing ballades by Villon, Lyonnet de Coismes, and Théodore de Banville, translated by Dante Gabriel Rossetti, Andrew Lang, and John Payne. (See Sutcliffe, pp. 142-143.)

In 1894 he confessed to "a weakness for the suggestiveness of those artificial forms" (Sutcliffe, p. 146), but by 1932 he had changed his refrain somewhat: "I tried many experiments — ballads, quatrains, villanelles. I tried many forms, but I was not really interested in them except as exercises." (Evans, p. 676.)

5 Robinson to Laura E. Richards in 1902: "The funny parts will not be apparent to those who have had too much of the sunny side of life, and they will wonder why it seems so queer when they try, as they will, to take it seriously. This is the difficulty (or possibly the vital advantage) of being born a comedian under the wrong (or again possibly the best) conditions." (Richards, *E.A.R.*, p. 55.) He was not writing specifically about the Nordau poem but his words are applicable to its burlesque intent.

6 "Among his favorite poets [was] Arnold. . . . He liked 'Sohrab and Rustum.'" (Tryon, p. 11.)

7 Robinson went through several phases in his estimation of Walt Whitman. While at Harvard: "When [Mowry] Saben filled a memorable evening with extracts from Walt Whitman, ending with 'When Lilacs Last in the Dooryard Bloom'd,' Robinson mused, 'If that's not poetry, it is something greater than poetry.'" (Hagedorn, p. 73.) Yet James L. Tryon (p. 12) did not recall that Robinson "said anything to me about Whitman."

At the MacDowell Colony: "For Whitman he could say little. 'I may be wrong; I probably am. But I have never been able to find so much in him.'" (Rollo Walter Brown, *Next Door to a Poet* [New York, 1937], pp. 36-37.)

To Nancy Evans (p. 679): "Somehow I feel that Whitman seems greater than he is. Anyway, I feel that whatever power he had was as a poet — not as a thinker."

And to Winfield Townley Scott (p. 167): "He wondered, too, if Whitman were 'as great as some people think he is.' Parts of *Leaves of Grass* were all right and 'some of the shorter things he wrote as an old man are good.' When I spoke of an early Robinson 'sonnet' commemorating Whitman's death, (not included in the *Collected Poems*), he said 'It wasn't a sonnet; it was a piece of blank verse. I was very young when I wrote it, but I knew all the time I was writing it that I didn't really mean it.' "

8 Reference is to line 5 of this poem: "To put these little sonnet men to flight."

Robinson's first published poem, "Thalia," is a sonnet, and he had such affection for the form that he issued a volume of *Sonnets 1889-1927* in 1928, all of which had previously appeared in print.

In the biography Hagedorn asserts, "The boy himself learned to write a sonnet in twenty minutes — and to work over it for twenty days" (p. 37); and relays Kate Vannah's remark to Mrs. Richards, "He says it takes him six weeks to write a sonnet" (p. 96). And in *The Edwin Arlington Robinson Memorial* (Gardiner, Maine, 1936), pp. [5-6]: " 'Some one line of a sonnet,' he admitted on one occasion, 'generally does, I suppose, come to me unaccountably, out of the blue ether. But then I have to work like a dog for three weeks to make the other thirteen lines sound as though they had come out of the blue ether, too.' "

After returning from England in 1923: " 'I'm in the sonnet business again,' Robinson wrote [Lewis M.] Isaacs, 'and rather enjoy the shackles after so much free running — only the running in blank verse is not quite so free as it looks.' " (Hagedorn, p. 337.)

To Ridgely Torrence, August 30, 1923: "I am trying to write sonnets, but when I consider that there are only about forty or fifty really good ones in the world, I wonder if I hadn't better be delivering milk." (Torrence, p. 135.)

In equally self-critical vein, to H. Bacon Collamore on October 18, 1928: "As the lines you quote from one of my very early sonnets seem solemn and pretentious for an inscription I have taken the liberty to substitute for them the closing lines of 'Captain Craig.' " (Colby College Library.)

In 1932: " 'There is no such thing as a sonnet,' he said, 'there are only individual sonnets.' " (Evans, p. 677.)

"He said that he used to get ten dollars for a sonnet and that he had sometimes polished and repolished it for a whole week — ten dollars for a week's work!" (Frederika Beatty, "Edwin Arlington Robinson as I Knew Him," *South Atlantic Quarterly*, XLIII [October 1944], 377.) "I wrote sonnets because at that time I'd rather write sonnets than do anything else." (p. 378.)

9 Despite this and other strong endorsements, Robinson never included this poem in his series of *Collected Poems*. "Robinson explains the suppression of this poem by saying that he considers it too boyish to go on permanent record, but. . . . A more plausible reason for the omission of 'The Children of the Night' lies in the fact that 'The Man Against the Sky' some twenty years later said very much what had been said in the earlier poem and said it in a poem notable for its imaginative power and extreme beauty of form." (Lucius Beebe, *Aspects of the Poetry of Edwin Arlington Robinson* [Cambridge, Mass., 1928], pp. 18-19.)

10 "The Night Before," pp. 34-44.

11 This "felicity" was hard won. Robinson sent an early version of the poem to Harry Smith on May 21, 1891, remarking: "You will find it rather too literal for a poetical translation — a little prosy in places. I have not tried Horace since and I doubt if I ever do again. It is too much work for the pay. I have never seen an English translation of Horace that seemed satisfactory to me; perhaps I am over particular, but I doubt if the thing can be done to catch the spirit of the original. Horace is Latin, or nothing." (Sutcliffe, p. 19.) On December 14 four years later, with a partial revision: "I have been rebuilding that sonnet translation of Horace's ode to Leuconoë. . . . I may get the thing to partly satisfy me some day, but I rather doubt it." (pp. 237-238.)

12 Robinson demonstrated intense interest in what these early critics had to say about his work; his memory of what they said was equally intense. Five years after Trent used the phrase, Robinson remembered it precisely. "By the way, there's jingle

... likewise in the wilderness thing," he wrote Laura E. Richards, "which some people cannot read on account of its 'lack of restraint.'" (Torrence, p. 48.)

. . / / . .

In the "Books Received" section of the *Conservator,* December 1896, *The Torrent and The Night Before* is noted, with Robinson's first name rendered Edward. In the issue of June 1897 (VIII, p. 61), Robinson's poem "Walt Whitman" is reproduced in entirety below this brief preface: "In his little pamphleted volume of poems written by Edwin Arlington Robinson I find these verses inscribed to Walt Whitman:" This item is signed "T," for Horace L. Traubel, Whitman's Boswell. Given his overarching enthusiasm for The Good Gray Poet — to say nothing of his natural volubility — it is astonishing that Traubel refrained from any pronouncement on Robinson's tight-knit performance. See Traubel's review of *Captain Craig,* October 1902, reprinted in this volume.

. . / / . .

Touch of modern consciousness

THE TORRENT AND THE NIGHT BEFORE
Helen Archibald Clarke

A pamphlet book of poems printed by the author is not a propitious form or condition in which to come into the austere presence of the reviewer; but a first glance at *The Torrent and The Night Before* makes one wonder why Mr. Robinson chose to appear as his own sponsor. If only a few more poets as good as he would do so, the prejudice against the self-published poet would disappear. This verse has more power to hold the attention than anything we have seen lately.

In this modest pamphlet a wide range in subject-matter as well as variation in treatment is shown. He describes a scene in nature or a human being with equally facile touch. Among the strongest of his poems are those to various writers. We note especially the sonnets to Zola and Whitman,[1] in both of which he shows a real appreciation of the meaning of such art as theirs. Has Whitman and his relation to the time been more penetratingly summed up than in these lines? —

> His piercing and eternal cadence rings
> Too pure for us — too powerfully pure,
> Too lovingly triumphant, and too large;
> But there are some that hear him, and they know
> That he shall sing to-morrow for all men,
> And that all time shall listen.

The "Ballade of a Ship"[2] has all the weird fascination of some old ballad, with an added touch of modern consciousness on the part of the poet. Utterly different in style is "The House on the Hill." Almost bald in its use of language, the form is yet so managed that a startlingly vivid effect is produced, reminding one of nothing so much as the pathos of a fife and drum corps playing a melancholy tune, — an effect produced by small means. The most ambitious piece in the collection is "The Night Before," — a dramatic monologue giving a murderer's confession the night before his execution. It suggests Gabriel d'Annunzio's *Episcopo and Company*,³ though the details leading up to the crime are not so entirely horrible, and there is no child to add to the anguish of the situation. His hand is not yet quite assured in this difficult form of poetry, but there is plenty of promise of a future mastery in it.

From "Notes on American Verse," *Poet-Lore*, IX (July, August, September 1897), 448-449.

Helen Archibald Clarke (1860-1926) wrote books on Browning, Hawthorne, and Longfellow. Co-founder with Charlotte E. Porter of *Poet-Lore* in 1888, she served as co-editor until her death.

1 "Walt Whitman" is not a sonnet; it consists of three stanzas in blank verse, the last line of each stanza foreshortened to iambic trimeter with feminine ending.
2 Miss Clarke either did not notice or thought it not worth mentioning that line 5 in stanza 2 of this poem was omitted in the printing, at top of page 7. Robinson filled in the missing words in some of the copies he sent out, but not all.
3 This is an extension of the analogy broached in the Cleveland *Leader* review six months earlier (see review in this volume).

. . / / . .

Feeling and power, insight and sympathy

THE TORRENT AND THE NIGHT BEFORE

Edward Abbott

There is real feeling and a certain power in these modestly printed poems of E.A. Robinson (printed by the author), which are preceded by the subjoined dedication: "This book is dedicated to any man, woman, or critic who will cut the edges of it. — I have done the top."

Mr. Robinson could well have afforded to take himself more seriously.¹ He does not belong to the order of "little sonnet-men," to employ his own language,

> Who fashion, in a shrewd mechanic way,
> Songs without souls that flicker for a day
> To vanish in irrevocable night.²

There are insight and sympathy and the sense of musical expression in his verses. We do not have, while reading them, the sensation that we are chewing wind — wind with a little tang of bitter or of sugar about it. We give one extract, which fairly represents the quality of the little volume: ["Credo" follows.]

From "Current Poetry," *Literary World*, XXVIII (August 7, 1897), 260.

Edward Abbott (1841-1908), youngest son of Jacob Abbott, was a Congregational and Episcopalian clergyman, also wrote histories, biographies, juvenile verses, and literary criticism. He was editor of the *Literary World* from 1877-1888 and 1895-1903.

1 When Edith Brower informed Robinson of her intention to publish a critique on *The Children of the Night* (1897), he responded with congenital modesty and complete incorrectness: "I do not think the poems are to be taken so seriously as that, and I am half afraid that you may have some difficulty in finding an editor who will agree with you in thinking them worthy of any elaborate criticism at all." (Cary, p. 60.)

2 "Sonnet" (Oh, for a poet), p. 12.

.. / / ..

William Henry Thorne rates the accolade for being first to proclaim in print the promise of genius in Edwin Arlington Robinson's poetic work. Two and a half years before *The Torrent* emerged, Thorne appended a postscript to the fourth of his excoriative essays on the cultural and religious spirit of New England, which said in part: "It gives me pleasure to add here that in spite of the Globe's severe criticisms of recent New England literature, and in spite of the admitted general dilettante dullness of the modern Massachusetts product, there is still a good deal of literary genius in New England, and that four of the writers in this number of the *Globe* — viz.: Miss Swan, Dr. Schumann, Judge Webster and Mr. Robinson — are from the little town of Gardiner, Maine. . . . Mr. Robinson — a much younger person — bids fair to outshine all competitors in his native state." ("Wreck of the Mayflower," *Globe*, IV [July-September 1894], 801.) In the pages preceding this afterthought Thorne had sneered at the "quasi-chromo culture" explicit in Howells, and the "windy Oscar Wilde-ism, London West End milk and rose-water plaque-ism" of Henry James. Robinson could well thank his stars that this explosive style, this gift for invective was bent in his favor. Pleased, but as always self-defensive, he exclaimed to Harry Smith: "Do not hold me responsible for Thorne's nonsense at the close of the 'Wreck of the Mayflower.'" (Sutcliffe, p. 171.)

A genuine chip of this New England block

THE TORRENT AND THE NIGHT BEFORE

William Henry Thorne

Edwin Arlington Robinson, of Gardiner, Me., is already known to and appreciated by the discriminating readers of the *Globe Review*. Some of the best of the poems that go to make up *The Torrent and The Night Before*, recently published for the author, have already appeared in this magazine[1]; but I select one of the new ones, and one which is very characteristic of the quick and subtle gleaminess of the author's mind and of his great gifts as a poet. He calls it ["Supremacy" follows.]

This sonnet indicates alike the author's clear-cut work and the somewhat startling boldness of his thought.² The one feature is clearly the result of many years of closest study and application; the other a part of that transcendental mood into which New England has fallen since its amateur idolatry of Emerson³ became the ruling fad of the hour. It is due to the position the *Globe* has taken from its first issue until now, as it is due the gifted author here under review, that while admitting and welcoming his beautiful art I should call attention to the limited — doubting, if not utter — unbelieving character and quality of his mind.

I do not blame him for this. It is simply the natural inheritance of two hundred years of down-east Protestant skepticism; and the same dry-rot, unfortunately, has invaded and ruined the work of most of our younger American writers.

I believe that the Scotch parson and novelist, Maclaren, has recently invented a creed that one may well dismiss with pity and laughter.⁴ But Robinson and all New England — except the Catholic portion of it — has passed the Scotchman's halting-place long ago and are all in the depths of absolute negation.

Mr. Robinson has a sonnet that he calls "Credo," and here are its first two lines:

> I cannot find my way: there is no star
> In all the shrouded heavens anywhere.

Poor, deluded, hoodwinked, deceived, misled, unguided, self-willed, but sternly persistent New England! God pity her, and hasten the newer pentecostal day that shall forever burn the blackened scales from her eyes. Mr. Robinson is a genuine chip of this New England block — hard of unbelief.

From "Gems by the Wayside," *Globe*, VII (September 1897), 344-346.

William Henry Thorne (1839-1907), born and schooled in England, was at one time an orthodox clergyman, then a "cosmotheist" and freethinker. After a stint as professor of literary criticism in a small Illinois college, he founded the *Globe* in New York, "A New Review of World-Literature, Society, Religion, Art and Politics," for which he wrote much of the material himself on a boundless scope of topics with hellzapoppin verve — on the Pope's temporal sovereignty, labor problems, Bismarck, book reviews, isms of art, national morality, Ruskin — no theme beyond his boot or ken. He published two volumes of verse and one of biography and criticism.

Thorne was introduced by Kate Vannah to Caroline D. Swan, who invested in the *Globe*, which Hagedorn (p. 103) called "a quarterly of limited circulation and unlimited impudence." Thorne visited Miss Swan in Gardiner and thus came to know the group that met in her house for discussions of poetry, notably Schumann, Webster, and Robinson. In the issue of July-September 1894, quoted above, the *Globe* included two essays by Miss Swan, a poem by Webster, and two each by Schumann and Robinson.

Of the January 1895 number of the *Globe*, Robinson said to Harry Smith: "The *Globe* is rich — Thorne being omnipresent and not very good natured." (Sutcliffe, pp. 200-201.)

Hagedorn (p. 168) avows that Thorne was one of the prototypes of "Isaac and Archibald."

1 Thorne published eight by Robinson: "The House on the Hill" and "The Miracle" (July-September 1894); "Kosmos" (October 1895); "Thomas Hood" (February 1896); "I Make No Measure of the Words They Say" (May 1896); "God's Garden" (September 1896); "Shooting Stars" (December 1896); "An Octave" (June 1897). The first four and the sixth were collected in *The Torrent* with some changes; the fifth and seventh were never collected; the eighth reappeared in *The Children of the Night* (1897); only half (nos. 1, 4, 6, 8) are in *Collected Poems*.

2 On April 17, 1892 Robinson wrote Harry Smith that he planned to submit to the *Harvard Advocate* a sonnet beginning:
>There is a drear and lonely tract of Hell
>From all the common woe removed afar, —
>A flat sad land where only shadows are
>Whose lorn estate no word of mine can tell, etc.

The *Advocate* ran it on June 16, with Robinson's first initial as *F* instead of *E*. Robinson's letter continues: "I don't know how long this Hell business will last, but I may sigh out two or three more. It is a damned cheerful subject and my muse is merry whenever she gets into it. Sometimes I think that Hell may not be such a bad place after all," and he tells why. (Sutcliffe, p. 60.)

On October 1, 1893 Robinson returned to the subject. "Fancy and imagination brings to my mind the 'hell' sonnet. . . . My fancy gets a little lively in those fourteen lines. I have never been quite able to know what to make of them. They may be nothing but rot — they surely are if the reader can make nothing of them — but I have always cherished the idea that there is a thought mixed up in them that is worth the trouble of the thinking. . . . it really seems to me that I have brought out the idea of the occasional realization of the questionable supremacy of ourselves over those we most despise in a moderately new way. If there is a little poetry in it, then all the better. . . . I will state here that the verses in question must be taken as rather vague generalities: they will not bear, and I never intended them to bear, any definite analysis. To me they suggest a single and quite clear thought; if they do as much to you and to any other person who has seen them, I am satisfied." (Sutcliffe, pp. 108-109.) He enclosed a complete version of the sonnet, differing from the quatrain above and from the rest of the poem in Thorne's review.

3 Robinson spoke out on Emerson's prose and poetry several times. To Harry Smith he puffed "The Over-Soul" but groused about "that eminently unsatisfactory essay on 'Compensation.' " (Sutcliffe, p. 274.) "Emerson is rotten with good things," he wrote to Daniel Gregory Mason, "but he nailed them with cold hands and an empty stomach. . . . Every sentence of his cost Pain." (Emery Neff, *Edwin Arlington Robinson* [New York, 1948], p. 153.) On another occasion, "In the essay on Power he takes me over his paternal knee and wallops me with a big New England shingle for about three-quarters of a New England hour. He really gets after me. . . . I am ready to confess, however, that the human note has a faint suggestion of falsetto here and there, but, on the other hand may not that suggestion be the product of my own diabolical system rather than of Emerson's idealism?" (Mason, "Edwin Arlington Robinson: A Group of Letters," *Yale Review*, XXV [June 1936], 861.)

For Emerson as poet Robinson had nothing but panegyric. "Emerson is the greatest poet who ever wrote in America. Passages scattered here and there in his work surely are the greatest of American poetry. In fact, I think that there are lines and sentences in Emerson's poetry that are as great as anything anywhere." (Kilmer, p. 12.) "Emerson wrote some of the purest poetry we have in America — though not a great deal of it." (Brown, p. 37.) "He had the real juice," Robinson exclaimed to Winfield Scott (p. 175).

4 Ian Maclaren, pseudonym of John Watson (1850-1907), outspoken cleric, was a highly popular author of rural sketches and stories of which *Beside the Bonnie Briar Bush* (1894) is best known. Among his theological works, he published in 1896 *The*

Cure of Souls in which he declared theology similar and equal to "every other science, mental or physical," with "the same right to formulate her conclusions as physics." He was rather generally being denounced for "Pelagianism" during this period.

.. / / ..

As has been seen, Robinson was hungrily regardful of the published critical reactions to his poetic debut, reaped them assiduously, sent excerpts and his responses to Smith, and quoted phrases from them as long as decades later. He made the statement that "There was far more neglect than hostility," the first half of which is untenable in the face of at least twenty reviews in newspapers and magazines of substantial circulation and prestige — not a bad record for a first, minuscule volume of verses in paper wrappers by an utterly unknown poet who had issued them under his own auspices and had distributed them personally. He came off middling well under the circumstances, smarting at the occasional "protesting voice ... that was not especially complimentary or true." At this incipient stage — belated, frustrated, hopeful, confident, aggrieved, and indomitable — he bravely maintained that "My incurable belief in what I was doing made me indifferent alike to hostility or neglect." Notwithstanding, he needed some indisputable testimonials to the enduring quality of his art. These he received in abundance from editors, authors, academics, and friends to whom he had dispatched *The Torrent*. While their private letters had no bearing on the course of his public recognition, it is worth noting the names of the more prominent persons who ratified him at this time: John Vance Cheney, Barrett Wendell, Charles Eliot Norton, Titus M. Coan, George Pierce Baker, Horace E. Scudder, Edgar Fawcett, Edmund Gosse, Clinton Scollard, Edward Eggleston, George Wharton Edwards, S. Weir Mitchell, and Charles G.D. Roberts. (See Sutcliffe, pp. 267-276.) Certainly, acclamation from so impressive a concourse of littérateurs must have stiffened Robinson's determination, if indeed any stiffening was required. (Quotations in this paragraph are from Robinson's "The First Seven Years," *Colophon*, Part IV [1930], n.p.)

THE CHILDREN OF THE NIGHT (1897)

After the blue column of *Torrents* had been addressed and dispatched to far corners of the United States and to England, during the interlude before reviews began arriving and then months of manic response to their freckled verdicts, Robinson's stance in the parentless Gardiner household assumed a peculiar angle. Though the youngest of three brothers, the brunt of stability fell upon his shoulders, Horace and Herman having health and financial problems more bluntly imperative than Edwin's invisible psychological and esthetic tensions. He took on the quotidian masculine chores around house and barn, comforted Herman's wife, and with his three little nieces played games and the violin. By preference an isolate, he consigned his time mostly to books, collected stamps, and attended occasional performances of music and drama in the town theatre. Conventional social gatherings he eschewed though he did now and again take a hand a poker with Blair, Pope, and Robbins (The Quadruped) in their upper-story back room on Water Street. He also fell in serenely with Laura E. Richards and her bustling family, which included cousin John Hays Gardiner, a professor of English at Harvard.

The stresses of domestic responsibility were inimical to his temperament but he submitted to them at first with unblinking Puritan resolve. "There are things here at home that are pulling me back, and I've got to look out for them,"[1] he confided to Harry DeForest Smith. Once he had contemplated Christian Science as the golden avenue that would lead him out of mundane obscurity into the realms of truth and light; now he knew that for him that way was barred. In the midst of a progressively darkening situation, he reached out once more for his pen and — the only satisfactory solace and solution in his life so far — poetry. He spent the greater part of morning and afternoon in his study, staring out at apple orchard and greening ravine, reading poems and writing poems. In this period he cast them prominently into a form he called "octaves," terse, eight-line constructs in blank verse expressing grim cogitations on life and God and hell and Truth and death. He produced scores of these ruminative stanzas and in the end preserved a bare two dozen. His letters to Harry Smith at this time expose a loneliness verging on desperation. With palpable eagerness he clung to his newfound epistolary friend Edith Brower, coming as close to self-divulgence as his New England diffidence ever allowed. In Gardiner, murmurs over his continued unconcern about a breadwinning job rose. "I can't do anything but write poetry," he protested to his sister-in-law, "and perhaps I can't do even that, but I'm going to try. I don't expect recognition while I live but if I thought I could write something that would go on living after I'm gone, I'd be satisfied with an attic and a crust all my life."[2] The psychic wall around him seemed to be contracting exponentially.

By the last days of March 1897 Robinson had conceived a script which would comprise almost all of *The Torrent and The Night Before* and an equivalent number of selections from his new work. He took a trip to Boston in search of a publisher, stopping first at Harvard where he was repulsed by the obsequiousness of "men who never knew me" and "the sight of that blue-covered experiment of mine on Barrett Wendell's desk."[3] In Boston too he was "treated magnificently" and "much lunched," one publisher signifying that he might "possibly do something with it in the fall."[4] When all was said, however, no contract eventuated. Subconsciously, Robinson was relieved by this setback. He was not yet ready to shake off Tilbury Town. He unbosomed himself categorically to Miss Brower: "Sometimes it made me grin to hear [the publishers] talk so seriously, and sometimes it made me glad to feel that I was 'fired' once more. I rather like to be rejected now. I am so used to it. If ever I achieve worldly success, I'm half afraid it will finish me."[5] His reaction to his reception in Cambridge followed the same line: "I don't know why, but I felt ashamed of myself. I felt that I had better go back to Maine and stay there."[6]

Back to Maine he went, though not to stay for long. In the next seven months Robinson read avidly in Zola, Merimée, Pater, Kipling, Clough, Jefferies, Stevenson, and Edward Rowland Sill. He spoke of going often to Mrs. Richards' home. Conscientiously he reworked some of the poems in *The Torrent*, pondered the exclusion of several from his projected volume ("ready to cancel the Hardy sonnet" and "very shaky about 'For Calderon'"), and discussed a number of recently written ones to be incorporated: "Calvary," "L'Envoi," "Romance," "Richard Cory," and the surviving octaves. In May he described the new venture conditionally to Harry Smith as *"The Torrent . . .* with a little additional water," and in June wrote glumly to Miss Brower that he had not the slightest notion what his latest poems were good for, while already hopeful that his "partly new" book would be out in November. By September 7 he had fixed upon a title, *The Children of the Night*.

At the approach of autumn Robinson had completed arrangements with Richard G. Badger of Boston for issuance of the book in two formats. Badger was a "vanity" publisher who, for a price, would accommodate any desirous poetaster. His imprint doubtlessly alerted reviewers that the book in hand was probably otherwise unpublishable, and to that extent induced a judgmental hazard. Yet, as Hagedorn suggests, it was better than no imprint at all. William Edward Butler, son of a Boston department store owner and a friend from Robinson's Harvard days, volunteered to defray the cost. By the end of September Robinson began looking for galley proofs. Soon after a purported quarrel with brother Herman in

October, Edwin formulated plans to leave Gardiner. " 'I am going away,' Robinson said abruptly to his sister-in-law. 'I can't sleep. I can't do any work.' "[7] From this wallow of dejection he sent forth another cry to another female: "I know as well as anyone that the book is full of flaws and that the touch of the novice is everywhere, or almost everywhere, apparent.... I don't expect very much from it but I hope it may be [the] means of my feeling a little more certain in regard to what I am here for."[8] But the unquenchable volition which was to carry him through crises more precarious than this one reasserted itself in a note to Smith:

> From the *Children* I do not expect much, if anything, in the way of direct remuneration but I shall always feel, even if I starve to death someday, that the book has done a good deal for me. Perhaps the knowledge that I have done a good deal for the book has something to do with this feeling. When I think of the hours I have spent over some of the lines in it I wonder if it is all worth while; but in the end I cease wondering. If anything is worthy of a man's best and hardest effort, that thing is the utterance of what he believes to be the truth.[9]

A bequest of $600 from his father's estate enabled Robinson to leave Cambridge in late November, where he heard from Badger that the book would be ready in about a week. Robinson moved on to New York City, quartering with another Harvard friend, George Burnham, in a rooming-house on West 64th Street. It was here he received the first copies of *The Children of the Night* to come off the press.

. . / / . .

By way of purely numerical comparison, *The Torrent and The Night Before* contains forty-three titles, forty-six poems; *The Children of the Night* fifty-seven titles, eighty-seven poems. Although Robinson vacillated over the fate of several poems in *The Torrent* he left only two out of *The Children*: "For Calderon" and "A Poem for Max Nordau." He introduced forty-three new poems:

>Two Men
>Richard Cory
>Two Octaves (2)
>Calvary
>The Story of the Ashes and the Flame
>Amaryllis
>The Pity of the Leaves
>Cliff Klingenhagen
>Charles Carville's Eyes
>Fleming Helphenstine
>Reuben Bright
>The Tavern
>Octaves (25)
>Two Quatrains (2)
>Romance (2)
>L'Envoi

Whereas every title and line in *The Torrent* is flush with the left margin, titles in *The Children* are centered over each text, and many poems carried over from *The Torrent* are now variantly indented. This may of course have been none of Robinson's doing, and is of small consequence in any case, but the revised configuration is retained in all subsequent collections.

No significant pattern or criterion of concentration by genre or theme is immediately evident in Robinson's reallocation of poems in *The Children*. The four ballades, spread out in *The Torrent*, are here grouped compactly. However, quatrains, sonnets, and octaves are scattered, with character sketches interspersed. A kind of envelope-logic attends the placement of the title poem at the head of the book and "L'Envoi" at the close.

By far the most prevalent brand of textual change made by Robinson in poems transplanted from *The Torrent* to *The Children* is punctuational — excising or inserting ubiquitous dashes; substituting commas, colons, semicolons, and periods for each other or by exclamation points, quotation marks, and triple dots. It cannot be said that he notably altered tempo, rhythm, emphasis, or meaning by this wholesale juggling (some 230 instances), so the full docket of these minutiae is not offered here. Other modifications largely typographical in character include:

1) "The Dead Village," line 14: in *The Torrent*, his; in *The Children*, His.
2) "Ballade of a Ship," stanza 2, line 5: (*TT*), omitted by oversight; (*TC*), "But they danced and they drank and their souls grew gay." (This of course affects every aspect of the previously dismembered poem.) The caption "Envoy" is inserted at the head of the final four-line stanza (*TC*).
3) "Sonnet (When we can all so excellently give)," line 9: (*TT*), O; (*TC*), Oh. Line 13: (*TT*), Till; (*TC*), 'Till.
4) "Ballade," (*TT*), title; (*TC*), "Ballade of Broken Flutes." (No significant change in meaning inasmuch as the added phrase occurs four times in the refrain.
5) "Horace to Leuconoe," (*TT*), title; (*TC*), "Horace to Leuconoë." The diaresis is also added in line 1.
6) "The Ballade of Dead Friends," (*TT*), title; (*TC*), "Ballade of Dead Friends."
7) "A Ballade by the Fire," (*TT*), title; (*TC*), "Ballade by the Fire." The caption "Envoy" is inserted at the head of the final four-line stanza (*TC*).
8) "Two Sonnets: II," line 4: (*TT*), for evermore; (*TC*) forevermore.
9) "The Night Before," lines 1, 6, 19, 359: (*TT*), Domine; (*TC*), Dominie — earlier preference discarded (see Sutcliffe, p. 158). Line 54: (*TT*) marvelous; (*TC*), marvellous. Line 153: (*TT*), heaven; (*TC*), Heaven. Line 210: (*TT*), When love goes; (*TC*), When loves goes — an ironic reversal of typographical error, perpetuated in the 1905 edition of *TC*. Line 348: (*TT*), whiskies; (*TC*), whiskeys. Line 367: (*TT*), shrieve; (*TC*), shrive.

Typographical changes affecting metric duration or phonic value:

1) "Thomas Hood," line 10: (*TT*), sorrow swept; (*TC*), sorrow-swept.
2) "The Children of the Night," stanza 4, line 3: (*TT*), embittered; (*TC*), imbittered.

In *The Children* Robinson not only elongated the title of "Ballade" to "Ballade of Broken Flutes," he also affixed the dedication "To A.T. Schumann" between title and first line. Conversely, he removed the epigraph, "As if God made him and wondered why," from the same position in "The Night Before." At line 28 of this poem Robinson eliminated the original stanza break, as he did at line 66; in the blank space indicating a stanza break between lines 184-185 he inserted six dots. Heightened or slackened narrative tension may be assumed as Robinson's intention through these devices.

After fretting lugubriously about his exertions on the old poems brought forward to *The Children*, Robinson made remarkably few verbal changes in them, three in all. Two are relatively trivial: in "The Torrent," line 8, he supplanted *But* with *Yet*; in "The Night Before," line 180, he dropped the definite article from "But the scenes." The only true dramatic and interpretive shift occurs in the latter poem, line 38: "Not one of those little black lawyers were told it" becomes "had guessed it." Surprisingly, "For a Book by Thomas Hardy," over which he had audibly agonized, he made the transfer without a single verbal mutation. Given these meager revisions, and assaying the properties of his new poems in this second volume, it may fairly be said that during the darkly procreant year between *The Torrent* and *The Children* Robinson's eye was less on the Word of the past than on the Light of the future.

One noteworthy evolvement has its start in this volume. From its position near the end of *The Torrent* Robinson promoted "The Children of the Night" to first place and bestowed its title upon his second book. Yet, in a puzzling about-face, he completely disowned the poem thereafter. Years later he explained to an inquisitor: "I omitted 'The Children of the Night' from my *Collected Poems* in the hope of exterminating it."[10]

. . / / . .

THE CHILDREN OF THE NIGHT. Published December 6, 1897 by Richard G. Badger & Company, Boston. Bound in light tan cloth, with green and red *art nouveau* design by T.B. Hapgood, Jr. inside green rule, title and author's name green stamped on both covers and spine. On rear colophon page: Printed by John Wilson and Son at the University Press, Cambridge, for Richard G. Badger and Company, Publishers, Boston. Leaves measure 17.5 by 11.3 centimeters. Issued in two formats: 500 copies on Batchword laid paper, all edges trimmed, at $1.25; 50 copies on Imperial Japanese vellum, with vellum wrapper, at $3.00. Dedicated TO THE MEMORY / OF / MY FATHER AND MOTHER.

The Children of the Night

A Book of Poems

BY

EDWIN ARLINGTON ROBINSON

BOSTON
RICHARD G. BADGER & COMPANY
M DCCC XCVII

THE CHILDREN OF THE NIGHT (1897)

Contents

The Children of the Night	11
Three Quatrains	
I (As long as Fame's)	13
II (Drink to the splendor)	14
III (We cannot crown ourselves)	15
The World	16
An Old Story	17
Ballade of a Ship	18
Ballade by the Fire	20
Ballade of Broken Flutes	22
Ballade of Dead Friends	24
Her Eyes	26
Two Men	28
Villanelle of Change	29
John Evereldown	30
Luke Havergal	32
The House on the Hill	34
Richard Cory	35
Two Octaves	
I (Not by the grief that stuns)	36
II (When through hot fog)	37
Calvary	38
Dear Friends	39
The Story of the Ashes and the Flame	40
For Some Poems by Matthew Arnold	41
Amaryllis	42
Kosmos	43
Zola	44
The Pity of the Leaves	45
Aaron Stark	46
The Garden	47
Cliff Klingenhagen	48
Charles Carville's Eyes	49
The Dead Village	50
Boston	51
Two Sonnets	
I (Just as I wonder)	52
II (Never until our souls)	53
The Clerks	54
Fleming Helphenstine	55
For a Book by Thomas Hardy	56
Thomas Hood	57
The Miracle	58
Horace to Leuconoë	59
Reuben Bright	60
The Altar	61
The Tavern	62
Sonnet (Oh for a poet)	63
George Crabbe	64
Credo	65
On the Night of a Friend's Wedding	66

Sonnet (The master and the slave)	67
Verlaine	68
Sonnet (When we can all)	69
Supremacy	70
The Night Before	71
Walt Whitman	85
The Chorus of Old Men in "Aegeus"	86
The Wilderness	88
Octaves	
I (To get at the eternal)	91
II (We thrill too strangely)	92
III (To mortal ears)	93
IV Tumultuously void)	94
V (To me the groaning)	95
VI (While we are drilled)	96
VII (There is one battle-field)	97
VIII (When we shall hear)	98
IX (The guerdon of new childhood)	99
X (There is no loneliness)	100
XI (When one that you and I)	101
XII (Where does a dead man go)	102
XIII (Still through the dusk)	103
XIV (With conscious eyes)	104
XV (I grant you friendship)	105
XVI (Though the sick beast)	106
XVII (We lack the courage)	107
XVIII (Something as one)	108
XIX (To you that sit with Sorrow)	109
XX (Like a white wall)	110
XXI (Nor jewelled phrase)	111
XXII (The prophet of dead words)	112
XXIII (To curse the chilled)	113
XXIV (Forebodings are the fiends)	114
XXV (Here by the windy docks)	115
Two Quatrains	
I Unity	116
II Paraphrase	117
Romance	
I Boys	118
II James Wetherell	119
The Torrent	120
L'Envoi	121

Much of it is metaphysical

THE CHILDREN OF THE NIGHT

It requires considerable courage, in this critical period of literature, to launch a new book of poems. Mr. Robinson is fortified, however, in such a venture, by the beauty and the merit of his verse. While much of it is metaphysical in character, there are here and there bits of description and gems of simile, which exhibit a close acquaintance with and love of nature. The character of Mr. Robinson's theology is well shown from "The Children of the Night," the short opening poem from which the book takes its title:

> And if God be God, He is Love;
> And though the Dawn be still so dim,
> It shows us we have played enough
>   With creeds that make a fiend of Him.

Mr. Robinson's verse abounds in new and striking thought, and many beautiful images and word pictures. The typographical work is first class — although there is an evident effort to avoid conventional forms of arrangement that appears to us a trifle strained, and not altogether pleasing. Sometimes the conventional methods are best.

From "The Editor's Table," *Daily Kennebec Journal* (December 16, 1897), 3.

The *Daily Kennebec Journal* is still published in the capital city of Augusta, Maine, some seven miles north of Gardiner.

. . / / . .

Not of the brass-band brotherhood

A NEW POET

Among the books of this rather notable season[1] is one which from its size might well be passed over in the rush of the jostling quartos and octavos, yet which is likely to outlast many of its bulky contemporaries, *The Children of the Night: A Book of Poems*, by Edwin Arlington Robinson. This modestly announced, this small volume gives evidence that a new poet has arisen among us; one who, if not of the world-firing kind, not of the electric-light and brass-band brotherhood, is yet sure to win his place and keep it among the true singers. The poems are mostly short, grave and often sombre in tone, though never morbid or unhealthy. Many are in sonnet form; occasionally the writer follows the courtly fashion of villanelle or ballade, with sure and graceful touch; others again are simple and direct, with no special costume, "straight poetry," as someone says, "without stays." Among these are several imaginary portraits, which are too good not to quote. Here is ["Richard Cory"[2] follows.]

Here is a story told — or, better still, not told — in sixteen lines; and more stuff in them than in the average three-volume novel.[3] The man lives, and dies, before us; we should know him if we met him in the street; know him and walk aside, and wonder if it were himself or his ghost. It is the same with "Cliff Klingenhagen," "Aaron Stark," and two or three more. Mr. Robinson has a fancy for curious names, but they suit the owners well enough.

Mr. Robinson is evidently a thoughtful reader. Among the sonnets are several fine ones on different writers of our own and other days; the best is perhaps that on George Crabbe, and we shall be mistaken if it does not send many readers to the "darkest inch their shelf allows,"[4] in search of this poet, now well-nigh forgotten save by scholars: ["George Crabbe" follows.]

Such words as these need no praise. Mr. Robinson's philosophy is that of a wide and earnest charity, a deep sympathy, for all who suffer and struggle, and a lofty, serious, yet hopeful aspiration. His manner is noticeable for a certain grave restraint; yet he can be gay in a quiet fashion; witness the quaint song entitled "Two Men"; and here and there, as in "The Dead Village," and the "Ballade of Broken Flutes," music seems to linger along the lines, which fairly sing themselves into one's memory. Finally, in the first of a series of remarkable little poems called "Octaves,"[5] Mr. Robinson gives his own idea of what constitutes a poet; and we shall be greatly surprised if all lovers of real poetry do not feel that in these noble lines he describes fairly enough his own singing:

> To get at the eternal strength of things,
> And fearlessly to make strong songs of it,
> Is, to my mind, the mission of that man
> The world would call a poet. He may sing
> But roughly, and withal ungraciously;
> But if he touch to life the one right chord
> Wherein God's music slumbers, and awake
> To truth one drowsed ambition, he sings well.

From "The Christmas Bookstalls," Boston *Evening Transcript* (December 18, 1897), 13.

1 Not counting the popular successes that have since dropped out of sight, Robinson's book was battling for attention against Henry James's *What Maisie Knew* and *The Spoils of Poynton*, Kipling's *Captains Courageous*, Rostand's *Cyrano de Bergerac*, James Lane Allen's *The Choir Invisible*, S. Weir Mitchell's *Hugh Wynne*, William James's *The Will to Believe*, Mary Wilkins Freeman's *Jerome*, W.B. Yeats *The Secret Rose*, and Hall Caine's *The Christian*.

2 The concept of this poem may not have been entirely imaginary. On April 4, 1897 Robinson wrote: "Frank Avery blew his bowels out with a shot-gun." (Denham Sutcliffe, editor, *Untriangulated Stars: Letters of Edwin Arlington Robinson to Harry DeForest Smith 1890-1905* [Cambridge, Mass., 1947], p. 285.)

Hermann Hagedorn suggests his own candidate for the role, Sedgwick Plummer. (*Edwin Arlington Robinson: A Biography* [New York, 1938], pp. 53-54.)

Robinson to Karl Schriftgiesser, "An American Poet Speaks His Mind," Boston *Evening Transcript Book Section* (November 4, 1933), 1: "I am a little tired of hearing of 'Richard Cory' . . . I suppose it is because it is concise and clear and has a sharp conclusion that people like it and remember it."

3 See note on compression in the section *Olla Podrida* in the chapter "Preliminary Vistas" of this volume.

4 First line of "George Crabbe": "Give him the darkest inch your shelf allows."

5 During his indeterminate period between *The Torrent and The Night Before* and *The Children of the Night* Robinson proliferated these unrhymed, eight-line, single stanza forms which he read on inception to his chums of The Quadruped. The poems precipitated vigorous argument among them, the while Robinson sat hunched in his chair, smiling quizzically. (Hagedorn, pp. 118-119.)

He explained them thus to a friend in Wilkes-Barre: "I have done forty Octaves — there are to be about sixty in all — but I do not think they will be very well received. They are wicked things to make — infinitely harder than sonnets — and I have not yet succeeded in making one that even suggests completion. The one from the *Transcript* ["Saints of all times I love"] is altogether too rickety to be considered for a moment as a finished poem, though I don't know just what I can do with it." (Richard Cary, editor, *Edwin Arlington Robinson's Letters to Edith Brower* [Cambridge, Mass., 1968], p. 37.) "The form is impracticable and needlessly severe." (p. 59.)

Robinson wrote more than threescore of these octaves, published one in a newspaper, one in a periodical, twenty-seven in *The Children*, reduced to twenty-three in his final offering of *Collected Poems*.

. . / / . .

A day before the above review of *The Children* made its appearance, the poet expressed modified optimism over the volume's progress: "The book seems to be making a rather favorable impression wherever it goes and I cannot but feel that something will come from it. How much, of course, I have no means of knowing. Perhaps the fact that it has put me already in the way of meeting some people who are supposed to be worth knowing is something. (Sutcliffe, p. 293.)

During this initial visit to New York City Robinson met Titus Munson Coan, whom he had known only through correspondence, William Henry Thorne, and two others — Craven Langstroth Betts and Alfred Hyman Louis — who were, for good or ill, to make explicit marks in his life and writing. Robinson told both Harry Smith and Edith Brower about his evening at the Authors' Club, the membership at this time including Kipling, Stockton, Gilder, Eggleston, Stoddard, Stedman, and Garland, whose "illustrious cuticle" he had the honor of "pressing." He also had entry to the Century Association (Kipling, Howells, Theodore Roosevelt, Van Dyke, *et al*) but does not seem to have capitalized the opportunity.

On December 11 the New York *Sun* listed *The Children of the Night* among books received, as did the *Critic* on December 18, the New York *Evening Post* on the 20th, *Bookman* in its February 1898 issue, and *Current Literature* in March. In February the *Harvard Monthly* reprinted "Richard Cory" with a footnote detailing its source. None of these publications saw fit to assign the book to a critic, most likely because they mistook it for a rerun of *The Torrent and The Night Before* in refurbished title and larger format or dismissed it as too prohibitively the same. Later the *Post* picked up T.H. Higginson's review from the *Nation* of June 2, 1898 and repeated it whole.

The similitude of content in Robinson's first and second books probably also persuaded the *Independent, Bookseller,* Denver *Times,* Chicago *Record,* Cleveland *Leader,* and Bangor *Daily Commercial,* all of which had noticed *The Torrent,* to forego any discussion of *The Children.* For, it stands to reason that Robinson gave Badger a full accounting for purposes of promotion. *Time and the Hour,* New Orleans *Daily Picayune, Christian Register, Dial, Outlook, Sewanee Review, Poet-Lore, Literary World,* and the *Globe,* which had reviewed *The Torrent,* saw that as no obstacle to making a new judgment on *The Children.* As for the Boston *Evening Transcript,* it came through nobly with double measure, on December 18 and 24.

. . / / . .

Too serious? Perhaps.

THE CHILDREN OF THE NIGHT

'The Book of Poems in gilt and white' is one of the things it is good to bid farewell; for less daintiness combined with more art is what catches the fancy this year, and such is the make up of a volume of poems by Edwin Arlington Robinson. We like a book for its binding and its ragged edges. This is what first attracted us to *The Children of the Night.* But if a fine gown is a fine thing, there must be the girl to wear it, and so with the book-makers' trade. There is poetry inside the artistic covers of *The Children of the Night.* Thus run the first lines:

> For those that never know the light,
>   The darkness is a sullen thing;
> And they, the Children of the Night,
>   Seem lost in Fortune's winnowing.
>
> But some are strong and some are weak, —
>   And there's the story.
>
> . . . .
>
> And if there be no other life,
>   And if there be no other chance
> To weigh their sorrow and their strife
>   Than in the scales of circumstance,
>
> 'Twere better, ere the sun go down
>   Upon the first day we embark,
> In life's imbittered sea to drown,
>   Than sail forever in the dark
>
> . . . .
>
> It is the crimson, not the gray,
>   That charms the twilight of all time;
> It is the promise of the day
>   That makes the starry sky sublime;
>
> It is the faith within the fear
>   That holds us to the life we curse; —
> So let us in ourselves revere
>   The Self which is the Universe!

THE CHILDREN OF THE NIGHT (1897)

> Let us, the Children of the Night,
> > Put off the cloak that hides the scar!
> Let us be Children of the Light,
> > And tell the ages what we are!

A book that strikes this keynote on its first page promises good things and Mr. Robinson's muse seldom falters in the whole 121 pages.[1]

The ideal poet must be an all-sided man. He must sing, and preach. Mr. Robinson's volume of poetry contains many gems. Too serious? Perhaps. He lacks the rollicking, rushing gift of Kipling[2] and we would that he liked to make us laugh oftener.

He writes for the more serious mood, but his thoughts are good and strong and his lines have the rhythm of the sea when the wind is from the south'ard.

From "The New Publications," Lewiston *Saturday Journal* (December 18, 1897), 11.

The Lewiston (Me.) *Saturday Journal* should also be inscribed on the scroll of publications that gave critical attention to both of Robinson's first two books. With a tint of bar sinister, however, for the *Journal* simply reprinted Joseph E. Chamberlin's critique of *The Torrent* rather than judging for itself.

1 The poems in this book start on page 11, thus allowing Robinson ten pages less than the given total to exercise his muse.

2 Robinson made no bones about his debt to Rudyard Kipling. "When I was younger," he wrote to Lewis N. Chase in 1917, "I was very much under the influence of . . . Kipling." (Ridgely Torrence, editor, *Selected Letters of Edwin Arlington Robinson* [New York, 1940], p. 102.) Yet, he made it twice plain that he objected to Kipling's "professional super-journalistic touch," and that "his things have been marred by journalism." (Edwin S. Fussell, *Edwin Arlington Robinson: The Literary Background of a Traditional Poet* [Berkeley, 1954], p. 112; Winfield Townley Scott, *Exiles and Fabrications* [Garden City, N.Y., 1961], p. 159.)

Robinson stated flatly in January 1891 that "Kipling's poetry is better than his prose." (Sutcliffe, p. 9.) Three months later he exclaimed: "I am tired of him. There was a time when I thought that he was booked for something great, but my ideas have changed since. . . . I don't think five years hence will hear a great deal of Rudyard. . . . It is a relief to turn from him to Mr. Thomas Hardy." (p. 17.) Again in 1894 and 1895 he registered distaste for Kipling's stories, then said to Harry Smith: "I am still of the opinion that if Kipling leaves any name to posterity it will be almost wholly for his poems. He is the greatest poet now writing English and I have said so ever since the death of Tennyson." (pp. 160, 195, 224.)

As Robinson was reaching the height of his own poetical powers, he teetered once again. "I am always revising my opinion of Kipling," he said to Joyce Kilmer. "I have changed my mind about him so often that I have no confidence in my critical judgment." ("Edwin Arlington Robinson Defines Poetry," New York *Times Magazine Section* [April 9, 1916], 12.) In 1929 he told Lucius Beebe it would be difficult to estimate Kipling's relative position because he was "essentially" a writer "of the present." (Lucius Beebe, "Robinson Sees Romantic Strain in Future Verse," New York *Herald Tribune* [December 22, 1929], I, 19. But in his last year he assured Carl Van Doren, "Kipling's poetry is better than most people think." ("The Literary Twenties," *Harper's*, CLXXIII [June 1936], 155.)

. . / / . .

On January 1, 1898, the Lewiston (Me.) *Saturday Journal* injected this lateral intelligence among its "Literary Notes": "Maine people will be interested to know that Mr. Prescott Warren . . . has recently entered the firm of Richard G. Badger & Co., an enterprising young publishing firm of Boston. A book of delightful poems entitled *The Children of the Night* by Edward [sic] Arlington Robinson of Gardiner, Me., reviewed recently in these columns, is one of the recent books from this house. Badger & Co. are also publishing the *Literary Review* which is one of the best of its kind. The matter is always newsy and readable and typographically, the *Review* is a work of art."

. . / / . .

Direct prosaic power

THE CHILDREN OF THE NIGHT

Rather less than a year ago Mr. Edward [sic] Arlington Robinson sent down from Maine a little privately-printed pamphlet of his poems, which made, wherever it reached, a decidedly favorable impression. *The Children of the Night*, revised and enlarged, is now issued in a bound volume (Richard G. Badger & Co.). The book is a beautiful one, with a remarkably attractive cover design by Mr. T.B. Hapgood.[1] The poems themselves are quite unlike the run of contemporary verse; they descend, in a way, from Crabbe and Dr. Thomas Gordon Hake.[2] They are accomplished and show the literary instinct; but rather than grace or fancifulness, one feels in them occasionally the stirrings of something that very closely resembles direct prosaic power. Witness the sonnet, "Reuben Bright" (the name itself significant of Mr. Robinson's traditions: [The poem follows.]

The volume abounds in good criticism on literature. Here is the sonnet on Crabbe himself: ["George Crabbe" follows.]

From "Books," *Time and the Hour*, VI (December 18, 1897), 8-9.

1 Thomas Brown Hapgood (1871-1938), a Boston-trained designer of monuments, plaques, inscriptions on wood, bronze, and marble tablets, bookplates, and illuminations on vellum, created striking title pages and press insignia for Ginn & Company, Atlantic Monthly Press, Craftsman's Guild, and others.

2 Thomas Gordon Hake (1809-1895), physician, poet, and dramatist, published a book at 31 but did not seriously devote himself to writing until 50. *New Symbols* (1876) and *Maiden Ecstasy* (1880) are his finest volumes of verse; "The Blind Boy," based on Philip Bourke Marston, and "Ecce Homo" his most widely known poems. Hake risked obscurity for depth, sacrificed grace to the grotesque, and employed diction and symbolism too disconcerting to suit the general public. In some respects he was indeed not unlike Robinson.

. . / / . .

Lacks subtlety, lacks poetry

MEDIAEVAL ROMANCE AND MODERN ART

. . . Mr. Edwin Arlington Robinson's fancy runs to portraiture. He specifies his "Children of the Night," sings of John Evereldown,[1] Luke Havergal, Richard Cory, Aaron Stark, Fleming Helphenstine and others until the reader wonders where all the names come from. These vignettes attempt to hit off some salient trait, and sometimes the stroke is vivid, as in the sketch of Aaron Stark —

> A miser was he, with a miser's nose.
> And eyes like little dollars in the dark.

But in the main Mr. Robinson's art lacks subtlety, lacks poetry. The best thing in the book is the "Ballade of a Ship," a really spirited performance. In fact, the verses in the collection are almost invariably nimble, they move naturally, if not with grace, and if it were not that Mr. Robinson wanted imagination his book would be of uncommon interest. As it is the work is decidedly readable.

From "Poetry," New York *Daily Tribune* (December 20, 1897), 8.

This review is fifth among seven anonymous reviews, sandwiched between M.A. DeWolfe Howe's *Shadows* and William Edward Penney's *Ballads of Yankee Land.* This kind of submergence among "decidedly readable" mediocrities, so often Robinson's lot in these early days, is one of the factors that hindered his gaining stronger recognition.

1 To Lewis N. Chase, Robinson described "John Evereldown" as one of his "purely fanciful sketches, without ethical or symbolical significance." (Torrence, p. 104.) He called it and "Luke Havergal," written when he was 23, "young poems." "I don't know where they came from. They just came, out of the air." (Schriftgiesser, p. 2.) To Edith Brower, September 8, 1899: "If I am not erotic I have been accused of being very immoral in 'John Evereldown.' I thought all the time that he was merely unfortunate." (Cary, p. 105.)

. . / / . .

A voice crying in the wilderness

EDWARD[1] ARLINGTON ROBINSON
Edith Brower

People say a great deal about the world's not wanting poetry any more. "This scientific age"; "age of materialism"; "cycle of invention and discovery"; "the almighty dollar, etc., etc." — such phrases are eternally in our ears. And because they all point to a truth which is on every side evident — namely, that the present period really is astonishingly and unprecedentedly practical and materialistic — they have come to be accepted as expressing the entire truth.

This they are far from doing. Discouraging as the spiritual outlook often appears, yet if a man will only use his own eyes and not those of others; if he will forget for a few moments the phrases just quoted, and listen to certain quieter but just as insistent world-voices, he shall be cured of all transient pessimism to which he may have yielded; he shall see and hear enough to prove to him the full truth of Keats's saying, that "the poetry of earth is never dead," — poetry here standing for all that excites or expresses the aesthetic in man's nature, not to mention any ethical or spiritual import it may have. It surely is not dead in our own land. That we have at the present moment in painting a Lafarge and a Sargent, in sculpture a St. Gaudens, in music a MacDowell, sufficiently proves it. These men, though working in different art materials, represent, each in his own person, the highest type of artist; that is, one whose faultless technical skill serves as the expression of a profound spirituality.

If one says, "but men such as these are scarce," I reply: Most certainly they are, and have been in every age and country. When nature executes her superfine in human shape, she does it after the artistic, not the mechanic, fashion; — in other words, she does not turn out her chefs-d'oeuvres by the gross, but makes only one of a kind. The multitude does not require individual teachers; a single pre-eminent soul, gifted with whatever mode of speech, will speak to thousands. From the very nature of printed matter, the poet can reach a larger number of his fellowmen than any other kind of artist. This is fortunate, since his direct ethical force and influence are far greater than those of the painter or composer. I say, fortunate, always supposing him to be of the first order — ranking poets first by the importance of the message they have to deliver, and second by the power and beauty of their utterance.

That the poet whose name heads this article voices with a quite overcoming boldness and in an entirely individual manner some of the loftiest and most comprehensive thoughts that are stirring a few brave, unconventional spirits today, is not to be questioned. That certain large, plain, wholesome truths have uncovered to him depths and breadths of meaning not understood by "the general" without aid, is a claim verifiable upon almost every page of his little book, *The Children of the Night*. Yet, whether he has succeeded in uttering what he knows or divines of the World beyond the world, in a way that shall be acceptable and useful for all time, those who come after us must be the judges, not we. We can tell only if he has proved acceptable to us, if he has helped us; and if he has, and so filled the part assigned for him to fill, what more could an eternity of fame do for him? Edwin Arlington Robinson is not the man to ask for more.

Let him tell us in his own words what he thinks he is here for. This is the first of twenty-five consecutive short poems written in that highly condensed and severely artistic form known as the octave.[2]

> To get at the eternal strength of things,
> And fearlessly to make strong songs of it,
> Is, to my mind, the mission of that man
> The world would call a poet. He may sing
> But roughly, and withal ungraciously;
> But if he touch to life the one right chord
> Wherein God's music slumbers, and awake
> To truth one drowsed ambition, he sings well.[3]

These eight lines show us we need not expect to find much verse of the light, soft, sensuous sort in Mr. Robinson's book. Those who desire to remain in their sins and be soothed must go elsewhere.[4] Poetry with him is not mere music, though he scorns not the music of it; it is more than a pleasant entertainment of thoughtless, idle hours. It comes, rather, as the voice of one crying in the wilderness, calling upon men almost sternly, at times, to look at Truth as she has been shown to him. The gist of that revelation seems to be that there is no commonplaceness in life, unless we view life through commonplace eyes; that man was not made to mourn but to rejoice; — to rejoice even in the darkness, since darkness presupposes "the coming glory of the Light"[5]; that there is no evil in the universe to those who have once glimpsed the true Real, in other words, the Divine Ideal, which must embrace all things.

> And if God be God, He is Love;
> And though the Dawn be still so dim,
> It shows us we have played enough
> With creeds that make a fiend of Him.
>
> There is one creed, and only one,
> That glorified God's excellence;
> So cherish, that His will be done,
> The common creed of common sense.
>
> It is the crimson, not the gray,
> That charms the twilight of all time;
> It is the promise of the day
> That makes the starry sky sublime;
>
> It is the faith within the fear
> That holds us to the life we curse; —
> So let us in ourselves revere
> The Self which is the Universe![6]

Perhaps this is not a new communication. If it is not, so much the better for its success. Humanity rarely listens to what is wholly new; it is the reiterated word in fresh forms that causes it at last to prick up its ears and give heed. But no prophet who brings an earnest message, learned out of his own soul, and delivers it in a way that is his very own, has ever yet failed to make some impress, if only on a small portion of the "remnant that saves." This being true, we boldly and publicly bid Mr. Robinson to be of good courage, which, however, he appears disposed to be without our bidding.

A little paper edition printed by the author a year ago, containing the greater part of what the present bound volume contains, met with small notice and that hardly of an adequate quality. The most prominent of these notices dismissed Mr. Robinson as a pessimist; but the critic (?) must have had a curious idea of pessimism, or else he read superficially.[7] There is undoubtedly a tinge of sadness in nearly everything this young poet writes — what we might call a New England sadness, arising from deep thought experience, never from despair. There is nowhere discernible to one who reads him thoroughly any faith in "hell's fulfilment of the end of things"[8] — to quote a line of his own. It is Heaven's fulfillment that he looks for, nay, actually sees with those far-piercing poet's eyes. Hear him again, O dispassionate reader, and say if there is any lack of a right brave hope in him:

> Forebodings are the fiends of Recreance;
> The master of the moment, the clean seer[9]

> Of ages, too securely scans what is,
> Ever to be appalled at what is not;
> He sees beyond the groaning borough lines
> Of Hell, God's highways gleaming, and he knows
> That Love's complete communion is the end
> Of anguish to the liberated man.

Elsewhere he sings of:

> Life's all-purposeful
> And all-triumphant sailing,[10]

of:

> Man's unconjectured godliness —[11]

can any despair for the race be extracted out of this?

of:

> indissoluble Truth,
> Wherein redress reveals itself divine,
> Transitional, transcendent.[12]

of:

> the glorifying light
> That screens itself with knowledge,[13]

as if the much-valued earthly learning were less for our immediate enlightenment, than for a merciful shade to eyes now spiritually too dim to endure real Truth's bright shining. That we shall some day be strong-sighted enough to endure it, there is no doubt in our poet's mind, though he gives us small hope in this direction so long as we continue to pursue knowledge only for knowledge's sake; for he has the bard's true scorn for the shell without the meat; for:

> Songs without souls, that flicker for a day,
> To vanish in irrevocable night.[14]

for:

> altars where we kneel
> To consecrate the flicker, not the flame.[15]

and for:

> The prophet of dead words

who, he tells us, "defeats himself."[16]

Not for a moment will he tolerate the laziness or the cowardice of soul that makes men to dawdle around the outside of things, indifferent if there be any inside, or unfaithfully fearful of the consequences of investigation. Never to such are the spiritual secrets of the material universe unfolded. "Never," he says:

> Never until our souls are strong enough
> To plunge into the crater of the Scheme —
> ... are we to get
> Where atoms and the ages are one stuff.

> Nor ever shall we know the cursed waste
> Of life in the beneficence divine
> Of starlight and of soul-shine
> That we have squandered in sin's frail distress,
> Till we have drunk, and trembled at the taste,
> The mead of Thought's prophetic endlessness.[17]

That mead, terrible draught though it be, concentrated essence of the ages, oppressing weak spirits almost to death, is to him God's philter, the veritable love-potion of Divine Truth. He believes with Pater[18] that "for man, in proportion as man thinks truly, thought and being are identical."

But this view is not to be interpreted as indicating that all of life — this present life — is in pure, inactive thought. Such thought is not God's, the Creator's. Man too, rejoicing in "The glory of eternal partnership,"[19] must create. The poet, nearest partner of God in his preeminent capacity of Seer — the man who most clearly sees the underlying meaning of things — must make, nor ever cease from making, and thus working faithfully, will he perhaps be able to show to others something of what he sees. And in proportion to this ability will he be Lord of the world, but at the same time the world's servant. ["Sonnet" (The master and the slave) follows.]

And so the poor poet is a slave to himself as well as to the world, but he will work on, knowing well that:

> There is one battle-field whereon we fall
> Triumphant and unconquered;[20]

The sonnets on Zola, Verlaine, Thomas Hood, Crabbe, and the short poem on Walt Whitman furnish what never fails to be interesting: A poet's characterization and estimate of poets. In "Cliff Klingenhagen," "Aaron Stark," "Charles Carville's Eyes," "Fleming Helphenstine," and "Reuben Bright," we find the sonnet form put to an entirely new use: That of a lightly touched, yet seriously conceived character study.[21] These studies — seemingly of the fictitious order — remind us, in their quick typical short story in prose, which par excellence, is "brief as woman's love" yet contains the essence of a life.

Upon "Luke Havergal," a little poem of four double stanzas, Mr. Robinson might rest his reputation for the pure poetical gift. Doubtless, a delicate spiritual discernment is needed to penetrate the supernatural atmosphere suffusing it, and to read under the paradoxes of its uncannily suggestive situation the true mystery of Love and Death; yet the lines have in themselves a weird attractiveness, whether they be meaningless or meaningful to the reader.[22] The entire piece shall be given here to show the poet in a different mood from his usual one; — not less serious, for he is always that, but less oppressed by his sense of his mission, and indulging for the moment in the romance of poetry. Possibly he needs what Lowell attempted to teach himself in his "Fable for Critics": — to "learn the distinction twixt singing and preaching"; — not that he should cease preaching, but that he should sing more, remembering that the "lyric cry" reaches souls that are beyond being touched by "strong songs" however "fearlessly" made. But the following is a strong song too, though it does not preach: ["Luke Havergal"[23] follows.]

"The Night Before," the only long poem in the book, can be little more than referred to here. Not to refer to it would be absurd in any review of this collection of poems, yet the foundations are laid almost too broad and deep for a touch-and-go comment. It is the very innermost history of a crime related by the criminal himself on the eve of his execution. A simple enough tale and all too common: — Love, the murder of love, and then murder of love's murderer. The telling of a tale is the thing; — not the mere narration of facts, but "That reality, that substance, that precious and eternal treasure — the Meaning, the Object, the Gist of all we know as fact; this is the reality of revelation — spiritual and material — and more, Divinely Natural."

It is the Divinely Natural quality of the narration in "The Night Before," which makes it worth the reading.[24]

This article, insufficient though it be as a criticism, aims to offer for the benefit of any who may care to use it, a key to what would seem the real intent of the little book under consideration. It does not aim to fix the standing of the author as a poet. Whatever that standing may be, is already fixed and unalterable, and will be known when the time comes for knowing. But even as the poet has felt compelled to speak out to the world what was given him to utter, so has one of his readers been urged from within to reinforce, by calling attention to it, his message which seems to her full of help, comfort and stimulus — help which does not emasculate; comfort which is not coddling; stimulus that is not a stimulant producing temporary excitement, but that reaches to the very roots of soul-activities and stirs the eternal life that is there.

Let the last word here be his, as it is also the last in his book: ["L'Envoi" follows.]

From Wilkes-Barre *Times* (December 20, 1897), 15.

Miss Edith Brower (1848-1931) of Wilkes-Barre, Pennsylvania, first became conscious of Robinson's existence during one of her periodical trips to the New York City office of Titus Munson Coan, for whom she worked as a reader of manuscripts by aspiring amateurs. Coan showed her his recently received presentation copy of *The Torrent and The Night Before*. An accomplished writer of essays and fiction for the *Atlantic Monthly, Harper's Weekly, Catholic World,* and *Lippincott's,* she immediately discerned its pithy character and sent Robinson a note which sparked three decades of correspondence between them. For an account of her life and their friendship see Richard Cary's introduction to *Edwin Arlington Robinson's Letters to Edith Brower*, which also contains Miss Brower's memoir on Robinson. See also the references to her in Sutcliffe's edition of Robinson's letters and in Hagedorn's biography.

On October 7, 1897 Robinson wrote to Miss Brower: "Nothing would give me greater pleasure than to have you criticize my new book, though I should feel very bad to have you perish in the effort. I do not think the poems are to be taken so seriously as that, and I am half afraid that you may find some difficulty in finding an editor who will agree with you in thinking them worthy of any elaborate criticism at all." (Cary, p. 60.) Miss Brower, a highly influential civic figure in her community, seems to have encountered no such complication. Her critique, the lengthiest on

Robinson to date, took up three page-length columns in this full-size newspaper.

After perusing it, Robinson said: "I read your criticism with a great deal of pleasure — not for the praise that was in it (I forgot myself — you told me there wasn't any) but for the intelligent sympathy of the thing. No doubt you are right in what you say regarding my tendency to forget singing for preaching." He expostulated over some of his myopic critics, and continued, "Then you come along and find no difficulty in seeing what I am driving at and I feel encouraged again. I do not mean that you are alone, but still you are one of an apparently hopeless minority." (Cary, p. 68.)

1 The distortion of Robinson's given name in this caption is in all probability the fault of the typesetter; Miss Brower renders it correctly in the body of the essay. She was less likely to misname him than anyone outside his immediate family.

2 On September 7, 1897 Robinson had written Miss Brower regarding octaves: "I have written sixty-four of them, but, partly by my own persuasion and partly by the merciless scavenging of Pope, I have cut them down to about 25 — I don't remember just how many there are, but I know there are enough. I rather fancy some of them are pretty good but can't feel at all sure of them as they have not yet been tested by disinterested readers. The praise of friends is pleasant, but it is not to be taken too seriously." (Cary, p. 55.)

Seth Ellis Pope was a schoolteacher who fell into disfavor with the authorities in Gardiner, and he was a member of The Quadruped. Years later Robinson roomed with him in Brooklyn.

3 Prior to the June 1914 reprint of *The Children* Robinson forewarned Miss Brower: "You are good to think of writing another article, but I don't like to give you much encouragement. I'm afraid you will have the devil and all of a time in disposing of me. And when you do, please don't quote that incriminating first 'Octave,' which is a little the worse thing that I have done — and that is saying much." (Cary, p. 156.) He is referring to this octave, which he retained in reprints of *The Children* but never included in any of his *Collected Poems*.

4 In his letter of January 7, 1901 Robinson corroborated Miss Brower's feeling about the purpose and effect of his octaves. After citing William Vaughn Moody's opinion that the "octaves are rubbish," Robinson declared: "Not that the Octaves, as literature, necessarily amount to anything; but I always take it upon myself to feel that a fellow has not quite grown up when they mean nothing to him. Moody has not grown up in that way." (Cary, p. 135.)

5 "Credo," p. 65.

6 "The Children of the Night," p. 12.

7 There are in fact several *Torrent* notices that "dismissed Mr. Robinson as a pessimist" (see the section *Pessimism* in the chapter "Preliminary Vistas" of this volume). Louis V. Ledoux said, "E.A. used to refer to himself as an 'insane optimist,' because he saw the possibilities of good in thwarted lives that seemed wholly evil." ("Psychologist of New England," *Saturday Review of Literature*, XII [October 19, 1945], 4.)

8 "Verlaine," p. 68.

9 Over this phrase in "Octaves" XXIV, p. 114, Robinson chided Miss Brower. "Why do you think I meant to say 'clear seers.' Certainly not. 'Clear' would spoil the whole thing, it seems to me. At any rate, I never thought of it." (Cary, p. 65.) Robinson had sent her a prepublication copy of the poem in his microscopic handwriting. Although he protested a week before the review appeared, the word was printed "clear" in her critique. As with other mishandlings of Robinson's text, the present editor has provided the correct version in order to forestall future misquotations.

10 "Octaves" XXV, p. 115.

11 "Octaves" XX, p. 110.

12 "Octaves" XVI, p. 106.

13 "Octaves" XIV, p. 104.

14 "Sonnet" (Oh for a poet), p. 63.

15 "George Crabbe," p. 64.

16 "Octaves" XXII, p. 112.

17 "Two Sonnets" II, p. 53. Robinson was disappointed in the paucity of comment on this sonnet pair. "I guess they are too rank," he said to Harry Smith. (Sutcliffe, p. 269.) Of line 7, not quoted here, he told Nathan Haskell Dole in 1928, "I wrote 'scared years' when I was young, meaning something between bewildered and frightened. 'Scarred' would go but it wouldn't mean what I had in mind." (Torrence, p. 154.)

18 Robinson to Harry Smith, June 17, 1897: "Some day I must . . . find out what Pater really stands for." (Sutcliffe, p. 288.) Robinson had apparently read Walter Pater's *Plato and Platonism*; he read *Gaston de Latour* on Miss Brower's behest at this time but sent a disavowal: "As long as I have not read *Marius*, however, I ought not to say much about Pater, for I cannot know much about him." (Cary, p. 49.)

19 "Sonnet" (When we can all), p. 69.

20 "Octaves" VII, p. 97.

21 Much of the essential intent was dissipated from "Reuben Bright" by a typographical error in the first printing of the climactic line in *Collected Poems* (1921) — "and tore down *to* the slaughter house" — thereby degrading a poignant symbolic action to the level of a pointless colloquial expression. Often dogged by printers' lapses, Robinson shrank most from "those diabolical errors that make a sort of sense." (Cary, p. 180.)

22 Robinson's words to Miss Brower on April 21, 1897 are particularly apt here: "Of course the meaning is all suggested, and is not capable of a definite working-out by anyone who doesn't happen to sympathize with the writer's fancy." (Cary, p. 39.)

23 When Robinson made his one visit to Miss Brower's home in Wilkes-Barre, she told him "Luke Havergal" was the "most utterly poetic thing" he had done. " 'It has a lot that spoils it,' he replied, and pointed to his use of the word *some* [in stanza 1, line 4] — 'The wind will whisper some' — for *somewhat, or a little*. 'It's provincial,' he said." (Cary, p. 208.) It remained unchanged in editions of *The Children* but Robinson revised the passage to read: "The leaves will whisper there of her, and some, / Like flying words . . ." in *Collected Poems* (1921).

24 Miss Brower's extended consideration of "The Night Before" may well have been stimulated by Robinson's remark about William Peterfield Trent's note on the poem in his review of *The Torrent and The Night Before* in the *Sewanee Review*, April 1897, reprinted in this volume.

. . / / . .

Yet, at times, he can laugh

THE CHILDREN OF THE NIGHT

. . . Quite different is Edwin Arlington Robinson's *The Children of the Night* (Richard G. Badger & Co.). He sings:

> To get at the eternal strength of things,
> And fearlessly to make strong songs of it,

>   Is, to my mind, the mission of that man
>   The would would call a poet. He may sing
>   But roughly, and withal ungraciously;
>   But if he touch to life the one right chord
>   Wherein God's music slumbers, and awake
>   To truth one drowsed ambition, he sings well.[1]

Mr. Robinson's verse is not often so prosaic as this, but much of it is written in the spirit of these lines; while yet, at times, he can laugh himself and make us laugh most heartily.

From "Recent Poetry," *Christian Register*, LXXVI (December 23, 1897), 822-823.

This was one of seven reviews, the first on Evaleen Stein's *One Way to the Woods*, in which the critic finds that occasionally " 'the still, sad music of humanity' comes and relieves a strain that otherwise might be monotonous." Robinson, he opines is "quite different."

1 "Octaves" I, p. 91.

. . / / . .

Inspired and triumphant common sense

A NEW POET

John Hays Gardiner

Mr. Edwin Arlington Robinson, the author of the little book of poems which is published under the title — and it is a happy title — *The Children of the Night*, first made its appearance in a little pamphlet, privately printed, which he sent out last year in a quiet and limited way. The very favorable comment which then appeared from various sources seems to have encouraged him to offer the same poems with some strong additions to the public at large. The volume before us justifies his confidence. It is essentially a modest effort; its range is not large; and the mood which marks almost all of it is contemplative. But it is so free from the turgidity and undeveloped obscurity[1] which so many young poets look on as the promise of genius, it is so freshly and not unduly phrased, it is so sane and so concrete, and it puts forward so high and so brave a standard for life in a gray and troubled world, that the modesty may be interpreted not as a consciousness of weakness, but as a sign of reserved strength. We may look on this book then as promising first-fruits of what Mr. Robinson may do when he enlarges his experience and the scope of his effort.

The book contains, except for the poem called "The Night Before," only short poems; it is composed largely of sonnets, quatrains and unrhymed octaves; and but for this one long poem there is nothing that can be called narrative. Many of his sonnets are sketches, hauntingly suggestive and real, of imaginary characters. A few of these imaginary sketches are worked out in longer lyrics, in which the refrains are used with great expressiveness. In these and in the sonnets there is a kind of natural realism of method which reminds one of Wordsworth, and withal a shrewd and

Yankee directness[2] which is like nothing that we remember. Here is an example: ["Cliff Klingenhagen" follows.]

This is only one of a half dozen or more, in each of which Mr. Robinson has with a touch that in its realism and directness reminds one of the old German etchers fastened to an imaginary name that solidity and warmth of impression of real life. In another one, "Amaryllis," to this vivifying concreteness he adds a touch of tenderness: [The poem follows.]

The haunting pathos of this little fable — for one feels that it has a deeper significance behind the words — is characteristic of the mood in many of the poems. This mood, however, nowhere falls into sentimentality. The note is everywhere sane and manly; it is the note of a man to whom life has not been lavish of rich color and gayety, but who for all that sees no reason for burdening the world with his distress or discouragement. Though the book dwells almost insistently on the sadder aspects of life, the poet shows no signs of depression; rather he seems like a man mellowed by meeting misfortunes bravely, and girding up his loins to meet his God cheerfully and unabashed. One of the octaves he ends:

> We do not fight to-day, we only die;
> We are too proud of death, and too ashamed
> Of God, to know enough to be alive.[3]

And the charming "Ballade by the Fire" ends:

> But then, what though the mystic Three
>   Around me ply their merry trade? —
> And Charon soon may carry me
>   Across the gloomy Stygian glade? —
>   Be up, my soul! nor be afraid
> Of what some unborn year may show;
>   But mind your human debts are paid,
> As one by one the phantoms go.
>
>   ENVOY
> Life is a game that must be played:
>   This truth at least, good friend, we know;
> So live and laugh, nor be dismayed
>   As one by one the phantoms go.

Obviously the fine spirit of indomitable and determined cheerfulness has little to do with the playing at pessimism and atheism which has been the affectation of so many young poets of late.

The book is not without its note of fun, though the fun is of a subdued sort, rather quizzical than gay. The poem, "Two Men," who are Melchizedek[4] and Ucalegon, the latter

> Ucalegon he lost his house
>   When Agamemnon came to Troy,

gives a gleam of sober amusement that is very pleasant. It seems a pity that Mr. Robinson did not find it worth while to reprint the "Poem for Max Nordau" from his former pamphlet, the poem which began:

> Dun shades quiver down the lone long fallow,
> And the scared night shudders at the brown owl's cry;

It was a piece of most excellent fooling,[5] and it bore more testimony to the sanity and wholesomeness of Mr. Robinson's talent.

The philosophy of the book, for nowadays it seems that we cannot separate poetry from philosophy, is that of a high and independent trust in the righteousness and omnipotence of God. In the first poem that gives the title to the book, he declares:

> If there be nothing, good or bad,
>   But chaos for a soul to trust, —
> God counts it for a soul gone mad,
>   And if God be God, He is just.
>
> And if God be God, He is Love;
>   And though the Dawn be still so dim,
> It shows us we have played enough
>   With creeds that make a fiend of Him.
>
> There is one creed, and only one,
>   That glorifies God's excellence;
> So cherish, that His will be done,
>   The common creed of common sense.

This creed of inspired and triumphant common sense, strongly and convincingly phrased, is the keynote of the book. Mr. Robinson maintains it even when writing of Zola, of Mr. Thomas Hardy,[6] and of Verlaine. Man's view is limited; conventions may be shattered by the uncontrolled excursions of art; but behind all the clamor and delirium of the men who delight in the shattering is the calm and omniscient view of God. The message of the book is really this declaration, in a new way — for the book is entirely modern in its interests and attitude — of the old and eternal verities. The philosophy of this book then is, in spite of the subdued and meditative tone and all the dwelling on the sadness of things, a triumphant and deep-seated confidence in the ultimate heritage of man in the divine.

We have no space to comment at length on the high passion and indubitable power of the long poem of the collection — "The Night Before"; nor on such fine phrasings of literary appreciation as the sonnets on Matthew Arnold, Thomas Hood and George Crabbe; nor on the thoroughly modern, even Yankee spirit of such a poem as "The Torrent," with its happy justification of the somewhat Philistine progress of this age of ours. It is worth while, however, to point out that Mr. Robinson has not been content to pile up words and phrases from which his reader might thresh out for himself what meaning he could. Though some of the quatrains and octaves are condensed to the point of obscurity, still one never has the feeling that he did not know exactly what he meant himself. The difficulty seems due rather to too great condensation than to any crudity and lack of pains in the expression. And at his freest Mr. Robinson shows much command of that singing quality of the verse which expresses almost more than the words themselves.

It is dangerous to prophesy or even to praise too highly in the case of a volume of verse; but it is easily within the bounds of caution to say that this little book is worth having and reading; that its message is ennobling and stimulating; and that no one can doubt its promise for the future. It bears what is after all the only test that one can apply in the case of one's contemporaries, the test of a repeated reading.

From Boston *Evening Transcript* (December 24, 1897), 5.

    The title of this review is identical to the one published by this newspaper six days earlier. "The long (second) notice in the *Transcript* was written by Gardiner," said Robinson to Harry Smith. "Don't know who wrote the first one." (Sutcliffe, p. 295.)

    John Hays Gardiner (1863-1913) was a cousin of Laura E. Richards, at whose home Robinson met him, enjoying his pleasant commentary between selections of music. Gardiner was a professor of English at Harvard, author of four books on composition, rhetoric, forms of prose, and the Bible as English literature. He edited the Harvard alumni bulletin for two years, and he helped Robinson secure a job in the administrative offices of the college. He and Mrs. Richards provided funds for the publication of *Captain Craig* in 1902, and when he died, Gardiner left Robinson a legacy of $4,000.

1 See the section *Obscurity* in the chapter "Preliminary Vistas" of this volume.

2 Robinson to Lewis N. Chase, July 11, 1917: "When I was younger I was very much under the influence of Wordsworth." (Torrence, p. 102.) In 1895 Harry Smith gave him a volume of Wordsworth. "Hereafter it will be a part of my life. Of course a great deal of it is slow and of not much value; but the general tone and effect of it is so clear and wholesome, not to say magnificent, that we must all own it power to some extent." Robinson esteemed *The Excursion* a masterpiece and "Ode on Intimations of Immortality" as "worth all the rest of his work put together." (Sutcliffe, p. 207; see also Chard Powers Smith, *Where the Light Falls: A Portrait of Edwin Arlington Robinson* [New York, 1965], p. 61.) One may in fact ally Robinson's sonnet "The master and the slave" with stanza 8, lines 11-13 of the "Ode" — "Thou, over whom thy Immortality / Broods like the Day, A Master o'er a Slave, / A Presence which is not to be put by."

    Gradually Robinson disentangled himself from Wordsworth's spell. In "Momus" (1910) he proposed irreverently: "Some of / Wordsworth lumbers like a raft?" And ten years later he said to Herbert S. Gorman: "The poets who influenced me most in those days seem to have been those who have eventually influenced me in the least. Probably Wordsworth was something of a formative influence, though I was not aware of it at the time." ("Edwin Arlington Robinson, and a Talk With Him," New York *Sun* [January 4, 1920], 7.) Robinson's contradictory statements and willful vagueness about Wordsworth is of a piece with his ambivalence over Browning, doubtless a desire on the part of the matured poet to be gauged as his own man. Substantial wisdom is expressed by a later critic, Ben Ray Redman in his *Edwin Arlington Robinson* (New York, 1926), p. 11: "When he looked at nature it was not through Wordsworth's eyes; and the waters upon the strand at Dover Beach told him nothing of 'the turbid ebb and flow of human misery' that he had not already learned from the rising and receding tides of Maine." (See Index for Robinson's comments on Matthew Arnold.)

3 "Octaves" VI, p. 96.

4 Augustus Jordan and his sister Alice, who lived across the street in Gardiner told how Robinson's "greatest delight seemed to be 'hunting difficult words.' This became a sort of game between the three, he being then ten or twelve years old. He would appear suddenly in the doorway, face alight, eyes glowing, and cry 'Nebuchadnezzar!' 'Melchizedek!' or the like." (Laura E. Richards, *E.A.R.* [Cambridge, Mass., 1936], p. 11.) Hagedorn echoes this anecdote in his biography (p. 20).

5 Gardiner is virtually alone among the early critics to recognize the parodic elements of this poem.

6 In 1896 Robinson's regard for Hardy was such that he mailed him a presentation copy of *The Torrent and The Night Before,* which Hardy did not trouble to acknowledge.

Esther Willard Bates said it all succinctly: "Hardy he know thoroughly and always admired, though his esteem rose at times, and at times diminished." (*Edwin Arlington Robinson and His Manuscripts* [Waterville, Maine, 1944], p. 31.) After reading *The Hand of Ethelberta, Far From the Madding Crowd,* and *Under the Greenwood Tree* Robinson wrote Arthur R. Gledhill on April 20, 1891 that Hardy "in his own quiet way it seems to me that he stands without an equal." (Fussell, p. 107.) In the same year he told Harry Smith that *The Mayor of Casterbridge* was "a revelation," that *The Return of the Native* "lacks a certain naturalness," and that he could not understand how a writer of such power failed to become popular. (Sutcliffe, pp. 11, 16, 17.) In 1895 he pointed out that *Madding Crowd* and *The Woodlanders* had "something that you will have never seen before, and I am afraid, you will never see again — modernized Shakesperian comedy." (pp. 196-197.) Nevertheless, in 1901 he predicted to Daniel Gregory Mason that "Nearly all of Hardy will die," regretting the funeral of *The Return of the Native,* and rating *Jude the Obscure* "his one book that is true." (Torrence, p. 45.)

Miss Bates, who became Robinson's close friend and helper at the MacDowell Colony, attests that "There was never any lessening of his high opinion of *The Dynasts*" (p. 31), yet equate this with his remark to Mrs. Richards that it "is pretty bad poetry, but still is probably the great book of the last half of the nineteenth century." (Fussell, p. 197.) He repeated the encomium almost verbatim to E.R. Leippert (p. 112), and extended both portions to superlative degree in an interview with Carty Ranck: "the greatest long poem of the nineteenth century." ("Edwin Arlington Robinson," New York *Herald Tribune Magazine* [December 14, 1930], 8.) He summarized and rhapsodized to Thomas Sergeant Perry on July 25, 1926: "To me, it is beyond a doubt the great book of the latter half of the nineteenth century perhaps of the whole century — though I'll hardly go so far as that. The verse, or most of it, is rather bad, but somehow that doesn't matter. Hardy has an indomitable way of driving his poetical horse and cart over the roughest roads and getting home with nothing really broken. I have no doubt that Homer's name was Thomas." (Colby College Library.)

Robinson espied a common attribute between himself and Hardy as poets, which he broached impishly to Laura Richards: "Hardy's poetry, by the way, fares about as badly with a single reading as that of another spreader of sunshine whom I might drag in." (Torrence, p. 130.) He assured Leippert that the more he read Hardy's work the better he would like it, but that some of it is "miraculously bad." (Fussell, p. 112.) "In Hardy he found much. 'He stumbles along a good deal, but somehow he usually manages to get there.'" (Rollo Walter Brown, *Next Door to a Poet* [New York, 1937], p. 36.) Specifics aside, Robinson believed that Hardy would "take his place among the solid poets of England." (Torrence, p. 129.)

As philosopher, Hardy jarred Robinson's Emersonian faith in the dignity of man. "Mr. Robinson said, apropos Hardy's pessimism, that Hardy's blunder, both philosophic and artistic, was his reiteration of the idea of God jesting with mankind." (Bates, p. 14.)

In 1929 Robinson told Lucius Beebe it would be difficult to estimate Hardy's relative position because he was "essentially" a writer "of the present." (Beebe, I, 19.)

. . / / . .

Genuine song-swing and underlying seriousness

THE CHILDREN OF THE NIGHT

A charming book from the publisher's standpoint is Mr. Edwin Arlington Robinson's *The Children of the Night,* and a charming book, too, from the reader's. Mr. Robinson's verses are of unequal merit; some lines have misplaced emphasis[1]; many have a genuine song-swing; all have an underlying seriousness. The "Octaves" are peculiarly characteristic in this respect; there is the adequate expression of one who is both thinker and artist in "The Pity of the Leaves," and there is an *In Memoriam*[2] faith in the final "L'Envoi."

From "Books and Authors," *Outlook*, LVII (December 25, 1897), 1013.

---

[1] This phrase by the anonymous reviewer nettled Robinson. He wrote to Edith Brower on July 22, 1898 (another instance of his amaranthine memory in these matters): "I am quite ready to have Mr. Higginson call me crude but I don't want the *Outlook* man, or woman, to write about my 'misplaced emphasis.'" (Cary, p. 80.) See Thomas Wentworth Higginson's review, *Nation*, June 2, 1898, in this volume.

A year and a half later he aired his discontent again. "I call it blank verse, but you may call it what you please," he said to Harry Smith, "as long as you don't have anything to say about 'misplaced emphasis.' That is the one thing that makes me raw." (Sutcliffe, p. 303.)

[2] There is indeed more of Tennyson's *In Memoriam* in Robinson's "The Children of the Night." "There lives more faith in honest doubt, / Believe me, than in half the creeds" (Part XCVI, stanza 3) is quoted by Robinson in his stanza 6: "No faith for 'honest doubt' to keep." Robinson's "The common creed of common sense" (stanza 9), and "the faith within the fear" (stanza 11) have distinct Tennysonian vibrations.

. . / / . .

A most disheartening amount of chaff

THE CHILDREN OF THE NIGHT

The Children of the Night by Edwin Arlington Robinson, 10mo. cloth, ornamental cover, pp. 121 (Richard G. Badger & Co., Boston). In this book of poems we find sprinkled here and there, among a most disheartening amount of chaff, a few grains of good wheat. In other words, trashy rhymes alternate with real poetry in such puzzling fashion that the reader is disposed to believe the book is the work of two writers. On one page is poetic sentiment, graceful play of fancy, powerful imagery and strength of diction, while the next page may hold the rudest twaddle. The work should have been carefully edited before publication.

From "New Publications," Denver *Republican* (December 26, 1897), 14.

This is the most abrasive review leveled at the book. The judgments are journalistically arbitrary, offering no examples or explanations to substantiate its own series of stylized polarities. Badger gleefully misused the penultimate sentence in his advertisement of the book in Mosher's *Bibelot* for February 1898, quoting the four favorable phrases but omitting the pejorative conclusion.

. . / / . .

Gentle and contemplative sadness

THE CHILDREN OF THE NIGHT

In these times one opens a book of poems by a new poet with many misgivings. Happily, however, Mr. Robinson's muse sings with so sincere a voice, and in such musical numbers, that the preliminary qualms soon disappear. The reader will find here many charming pieces, all tinged with a gentle and contemplative sadness. The verses are not uniformly excellent, and the poet has many limitations, but he strikes the right note now and then, and when he does, the effect is very pleasing.

From "Recent Publications," New Orleans *Daily Picayune* (December 26, 1897), 9.

.. / / ..

A touch of the divine afflatus

GOOD VERSE

In these days when everybody writes poetry, and what is worse finds someone to publish their verses, it is a real oasis to the jaded reviewer to encounter a little book of verse that rings true and that has at least a touch of the divine afflatus. *The Children of the Night*, by Edwin Arlington Robinson, is a daintily clothed little volume containing some real poetry. Many of the songs are of common things and common people, but not sung in a common way. Mr. Robinson also attempts to probe for the reason of things and touches some deep chords that thrill us. "The World" is a pretty rendering of the thought that our environment is what we make it, and a "Ballade by the Fire" is a pretty plea for cheerfulness in life. "Her Eyes," "The Clerks," and "Dear Friends," have much of thought and beauty in them. There are some pleasing tributes to some of the master singers as Verlaine and Whitman and appreciations of Zola, Hardy and Thomas Hood.

The longest poem in the book is "The Night Before," in which is related the story of a man about to be hung. Perhaps the daintiest bit is "The Miracle" and all ends fitly with "L'Envoi," in which the author apostrophizes the deathlessness of true poetry.

From "Literary," Hartford *Post* (January 6, 1898), 8.

.. / / ..

Music in a proper name

THE PROMISE OF FAME

Late in 1896, Mr. Robinson sent out a slender little pamphlet which he had caused to be privately printed, with the title *The Torrent and The Night Before*, dedicating it "To any man, woman, or critic who will cut the edges of it," and adding, "I have done the top." The author has probably changed his mind about the place of critics in the physical world, since most of them had kindly things to say of a modest little book which deserved them. For this, his second volume, he has taken all the poems in the former book, with one exception, and has added a very few more numbers.[1]

The most characteristic thing in Mr. Robinson's verse is his complete appreciation of the music in a proper name — and not the music merely, but its general poetic value. He has poems to John Evereldown, to Fleming Helphenstine — which is a mere misspelling of the German helfenstein, or stone of succor, — to Aaron Stark,[2] a miser, to Reuben Bright, an amiable butcher, and to others, the character he assigns each fitting the name like a glove.[3] One may see how it works out in such a complete poem as this, which he calls a "Romance":

> We never half believed the stuff
> They told about James Wetherell;
> We always liked him well enough,
> And always tried to use him well;
> But now some things have come to light
> And James has vanished from our view, —
> There isn't very much to write,
> There isn't very much to do.[4]

This simplicity of treatment runs through all of the lines except those on classical topics, and it is a welcome note. Here is another instance of this recondite knowledge of proper names: ["Fleming Helphenstine" follows.] The situation there is Maeterlinckian.[5]

Though we have dwelt upon one salient point, and trusted to quotation to bring other beauties of Mr. Robinson's verses into view, we are not to be understood as having more than hinted at the contents of a very worthy book, filled with varied promise.

From "Reviews," *Chap-Book*, VIII (January 15, 1898), 219.

---

[1] Robinson actually omitted two poems, "For Calderon" and "A Poem for Max Nordau," and added forty-three new ones, just one short of the total carried over from *The Torrent*.

[2] Robinson to Laura E. Richards, March 9, 1902: ". . . little John Evereldown. I call him little because he isn't big. He is merely John Tarbox plus a superannuated projection of. . . . Aaron Stark, on the contrary, has nothing whatever to do with the late N.M. Whitmore, or with anyone else." (Torrence, pp. 50-51.) Torrence deletes the name of Henry S. Webster in connection with John Evereldown but Mrs. Richards perserves it in her typewritten copy of Robinson's letter, now in Colby College Library.

[3] Although Robinson's penchant for "curious" names had been noted before, this is the first worthy insight and treatment of this surpassing utilization of symbolic nomenclature. See the section *Nomen Est Omen* in the chapter "Preliminary Vistas" of this volume.

[4] "Romance" is a poem in two parts: the first entitled "Boys" (originally "The Brothers"), a quatrain in iambic pentameter; the second, "James Wetherell," this octave in iambic tetrameter. Robinson wrote in this vein about them to Edith Brower in May and June of 1897: "The 'Brothers' was another wicked grind. A year ago

it was a sonnet; now I'm not sure that it is anything. 'J. Wetherell' was an 'inspiration'; and is about on the level I think with the bulk of inspirational work. The first draught comes easily, then comes the struggle." (Cary, p. 45.) "As far as I know, 'James Wetherell' is the best thing I have done." (p. 52.) Robinson obviously changed his mind. He never included either part of "Romance" in any edition of his *Collected Poems.*

5 Robinson undoubtedly read Maurice Maeterlinck (see Sutcliffe, p. 187, and Cary, p. 106), but he gave no indication of direct "influence."

.. / / ..

Strong and distinctive note of song

THE CHILDREN OF THE NIGHT
William Morton Payne

It was a year ago that we hailed in a modest pamphlet a verse sent us by Mr. Edwin Arlington Robinson[1] a strong and distinctive note of song, and we are glad that the privately printed booklet has now been brought to the sight of a wider public. It is not strictly the same volume, for there are a number of new pieces, while the old ones are revised and rearranged.[2] "The Children of the Night" gives a title to this new volume. Noteworthy among the added verses are a number of gnomic "Octaves," for one of which we may find space.

> Nor jewelled phrase nor mere mellifluous rhyme
> Reverberates aright, or ever shall,
> One cadence of that infinite plain-song
> Which is itself all music. Stronger notes
> Than any that have ever touched the world
> Must ring to tell it — ring like hammer-blows,
> Right-echoed of a chime primordial,
> On anvils, in the gleaming of God's forge.

From "Recent American Poetry," *Dial*, XXIV (January 16, 1898), 49.

1 See his review of *The Torrent and The Night Before*, *Dial*, February 1, 1897, in this volume.

2 See collation of *The Torrent* and *The Children* in the introduction to this chapter. The tables of contents for both these books are also provided in this volume.

.. / / ..

Robinson vented delight and wonder over the prolific circulation of his book. On January 26, 1898 he wrote Miss Brower: "I had some astounding news the other day. Badger writes me that he has got rid of three hundred copies of *The Children*. I can partly account for 150 of them but the rest have gone off into the unknown and the unknowable. That's where I like to have them go." (Cary, p. 71.) Two new ingredients had been added since his personal distribution of *The Torrent* — the magic of advertising and Richard Badger's unscrupulous use of it. He placed in Thomas B. Mosher's *Bibelot* for February 1898 a four-inch, enframed ad extolling

The Children in glowing statements plucked from the two Boston *Evening Transcript* notices, the *Outlook*, New Orleans *Daily Picayune,* and Denver *Republican* (see note on his manipulation of this one following the review, above). On February 4 Robinson repeated the sales statistic to Harry Smith, then: "What notices have come in are very good. . . . I am very well satisfied with the way things are going — didn't expect any howling success." (Sutcliffe, p. 295.)

. . / / . .

In this oddest of all critiques written on Robinson's poems, Thorne foregoes esthetic scrutiny, focuses on the philosophic, plunges into moral stricture, and winds up with a florid religious harangue. By way of elucidation it must be noted that Thorne was originally a Protestant clergyman, attended Union Theological Seminary, converted to Catholicism, and underwent more than one other creedal mutation.

Under his encompassing title Thorne first reviewed Edwin James Dunning's *The Genesis of Shakespeare's Art* and Sam Walter Foss's *Dreams in Homespun,* then turned to Robinson. His guiding thesis is stated most concisely on page 22: "Over and over again, in the pages of this magazine during the past eight years, I have pointed out the truth that the most fatal malady of modern times is our almost universal lack of all true knowledge of, reverence for or belief in the ancient landmarks or standards of true morality, true philosophy, true religion, true literature, or true poetry, and I count among the basest enemies of modern culture those literary gentlemen of our day — Catholic and Protestant and Infidel alike — who are debasing their own God-given capacity for doing things that are beautiful by doing things that are merely popular, for pay, and at the same time advocating this infernal heresy that literature is a matter of taste — that is, of popular taste — that is, of frog spawn and the mud-gutter."

Inimitable art and pitiable unfaith

SHAKESPEARE, FOSS AND CO.

William Henry Thorne

. . . The third and last member of our present firm of Shakespeare, Foss & Co., to be noticed here, is Mr. Edwin Alington[1] Robinson, some of whose poems have time and again appeared in the pages of the *Globe Review,*[2] and whose first little book, *The Torrent and The Night Before,* was noticed in a recent issue of this magazine.[3]

The Children of the Night is simply a little larger than *The Torrent,* printed in the same dainty style, and with all the faults and merits of its predecessor intensified. In truth, the opening poem, which also gives name to Mr. Robinson's new volume, tells the whole story of his inimitable art and of his poor pitiable unfaith and negation.

His work is beautiful, clear-cut, and well done beyond that of any of our younger American poets, but he has no message to deliver — nothing to say to this floundering age of imbecile newspaper and shoddy-fed boobies — only a wail, as if there were really no heaven above us, no God above the heavens, no Christ of glory to lift us thither — nothing but the lies of hypocrites and the laughter of clowns.

I quote "The Children of the Night" entire, that readers of the *Globe* may judge for themselves: [The poem follows.]

As a poem, pure and simple, and regardless of its philosophy, I call this "Children of the Night" one of the very best that has appeared in the English language since the best portions of Tennyson's *In Memoriam* brought down upon that poet's brow the plaudits and the love of mankind.[4]

Moreover, there are sonnets and octaves in this book, as there were in *The Torrent*,[5] that, as a matter of strong and beautiful poetry, are equal to the best that Keats[6] and Shelley[7] ever wrote, and, unfortunately, they are, as a rule, scarcely less despairing and atheistic.

In the present instance, and having avowed my praise of this first poem, I shall confine my remarks to a few criticisms of the conceited and abominable and impertinent philosophy which it contains.

To begin at the end of the poem, the children of the night — that is, the atheists, the unbelievers, the croakers, the dissatisfied, the children without faith, hope, or God in this world, and the world at large with all its teeming millions of children of the night are to be cured, saved, enlightened, uplifted, glorified, made men and women of virtue, hope, integrity, saints, heroes, angels, and archangels of light ineffable and eternal, for such are the dreams which our fellow-men and women have ever dreamed, simply by following "common sense" — that is, when pressed to its logical consequences, by following what is known as the philosophy of Tom Paine & Co., including Walt Whitman & Co., W.D. Howells[8] & Co., T.B. Aldrich[9] & Co., — that is, again, when sifted to the bone and marrow, by becoming devotees of Mammon, by putting money in their purses, by robbing the poor, by robbing the world, by robbing God and trampling upon all the dreams and prayers, and hopes and visions, the bravest and best souls of the human race have ever dreamed and died to realize.

I do not pretend to charge that Mr. Robinson has himself carried his thought to its logical consequences, or that he pretends or would dare or desire to teach such blasphemy if he really understood his own meaning.

I know the man and love him, and I know that his purposes are high and pure; nevertheless, his infernal philosophy means all that I have depicted, and far worse than this.

In fact, with the characteristic arrogance of the race of Yankees whence he came, he makes his own definition of God, admits no higher mind or power than his own untaught and youthful intellect as a possible higher power than his own for the definition of God.

Worse than this, he defines such definitions as have been made by the prophets, by Christ, by his apostles, by the Church, as simply "a prophet's lie," and presumes that because he himself has never risen above the sphere of "honest doubt," therefore, all those who have so risen — and glory be to God, they are to be counted by millions of better, braver, and stronger men and women than Edwin Arlington Robinson — are either knaves or fools, the mere children of "a prophet's lie."

"And if God be God, He is Love." Where did Mr. Robinson learn this — from Jesus Christ[10] or Thomas Paine? A pox upon such everlasting duplicity and ignorance as our modern poets of atheism and boyish conceit everywhere manifest.

Did Mr. Robinson learn how to write good poetry without studying the masters of his art? Can he expect to know God, or his ways in this world, without studying the prophets of God and the masters in the science of theology, which he clearly despises?

I do not blame this young man for these flagrant and outrageous ignorances and conceits.

He cackles but the pride, the rebellion, the hard-hearted, hard-headed obstinacy of the long beaten broods of Plymouth Rock hens and roosters out of which he has been evolved.

The rebels of the Mayflower are to blame for Robinson's pride and atheism.

The Down East Yankee-English robbers and murderers of the French Canadians of Acadia, the high-headed witch-burners, the Yankee persecutors of innocent Quakers, Baptists, and other Protestant brethren of their own, are to blame for the darkness and madness of this young man's gifted brain. They were thieves and rebels and murderers from the start, and what can be expected of their children except so far as these have been brought under the pure and holy teachings of Christ and His Church?

I do not blame Mr. Robinson or any modern Yankee for his rebellion, his hardness of heart, his conceit, or his ignorance. These have all been entailed for three long centuries.

On the contrary, I love this man and bid him try to see the truth of God through the visions of God's true prophets, and forget his Yankee ancestral prophets of lies.

Whether Mr. Robinson sees it or believes it or not, the fact remains that the God of Love, he fain would sing, has manifested himself in the person of a man, who, having lived the life of God's truth among us, was crucified as a liar, which is still the fate of many of his true followers; and, whether Mr. Robinson sees and admits the truth or not, millions of the bravest souls God ever made and the world tried to throttle have followed the life of this divine man to the limitless realms of light and glory, singing on their way, and, whether Mr. Robinson sees and admits it or not, these and the likes of these are the only true guides and hope of the world to this hour, and will and must remain so to the end of time.

My prayer is that the God of love, the God of all light and truth, in His dear Son, through His own Church, may bless this young man and gift him with faith equal to his art. Then the future Americans of the next generation and for generations to come would have poetry worthy the name of art, and also worthy the nameless and ineffable glories of divine love and Christian heroism that have folded our world as with the garments of sunrises and sunsets of blessing, and hope and faith and human tenderness during these last nineteen hundred years.

Lay down thy Tom Paine and thy mere brutal Walt Whitman, and take up thy Tennyson,[11] thy Bible, and, hand in hand with God and truth, sing us a song worth singing, my dear young friend, and so I bid thee God speed.

From *Globe*, VII (March 1898), 29-33.

1 This was quite evidently a typographical slip, for the name is spelled correctly later in the text, but it no doubt added to Robinson's annoyance and sense of belittlement in the continual bungling of his name in this early period.

2 Thorne had published eight Robinson poems, more than any other single source up to this time: "The House on the Hill," "The Miracle," "Kosmos," "Thomas Hood," "I Make No Measure of the Words They Say," "God's Garden," "Shooting Stars," and "An Octave."

3 See *Globe*, September 1897, reprinted in this volume.

4 See note 2, *Outlook*, December 25, 1897, in this volume.

5 There are no octaves in *The Torrent and The Night Before*.

6 Robinson to Harry Smith, October 12, 1890: "Did you ever read any of Keats' sonnets? They are great. To my mind they are the greatest in the English language." He specifically mentions "Kosciuscko," "On Reading Chapman's Homer," "Homer," and quotes most of "To Fanny." (Sutcliffe, pp. 4-5.) Robinson once playfully signed a letter to Josephine Preston Peabody "Fred Keats."

7 Robinson was considerably less impressed by Shelley. "The Revolt of Islam," he told Laura Richards, is "too much for me" (Fussell, p. 84); Mrs. Louis V. Ledoux that he liked the Policeman's Chorus in *The Pirates of Penzance* "better, in some ways, than the last act of *Prometheus Unbound*, which somehow doesn't quite come off" (Torrence, p. 86); and Thomas Sergeant Perry, December 26, 1925, "If Shelley had been an artist as well as a poet he would have been such a poet as never was." (Colby College Library.)

8 Robinson and William Dean Howells apparently shared fairly low opinions of each other. "Howells, I doubt not, is really good for something, even if he does write 'literary passions' for the *Ladies' Home Journal*," Robinson said to Harry Smith not without malice, after conceding that he knew "next to nothing" about him. (Sutcliffe, pp. 225-226.) Less scornfully to Lilla Cabot Perry on December 3, 1914: "For some queer reason Howells doesn't [produce the personal thrill], although I admire much that he has done." (Colby College Library.) And it comes as a distinct jolt that, among the thousands upon thousands of words Howells dispensed in his agglomeration of book reviews for the *Atlantic Monthly*, *Harper's*, and others, not even one full sentence is allotted to Robinson. The best Howells could muster was: "There is such fine, manly *go* in 'The Klondike' of Mr. Edwin Arlington Robinson's *Captain Craig: A Book of Poems* as makes you wish to read the whole book;" Anna Hempstead Branch being awarded the nether side of the semicolon. On this occasion Howells crammed twelve notices into four pages, with Amy Lowell, Edgar Lee Masters, and Robert Frost receiving lions' shares. ("Editor's Easy Chair," *Harper's*, CXXXI [September 1915], 637.)

9 During the discouraging autumn after his return from Harvard, Robinson wrote Harry Smith: "If I turn out a failure after all, and go hopelessly to the devil, I shall have [Thomas Bailey] Aldrich's lines to console myself with:
    Then if at last thine airy structure fall,
    Dissolve, and vanish, take thyself no blame:
    They fail, and they alone, who have not striven.
For I am going to strive, and strive hard this winter." (Sutcliffe, pp. 107-108.)

10 Robinson to Arthur R. Gledhill, October 28, 1896: "I have been slowly getting rid of materialism for the past year or two, but I fear I haven't the stamina to be a Christian — accepting Christ as either human or divine." (Torrence, p. 13.) To Harry Smith on November 6, 1896 Robinson summarized Carlyle's *Sartor Resartus* as "a denial of the existence of matter as anything but a manifestation of thought. Christianity is the same thing, and so is illuminated commonsense." After commenting on Mary Baker Eddy's doctrines of Christian Science, he proceeded: "Epictetus and Socrates, Emerson and Carlyle, Paul and Christ (or Jesus, if you prefer) tell pretty much the same story from a more general point of view." (Sutcliffe, p. 263.)

11 Robinson had in fact taken up the Poet Laureate earlier with the sturdiest kind of appreciation. In 1894 he had exulted over one of Tennyson's blank verse poems, quoting a particularly splendid line to Harry Smith. "His greatest charm lies in the fact that one can read him over and over again without tiring of him. I have read *Maud* aloud three times, and am quite ready to do so again." (Sutcliffe, p. 163.) Alas, within seven years he was saying to Josephine Peabody, "Tennyson is so much worse than Browning that I am willing to be content with what I have tried to read of his other things in 'dramatic form'.... Anyhow I am sure that a fairly good trial for dog-stealing would make a better play than *Luria*." (Torrence, p. 47.) During the later MacDowell Colony days he trod the same mill. He said testily to Esther Willard Bates "that Tennyson was a terrible ass, that the adulation of the British public was too much for him." (Bates, p. 2.) Yet, and probably to deflate an overblown ego, "When he listened to a fellow Colonist belaboring Tennyson heavily at the supper table he remarked dryly: 'He wrote some poetry.'" (Brown, p. 37.) One last, moderated judgment, to Lilla Cabot Perry, August 15, 1925: "Tennyson's *Idyls* are strangely thin nowadays, just as Swinburne's *Tristram of Lyonesse* is strangely prolix and saccharine, — and yet Tennyson and Swinburne, when all the worst has been said about them remain rather creditable poets." (Colby College Library.)

. . / / . .

Noticeable for imaginative force

THE CHILDREN OF THE NIGHT

William Peterfield Trent

Some months ago we reviewed a little volume of verse by Mr. Edwin Arlington Robinson, which struck us as having many fine and commendable qualities.[1] We are glad to note that he has republished his poems, with some additions, in quite a handsome volume (Boston: Richard G. Badger & Co.) entitled *The Children of the Night*. A reperusal of Mr. Robinson's verses confirms us more than ever in the judgment we first passed upon them. He has merits that will stand the wear and tear of the success that we believe he will attain in time, if he goes on steadily devoting himself to his work. Some of his octaves and sonnets are particularly noticeable for imaginative force.

From "Notes," *Sewanee Review*, VI (April 1898), 254-255.

1 See his much longer review of *The Torrent and The Night Before* in the *Sewanee Review* of April 1897, reprinted in this volume.

. . / / . .

A whole life in fourteen lines

THE CHILDREN OF THE NIGHT

Thomas Wentworth Higginson

The poet Tennyson, pointing a quarter of a century ago to a copy of Miller's early poems that stood on a shelf of his library, said briefly to an American visitor: "There's power there, but crude."[1] Among all the new

American poems which have lately passed across the critic's desk, there is no question which is entitled to just this praise so far as it goes. It is *The Children of the Night*, by Edwin Arlington Robinson (Boston: Badger). Nay, one can go farther than this, for, while the variety of Mr. Robinson's measure is as yet small, he does his work deftly and thoroughly within that plot of ground, and packs even his sonnets with such vigor and such creative imagination that the whole story is told. He writes of men and women, not of external nature, and uses the latter only as the Greeks did,[2] for a setting, not a theme, which is the better way. When he deals of books, there is the same power of characterization. We expect young poets to have their say about Verlaine and Whitman, but we hardly expect them to have heard of Crabbe; and yet what prose critic ever summed up Crabbe and placed him in his niche so completely as this young American? (p. 64): ["George Crabbe" follows.]

And when the young poet, looking away from his bookshelves, turns his lens upon the village street which he knows so well, the result shows the same power of putting a whole life, or a whole generation of lives, into the same narrow compass of fourteen lines[3] (p. 54): ["The Clerks"[4] follows.]

Mr. Robinson is not afraid of odd words where they give just what he needs. In this last verse, "tiering" is, we take it, arranging in tiers, and "alnage" means ell-measure.[5] To show him capable of a lyric flow and of producing something which shall haunt the reader, take this (p. 32): ["Luke Havergal" follows.]

From "Recent American Poetry," *Nation*, LXVI (June 2, 1898), 426.

Robinson identified the author of this unsigned critique in a letter to Edith Brower, July 22, 1898: "I am quite ready to have Mr. Higginson call me crude . . ." (Cary, p. 80.) The New York *Evening Post* reprinted the review in full on June 4.

Thomas Wentworth Higginson (1823-1911), Unitarian minister, colonel of the first regiment of Negro soldiers in the Civil War, mentor of Emily Dickinson, social activist, novelist, and biographer of Whittier, Longfellow, and Margaret Fuller, wrote all the poetry reviews for the *Nation* from 1877-1904.

1   Joaquin Miller (1839?-1913), American frontiersman who shed his given name Cincinnatus for that of the Mexican bandit Murietta, was variously a horse thief, Indian fighter, pony-express messenger, judge, editor, and poet. His colorful personality and wild-west dress brought him as much acclaim during his stay in England as did his most widely known volume, *Songs of the Sierras* (1871). While in England in 1872 Higginson visited Tennyson.

2   Robinson disavowed all but "a few scraps" of Greek. (Torrence, p. 129.) In high school "Win took the 'scientific' course, not because he had any interest in science but because it absolved him from Greek." (Hagedorn, p. 30.) He tried to read Xenophon in the original and planned an ambitious rendition of Sophocles' *Antigone* in meters, which Harry DeForest Smith first translated into English prose (see references to this collaboration in Sutcliffe's Index.) Poems displaying Robinson's knowledge of Greek literature include "The Chorus of Old Men in 'Aegeus,'" "As a World Would Have It," "The White Lights," "Variations of Greek Themes," and "Captain Craig."

3   See the note on *compression* in the last section of the chapter "Preliminary Vistas" of this volume.

4   Robinson said that he "tinkered" with this sonnet "for a month." (Torrence, p. 103.)

Notwithstanding, he expressed misgivings about the final result to Harry Smith: "I enclose a sonnet which appeared in the *Transcript* the other day. I cannot see that it amounts to anything, though it may be a trifle odd." (Sutcliffe, pp. 250-251.)

5 Robinson to Lewis N. Chase, July 11, 1917: "Ten years ago I was called a radical, and most readers looked sideways at my work on account of its unconventional use of so-called simple language." (Torrence, pp. 101-102.)

.. / / ..

Worthy little sonnet

THE CHILDREN OF THE NIGHT

In major poetry England easily leads, but American minor poetry is perhaps a few degrees better than our own. There is a crisper manner across the Atlantic, a clearer sense of what is to be said, a gayer movement. In a recent *Nation* we find some dozen native singers dealt with,[1] and nearly all repay notice. Among them is Mr. Edwin Arlington Robinson[2] with a slim volume, entitled *The Children of the Night*, from which we take this worthy little sonnet: ["The Clerks" follows.]

From "Notes and News," *Academy*, LIII (June 18, 1898), 664-665.

1 Despite the condescension redolent in the first clause and last phrase of this first English review (of a review), Robinson fared well in being cordoned off for notice and quotation. Reference is to Thomas Wentworth Higginson's critique, preceding this one in this volume. Higginson actually took seventeen poets to account in this judgmental hippodrome, of whom only Robinson, Joaquin Miller, and Lloyd Mifflin are recognizable names today.

2 Robinson's name escaped adulteration in this text but his gremlin caught up in the "Contents" page, where he is rechristened Edward.

.. / / ..

Lines that will haunt you all night

A NEW POET
Vance Thompson

In *The Children of the Night* (Richard G. Badger & Co., Boston) Edwin Arlington Robinson reveals himself as a poet of rare sincerity, force and delicacy. Years have brought us nothing quite so good. Many of the verses, to be sure, are merely exercises in technical achievement, and it is hard to keep up one's interest in verses that Swinburne[1] has written, or might have written, in villanelle, rondeau, and pantoum. Fortunately Mr. Robinson has not devoted much of his time to this word-juggling.

At his best he is earnest, unaffected, with a certain Wordsworthian love for the fugue-like thought and a certain directness of expression that is the mark of our poets since Henley.[2] These lines are typical:

> Still through the dusk of dead, blank-legended,
> And unremunerative years we search

>   To get where life begins, and still we groan
>   Because we do not find the living spark
>   Where no spark ever was; and thus we die,
>   Still searching, like poor old astronomers
>   Who totter off to bed and go to sleep,
>   To dream of untriangulated stars.³

To see things and say them — it is the poet's art. There is a serene, far-seeing philosophy in this sonnet, "The Clerks" — *i.e.*, shopmen — that sets one thinking again of Wordsworth: [The poem follows.]⁴

"Luke Havergal" has already been printed in the *Courier*; quite as striking is the ballad of "John Evereldown," who "followed the women wherever they call." Mr. Robinson has objectivity in a degree. He spends little time hymning himself. And his verse is always best where it is mirroring the souls of the villagers he knows — those dwellers among the "northern pines." *The Children of the Night* is Mr. Robinson's first volume⁵; it is more than a promise — it is a very fine achievement. This new poet has strength and tenderness and, above all, he knows the "web of our life which is of a mingled yarn, good and ill together."⁶ He has no undue love for the sorceries of the seas and stars and all the stock-in-trade of young poets. He has discarded these shopworn superfluities. His strenuousness of thought is matched by frugality of word. In no book of verses of recent years are there so many lines that will haunt you all night and come to you fresh the next day. Rare epithets are the sign of a good style, and Mr. Robinson has rare epithets, but in addition he has a style that fits his thought — sober, quiet, evening-colored — with marvelous exactitude. By way of example let me quote this sonnet, "Supremacy": [The poem follows.]

From *Musical Courier*, XXXVII (July 13, 1898), v.

This is the third review of *The Children of the Night* identically titled.

Charles Vance Thompson (1863-1925) rounds out the quintet of Robinson's reviewers most closely approximating some of his own poetic characterizations (see William Henry Thorne, Harry Thurston Peck, Joseph Lewis French, and Edwin Carty Ranck). Poet, essayist, novelist, dramatist, critic of music, theatre, and literature, he exuded deftness in all of these forms. In 1895 he established and edited *M'lle New York*, a vivacious mirror of metropolitan goings-on. He was hailed as one of the "most interesting and eccentric" young American writers of the day, while spending the greater part of his time in Paris "monocled and trying to pass for a Parisian *flâneur*." He wrote a weekly department of breezy, anecdotal commentary on current plays, here and abroad, for the *Musical Courier*, interpolating his own original poems and reprints of any others that caught his fancy. Robinson gives no indication of having ever met him.

1 In 1893 Robinson spoke of the predilection for Swinburne held by his Gardiner friend A.T. Schumann, who nurtured young Robinson in the composition of French forms, and in 1895 Robinson records reading Swinburne's *Tragedies*. (Sutcliffe, pp. 111, 215.) It is not until 1916, however, that he makes any significant remarks about his English contemporary who, he felt, had "gone altogether too far in trying to make words do the work of tones." (Torrence, p. 96.)

Three of his observations came in the twenties, the most dour: "For the past two days I've been reading *Songs Before Sunrise* and deciding that most of it won't do. Swinburne should have been permitted to drink himself to death. . . . By doing so he would have saved you a lot of shelf-room." (Letter to Louis V. Ledoux, June 23, 1921 in Fussell, p. 102.) To Laura E. Richards he pontificated that Swinburne "isn't any too real — except in a few places." (Torrence, p. 129.) And yet, and yet: "I am not sure that there has been any really great name, with the possible exception of Swinburne, added to the list of English poets since Tennyson." (Beebe, I, 19.)

In *A Threshold in the Sun* (New York, 1943), pp. 191-192, Lloyd Morris tells this poignant story. "With a youthful poet's enthusiasm, E. A. had posted a copy [of *The Torrent and The Night Before*], suitably inscribed, to Algernon Charles Swinburne. But no word ever reached him from the venerable master. Some years after Swinburne's death, his library was dispersed at auction in London. An American bibliophile, a friend of both E.A. and Morris, bid a few shillings for the bundle of uncataloged books, and acquired it. When he examined his purchase, he found that it contained E.A.'s presentation copy of his first book — with all the leaves uncut. Knowing that E.A. himself possessed no copy, he decided to present his prize to its author and, with a tact which matched his unselfishness, carefully cut all the pages. The gift deeply delighted E.A. for, after a quarter of a century, it seemed to prove that Swinburne had not, indeed, ignored his early work. 'He read it! He really read all of it!' E.A. told Morris with astonished happiness. 'Just think of his cutting every page! He wouldn't have done so, you know, if he hadn't thought well of my work.'"

2 Robinson had a favorite anecdote about James Whitcomb Riley, the Hoosier poet. "It seems that shortly after William Ernest Henley's poem 'Invictus' was published some one read it aloud to Riley. When the reader came to the concluding lines:
   I am the master of my fate,
   I am the captain of my soul.
Riley smiled grimly and remarked: 'Like hell he is!' 'Which is just about the way that I feel about it,' Robinson always adds." (Ranck, pp. 9, 24.)

3 "Octaves" XIII, p. 103.

4 Robinson to Edith Brower, July 22, 1898: "The man in *The Musical Courier* changes 'alnage' to 'selvage' and 'removed afar' to 'removèd far,' all of which is unpleasant, but he praises me most outrageously, so I suppose I ought not to growl." (Cary, p. 80.) Thompson made the second change in his following quotation of "Supremacy."

5 Thompson is one of several reviewers not aware of *The Torrent and The Night Before*.

6 From Shakespeare's *All's Well That Ends Well*, Act IV, Scene III. Thompson, a freewheeling transcriber, injected the word *which*.

. . / / . .

Unusual promise of strength

THE CHILDREN OF THE NIGHT

Helen Archibald Clarke

We are glad to see that the poems of Edwin Arlington Robinson, which were privately printed about two years ago, have now been reissued in an attractive little book called *The Children of the Night*. Upon the first appearance of these poems we took pleasure in calling attention to them as showing unusual promise of strength, and upon re-reading them are still of the same opinion.[1] It is to be hoped that such a successful attempt in dramatic monologue as "The Night Before" may be the forerunner of more work in the same line.

From "Some American Poets," *Poet-Lore*, X (No. 4, 1898), 597.

1 This critic seems oblivious of the fact that Robinson added almost as many new poems to this volume as had appeared in his first, *The Torrent and The Night Before*.

. . / / . .

Careful workmanship, but it stops there

THE CHILDREN OF THE NIGHT
Edward Abbott

That hope which springs eternal in the breast, the breast even of the editor of a journal of literary criticism, had risen within this particular breast that encomiums, or otherwise, which we have lately felt obliged in justice to bestow upon some living writers of poetry would deter followers by reason of the difficulty of imitation and achievement along that line. We regret to say that hope is again disappointed, and that a new relay of these poets — with one or two happy exceptions — are at our elbow asking for attention. . . .[1]

Paper maker, typesetter, printer, and binder, all have done their best to help Mr. Edward[2] Arlington Robinson into the rank of poets with his *The Children of the Night* (Richard G. Badger & Co., $1.25), and he helps himself somewhat with the combined skill of a musical ear and a delicate pen, real thought, and pure sentiment; but it is not possible always to sympathize with his point of view, and while his verse shows careful workmanship, it stops there.

From "Current Poetry," *Literary World*, XXIX (September 3, 1898), 284.

1 Abbott takes on eighteen poets in this marathon review, bestowing upon each one brief paragraph and epithets reminiscent of Poe at his roughest. Robinson's book is second in order and among the lower half in esteem. Although he was obviously not one of the "happy exceptions," neither was he the most vilely treated in this slate, of whom only Madison Cawein still retains a semblance of stature. Abbott's preference ran to John Lucas Tupper, R.P. Broroup, and Mathilde Blind.

2 This plaguish misrepresentation of Robinson's name adds injury to the generally insulting tone of the critique.

. . / / . .

Slightly more than a year after publication Robinson wrote to Edith Brower: "*The Children* are keeping very quiet now but once in a while there is a call for one of them — perhaps once in two or three weeks. It is hardly probable that a second edition will be called for." (Cary, p. 87.) Robinson was right, for the moment. A second edition did come to life under another aegis in October 1905, with reprints in 1910, 1914, 1919, and 1921.

In August 1899, deeply immersed in his next poetic project, he informed Miss Brower that "I have sold *The Children* to a business man in Boston who thinks he would like to do a little gambling on future possibilities and at the same time see my other work brought to some sort of finish." (pp. 101-102.) He had been advised that publishers would be more amenable to his next book if sales of *The Children* were more robust. When Badger & Co. went into bankruptcy in December 1900 Robinson's Harvard friend William E. Butler induced his father to buy out the remaining copies and put them on sale in his Boston department store.

Two influential critics of our own generation had this to say about *The Children*:

Allen Tate — "*The Children of the Night*, a volume little noticed at the time but one which marks the beginning of a new era in American poetry." (*On the Limits of Poetry* [New York, 1948], p. 358.)

Louise Bogan — "*The Children of the Night* is one of the hinges upon which American poetry was able to turn from the sentimentality of the nineties toward modern veracity and psychological truth." (*Achievement in American Poetry 1900-1950* [Chicago, 1951], p. 20.)

CAPTAIN CRAIG (1902)

Robinson's first visit to New York City in December 1897 convinced him he would rather live there eventually than in Boston. For the first time he savored a free existence among free spirits — Titus Munson Coan, William Henry Thorne, Craven Langstroth Betts, Alfred Hyman Louis — much more to his taste than the taut society of Gardiner with its morality of disapproval. One month after publication of *The Children of the Night* Robinson accepted Edith Brower's invitation to spend a weekend at her home in Wilkes-Barre, Pennsylvania, the farthest west he ever traveled. On January 15, 1898 he told her that he had for the past week "been trying to get started on a piece of blank verse which, if it is ever done will be a book by itself — not a very big one, but still a book."[1] Two days earlier he had described this "long thing in blank verse" to Harry DeForest Smith as "George Annandale."[2]

On that first afternoon Robinson produced twenty-four painstaking lines. Two weeks later his intent hardened immutably: "The blank verse affair is to be a book even if I print it on bag-paper and without covers."[3] His will to be heard had suffered no deflation from the pricks of so many critics over his self-published, self-distributed *The Torrent and The Night Before*. His teeth were bothering him now and the work moved sluggishly; by February he had "but 220 lines or so" done. Suddenly, on March 2, he announced to Miss Brower, "I have thrown my blank verse effusion aside for a time and am slowly writing — in my head — another of an entirely different sort."[4] This was no tactic to rid himself of an unmanageable gambit, nor was it a temporary diversion before returning to the attack. The concept that severed him from his fixed aim was to eventuate as "Captain Craig," Robinson's most audacious departure from current praxis, the Rubicon he breasted now but would fail to cross in years to come.

From the beginning Robinson sensed that he had a tiger by the tail, doubting that Miss Brower could tolerate parts of it and sure that Titus Coan would find it "a wicked dose." Still, his first expressed hope was that he might complete it and the "Annandale" poem by December of '98. He went to Cambridge to look for work, money being his scarcest commodity at this point and for the next two decades. Back in New York empty-handed, he pondered the effects upon him of the past winter and spring. Strange as it may sound to most sojourners in the metropolis, his nerves had had "a chance to settle back to where they belong. When I came here they were like the E string of a fiddle."[5] Because he was broke he returned to Gardiner, where brother Horace was succumbing rapidly to drugs and relations with brother Herman were none too cordial. Despite this enervating emotional vortex, "The Pauper," as Robinson was calling the new poem, flourished.

In June other poetic projects intruded — he laid the seed that grew into "Isaac and Archibald." His bulletins to Miss Brower in July and August are instructive. He was "still hard at work," had enough in first draft "to make a good-sized book," yet felt he would need eighteen months more "at the least" before he had a presentable script. By next June it would be "pretty well straightened out" though not "in any condition to print." He reaffirmed his determination to bring out the book himself as a last resort.[6] In September his work seemed in "a most chaotic uncertain state" and "a little too big" for him[7]; in October the possibility of a job at Harvard began to solidify; in November he declared the book "nearly all written in the rough, but the real labor is still to come"[8]; in December he moved to a friend's house in Winthrop, Maine, for greater privacy and concentration. From there he wrote Miss Brower: "The work is going on, but there is a possibility that it may be interrupted. I am threatened with compulsory prosperity in the shape of a job . . . . the book will probably be delayed a year, but that will make no particular difference."[9]

Early in January 1899 the job John Hays Gardiner had been trying to get for Robinson came through: he was hired as a clerk in the administrative offices at Harvard. His duties, as Hagedorn puts it, were dry and unexacting, "in effect, an office-boy, and cleaning inkwells was the most taxing of his responsibilities."[10] Realizing that he had been chosen solely because of *The Children of the Night* and not for any demonstrable work expertise, Robinson gulped his pride and went through the motions as "a sort of assistant secretary and metaphorical bottle washer to the whole concern."[11] When the academic year closed in June, the university dispensed with his services. He admitted without guilt that his performance had been "pretty bad," and looked back at his "six months in hell" with "the joy of a liberated idiot."

On the credit side, he met during this period three people who in one way or another made perceptible imprints on his future literary life: Daniel Gregory Mason, Joseph Lewis French, and Josephine Preston Peabody. Additionally, in February he made a decision which indubitably affected his career — he turned down the position of literary editor for the Kansas City *Star* with its tempting salary of $2000 per annum, wisely foreseeing what its timetable restraints might do to his poetic flight.

In the spring Robinson had resolved that "The Pauper" would consist of "something like a thousand lines." He would settle down to it between 11 and 1 at night, after eight or nine hours of galling work at the office, the result under these circumstances seeming to him "worthless." The end of his servitude in view, he wrote with renewed heart to Miss Brower on June 6: "I am going to finish up my two books and then if things go at all decently I am going after bigger game." To Mason he reported: "I am in ridiculously good spirits just now [July 14], sending the *Pauper* along at a rate that makes him red in the face." He began referring to "The Captain" by mid-August and by the 27th had raced beyond his self-inflicted quota of a thousand lines. On September 4 he estimated "it will be cruelly long, nearly two thousand lines"; on September 8 told Miss Brower definitively, "Captain Craig, his name is."[12]

Robinson's brother Horace died in September 1899. Edwin attended the funeral in Gardiner and, before he left two days later, knew he would never come back there to live. In October he was once more ensconced with George Burnham in New York City, this time in a boardinghouse near Gramercy Park. He took up again with Betts, Coan, and Louis, came to know Ridgely Torrence and Edmund Clarence Stedman, drifted happily in the looser rhythms and accountabilities of the big city. His mood conduced a spate of productivity. Within two months of his arrival he wrote Harry Smith: "I have done a big lot of work since I came here and I hope to have something between covers before very long." On April 7 he "packed off" two-thirds of the manuscript to a typist.[13] Eleven days later he was feeling "particularly optimistic just now because I am on the home stretch with *The Pauper*. It gags me to look at the twelve-hundred odd lines that have come back from the machine, but I have a satisfying consciousness of having done something and that's what makes me an optimist. By the time the thing has come back from six or seven publishers, I may be more rational."[14] His last statement wears an air of sardonic levity. He could not know how grievously close to fact his prognosis was to be.

On May 16, 1900 Robinson informed Miss Brower that tomorrow he planned to mail "the Big Thing" to Scribner's, "from which it will undoubtedly come back in due time." He hedged expectations of failure by crowing that he had "no end of other stuff in my head," and that two of his friends had read it "and are still friends of mine."[15] The tortuous *Wanderschaft* of Captain Craig had begun.

From the start Robinson lacked confidence that "the ancient house" of Scribner would really publish what he aciduously called his "piece of conservative and wholly legitimate Art,"[16] and he was right. After holding *Captain Craig* for more than a month, Scribner's returned it. Prompted by Mason, Robinson dispatched the poem to Small, Maynard & Company of Boston in June. He heard no word for weeks but lulled himself with the conviction that "The one thing the Pauper will not stand is a hasty examination,"[17] an excruciating irony in view of subsequent events. After further delay, Josephine Peabody interceded and Maynard agreed to print the book. Another long interval of silence ensued, during which Robinson's typescript was mislaid for the winter in a Boston bagnio and the firm of Small, Maynard went into receivership in the spring. In May 1901 the script, fortuitously retrieved from the conscientious madame, was back in Robinson's hands. Almost immediately he shipped it to a New York house. By September *Captain Craig* had been rejected three more times but was "still on the march," at McClure, Phillips & Company.

In the meanwhile Robinson had been gradually formulating another book. Part of it he had "written two years ago, in the rough, but the greater part of the work ... yet to be done" he had been toiling at since coming to New York.[18] The title, he explained to Mason, was to be *Isaac and Archibald*, two-thirds of which "will be taken up by four things in blank verse, of which 'I & A' will be the longest. Those four things, thank heaven, are done, and the other things are in various stages of doing."[19] Some of these poems in progress he discussed at length with Brower, Peabody, Richards, and Mason: "The Return of Morgan and Fingal," "Aunt Imogen," "The Klondike," "The Growth of 'Lorraine,'" "The Sage," "Erasmus," "The Woman and the Wife," "Sainte-Nitouche," "The Wife of Palissy," "Twilight Song," and a revision of "George Annandale." He sent out a number of these. When they were "refused by nearly all of the magazines," he made up his mind to "stick to books hereafter."[20] Between August 1897 and August 1905 Robinson published precisely two poems in periodicals, both in the *Harvard Monthly*.

On the 7th of January 1901 Robinson informed Miss Brower that "that other book" was slowly but surely nearing completion. "It will be as unlike *Captain Craig* as any two things of mine can possibly be. ... This new book is not funny, or not so funny as *C.C.*" On April 1 he told her he would soon be finished with "the book I have been pegging at for the past three years. It could have been done long before this, but it was interrupted by C.C. — and several other people. It won't be a big book ... but it will be a book."[21] To Mrs. Richards he said bleakly, "About half of the new book is, relatively speaking, rubbish."[22]

In October the volume of new poems, now retitled *The Book of Annandale*, was typed and ready for consideration. As he had for *Captain Craig*, John Hays Gardiner took the initiative in prevailing upon Scribner's to publish it. Despite the imposing phalanx of notables he marshaled in support, Scribner's once more declined, damning these shorter poems as "at once too simple and too sophisticated" for its bracket of readers.[23] A follow-up appeal, naming several people willing to underwrite publication, was also vetoed.[24] Undeterred, Gardiner rallied William Vaughn Moody to the cause and sent the script on to Houghton, Mifflin & Company. Bliss Perry, editor of the *Atlantic Monthly* and literary adviser to Houghton, gloats in his autobiography that although he might have been too timid to publish Robinson's "Aunt Imogen" in the *Atlantic*, he at least "atoned for that blunder by persuading the sceptical House to publish Robinson's *Captain Craig*."[25] The facts are less ebullient. In his report Perry classified the manuscript as "A volume of obscure verse, often eccentric & prosaic in character but with flashes of genius occasionally"; then recommended "The only ground of acceptance is the faith of Robinson's friends and the possibility of a more popular book later."[26]

So, it was back to a matter of guaranteeing the expense of printing. Gardiner and Mrs. Richards quickly agreed to put up the money. On Moody's suggestion Robinson combined the contents of *Captain Craig* and *The Book of Annandale*, which Houghton Mifflin accepted in April 1902, "partly at my solicitation" wrote Moody proudly,[27] and somewhat to

Gardiner's surprise. Out of gratitude, but unsure, Robinson meditated the insertion of Gardiner's name at the head of the book. "I was wrong about the dedication in *C.C.*," he told Lewis M. Isaacs a quarter-century later. "I remember now that Gardiner was so bewildered by the poem, which was pretty radical in those days, that I had not quite the heart to dedicate it to him as I had intended. But he came to think better of it before he died, and after his death I ventured to use his name."[28] It appears in the 1915 reprint and the *Collected Poems*.

The route had been steep, the duration wearing, the mood dolorous. Now that this book which "was to be his justification, his answer to Tilbury Town, his passport to recognition and a livelihood" had become a reality, Robinson should have been "immensely elated." Or so thought Ridgley Torrence. "Absolutely not," Robinson retorted. "I don't feel any thrill in it. It's been delayed too long."[29] It would be silly, he wrote Miss Brower "to pretend that I am not glad to get C.C. and the rest of them off my hands, for I am."[30] And yet, aside from his dogged disclaimers, he was awed and completely enthralled by his novel concepts and ingenuities in "Captain Craig." During its lentitudinous progress he made many statements about it, some of them contradictory.

Of its origins he revealed these details to Smith in June 1900:

I am half inclined to think that the whole thing was suggested, indirectly enough, as you will see when you read it, by the alarming pageant on the day when E.R. Protheroe was 'carried to his final resting place' — and I am sure that you will see that I am talking now about the principle of the thing, not about Protheroe: there is not so much as the ghost of him in the poem, but I fear there's rather more of old Mr. Louis . . . than I first intended there should be. There is not very much of myself. . . . I should never have written it, as it stands, if I had not passed through those six months of hell in the College Office, and I should never have written it at all if I had not got out of that same hell at about the time I did.[31]

The cemetery in Gardiner is a short walk past the Robinson house. Protheroe, a popular teacher of music, was conveyed slowly there by the town brass band and the Knights of Pythias in full regalia. Alfred H. Louis is the aged, brilliant, unpredictable English intellectual Robinson met in New York City, now reduced to virtual mendicancy.

Robinson was seldom loath to admit that Louis was the prototype for Craig, "more or less," but he usually maintained that "the other people are entirely imaginary, so far as I can say."[32] However, he said to Josephine Peabody of the character Wocky Bocky: "He is a real being, by the way — or was (the poor devil is dead now) — and I used to go on the trail with him. This and the few lines where Killigrew stretches himself and lights his pipe are the only things in that book that are drawn directly from life. That particular part of Killigrew is now in the Library School at Albany."[33] That model was his friend Seth Ellis Pope.

As regards himself in the poem, Robinson qualified a bit. On September 7, 1899 he assured Daniel Mason that Craig "is something of a scholar but not 'me' "; on the following day to Miss Brower: "There is undoubtedly a certain amount of self-caricature in him."[34]

The protagonist's name Robinson expropriated while working at Harvard. He read "the application of a Divinity School man who gloried in the name of Louis Craig Cornish, and the Craig part stuck."[35]

Robinson suffered sporadic uncertainties over the quality of this new product he was concocting. "I fear I have tried to do too many things — tried to cook too many things in one dish," he wrote Miss Peabody; and again, "In Captain Craig, I did whatever I liked; and I'm beginning to fear that the self consciousness in the thing, rather than the prosiness . . . will prove to be its worse obstacle. . . . Still it is very amusing and sometimes hilarious; and, as a whole, it is elevating."[36]

He was acutely aware of the innovative aspects of this work, calling the poem "a queer sort of thing," "just a little queer," "a strong dose," and the Captain "rather a queer sort of devil."[37] To Laura E. Richards he described the book: "If you will multiply Isaac and Archibald by sixteen, subtract the barnyard element and add two drops of Milton you may have a suggestion of what the new animal is like. He is something like the new animal that has been discovered in Africa, only without quite so much yellow in him; in fact he has no yellow at all except for a moment or two when he drivels a little about spring — all the spring I ever wrote."[38]

There, as in this note to William Vaughn Moody, Robinson seemed to be reaching for some word of confirmation: "It is pretty good stuff in its way, but I am not altogether certain that it has unity. . . . During the past year I have invented a unity of my own, which you will have a chance to inspect when the book is out. I call the book funny, but you may call it prosaic."[39] In the same vein to Miss Brower: "It's a rather prodigious piece of business and a thing that must necessarily be pretty good or very bad."[40] With Mason he was more positive. "The thing is artistic," he asserted. And he implied depths of parable as well: "a sort of humorous poem with something else underneath."[41]

How would people receive this noble experiment of his? This "sort of development of the octaves," he told Miss Brower, "will disgust and frighten some people, and, I hope, please others."[42] The Captain "will be hooted at, if he is noticed at all," he predicted to Miss Peabody.[43] As to Mason, Robinson was sure the first part would "jar your nervous system" and the second part would "make you thirsty."[44] He summed up his expectations for Harry Smith: "I can see how it will repel a good many delicate readers, but I don't see [how] it can fail to make them a little more sensible in their attitude toward the sentimental of life and death."[45]

Before the book was off press Gardiner and Mrs. Richards laid out a strategy of widest possible promulgation. Copies were to be placed in the hands of "this influential editor and that" — Franklin B. Sanborn, Talcott Williams, Thomas Wentworth Higginson, Jeannette Gilder, William Dean Howells; of Alice Meynell, Henry James, Edmund Clarence Stedman; of the *Atlantic Monthly*, and well-connected friends in Missouri, California, Bangor, and Chicago. Of these, the only one named who did produce a review was Higginson; Stedman wrote a blurb of less than a hundred words. Two newspapers in Chicago, the *Argonaut* in San Francisco, and the *Atlantic* also accommodated the ardent guarantors. A number of unanticipated worthies (Traubel, Sherman, Carman, Payne, Scollard) contributed judgments from their various niches. One effusion — from Joseph Lewis French — emerged tardy, unsolicited, and distinctly unwelcome. Robinson took all of this in his customary way — amused, irate, and not a little self-depreciatory. In his heart he knew it was up to the readers now.

. . / / . .

CAPTAIN CRAIG, A Book of Poems. Published October 4, 1902 by Houghton, Mifflin & Company, The Riverside Press, Cambridge, Massachusetts. First trade edition: bound in light green cloth, blind-stamped rule around edges of both covers; gold-stamped spine; top edge gilt, front and bottom edges rough-trimmed; leaves measure 18.7 by 12.6 centimeters; 375 copies at $1.00. First limited edition: bound in dark green cloth; white paper label on spine, lettered in red; top edge rough-trimmed, front and bottom edges untrimmed; leaves measure 19.1 by 12.7 centimeters; 125 copies at $1.25. There is also an English edition of undetermined number with A.P. Watt & Son imprint, shipped to England on August 12, prior to the American issue; format equivalent to the trade edition.

CAPTAIN CRAIG

A Book of Poems

BY

EDWIN ARLINGTON ROBINSON

Boston and New York
HOUGHTON, MIFFLIN & COMPANY
The Riverside Press, Cambridge
1902

CAPTAIN CRAIG (1902)
Contents

Captain Craig	1
Isaac and Archibald	85
The Return of Morgan and Fingal	103
Aunt Imogen	108
The Klondike	115
The Growth of "Lorraine"	121
The Sage	123
Erasmus	124
The Woman and the Wife	
I The Explanation	125
II The Anniversary	125
The Book of Annandale	127
Sainte-Nitouche	150
As a World Would Have It	159
The Corridor	163
Cortège	164
The Wife of Palissy	166
Twilight Song	169

Robinson you are almost arrived

CAPTAIN CRAIG
Horace Traubel

Having so much talent for recitative I wonder that Robinson has not more. Being so simple I wonder that he is not simpler. Having a philosophy of style so nearly free I wonder that he is not free. Possessing pith I wonder why his poems are so long. He did so well in his first book he compelled us to expect him to do better in this. Robinson you are almost arrived. But you have not arrived. First you excite my suspicions. Then I feel myself persuaded. Yet you do not touch me. What do you lack? What do I lack? Why can we not connect? You have enough art. But have you art? You can go high and sustain a strong note. I have quoted you as the scripture of this department. But you who can accomplish such a feat half a dozen times or even only once in the compass of a songster would be able to do it oftener. What do you suppose is the trouble? Or is there no trouble? Is it only my defect of ear? Where you please me you please me very much. But so much of your verse is drawn so taut. It measures up and around and down. It is ruled and ruined. I can see you at work. I should not see you at work. For after the workman's work is done the workman should disappear. Yet you have nerve. Your hand is unerring. And now and then your spirit breaks loose and sings. I often think of your *The Night Before*.[1] It is irresistible. It seems like a promissory note issued on a certain future. What are you doing, Robinson, to keep faith with that credit? Are you quite at ease with yourself? Are you not giving words a possible too free being? Are you not retiring before words? You will only use words to escape them. The master is the friend of words. He treats them well. But he is at his best without them.

From "As to Books and Writers," *Conservator*, XIII (October 1902), 125.

Horace Logo Traubel (1858-1919), devotee and companion to Walt Whitman, is remembered for his invaluable five-volume Boswellian compilation, *With Walt Whitman in Camden*. A Marxist socialist, Traubel published other studies of Whitman and several books of Whitmanesque poems. He founded the *Conservator* in 1890 and regularly conducted the book review section. In italic at the head of each monthly set of reviews Traubel quoted from one of the books under consideration, here (pp. 122-123) thirty lines from Robinson's "The Book of Annandale." Traubel's hortatory tone and approach bring to mind William Henry Thorne's March 1898 review of *The Children of the Night*.

1 Traubel received a copy of *The Torrent and The Night Before*, ritually observed the presence of Robinson's poetic tribute to Walt Whitman, but did not review the book. See the note on Traubel and the *Conservator* for June 1897, in this volume.

. . / / . .

In the biography (p. 191), Hagedorn relates that "A western critic called Robinson, not without acumen, a 'forlornly joyous cuss,'" but he does not document the source of this comment. No solid clue on its possible location turned up during the period of research for this volume.

. . / / . .

Why can't Mr. Robinson be himself?

CAPTAIN CRAIG

If the principal poem in Mr. Edwin Arlington Robinson's *Captain Craig* (Houghton, Mifflin & Co.) had been written by Robert Browning, it would have afforded keen joy and much occupation to the Browning societies. There are passages in these eighty-four pages of blank verse that suggest the difficulties of *Sordello* and *The Ring and the Book*. Browning's trick of roughness is imitated in lines that you can't scan even by standing on your head.

Why can't Mr. Robinson be himself? Why do he and others forget that Browning[1] and water is as bad as Whitman and water, or Carlyle[2] and water? Here is a man with certain gifts, who apparently strives deliberately to be an echo and nothing more.

Mr. Robinson shows in this poem, in spite of its cracks and flaws and crudities, that he can manage a narrative in verse. His hero emerges at times as a sort of mad humorist. But you ask, "What is it all about?" Apparently it is the story of an interesting old gentleman who had read a lot, had views on life, and wished to be conveyed to the grave behind a brass band playing the Dead March in *Saul*. Says he, just before the end:

"For example:
When I go riding, trimmed and shaved again,
Consistent, adequate, respectable, —
Some citizen, for curiosity,
Will ask of a good neighbor, 'What is this?' —
'It is the funeral of Captain Craig,'
Will be the neighbor's word. — 'And who, good man
Was Captain Craig?' — 'He was an humorist;
And we are told that there is nothing more
For any man alive to say of him.' —
'There is nothing very strange in that,' says A;
'But the brass band? What has he done to be
Blown through like this by cornets and trombones?
And here you have this incompatible dirge —
Where are the jokes in that?' — Then B should say:
'Maintained his humor: nothing more or less.
The story goes that on the day before
He died — some say a week, but that's a trifle —
He said, with a subdued facetiousness,
"Play Handel, not Chopin; assuredly not
Chopin."' — He was indeed an humorist."

We should have thought that "Captain Craig" was a joke on Browning,[3] but for the fact that in another piece there is a suggestion of the Irish literary school manner. And Yeats & Co.[4] are as bad examples as Browning is.

Mr. Robinson has talent. Let him read nothing modern for a year and see what the result will be.

From "Books and Their Makers," New York *Evening Sun* (October 17, 1902), 10.

1 "Browning he said he rarely went back to and, speaking of critics' comparisons of his own work with Browning's, he insisted he couldn't see it. He thought he would have done the dramatic monologues whether or not there had been a Browning." (Winfield Townley Scott, *Exiles and Fabrications* [Garden City, N.Y., 1961], p. 167.)

2 Robinson wrote frequently to Harry Smith and occasionally to Edith Brower about Thomas Carlyle. To Smith he confessed being "completely soaked with [the] fiery philosophy" of *Sartor Resartus* (Denham Sutcliffe, editor, *Untriangulated Stars: Letters of Edwin Arlington Robinson to Harry DeForest Smith 1890-1905* [Cambridge, Mass., 1947], p. 12.); yet he could see that "there is, even in Carlyle, a distressing percentage of fool talk mixed in with the world's time-honored precepts about thoughts and deeds." (Richard Cary, editor, *Edwin Arlington Robinson's Letters to Edith Brower* [Cambridge, Mass., 1968], p. 98.) See Indexes of both books.

3 Robinson acknowledged "Captain Craig" as a comic composition, not, as this reviewer charges, an imitation or parody of Browning, but as "a rather particular kind of twentieth century comedy." (Sutcliffe, p. 306.) "I call it funny," he said to William Vaughn Moody, "because it begins with a line that will not scan (so I am told) and ends with a brass band." (Edwin S. Fussell, *Edwin Arlington Robinson: The Literary Background of a Traditional Poet* [Berkeley, 1954], p. 177.)

4 William Butler Yeats and his contemporaries of the eighties and nineties lent themselves to an excess of Pre-Raphaelite and Romantic practices, blending Shelley-Keatsian richness with Mallarmé Symbolism, Walter Pater estheticism, and Irish mythology — all negligent of objective reality, highly imagistic, vague, mysterious, sad, passionate, sonorous, and iridescent. Robinson's "The House on the Hill," "The Dead Village," "The Wilderness," and "Twilight Song" are of this stripe. Still he could say in 1894: "Mr. W.B. Yeats looks as if he might have the afflatus, and pretty badly, too. His picture is not just what one has a right to look for in this nineteenth century, and I am too conservative to admire the taste that leads a man to make such a 'holy show' of himself." (Sutcliffe, pp. 180-181.)

. . / / . .

Penetrative, powerful masque of life

AN ALTRUISTIC VAGABOND

American versifiers are numerous as candidates for public office, but our poets are few. One of them is Edwin Robinson,[1] revealed by *The Children of the Night*, and again encountered with added pleasure in *Captain Craig*.

Through that altruistic pensioner of Tilbury Town: —

> A vagabond, a drunkard, and a sponge,
> But always a free creature with a soul — [p. 34]

he composes a masque of life, penetrative, powerful and ethically strong. Angular in form, his lines are lit by high spirit. He has pictorial gifts and nice discrimination in use of words, ability to suggest, —

> things that are not words alone
> Which are the ghosts of things — but something firmer.
> [p. 4]

Summarized, the captain's cheerful creed of life amounts to this: —

> The more we measure what is ours to use,
> The less we groan for what the gods refuse.[2]

In other poems Mr. Robinson drops into Whitmanesque form. "The Klondike"[3] is an example: —

> Far we came to find it out, but the place was here for all of us;
> Far, far we came, and here we have the last of us.
> We that were the front men, we that would be early,
> We that had the faith, and the triumph in our eyes:
> We that had the wrong road, twelve men together, —
> Singing when the devil sang to find the golden river.

From "Books and Authors," Boston *Daily Advertiser* (October 25, 1902), 8.

---

1 Peculiarly, this critic omits Robinson's middle name in both the listing of the book and in the text, as well as the *The* from *The Children of the Night*. He also seems unaware of *The Torrent and The Night Before*, and spells Tilbury with a double *l*.

2 By telescoping, this critic conveys a false impression of metric neatness and rhyme which Robinson deliberately avoided. These words occur on page 36 of "Captain Craig" not in rhymed couplet form, but spoken by Craig as part of a four-line sequence without the pat end rhyme. Robinson's own summary of the theme, made for Laura E. Richards: "[Captain Craig's] theory that it is possible to apply good natured common sense even to the so-called serious events of life." (Ridgely Torrence, editor, *Selected Letters of Edwin Arlington Robinson* [New York, 1940], p. 51.)

3 The friends to whom Robinson showed this poem before publication must have derogated it. "I thought 'Shiras' and 'The Klondike' were rather the best things in the book — all of which goes to show that a fellow is not a very good judge of his own performances," he wrote Laura Richards. (Torrence, p. 48.) "Shiras" he discarded before submitting his final version of *Captain Craig*; "The Klondike" came off quite well with reviewers who cited it at this time.
"It's a pretty amusing piece of literature, I fancy," he told Miss Peabody, "and it ought to be a good antidote for the thermometer even if it isn't very good poetry. I'm not sure that it is poetry [at] all." (Torrence, p. 42.) This in the last week of June 1901.
"By the way, there's jingle in 'The Klondike' if you get my notion of quantity." (To Mrs. Richards, Torrence, p. 48.)

. . / / . .

A new poet worth watching

POET ROBINSON RECEIVING RECOGNITION

John A. Macy

It is a relief to find among the season's books a volume of poems which have genuine distinction, by a new poet worth watching. Houghton, Mifflin & Co. have published Edwin Arlington Robinson's second book of verse, *Captain Craig*.[1] Mr. Robinson's first book, *The Children of the Night*, was printed two years ago by Badger & Co.,[2] and Mr. Stedman immediately gave a considerable space to Mr. Robinson's verse in the *Victorian Anthology*.³ Mr. Robinson's poems will mean nothing to people who like Will Carleton and Ella Wheeler Wilcox.⁴ But those who know English poetry from Spenser to Stephen Phillips will recognize in Mr. Robinson's work the most important new voice in poetry since Mr. Phillips's *Marpessa*.⁵

Mr. Phillips is in the decadence of Victorian romanticism. His beautiful lines are reminiscent of English lyrics from Keats to Swinburne, and they have a later day wanness, a pallor that seems not to promise long life. Mr. Robinson is a revolter against the remote literary phrasing that has become so much a convention that nearly all modern poetry tastes the same. He has returned to plain speech, and if he should do enough better in the direction he has taken to justify the comparison, he would stand to our age as Wordsworth did to his. His view of life is straight-eyed and truthful with the seriousness of a deep humor. He is so afraid of the modern poetic manner that he makes his verses often bald and hard, and does not sing as well as he can. His thought is new, finely cultivated and sincere. He is a poet inside; not, like William Vaughn Moody,⁶ a poet by virtue of a trained skill in phrase making. One should read Mr. Moody's "Daguerreotype" and Mr. Robinson's "Aunt Imogen"⁷ to see the difference between the surface beauty of literary locutions and unaffected truth.

Robinson has not come to the full power of plain speech, for he has got its strength without its perfect clearness. His kind of vocabulary ought to rid his work of obscurity. Then he would not be so afraid of singing. There should be more work like his "Twilight Song"⁸ and "The Klondike," fewer of the rough, bathetic prose passages of "Captain Craig."⁹

From "What Book Folk of Boston and New York Are Talking About," Chicago *Evening Post* (October 25, 1902), 9.

John Albert Macy (1877-1932), currently special Boston correspondent to the *Evening Post*, was a student (and later instructor of English) at Harvard while Robinson was working in the administrative offices there. At Miss Brower's impulsion they met, Robinson pronouncing Macy "the real thing," although feeling thereafter that he treated him rather shabbily. Macy wrote a vanguard study, *The Spirit of American Literature* (1913) and was a liberal staff member of the *Nation* in the twenties.

1 Macy, like the preceding critic, did not know *The Torrent and The Night Before*, and similarly omits the initial *The* in Robinson's second book.

2 *The Children of the Night* was published by Richard G. Badger & Company, but in 1897.

3 Macy is confusing the titles of two Edmund Clarence Stedman collections. *A Victorian Anthology, 1837-1895* (New York, 1895), subtitled "Selections Illustrating the Editor's Critical Review of British Poetry in the Reign of Victoria," contains no American poems. *An American Anthology, 1787-1900* (Boston, 1900), subtitled "Selections Illustrating the Editor's Critical Review of American Poetry in the Nineteenth Century," contains "Luke Havergal," "The Ballade of Dead Friends," "The Clerks," "The Pity of the Leaves," and "The House on the Hill," pp. 727-729. In his "Biographical Notes" at the rear of the anthology Stedman gives Robinson's place and date of birth, then seven lines of identification: "Now a resident of New York City. Engaged in literary pursuits. His poetry has an individual cast, and is contained,

thus far, in his two collections *The Torrent and The Night Before*, 1896; *The Children of the Night*, 1897."

4   Two Midwest poetasters who reflected the subliterary tastes of the time. Will Carleton (1845-1912) specialized in homespun ballads, the best known, "Over the Hill to the Poor House"; Ella Wheeler Wilcox (1850-1919) proliferated sentimental, platitudinous, and popular verses, notably "Solitude" in which appears the line, "Laugh and the world laughs with you."

5   Stephen Phillips (1868-1915), English poetic dramatist, reached his greatest height in these years with *Paolo and Francesca* (1900) and *Herod* (1901), which would strike today's reader as ponderously rhetorical and full of fustian. *Marpessa* (1900) is seldom listed among his best works.
    Robinson was in essential agreement with Macy on Phillips' basic qualities. In February 1898 he said to Harry Smith: "Phillips is getting a big boom and I think he has done something to deserve it. Perhaps a bit too much straining for effect." (Sutcliffe, p. 295.) In 1899 he presumed *Paolo and Francesca* would be "too flowery." (p. 303.) To Daniel Gregory Mason he wrote twice in January 1900: "Have you read Stephen Phillips' tragedy? From quotations I have seen, it seems to be a piece of rather magnificent rant. I should say that four acts of it might be something like Benedictine from a stein, but I have really no right to criticize it on so slight an acquaintance" (Mason, "Early Letters of Edwin Arlington Robinson: First Series," *Virginia Quarterly Review*, XIII [Winter 1937], 59); "*Paolo and Francesca* is a mixture of the magnificent and the pitiful. Read it. The last act is very beautiful but curiously anachronistic." (p. 60.)

6   Of this review Robinson wrote to William Allan Neilson, November 6, 1902: "He hit me off pretty well in some ways, but I can't have him calling Moody a phrasemaker. He is that, to be sure, but he is also many other things — the author of 'The Daguerrotype,' for instance." (Robert Liddell Lowe, "Two Letters of Edwin Arlington Robinson: A Note on His Early Critical Reception," *New England Quarterly*, XXVII [June 1954], 258.)
    William Vaughn Moody (1869-1910), poet and playwright much honored in his own time, is remembered for the poetic dramas *The Great Divide* and *The Faith Healer*, and for *Lyric Poems* (1901). Robinson's course converged with Moody's at Harvard in 1891-1893, but they were otherwise poles apart. At Harvard Moody was a brilliant student and editor, Robinson a nonmatriculating special student; Moody's personality glittered, Robinson preferred the shadows; Moody went on to an outstanding career as teacher, poet, literary historian, Robinson returned to Gardiner, then the menial job at Harvard; Moody attained immediate recognition as poet, Robinson had to wait twenty years. Moody was an undergraduate editor of the *Harvard Monthly* and as such had a hand in rejecting every poem that Robinson submitted. By the time 1902 rolled around both were conscious that the other constituted a rival in the highest echelon of American poetry. (See Hermann Hagedorn, *Edwin Arlington Robinson: A Biography* [New York, 1938], pp. 180-181.) While both pecked a trifle at each other's ways and individual efforts, neither belittled the other in general. Said Robinson to Mason: "Give Moody ten years of tolerably decent existence, I think he ought to produce almost anything.... He is pretty big." (Mason, "Edwin Arlington Robinson to Daniel Gregory Mason: Second Series," *Virginia Quarterly Review*, XIII (Spring 1937), 234.) And: "There is a possibility of his growing up someday and writing like Shakespeare — or maybe like a new Ibsen without smoky spectacles." (p. 236.) Said Moody to Ridgely Torrence: "When we're all dead and buried, EA will go thundering down the ages." (Hagedorn, p. 250.)
    For an account of their relationship see Fussell, above; Maurice F. Brown, "Moody and Robinson," *Colby Library Quarterly*, V (December 1960), 185-194; Richard Cary, "Robinson and Moody," *CLQ*, VI (December 1962), 176-183; Hagedorn, *passim*.

7   Moody was writing in memory of his mother, while Robinson explained to "his sister-in-law that in 'Aunt Imogen' it was himself that he was revealing — or concealing, as you will." (Laura E. Richards, *E.A.R.* [Cambridge, Mass., 1936], p. 59.) Moody's poem is shot through with the rhetoric of anguish and imploration as against

Robinson's controlled utterance and tone.

Robinson to Mason, July 31, 1900: "In the meantime I am wearing poetical petticoats and making a regular analysis of an Old Maid — 120 odd lines of blank verse. I did it in rough two years ago, when I had my eyrie over Brown's dry goods store and smoked 'Before the War' cigars. I had a good mill-pond to look out on and somehow conceived the notion of writing down this particular spinster. Maybe I thought she ought to have drowned herself; at any rate the mill-pond had something to do with it." (Mason, *VQR* [Winter 1937], 67.) In the middle nineties Robinson met frequently with a trio of his Gardiner friends ("The Quadruped") in their "down-town den" on Water Street, which they rented for two dollars a month, and where they could talk and smoke in complete privacy. (See Hagedorn, pp. 92-94.)

Robinson to Edith Brower, April 28, 1901: "I was rather puzzled at your objection to 'Aunt Imogen' as a title, for I had thought that for once at least I had struck one that no person could find fault with. If you thought it was too 'homely' or provincial, or something of that sort, you must have forgotten that I am an incurable myself in that way." (Cary, p. 141.)

Bliss Perry, *And Gladly Teach* (Boston, 1935), p. 177; "Only the other day, when I was praising Robinson's 'Aunt Imogen' to his face as one of his finest poems, E.A.R. gently reminded me that I had once rejected it for the *Atlantic*, on the ground that it was too difficult for a magazine reader to grasp at one reading."

8 On June 11, 1900 Robinson wrote Miss Brower that he had done seventy-two lines of a " 'symbolic' Twilight Song." Shortly thereupon he sent her a copy of the song. "I call it a song and say *marcato* to keep you from jigging its anapests (the accent is more than half of it, I fancy) — may mean pretty much everything or pretty much nothing; and I do not expect you, in either case, to try to bring the thought down to a clear outline. 'Feel' something of it, if you can, and be glad that it doesn't feel any worse." He had the feeling himself that it would make her wring her hands and drive his friend Betts to drink. He then asked her how many lines in the poem struck her as "inadequate," and whether she approved his changing the word *play* to *pray* in stanza 2, line 3. (Cary, pp. 117, 118, 123, 128.) In November he confided to Josephine Peabody that he was thinking of throwing out the whole "T.S. affair." (Wallace L. Anderson, "The Young Robinson as Critic and Self-Critic," in Ellsworth Barnard, editor, *Edwin Arlington Robinson: Centenary Essays* [Athens, Georgia, 1969], p. 82.) By middle December he had worked a considerable number of changes but by the first week of January "had come to the conclusion that I cannot produce the right sort. The four stanzas I have kept . . . seem to me now to be pretty doubtful." (Cary, pp. 132, 135.) The original version comprised six twelve-line stanzas. On Moody's suggestion Robinson excised two of these stanzas *in toto* yet remained unsatisfied, adjuring Miss Peabody, "If you can improve it by tearing out two more, do so by all means." (Torrence, pp. 36-37.) He predicted his "long-legged lyric" would be "hopelessly obscure to the lynx-eyed," and interpreted it to Miss Peabody as "an attempt to express in verse — 'impressionistic,' I fancy, — the dim consciousness we have of things going forward, and for that reason I am bothered by the certainty that everyone who reads it will try to read a thousand things into it that I never dreamed of putting there." (Hagedorn, p. 169.) "I tried to do something 'rather swagger,'" he told her, "and I did not quite succeed. I shall print it, I suppose, but I can't pretend that I am half-satisfied with it." (Torrence, p. 37.)

For a facsimile of the revised manuscript of this poem, see Cary, pp. 119-121.

9 "I suppose the book contains some of my best and some of worst work," Robinson remarked astutely. (Laura E. Richards, *Stepping Westward* [New York, 1931], p. 380.)

. . / / . .

Has still much to learn

CAPTAIN CRAIG

Mr. Edwin Arlington Robinson is for the long narrative poem, and the "criticism of life"; and some of the blank verse has character and some of it has not. The opening lines of "Captain Craig," for instance, are excellent: [the first twenty-eight lines follow.]

A poet of promise is Mr. Robinson, yet one who has still much to learn of his chosen art. Two sonnets may be quoted here to illustrate alike his merit and his failing: ["The Woman and the Wife"[1] follows.]

From "Recent Books of Verse," New York *Mail and Express* (October 25, 1902), Editorial Section, 2.

---

[1] In April 1900 Robinson wrote Miss Brower: "As for the sonnets, . . . I feel sure that there is something wrong in the way they 'connect' — or rather in the way they don't connect. When I tinker them to something like my satisfaction I'll send them along." Good as his word, Robinson enclosed them in a following letter, with this note: "You and other people seem to like this, but it is poison to magazine editors. Probably the 'me' in the last verse kills them. You would say 'him,' but I can't possibly see the question from your point of view." He tried in "seventeen different ways," but could not see that his psychology was misapplied in this case, and he continued to belabor the subject in several consecutive letters. "To me the 'me' is absolutely necessary to give a final turn or clinch to the whole thing; after the impassioned abstraction (wow!) of 'Do you think that Love etc' I came back to the concrete because it seems to me that I must do so in order to be ARTISTIC." The upshot was that he persevered in his own preference and staunchly retained that 'me' in every published appearance. The poem was one of the four he said "have been refused by nearly all of the magazines," remaining at *Cosmopolitan* more than five weeks without word. (Cary, pp. 111-116, 132.)

In February 1902, to Mrs. Richards: "Personally I should call the Woman and the Wife affair the best I have ever done or am likely to do, but next year I may throw it away." (Torrence, p. 50.)

. . / / . .

In the *Literary Digest* for October 25, 1902 *Captain Craig* was noted among the "Books Received" but was not subsequently reviewed. The same is true of the *Literary World* of November 1, 1902 under "New Publications." In the magazine *Outlook* good intentions must have yielded to contingencies of space, for on December 6, 1902 *Captain Craig* appeared in "Books of the Week" with this appended promise: "Reserved for later notice." However, on April 18, 1903 it was not among the critiques of five "Recent Books of Verse."

As far as has been ascertained, the elusive English edition elicited no reviews despite notice of sale of the book in the London *Times Literary Supplement* on November 21, 1902, a listing under "New Books Received" in the *Academy* of December 13, 1902, and the *Publishers' Circular* notice of June 13, 1903.

. . / / . .

Striking and memorable criticism of life

CAPTAIN CRAIG

Readers who had the good fortune to come across Mr. Robinson's former volume *The Children of the Night,* published five years ago, will remember its fine quality and unusual distinction of style and substance. It left one with the feeling that here was a man who would have some day a message worthy of attention. In the present volume Mr. Robinson, in no halting way, begins the delivery of his message, and one finds the promise of the earlier volume true; here is a man with something to say that has value and beauty. There are still shortcomings or perversities of style, but the thought is deep, and the ideas are high and stimulating.

To begin with, a critic, whether his final judgment be favorable or adverse, must take the book seriously. A poet must be measured by a high standard who strikes such notes as does Mr. Robinson in the following passages from the poem that gives the title to the book.

Speaking of the truth, he says:

> "we have heard
> A murmur now and then, an echo here
> And there, and we have made great music of it;
> And we have made innumerable books
> To please the Unknown God. Time throws away
> Dead thousands of them, but the God that knows
> No death denies not one: the books all count,
> The songs all count; and yet God's music has
> No modes, his language has no adjectives." [p. 5]

And again, toward the end of the same poem:

> "How, forsooth,
> Shall any man, by curses or by groans,
> Or by the laugh-jarred stillness of all hell,
> Be so drawn down to servitude again
> That on some backward level of lost laws
> And undivined relations, he may know
> No longer Love's imperative resource,
> Firm once and his, well treasured then, but now
> Too fondly thrown away? And if there come
> But once on all this journey, singing down
> To find him, the gold-throated forward call,
> What way but one, what but the forward way,
> Shall after that call guide him?" [p. 66]

And again in "Sainte-Nitouche":

> The fight goes on when fields are still,
>   The triumph clings when arms are down
> The jewels of all coronets
>   Are pebbles of the unseen crown;
>
> The specious weight of loud reproof
>   Sinks where a still conviction floats;
> And on God's ocean after storm
>   Time's wreckage is half pilot-boats;

The writer of such passages as these has ideas to offer us which will well repay the time that we may give him.

The book is composed of three longer poems, "Captain Craig," "Isaac and Archibald,"[1] and "The Book of Annandale,"[2] with a number of shorter poems, descriptive and lyrical. Of them all "Captain Craig" is the most important: here Mr. Robinson gives us a striking and memorable "criticism of life." The plot of the poem, though sketched with the fewest possible strokes, shows a singular command of narrative: an old man, in the worldly way a wreck and failure, is saved from starvation by half a dozen young men, who give him when the end comes, at his special request, a triumphant funeral with a brass band playing "The Dead March" from *Saul*. All the people, even those who appear in no more than a dozen lines, stay in your mind. The old man, with his fine humor and his tolerant patronage of the men who innocently suppose themselves the benefactors, is a new and inspiring figure in literature. Sitting in the sun, or writing to his friend, or propped up in bed over a perfunctory cup of gruel, he utters his deep reflections on human fate. He is often obscure, but it is the sort of obscurity that has a rich meaning underneath. And in the end his message is

> "Do you think the golden tone
> Of that far-singing call you all have heard
> Means any more for you than you should be
> Wise-heartedly, glad-heartedly yourselves?
> Do this, there is no more for you to do;
> And you have no dread left, no shame, no scorn. . . .
>
> What you take
> To be the cursedest mean thing that crawls
> On earth is nearer to you than you know:
> You may not ever crush him but you lose,
> You may not ever shield him but you gain —
> As he, with all his crookedness, gains with you." [p. 68]

Throughout these is a fine, large sense of humor,[3] which can liken the three Fates to sagacious hens without falling into flippancy; and which keeps the moralizing always human and sane.

Of the other poems "Isaac and Archibald" is a shrewd study of old age, but of old age which in spite of tremors and weakness holds to its faith in "the light beyond the stars."[4] It has such descriptive passages as this of "the cottage of old Archibald":

> Little and white and high on a smooth round hill
> It stood, with hackmatacks and apple-trees
> Before it, and a big barn-roof beyond;
> And over the place — trees, houses, fields and all —
> Hovered an air of still simplicity
> And a fragrance of old summers — [pp. 90-91]

Yet in spite of the fine passages which abound in the book, it must be said that the style is not infrequently marred by obscurity,[5] and in other places by a perverse plainness which brings some lines very near the level of prose. Mr. Robinson seems to belong to that school of poets of which Browning was the triumphant leader, and Mr. George Meredith[6] is today an unabashed sinner, who do not realize that expression is like a telephone in that it must have two ends working at the same time. No matter how pregnant and beautiful ideas a man may have in his head, if he is to get those ideas into other people's heads unstripped of their full radiance of meaning, he must consider not only whether the words and rhythms he uses fit themselves to the niceties of his own thought, but also whether they fit themselves to the normal reader's mind, and there awake images of like significance and wonder-working charm. Our modern poets do not go often enough to Shakespeare[7]; and hence are in danger of forgetting that the highest standard of poetry is the perfect balance of profundity of thought with clarity and beauty of expression.

In the case before us Mr. Robinson seems to be a wanton sinner; and one is tempted to quote against him Mulvaney's immortal distinction, "'Taint because you bloomin' can't. It's 'cause you bloomin' won't."[8] A man who can write the passages we have already quoted or those with which we will close this review cannot defend himself on the ground that the lyrical gift was not added in his making up to the gift of strong and penetrating thought. The first passage is from the poem called "The Klondike," the second is the last stanza of the "Twilight Song," which brings the book to a close:

> Say the gleam was not for us, but never say we doubted it;
> Say the wrong road was right before we followed it.
> We that were the front men, fit for all forage, —
> Say that while we dwindle we are front men still;
> For this is what we know to-night: we're starving here
> For this is what we know to-night: we're starving here together —
> Starving on the wrong road to find the golden river.

And the other:

> Through the shine, through the rain,
> We have wrought the day's quest;
> To the old march again
> We have earned the day's rest;
> We have laughed, we have cried,
> And we've heard the King's groans;
> We have fought, we have died,
> And we've burned the King's bones,
> And we lift the old song
> Ere the night flies again,
> Where the road leads along
> Through the shine, through the rain.

All in all, the more one reads in the book, the more one feels that here is the work of a man who not only can write beautiful verse when he will, but who can handle large subjects with the sure and steady hand of a master.

From "Books of the Day," Boston *Evening Transcript* (October 29, 1902), 18.

1 Robinson to Josephine Preston Peabody, April 12, 1901: "I have just sent a thousand lines of Imperishable Stuff to the typewriter and I feel a good deal better. Four hundred lines of it are about two old men and a small boy ["Isaac and Archibald"], and the other six hundred are a woman who promised her dying spouse that she would never repeat the ceremony and six years after pledged herself to a fellow who kept a queer sort of journal and went to sleep on the day of his wife's funeral" ["The Book of Annandale"]. I don't know just how people will like this sort of thing, but I shall be interested to find out." (Torrence, p. 39.) Robinson had told Miss Brower that "The next thing I do is going to be humorous" in June 1898; on April 1, 1901, "It is 400 lines long and perhaps a bit experimental. You will line it in spots, but whether

you will be able to stand the whole of it or not is another question." (Cary, pp. 79, 139.)

2 Originally titled "George Annandale" (see the first two paragraphs in the introduction to this chapter, and note 1, above). Robinson characterized it as "either good or bad" (Sutcliffe, p. 294), and described it to John Hays Gardiner as "Six hundred lines of blank verse without any bumble-bees or sunsets." (Fussell, p. 200.)

3 Robinson to Edith Brower, July 12, 1901: "Tell me if you find *C.C.* tedious in the opening. . . . I was cherishing a fond notion that it was rather frisky — for me." (Cary, p. 144.)

4 "The chief of the narratives had its birth in a chuckle. Alfred Louis and William Henry Thorne had each confided in Robinson that he was convinced that the other was crazy, and both, Robinson wrote Mrs. Richards, had not been 'far wrong.'" (Hagedorn, p. 168.)

5 See the section *Obscurity* in the chapter "Preliminary Vistas" of this volume.

6 Mowry Saben, friend of Robinson for forty years, says: "I have read a letter in which he speaks most disrespectfully of Meredith, but for years he was one of Meredith's warmest admirers." ("Memories of Edwin Arlington Robinson," *Colby Mercury*, VII [November 1940], 14.) The observation holds true. In 1893 Robinson found *Diana of the Crossways* "decidedly worth reading. Full of philosophy and sharp sayings, but rather heavy upon the whole for a novel. It might be called a 'study' and come nearer the truth." (Sutcliffe, p. 95.) In 1895: "Read every novel for the style and nothing else. Read every word and repeat the reading of every [illegible word] paragraph." (Fussell, p. 91.) In 1900: "Have you read *Beauchamp's Career* yet? It's part of everybody's education." (Torrence, p. 31.) Esther Willard Bates, who knew him well at the MacDowell Colony and did a considerable amount of typing for him, recalls: "Meredith he had apparently read with close attention, and compared novel with novel, especially liking *Richard Feverel* and *One of Our Conquerors*. 'You women,' he said, 'ought to be grateful to Meredith. See what he does for you!'" (*Edwin Arlington Robinson and His Manuscripts* [Waterville, Maine, 1944], p. 31.)

Robinson gave voice to his obverse view as early as 1914. On December 3 he wrote Lilla Cabot Perry anent producing "the personal thrill", "Hardy does it, but Meredith never did — and yet he was called the most magnetic being that ever lived." (Colby College Library.) By the thirties his admiration had taken a distinct turn. To Mrs. Richards in 1932: "[I] still cannot like the man. Something that I haven't liked has always leaked out through the cracks in his work"; and in 1934, "Meredith was too much a novelist to be a poet and too much a poet to be a novelist and too much a verbal snob to be either. And still he was a genius. . . . I have always smelt a disagreeable personality leaking its way out through Meredith's pages. I don't believe he had any feelings — except for himself." (Torrence, 166, 177-178.)

7 Robinson's letters reveal that his reading in Shakespeare was almost as important to him as writing poetry himself. In "Robinson at Harvard," George W. Latham asserts that "he was not ashamed to admit that his favourite poet was Shakespeare." (*Mark Twain Quarterly*, II [Spring 1938], 20.) His prime interest was in the Bard's humanity, for he frequently cut Professor Child's philological analyses of the works while managing to catch every performance of a Shakespearian play in Boston. He wrote four tributes to Shakespeare, the most celebrated being "Ben Jonson Entertains a Man from Stratford." The attraction endured to Robinson's last days. "I haven't read anything respectable this summer except some Bible and Shakespeare," he said to Mrs. Louis V. Ledoux, "which are still pretty good reading." (Fussell, p. 202.) "His desk was full of Shakespeare," noted Frederika Beatty in 1933-1934, "Sidney Lee's *Life*, numerous volumes of Shakespeare's works, nothing but Shakespeare." ("Edwin Arlington Robinson as I Knew Him," *South Atlantic Quarterly*, XLIII [October 1944], 376.)

8 From the short story, "On Greenhow Hill," in *The Writings in Prose and Verse of Rudyard Kipling* (New York, 1899), II, 203.

. . / / . .

Has this any earthly relation to poetry?

SAD STUFF

We have sometimes shuddered when we have found in contemporary criticism a reference to "the poetical output," and have wondered at the taste that could apply to any poetical question a term only to be used, one would think, in speaking of the production of pig iron or pills. But perhaps we have done injustice to those who have employed this word. Perhaps they were irresistibly influenced by a dim consciousness that what they were dealing with was, after all, not very superior in essence to pills or pig iron. A good deal of the minor poetry before us at this moment is nothing less than appealing in its mediocrity. This, for example, is the sort of thing by which we are greeted on the first page of *Captain Craig*, Mr. Robinson's book of poems:

> I doubt if ten men in all Tilbury Town[1]
> Had ever shaken hands with Captain Craig,
> Or called him by his name, or looked at him
> So curiously, or so concernedly,
> As they had looked at ashes; but a few —
> Say five or six of us — had found somehow
> The spark in him, and we had fanned it there,
> Choked under, like a jest in Holy Writ,
> By Tilbury prudence.

Has this any earthly relation to poetry? The whole volume is on the same prosaic level. Once Mr. Robinson seems to have had the glimmering of a poetic emotion, but "The Return of Morgan and Fingal" gives a promise in its first stanza which we look in vain for any of the twenty-one that follow to fulfil.[2]

From New York *Tribune Illustrated Supplement* (November 2, 1902), 11.

In these years Robinson was often the victim of collective contumely, one in a sizeable group under consideration by a man with an axe to grind, therefore hardly likely to devote concerted attention to the better qualities of any individual involved. Subtitled "The Works of Five Minor Poets," this cluster of reviews — of which Robinson's was the first — was dealt universal rough treatment. The other four are Anna Hempstead Branch, Mary Olcott, Madison Cawein, and Josephine Preston Peabody, her *Marlowe* dismissed as "a mere impertinence."

1 Robinson continually denied that the Tilbury Town of his poems was his home town of Gardiner, Maine, or that the people he portrayed were his neighbors and acquaintances there. He insisted to Esther Willard Bates that he did not "draw directly from life" in any of his poems. "He said he 'precipitated his own characters.'" (Bates, p. 5.)

"I have never yet been able to take a subject from real life," he wrote Thomas Sergeant Perry, "without having it run from itself beyond recognition. 'Isaac and Archibald,' for example, has a basis in fact, but the originals would never have known it. One of them was a . . . graduate of Trinity, and a protégé of the Rothchilds before he became a Roman Catholic, and the other was an English editor of a radical German [?] magazine in New York. Each thought the other crazy, and neither was wholly wrong." (Virginia Harlow, *Thomas Sergeant Perry: A Biography* [Durham, N.C.,

1950], p. 207.) Robinson is referring to Alfred H. Louis and William H. Thorne (see Hagedorn, p. 168). Harlow obviously misread Robinson's minute handwriting — Thorne was editor of *The Globe,* an English-language monthly.

To Lewis N. Chase: "While nearly everything that I have written has a certain amount of personal coloring, I do not recall anything of mine that is a direct transcription of experience." (Torrence, p. 103.)

His most definitive denial: "George Burnham has just recently told me — and I quote him literally — that Robinson said to him with emphasis 'that neither Tilbury Town, nor any of the portrait-sketches, nor the 'Town Down the River' referred to any particular place. In no instance whatever in any of his writings did he refer to anyone or any place. Tilbury Town might be any small New England small town.'" (James S. Barstow, *My Tilbury Town* [New York, 1939], p. 7.) And yet, in 1928, Robinson admitted to M.K. Wisehart that in the case of Alfred Louis, "I came to know him well, and to feel that I wanted to perpetuate his personality. . . . He is the central figure of 'Captain Craig.' He *is* Craig." ("'By Jove!' said Roosevelt 'It Reads Like the Real Thing!'" *American Magazine,* CV [April 1928], 78.)

2 Ironically, Robinson looked down on this poem as "merely an episode with overtones," and summarized it as "twenty-odd stanzas about the three chaps who ferried the dead girl and her half-crazy mother home through the storm and then went on with their hilarity as if nothing had happened." (Torrence, pp. 104, 40.)

. . / / . .

Strong and buoyant idealism

CAPTAIN CRAIG

M.L.B.W.

Of the recent interesting and valuable publications from Messrs. Houghton, Mifflin & Co. are: [*Captain Craig* is named as the third of six books reviewed here.]

Mr. Robinson's poems have the advantage of being quite unique in form and conception, dealing with fundamental questions of human life and fate in a spirit of strong and buoyant idealism. A dry and quaint humor pervades the verse, and prevents it from being too heavy and didactic, while following the longer poem which gives the volume its title, are others in somewhat lighter vein, though the general tone is intense, passionate and strenuous.

From "Concerning Books," Portland *Daily Press* (November 4, 1902), 6.

. . / / . .

A wholesome and virile force in American letters

CAPTAIN CRAIG, A BOOK OF POEMS

Lovers of good poetry will be glad to hear of the publication by Houghton, Mifflin & Co., Boston, of a book of poems by Edwin Arlington Robinson. In common with any work of true worth and serious purpose, it makes demands on the reader. But for the most part the author has assisted us by the clearness and elaboration of his thought. He has a message and there is no groping in the light. It is not a book to be picked up, read hurriedly and tossed aside. It deserves better treatment. It is strong, direct and in the subtlest of its parts convincing. There are some masterly passages which dominate us for the time being and an insistent quality in the style which compels interest. The book takes its name from the first poem, which is concerned with the character and utterances of Captain Craig, a beggar in rags whom everyone slights. Here is the way we are introduced to the Captain: —

> I doubt if ten men in all Tilbury Town
> Had ever shaken hands with Captain Craig,
> Or called him by his name, or looked at him
> So curiously, or so concernedly,
> As they had looked at ashes; but a few —
> Say five or six of us — had found somehow
> The spark in him, and we had fanned it there,
> Choked under, like a jest in Holy Writ,
> By Tilbury prudence.

This is the beginning of a poem whose narrative force carries us along through all the Captain's moods, his whimsical jokes, his keen analysis of character and the expression of his faith.[1] There was a false note in the Tilbury tune and people did not catch the meaning of a faith made up of sincerity and a struggle for the truth. He has succeeded in revealing all the vital impulses of this character not because he has studied character abstractly but by knowing the man or rather

>   — as if the child in him
> Had laughed and let him see; and then I knew
> Some prowling superfluity of child
> In me had found the child in Captain Craig [p. 13]

The author has explained, in his poem, the meaning of a life which in its outward aspect was all failure, and he has reconstructed it for us on the higher plane of the man's aims and his endeavors. He has created for us a real person of force and deep spiritual insight. We shall not attempt to give an outline of the poem, but the following extract will, at least, reproduce its spirit: —

>   It is the flesh
> That ails us, for the spirit knows no qualm,
> No failure, no down-falling: so climb high,
> And having set your steps regard not much
> The downward laughter clinging at your feet,
> Nor overmuch the warning; only know,
> As well as you know dawn from lantern-light,
> That far above you, for you, and within you,
> There burns and shines and lives, unwavering
> And always yours, the truth. Take on yourself
> But your sincerity, and you take on
> Good promise for all climbing: fly for truth,
> And hell shall have no storm to crush your flight,
> No laughter to vex down your loyalty. [p. 58]

"Isaac and Archibald," "The Book of Annandale," "Sainte-Nitouche," and some shorter poems make up the remainder of the book. In all of them we find the same mature thought accompanied by the most scrupulous regard for the structure and finish of the verse.

This book fulfils the promise of an earlier volume,[2] and it will show to those who read it the presence of a wholesome and virile force in American letters. Against a background of the great mass of contemporary verse these poems stand out with a distinctness and finish all their own.

From "The World of Books," Lewiston *Journal Illustrated Magazine Section* (November 22-27, 1902), 5.

1 Compare the diametric reaction of the New York *Tribune* (above) to these opening lines of "Captain Craig."

2 The Lewiston (Me.) *Journal* reprinted Joseph E. Chamberlin's review of *The Torrent and The Night Before* and ran a review of its own on *The Children of the Night* (see both in this volume), yet here appears ignorant of one of Robinson's first two books.

. . / / . .

Rough, crude, altogether prosaic blank verse

CAPTAIN CRAIG

Frank Dempster Sherman

Blank verse is the supreme test of a poet's powers. Mr. Edward [*sic*] Arlington Robinson in *Captain Craig and Other Poems*[1] manages to tell three or four very interesting stories, and in their telling he reveals a positive talent for narrative verse; but one cannot forgive him the rough, crude, and altogether prosaic character of the blank verse in which they are written. Some of his rhymed poems contain lines and passages of striking excellence, but others are marred by obscurities that baffle the most patient reader. They are more ambitious than those in the author's first book, *The Children of the Night*, but they might be improved by the file.[2] Poet though he be, Mr. Robinson is not great enough to disregard Gautier's injunction:

> Leave to the tyro's hand
> The limp and shapeless style;
> See that thy form demand
> The labor and the file.[3]

From "Recent Poetry," *Book Buyer*, XXV (December 1902), 429.

Frank Dempster Sherman (1860-1916), professor of architecture and graphics at Columbia University, published several volumes of genteel, manneristic verses — precisely the kind Robinson was getting away from — and collaborated with John Kendrick Bangs and Clinton Scollard on other books.

The *Book Buyer* was the house organ of Charles Scribner's Sons but it was also more than that. Subtitled "A Summary of American and Foreign Literature," it supplied reliable information about books published by other firms. It reviewed *Captain Craig*, despite Scribner's having rejected it for publication, and also Robinson's next two books, which Scribner's did publish. Robinson wrote to Harry Smith, April 14, 1895: "I like the *Book Buyer* for what it is, but it seems to me that one might naturally look for a little more serious criticism of Ibsen than that of *Little Eyolf* in the spring number.... The criticism of *Vistas*, on the other hand, was peculiarly fair and generous, — coming from the same pen, or apparently so." (Sutcliffe, pp. 217-218.)

1 For so short a review, there is a prodigality of error. Sherman not only misnames Robinson but also the title of the volume. He is wrong too about Robinson's first book. The extenuating circumstance: this is one of *thirty-nine* reviews under Sherman's byline in this issue.

2 Robinson commented frequently on his painful process of revision upon revision and told several droll anecdotes about this overweening meticulousness. One of these, remembered by Esther Bates: to a lady novelist bragging about writing never less than five thousand words per day, Robinson said dryly, "This morning I deleted the hyphen from 'hell-hound' and made it one word; this afternoon I redivided it and restored the hyphen." (Chard Powers Smith, *Where the Light Falls: A Portrait of Edwin Arlington Robinson* [New York, 1965], p. 46.) Of his own daily output: "My smallest was when I once spent a month on a couple of lines .... my idea is to put the first draft down as fast as I can, and then rewrite as slow as I can." (Rollo Walter Brown, *Next Door to a Poet* [New York, 1937], pp. 74-75.)

To Professor Lewis N. Chase: "I thought nothing when I was writing my first book of working for a week over a single line." (Torrence, p. 103.) And to Craven Langstroth Betts: "My ideal method of writing books of verse is to spend a year in getting together the first draft; let it soak six months; work on it another six months; soak it again — ditto; and then fix it up. This would mean one book every three years, which God knows is often enough." (Emery Neff, *Edwin Arlington Robinson* [New York, 1948], p. 97.)

His general philosophy on the subject he unveiled to Herbert S. Gorman: "Indeed, I am a terrible worker — always hammering away.... Labor in poetry consists for the most part in making the non-spontaneous lines read as if they had written themselves. This is all right as far as it goes, but the vital part of a poem is pretty likely to come of its own accord. I doubt if any poem worth reading was ever the result of sheer skill and labor." ("Edwin Arlington Robinson, and a Talk With Him," New York *Sun* [January 4, 1920], 7.)

See also, in this volume: note 12, "Genesis of a Poet"; note 9, introduction to "The Torrent and The Night Before"; note 8, *Sewanee Review*, April 1897; notes 4, 5, *Book Buyer*, November 1910.

3 Quoted with two variations in spelling (tiro's, labour) from Austin Dobson's "Ars Victrix (Imitated from Théophile Gautier)" in *Old-World Idylls and Other Verses* (London, 1889), p. 206. Also anthologized by Thomas B. Mosher in *Old World Lyrics* (Portland, Maine, 1893), p. lvii.

.. / / ..

A mistake rather than a failure

CAPTAIN CRAIG

Bliss Carman

I may as well confess that I feel like boasting at having read every line of "Captain Craig." I further confess that when I was half way through I was sorely tempted to lay it down,[1] and that then I was impelled to go on to the end, partly by the tattered voice of a reviewer's conscience, found somewhere in the gloomy lofts of memory, and partly (another confession) with expectation of self-laudatory remarks when I should accomplish my task. Now, I regret to say that I don't feel altogether like commending myself for anything but honesty. "Captain Craig" is worse than Browning — with all that statement implies. To read it through at a sitting is like a long swim under water — quite as much a feat as a pleasure.

"Captain Craig" is really a psychologic novelette in blank verse. You would say off-hand that such a thing is impossible. Indeed, I almost find myself beginning to argue against it, as being something far better fitted for prose treatment than for poetry. I would like to say that poetry cannot do such things because it is not exact and analytical enough. Poetry demands a plain story, if it be a ballad that is in building, and then proceeds to enhance its value with lovely and impassioned words. Or if the tale is really psychological and complex, then poetry resorts to the drama and translates the psychology into action before portraying it. But in either case poetry does not keep close to the original fact. It takes the original fact for granted as already in the reader's mind, and uses that as a text for discourse. An analytical novel is always something of a scientific achievement as well as an artistic one, and poetic expression can only be a hindrance to scientific exposition.

I feel, therefore, that "Captain Craig" is a mistake rather than a failure; and it is only saved from being the most dreary of failures by the very marked power of its author. Mr. Robinson made himself known by his first book of poems, *The Children of the Night*, two or three years ago,[2] and his present venture shows boldness of ambition and seriousness of aim. It shows more than that, too; for unless it has great cleverness, the sort of cleverness that Browning has in his monologues, it would be impossible. But, as I say, the subject is against him, and Mr. Robinson, I feel, will come to better things when he changes his purpose a little and sets himself other tasks. His arrow has gone very wide of the mark, not at all because he is a poor shot, but because his vision for the time being is not clear. At least, that is one reader's opinion; and it is advanced with a great deal of respect for the writer's sincerity and genuine force.[3] It is only that I found myself being bored by "Captain Craig"; but if others can enjoy it, why, then, I must admit it is altogether as admirable as it certainly is capable. And here is a further final confession that I find to make; it was the verse that bored and impeded me, while the story itself and the psychology lured me on. This fact makes me believe I am right in saying the book is a misdirected effort, for all its power.

From "Poetry of the Month," *Reader*, I (December 1902), 193-194.

Bliss Carman (1861-1929), Canadian poet laureate, collaborated with Richard Hovey on *Songs From Vagabondia* (1894) and two sequels of singable romantic verse, also wrote a score of books on his own. He edited the *Chap-Book* and began writing the "Poetry of the Month" department from the first issue of the *Reader* in November 1902.

As a prelude to his review of the next of three books, Carman made this remark by way of contrast: "If 'Captain Craig' is somewhat forbidding even at the outset, with its unmistakable prose accent [here he quotes the first five lines of the poem], Mr. [Edward Sandford] Martin's lengthy narrative, 'Eben Pynchot's Repentance,' is most engaging in manner."

1   On the other hand, Robinson to Harry Smith, November 22, 1900: "I heard once that Carman had recommended the old gentleman for publication." (Sutcliffe, p. 307.) And to Edith Brower, December 16, 1900: "I am told that Mr. Bliss Carman took a great fancy to him and desired that he should be published." (Cary, p. 132.) Around this time Robinson's script was languishing, unread, in the Boston brothel.

2   Carman stumbled three times in this half of the sentence: 1) *The Children of the Night* is Robinson's second book; 2) Carman omitted the initial *The* from the title; 3) it was published five years previously, 1897.

3   Not enough respect, however, to include a single poem by Robinson in his ten-volume anthology, *The World's Best Poetry* (Philadelphia, 1904). Carman's opinion improved visibly in time. His edition of *The Oxford Book of American Verse* (New York, 1927) contains "Two Men," "John Evereldown," "Miniver Cheevy," and "Flammonde."

.. / / ..

The most varied merit and demerit

UPS AND DOWNS OF A VERSIFICATION

There is no more promise of distinction in the older sense of being unlike the majority than can be found in the work of Edwin Arlington Robinson. His third book of verse bears the title of its major content, "Captain Craig," and this, unlike almost all the verse of the day not in dramatic form, is about two thousand heroic lines in length.[1] It is a poem of the most varied merit and demerit. Passages can be selected in many places which are poetry only because there are approximately ten syllables in each line, and because these lines do not go out to the edge of the page. Then there are little bits of description included, like this:

> " 'The toiling ocean thunders of unrest
> And aching desolation; the still sea
> Paints but an outward calm that mocks itself
> To the final and irrefragable sleep
> That owns no shifting fury; and the shoals
> Of ages are but records of regret
> Where Time, the sun's arch-phantom, writes on sand
> The prelude of his ancient nothingness.' "   [p. 60]

Taken as a whole, "Captain Craig" is a setting forth of a plain and good-natured philosophy,[2] placed in the mouth of an old man who had seen all that the world has to show and in old age and decrepitude is glad to exchange his impressions of life with a party of young men for a mere subsistence. There are flashes of characteristic humor throughout the poem, and all of it deserves reading. Where Americans will find themselves more at home, however, will be in the brief songs that close the book after two or three longer titles. The opening stanza, for example, of a "Twilight Song" has an irresistible lilt, curiously out of accord with any notion the singer may have of resting after the day's march:

> Through the shine, through the rain
> We have shared the day's load;
> To the old march again

> We have tramped the long road;
> We have laughed, we have cried,
> And we've tossed the King's crown;
> We have fought, we have died,
> And we've trod the day down.
> So it's lift the old song
> Ere the night flies again,
> Where the road leads along
> Through the shine, through the rain.

For those who are seeking characteristic expression Mr. Robinson's "The Growth of 'Lorraine' "[3] may be commended.

From "Most Recent Verse by American Singers," Chicago *Evening Post* (December 6, 1902), 16.

---

[1] The 1902 version of "Captain Craig" has 2026 lines.

[2] Robinson to Charles Eliot Norton, March 29, 1903: "If I was 'interpreting' anything in Captain Craig it was America, I should say, rather than life. I do not mean to leave a final impression of anything more than hope, more or less obfuscated may be, but still good-natured and real." (*Edwin Arlington Robinson: A Collection of His Works From the Library of Bacon Collamore* [Hartford, 1936], pp. 9-10.)

[3] On July 5, 1900 Robinson referred ironically to this sonnet-pair as "two comical sonnets." He too seems to have had a high opinion of the piece when he wrote Miss Brower later: "You may be right about 'Lorraine' but I hardly think I shall throw her away." (Cary, pp. 122, 132.)

. . / / . .

Any living poet with greater power?

CAPTAIN CRAIG

> I doubt if ten men in all Tilbury Town
> Had ever shaken hands with Captain Craig,
> Or called him by his name

Thus, abruptly, with a curious conversational note, begins one of the most remarkable poems published in recent years. From the first line, it possesses the reader; the thoughtful reader, *bien entendu*, not he who wishes to run as he reads. The thoughtful reader not only shakes hands with Captain Craig, but goes again, and yet again, to see him; becomes fascinated by him, seeks the friendship of the wonderful old man, poet, vagrant, philosopher, Socrates drifted back to earth to dream and reason through another pilgrimage. The story tells how this man, frail, old, and poor, is befriended by a little knot of young men, who club together to make his closing days warm and comfortable. The Captain is grateful, in his own way; and sitting on his one chair, "like a king," harangues his benefactors, "for longer time," says the story-teller, "than I dare chronicle." Most of the young men depart, "like brokers out of Arcady"[1]; but one, the story-teller, remains, and gains the friendship and affection of the old man. To him the Captain discourses at large; he listens, and we listen, in amazement and delight.

The Captain's talk, on the various occasions of meeting his friend, and the letters which form an interlude in it, are all his own; perhaps we ought to say Mr. Robinson's own, but we forget Mr. Robinson, as he means us to do; Captain Craig lives and speaks, and it is to him we listen. He gives us a philosophy of life, lofty yet broad, kindly yet austere and tinged throughout with a quaint and delightful humor.

> "First, would I have you know, for every gift
> Or sacrifice, there are — or there may be —
> Two kinds of gratitude: the sudden kind
> We feel for what we take, the slower kind
> We feel for what we give. Once we have learned
> As much as this, we know the truth has been
> Told over to the world a thousand times; —
> But we have had no ears to listen yet
> For more than fragments of it: we have heard
> A murmur now and then, an echo here
> And there, and we have made great music of it;
> And we have made innumerable books
> To please the Unknown God. Time throws away
> Dead thousands of them, but the God that knows
> No death denies not one: the books all count,
> The songs all count; and yet God's music has
> No modes, his language has no adjectives." [p. 5]

The style is often curiously rugged, often exasperatingly obscure; there are passages which one reads over and over, in a kind of despair, till at length the meaning flashes out like his own "shaft of dungeon-light"[2]; and this is all wrong, of course. We cry out, and we do well to cry out, for there is no reason why poets should not speak plainly, like other people, and this poet must look to it, lest "In Darkest James"[3] be followed by "In Cloudiest Robinson."

But clear or cloudy, rugged or smooth, the Captain, like the Ancient Mariner, holds us with his glittering eye, and we cannot choose but hear.

The third part, which tells of the closing days of the old man's life, is full of exquisite pathos, always gilded with the humor that is with him to the last. In what he calls his "last will and testament," he bids his young friends, who now are all gathered round him,

> "climb high,
> And having set your steps regard not much
> The downward laughter clinging to your feet,
> Nor overmuch the warning; only know,
> As well as you know dawn from lantern-light,
> That far above you, for you, and within you,
> There burns and shines and lives, unwavering
> And always yours, the truth. Take on yourself
> But your sincerity, and you take on
> Good promise for all climbing: fly for truth,
> And hell shall have no storm to crush your flight,
> No laughter to vex down your loyalty." [p. 58]

So on, and on; through strange figures, stranger visions. "A jocund instrument," [p. 53] the Captain calls this document; surely it is a marvelous one. And when he has done reading, they see "the tremor of an old heart's weariness" on his mouth.

> He gazed at each of us,
> But spoke no further word that afternoon. [p. 70]

At the end he falls into a gentle delirium, — if it be delirium — and it is Socrates himself who speaks.

> "Kind friends," he said, "friends I have known so long,
> Though I have jested with you in time past,
> Though I have stung your pride with epithets
> Not all forbearing, — still, when I am gone,
> Say Socrates wrought always for the best
> And for the wisest end . . . Give me the cup!
> The truth is yours, God's universe is yours . . .
> Good-by . . . good citizens . . . give me the cup" . . . [p. 80]

So he goes, with a smile, and the flash of a last quaint word; and we feel that we have lost — and gained — a friend, like no other friend.

One reads the poem through the first time because the narrative compels; one goes back and reads it again, and on the second reading one is struck by countless passages of such beauty that they sing themselves into the memory.

> Then shall at last come ringing through the sun,
> Through time, through flesh, God's music of the soul.
> For wisdom is that music, and all joy
> That wisdom: — [p. 9]

* * *

> "The world that has been old is young again,
> The touch that faltered clings; and this is May. [p. 19]

* * *

> for 'tis the child,
> O friend, that with his laugh redeems the man.
> Time steals the infant, but the child he leaves; [p. 20]

* * *

> on a day like this,
> When the chaff-parts of a man's adversities
> Are blown by quick spring breezes out of him —
> When even a flicker of wind that wakes no more
> Than a tuft of grass, or a few young yellow leaves,
> Comes like the falling of a prophet's breath
> On altar-flames rekindled of crushed embers, — [pp. 20-21]

* * *

> And the child —
> The child that is the saviour of all ages,
> The prophet and the poet, the crown-bearer,
> Must yet with Love's unhonored fortitude,
> Survive to cherish and attain for us
> The candor and the generosity,
> By leave of which we smile if we bring back

> Some first ideal flash that wakened us
> When wisdom like a shaft of dungeon-light
> Came searching down to find us. [p. 30]

We have not space to do justice to the shorter poems in the volume, many of which are as notable in their way as the title-poem. "Isaac and Archibald" is an exquisite picture of autumn, in nature and man; reading it, we see "the straw-shine of October" of which we read in "Captain Craig," [p. 55] and almost taste the cider that the old men drink. In the superb swing of "The Klondike," and the haunting melody of the "Twilight Song," we have glimpses of the lyric power which Mr. Robinson possesses in full measure, but of which for some reason he is singularly chary. Readers of his previous volume, *The Children of the Night*, will recall the remarkable poem called "The Wilderness" as another example of the lyric gift, and it is to be hoped that his future work will show more of it. In "Aunt Imogen" we have a study, tenderly and yet cruelly keen, of a lonely woman; while in "Sainte-Nitouche" and the still more wonderful poem called "The Woman and the Wife," Mr. Robinson touches perhaps his highest mark. In "Sainte-Nitouche," after telling of the death of Vanderberg, he says:

> I saw the dim look change itself
>   To one that never will be dim;
> I saw the dead flesh to the grave,
>   But that was not the last of him.
>
> For what was his to live lives yet:
>   Truth, quarter truth, death cannot reach;
> Nor is it always what we know
>   That we are fittest here to teach.
>
> The fight goes on when fields are still,
>   The triumph clings when arms are down;
> The jewels of all coronets
>   Are pebbles of the unseen crown;
>
> The specious weight of loud reproof
>   Sinks where a still conviction floats;
> And on God's ocean after storm
>   Time's wreckage is half pilot-boats; [p. 157]

After reading such words as these, we are tempted to ask: "Is there any other living poet who speaks with greater power and authority than this?"

From Gardiner *Daily Reporter-Journal* (December 6, 1902), [3].

With maddening consistency, Robinson's home town newspaper continues to call him Edward in the identification of the book at the head of this review.

1 All three phrases are on p. 4.

2 "Captain Craig," p. 30.

3 Reference is to the complexities and obscurities in the style of novelist Henry James.

. . / / . .

Has not yet mastered his own powers

CAPTAIN CRAIG
Thomas Wentworth Higginson

In *Captain Craig: A Book of Poems*, by Edwin Arlington Robinson (Houghton, Mifflin & Co.), we have the latest work of one of the most promising of our younger poets — one who, like so many persons gifted in the same way, has not yet mastered his own powers and has to follow his muse for a time, not direct it. His very singleness of mind sometimes defeats itself and leaves his meaning unconveyed. Obscure he may be and has a right to be, for his thoughts are always worth consideration, but it must be frankly owned that he sometimes draws near the unintelligible. He brings marvellous color and music into his verse when at his highest point[1]; yet, like Browning, he loses himself and his readers in regions of abstract thought. But he has a nature innately candid, has no desire to pose, and has been perhaps mainly embarrassed by working too much alone. It may be well for him that his surface has not suavity enough. If he said things with more uniform melody, he might be more easily flattered and perverted. A young poet needs some inaccessible domain of even rudeness to which he may retreat to assert himself. This book is likely to be passed unnoticed by all indolent readers, and with impatience by those a little more careful; but those more careful still will revert to it again and again, and wish health, fortune, and encouragement and still farther development to one who could write it. There is not a trivial or meaningless thing in it; and when there is obscurity, it is often like that of Emily Dickinson[2] when she piques your curiosity through half a dozen readings and suddenly makes all clear. Such a song ends at last, as this volume does, with a note of triumph (p. 169): [the first and last stanzas of "Twilight Song" follow.]

From "Recent Poetry," *Nation*, LXXV (December 11, 1902), 465.

This notice was reprinted verbatim in "Recent Poetry," New York *Evening Post*, December 13, 1902, p. 20.

1 When Robinson was putting together the book of poems which was to follow *Captain Craig* (all of those included in that volume excepting the title poem), he described it thus to Edith Brower: "I have not used the hydraulic press quite so much [as in *The Children of the Night*] and I have a notion that I have acquired something that has a faint suggestion of color. I don't make much of this, though, for I know that I am by nature a black and white man. I am going to be musical one day but I don't think I shall ever be crimson or purple. Still, I have some symptoms even of that now and then." (Cary, p. 140.)

2 Robinson to H. Bacon Collamore, July 12, 1930: "As for Emily Dickinson, I'm sorry to say that my acquaintance with her work is rather limited, and that I have to take her mostly on trust. Sometime or other I'll give her poems a real reading. Until then I can't say much." (Colby College Library.)

. . / / . .

New landmark in the world of books

SOME NOTABLE VERSE

The success of Mr. Edward [*sic*] Arlington Robinson's *The Children of the Night* has prepared his readers, in a measure, for the strength and originality of *Captain Craig*, his new volume of poems. Mr. Robinson, with the utmost daring, has taken his hero from squalid and, one would say, hopeless surroundings, and yet given us a picture of a soul and mind of absolute majesty, a new Socrates in a setting of wit and pathos.

With the charm of Mr. Robinson's character drawing is mingled a loftiness of tone that gives us reason to call him, as Emerson was once called, "the friend and helper of those who live in the spirit." For sheer force of intellect applied not in smoothing of verse or polishing of phrase, but in philosophy and creative thought, this volume stands alone among recent poetry.

Yet Mr. Robinson has not failed in the beauty that is poetry's reason of being, as we may see in such lines as:

> "The world that has been old is young again,
> The touch that faltered clings; and this is May."

or in the splendid spirit of

> "be myself
> Primevally alive, and have the sun
> Shine into me;"

or in the highest spirit of the book:

> "the rhythm of God
> That beats unheard through songs of shattered men
> Who dream but cannot sound it."

The wit and irony of the old Captain are as remarkable in their way, but they must be tasted in their entirety. The other poems are worthy of the first, the fascinating idyl of "Isaac and Archibald," like Tennyson trying his hand upon New England, and in all of the verses is the mixture of realism and poetic insight that seems to characterize Mr. Robinson. He is a new landmark in the world of books, and we believe the time will come some day, in his own words: "To shrine him when the new-born men come singing."[1]

From "New Books," Boston *Journal* (December 13, 1902), 5.

---

1 The four quotations in this review are all from "Captain Craig," respectively, pages 19, 20, 46, 33.

A philosophy of life not clearly formulated

CAPTAIN CRAIG
William Morton Payne

A slender volume of verse was put forth several years ago by Mr. Edwin Arlington Robinson,[1] and the few into whose hands it came, if they had any skill in literary discernment, felt that the voice that addressed them was at least distinctively individual, and took pleasure in an utterance that seemed to scorn rhetorical trickery, and came arrayed in the strength of sincerity and truth. The numbers were bare almost to harshness, and they made little appeal to the fancy or the imaginative sense, but they had qualities of earnestness and vitality that arrested the attention and impressed the memory. Now, after a long period of silence, Mr. Robinson has given us *Captain Craig: A Book of Poems*, and the impression made by the earlier collection is intensified. He has a philosophy of life, not clearly formulated in all respects, but traceable in its main outlines, and clearly held with the deepest conviction. It is a philosophy for which we should say that Walt Whitman was in large measure responsible, and in which Browning would seem also to have had a hand supplying the dramatic quality and the element of sardonic humor of which the *Leaves of Grass* is quite guiltless. It is the philosophy of the free spirit that has given no hostages to conventional life, and that seeks to divest from their adventitious trappings the fundamental verities of existence. If we can do this, and look the world squarely in the face, and realize that the subjective factor must play its part in the game, we shall find that it is a good world after all. But if we assume a supine or a merely receptive attitude, and trust to luck, we shall be the failures that we deserve to be.

> "There is no luck,
> No fate, no fortune for us, but the old
> Unswerving and inviolable price
> Gets paid: God sells himself eternally,
> But never gives a crust." [p. 13]

The long narrative poem, "Captain Craig," serves as the chief vehicle of Mr. Robinson's theory of life. Captain Craig is to outward seeming a disreputable enough person, but we, who make his acquaintance through the good offices of the poet, are permitted to know him in his true character, which may be roughly described as combining some of the traits of Socrates, Aristophanes, and Carlyle. In other words, he displays shrewdness in getting at the heart of life's problems, irony in his treatment of them, and zeal in his warfare upon their adjuncts of insincerity or hypocrisy. The substance of the poem's teaching may be found in two representative extracts.

> "Courage is not enough to make men glad
> For laughter when that laughter is itself
> The tribute of recriminating groans;
> Nor are the shapes of obsolescent creeds
> Much longer to flit near enough to make

> Men glad for living in a world like this;
> But wisdom, courage, knowledge, and the faith
> Which has the soul and is the soul of reason —
> These are the world's achievers. And the child —
> The child that is the saviour of all ages,
> The prophet and the poet, the crown-bearer,
> Must yet with Love's unhonored fortitude,
> Survive to cherish and attain for us
> The candor and the generosity,
> By leave of which we smile if we bring back
> Some first ideal flash that wakened us
> When wisdom like a shaft of dungeon-light
> Came searching down to find us." [pp. 29-30]

This is fine, and even finer is the following passage from Captain Craig's last will and testament, in which document he bequeaths "God's universe" to his friends:

> "Courage, my boys, — courage, is what you need:
> Courage that is not all flesh-recklessness,
> But earnest of the world and of the soul —
> First of the soul; for a man may be as brave
> As Ajax in the fury of his arms,
> And in the midmost warfare of his thought
> Be frail as Paris ... For the love, therefore,
> That bothered us when we stood back that day
> From Delium — the love that holds us now
> More than it held us at Amphipolis —
> Forget you not that he who in his work
> Would mount from these low roads of measured shame
> To tread the leagueless highway must fling first
> And fling forevermore beyond his reach
> The shackles of a slave who doubts the sun.
> There is no servitude so fraudulent
> As of a sun-shut mind; for 'tis the mind
> That makes you craven or invincible,
> Diseased or puissant. The mind will pay
> Ten thousand fold and be the richer then
> To grant new service; but the world pays hard
> And accurately sickens till in years
> The dole has eked its end and there is left
> What all of you are noting on all days
> In these Athenian streets, where squandered men
> Drag ruins of half-warriors to the grave —
> Or to Hippocrates." [pp. 79-80]

We have no space in which to discuss the remaining poems in Mr. Robinson's volume. They are often impressive in their direct appeal to the fundamental emotions, but none of them equals the titular poem in interest.

From "Recent Poetry," *Dial*, XXXIV (January 1, 1903), 18-19.

---

1 Payne's seeming ignorance that Robinson had published two books before *Captain Craig* is especially irking in view of the fact that he reviewed both *The Torrent and The Night Before* and *The Children of the Night* in the *Dial* shortly after each was

published. Perhaps he, like a number of others, considered them essentially identical in content, another inexcusable oversight.

. . / / . .

Set him off from the crowd

CAPTAIN CRAIG

Among some thirty or forty books of verse that poets and printing presses have produced for what is delicately referred to as "the fall trade," that of Edwin Arlington Robinson most strongly impresses us. It is not that this little volume, *Captain Craig: A Book of Poems* (Houghton, Mifflin & Co., Boston: price, $1.00), contains so much that is fine and bold, as it is that it inevitably impels to a faith in its author's ability to do something finer, something bolder. He has absolute originality. He gives to the most commonplace a flavor of rare, quaint humor, mingled with a constant perception of the pathos of things. Of modern poets, in methods he most nearly approaches Browning; yet there is no hint of imitation. He differs from the great mass of our minor poets in that his verse is dramatic in tendency, rather than lyric. These things set him off from the crowd. True, he is obscure,[1] but the conviction that Mr. Robinson's kernels of thought are worth earnest endeavor to find, is strong. Unfortunately for quotation, but in no other sense, the poems in this book are mostly long. "Captain Craig" runs to eighty pages, and "Isaac and Archibald" to over twenty.[2] Therefore we are obliged to give here a sonnet which has only a hint of the author's quality: ["Erasmus" follows.]

From "Some Recent Books of Verse," *Argonaut*, LII (January 5, 1903), 6.

1 See the section *Obscurity* in the chapter "Preliminary Vistas" in this volume.

2 In this edition "Captain Craig" is in fact 84 pages long; "Isaac and Archibald" three lines over 17.

. . / / . .

Whatever else, it is not commonplace

CAPTAIN CRAIG

Captain Craig, A Book of Poems by Edward [*sic*] Arlington Robinson, is a volume which has provoked a good deal of comment, on the whole favorable to the strength and originality, but not free from impatience with its very obvious faults, those of ruggedness which is not warranted by its effectiveness, obscurity and an effect of strain and unnaturalness; but whatever else it may be it is not commonplace and is the work of undeniable power. Captain Craig is a philosopher with whom life has gone hardly but not left him unconsoled, since he has found in it material for such utterances as are listened to by the group of friends which Mr. Robinson places about his bedside — utterances of speculation, learning, bitter satire and humanity. Among other poems in the book is one, "Isaac and Archibald," which has a quaint charm of reality and remembrance, a study of two old men and a summer afternoon. Mr. Bliss Carman in *The Reader* says of the book that it "is worse than Browning — with all that that statement implies. To read it through at a sitting is like a long swim under water — quite as much a feat as a pleasure," and that it "is a mistake rather than a failure and it is only saved from being the most dreary of failures by the very marked power of its author."

Unidentified newspaper, presumably February 13, 1903.

On the back of this detached newspaper clipping is a listing of what looks like Boston stocks, with the simple date February 13. The citation of Carman's recent review would seem to fix the year.

. . / / . .

Noble in conception, wearisome in humor

CAPTAIN CRAIG

The initial and most ambitious poem in this book of verse gives its name to the volume and shows an unusual gift in the management of blank verse,[1] which at times has much of the cadence of Tennyson's *Princess*. It combines in a strange way much that is high and noble in conception and expression, with a curious form of shrewd, if at times wearisome, humor.[2] In "Isaac and Archibald" there is a tender and quaint characterization of two old men, and at the close of the poem is this unique dream, which may serve as a taste of the peculiar humor of the book:

> And that night
> There came to me a dream — a shining one,
> With two old angels in it. They had wings,
> And they were sitting where a silver light
> Suffused them, face to face. The wings of one
> Began to palpitate as I approached,
> But I was yet unseen when a dry voice
> Cried thinly, with unpatronizing triumph,
> "I've got you, Isaac; high, low, jack, and the game."

"The Return of Morgan and Fingal" is a weird and effective description in ballad form of how three boon companions at night left their pipes, music, and punch, at the call of a half-crazed woman to ferry a dead girl home. Under the roar of the north wind and through "the flash of the midnight foam" they carried the dead body. Returning through the dark, bespattered with the sea, they once more sat down in the bright warmth of the cozy room:

> And there were the pipes, and there was the punch,
>   More shrewd than Satan's tears:
> Fingal had fashioned it, all by himself,
>   With a craft that comes of years.

> And there we were together again —
> Together again, we three:
> Morgan, Fingal, fiddle, and all,
> They were there for the night with me.

From "Songs of the Day," Chicago *Tribune* (February 14, 1903), 14.

---

1 In his reminiscent "The First Seven Years," Robinson said: "It was about my seventeenth year when I became violently excited over the structure and music of English blank verse, and in order to find out a little more about it I made — of all things possible — a metrical translation of Cicero's first oration against Catiline, which we were reading in school." (*Colophon*, Part IV [1930], n.p.)

Miss Bates reports that a volume of Milton was regularly on Robinson's studio table at the MacDowell Colony. "He said he liked to read Milton's blank verse when he was writing it himself." (Bates, p. 30.)

"If people should stop buying blank verse, there would be nothing left for me but that poorhouse, which you told me had burned down," he joked with Mrs. Richards in 1932. (Torrence, p. 167.)

2 See the section *Humor* in the chapter "Preliminary Vistas" of this volume.

. . / / . .

This colloquialism and commonplace, this Umgangssprache

A NEW POETRY

Take up a book of French verse, and, work of a novice tho it may be, you will have no difficulty in finding in it evidence at least to a first-hand impression of life, however little that impression may be worth in itself, and to a well set conception of poetry. Whatever debt it may owe its predecessors, it will show that its author has looked at life and thought about art for himself; it will strike a distinctly personal note and in so far an original one. You take up a new volume of English or American verse, on the other hand, and nine times out of ten you will find the contrary to be true. The book will be mainly derivative and vaguely reminiscent like all second-hand inspiration, which derives not immediately from life but from previous interpretations — a chamber of echoes, whose hollowness, in increasing the resonance, only confuses the listener the more. It will likely have no subject and no art of its own — in short, in most cases it will stand for nothing but what already has a place in letters and a following among the public.

But what is true, alas! of the majority is not true of Mr. Robinson's *Captain Craig,* and the contrast serves to make his book seem even more remarkable, if anything, than it actually is. He has a temperament, an outlook, a poetic nature which are his own, not because he is outside of all influence, but because he has assimilated them directly from the medium in which he lives, as the plant draws its nutriment immediately from its own inorganic surroundings. In this way he has produced an extraordinary piece — one, to use the consecrated expression, full of interest and instruction. Let us try to explain in a general way what are the characters of his work; for we think that, exaggerated as they will seem at present, they will be found symptomatic of certain tendencies of modern verse, the sum of which is making for what may be called the secularization of poetry.

In his title-piece, "Captain Craig," a poem of something over two thousand lines of blank verse, one is struck by three things. In the first place, neither the subject, nor what goes along with the subject, the sentiment, the spirit of the piece is poetic at all in any usual sense. The poem is not a story — it is too shapeless for that; it is rather a characterization of a bit of bombastical old social wreckage or *débris*, a sort of cross between Hamlet[1] and Captain Costigan,[2] further provided, not unlike Falstaff, with a glimpse of cosmic humor, tho, for all that, he takes himself very seriously indeed, and with a kind of transcendental optimism, the very fustian of a philosophy, rarely exploited by a dithyrambic eloquence very much in vogue among gentlemen of his kidney. Saved from the streets by some few good fellows, not too old to appreciate the charms of the higher paradox, he preaches to them his nebulous faiths a while, and finally makes an edifying Socratic end with equal rhetorical gusto and is buried to the music of a brass band, trombones, in accordance with his last words, not omitted:

> And all along the road the Tilbury Band
> Blared indiscreetly the Dead March in Saul. [p. 84]

Whether he is humbug or misfortune, failure or supersensible success you cannot tell for the life of you — there, indeed, is the man's charm; nor does it make any particular difference any way. It is enough to recognize his nature as a social problem and the streak of his philosophy. His mind is an emblem of his time, half-formed, undisciplined, vaguely emotional, full of scraps of classical lore, fragments of scientific information, incomplete, kaleidoscopic — amid all which chaos goes haunting some dim conception of human consanguinity and perfectibility.

If now we turn to the medium by which all this matter is conveyed we shall find the language no less diametrically opposed than the subject to all that we usually think of as poetic. There is absolutely nothing to distinguish it from prose either in diction, imagery, or rhythm.

> I turned about
> And having waved a somewhat indistinct
> Acknowledgment, I walked along. The train
> Was late and I was early, but the gap
> Was filled and even crowded. Killigrew
> Had left his pigeonholes to say good-by,
> And he stood waiting by the ticket window
> Like one grin-cursed of Orcus. — "You have heard?"
> Said he. — "Heard what?" said I. — "He! he!" said he; [p. 15]

and so on. There is nothing to choose. While with this singularity of style is joined, not much exaggerated either, that modern formlessness of which Browning stands as a conspicuous example and which consists in assuming that the art of writing is a monologing or communing with self, while the act of reading is a sort of licensed eavesdropping upon this performance wherein the reader is welcome to anything that he can contrive to pick up.

At first sight nothing could seem more incongruous and absurd than this formlessness, than the effect of all this colloquialism and commonplace, this *Umgangssprache*, as the Germans would say, jogging along contentedly to the measures of the iambic pentameter. But after a little while you begin, as in the author's words,

> Implacable, renascent, farcical,
> Triumphant, and American. [p. 46]

to calculate the profits for most readers and writers of a poetic medium which will allow any one to say any thing in any kind of a way as in the following sonnet:

> Carmichael had a kind of joke-disease,
> And he had queer things fastened on his wall.
> There are three green china frogs that I recall
> More potently than anything, for these
> Three frogs have demonstrated, by degrees,
> What curse was on the man to make him fall:
> "They are not ordinary frogs at all,
> They are the Frogs of Aristophanes."
>
> God! how he laughed whenever he said that;
> And how we caught from one another's eyes
> The flash of what a tongue could never tell!
> We always laughed at him, no matter what
> The joke was worth. But when a man's brain dies,
> We are not always glad ... Poor Carmichael! [p. 37]

In short, you begin after a time to recognize that here is indeed a poetry suited to all the uses of modern life — a sort of prose-poetry or poetical prose, which by virtue of its amorphousness strains out no jot of the welter of everyday things, adaptable to the commonplace, not incapable perhaps of rising to the usual degrees of emotional excitement, a suitable medium in its own confusion for hasty, turbid thinking, unhampered by an ideal of beauty or literary distinction, but compatible, like the present volume, with a great deal of vigor, humor, caricature, even satire and pathos. Can the lesson be lost; shall not the many merits of the book — for it has many, as we have just tried to suggest — rather emphasize than conceal the dangers to which poetry is exposed at present? For while we certainly should not be so rash as to assert that this is likely to be the poetry of the immediate future, or of any future for that matter, still we must repeat in closing that the piece we have been trying to analyze does display, more clearly than any other we have ever read, certain tendencies of the day which are generally overlooked or treated far too lightly.

From *Independent*, LV (February 19, 1903), 446-447.

---

1 Robinson to Laura E. Richards, August 31, 1932: "*Hamlet* ... is language and

character — and something else that no one has ever found a name for." (Torrence, p. 168). He considered Hamlet "a failure" because of his loss of personal vision, the inner truth of his own nature. (Nancy Evans, "Edwin Arlington Robinson," *Bookman*, LXXV [November 1932], 678.)

2 A bibulous, down-at-the-heels rake, father of Emily, an actress with whom Pen becomes infatuated in Thackeray's *Pendennis*. In Professor Lewis Gates's course at Harvard, Robinson wrote a paper on this novel. In 1895 he wrote Harry Smith: "I have read the book four or five times and shall soon be ready to read it again. There is something in the touch of the master that cannot be mistaken or explained, and — at least I find it so — cannot always be seen in a first reading." (Sutcliffe, p. 220.) George Latham observed that "In English fiction his choices were, I should think, Jane Austen, Thackeray, and Hardy." (p. 20.) This is corroborated with more pointed emphasis by James L. Tryon two years later in *Harvard Days With Edwin Arlington Robinson* (Waterville, Maine, 1940), p. 11: "His favorite novelists were Thackeray, Jane Austen and Thomas Hardy."

. . / / . .

Three of the more influential book reviewers of this time were Frank Dempster Sherman, Bliss Carman, and Clinton Scollard, all three also highly popular poeticules. It is Robinson's misfortune that their opinions as critics were defined by their practice as versifiers, infinitely more concerned with polish than with pith — "the attractive attire" Scollard eulogizes. They helped to preserve and further refine the prim role of hermaphroditic piper that American poetry had assumed between Whitman's eruption and the first World War. For most readers and reviewers of this era Robinson was playing too rough under current ground rules, a dissonant factor amid the general euphoria. An illustration of the lengths to which this viewpoint could mislead this breed of critic immediately precedes the following review, one of eleven Scollard included in this roundup. After commending L. Frank Tooker on his melody, gayety, and true tone, Scollard ascends to this evaluation: "His the happy phrase and the illuminating word; his both the voice and the vision! Decidedly he is a poet to be reckoned with." Then he turns to the recalcitrant Robinson.

Lacks not in matter but goes slovenly clad

CAPTAIN CRAIG

Clinton Scollard

There is a certain provoking fascination in Mr. Edwin Arlington Robinson's *Captain Craig: A Book of Poems*. We can but feel that the volume might have been vastly better from an artistic standpoint had the author so willed it. While there is strength, and to spare, there is also a seemingly perverse carelessness, a frequent disregard of the niceties of form. Surely if a poet has aught to say — and Mr. Robinson has clearly proven that he lacks not in matter — he owes it to his readers, if not to himself, to dress his thought in attractive attire, and not let it go slovenly clad. Blank verse that is little more than inverted prose chopped up into lines is continually elbowing passages that are shot through with real poetic fire in this disturbing volume. To glean any real and sustained satisfaction from Mr. Robinson's poetry one must turn not to the title-piece, nor to the two or three tales similar in manner, but to a sonnet entitled "The Sage,"[1] and to the swinging lyric with which the book closes.[2]

From "Recent Books of Poetry," *Critic*, XLII (March 1903), 232.

Clinton Scollard (1860-1932), professor of English at Hamilton College, published reams of poems in the precious French forms, in the same road-gypsy romantic strain as Bliss Carman, and collaborated with Frank Dempster Sherman in other delicate exercises. He also turned out quantities of essays, travel sketches, and prose fiction. Robinson sent a copy of *The Torrent and The Night Before* to Scollard who chose not to review it but wrote back in part: "Particularly I would congratulate you upon the pieces entitled 'The World' and 'The Children of the Night' and upon your sonnets." (Sutcliffe, p. 271.)

Robinson set no great store by the *Critic*. In May 1895 he said to Harry Smith: "Every man and woman who writes for the *Critic* seems to be cursed with a flippancy that I am getting very tired of." (Sutcliffe, p. 225.)

Two pages beyond this review is featured a photograph of Robinson occupying the larger portion of the page. This is the first of his likenesses known to accompany any text about him as a poet (he apparently never acceded to the request for his picture by the Bangor *Daily Commercial* in February 1897). With ineluctable irony, the caption reads: "Mr. Edward A. Robinson." (See frontispiece of this volume.)

[1] On May 16, 1900 Robinson forewarned Miss Brower: "You may look too for a sonnet on Emerson." Upon receipt, Miss Brower floundered in ambiguity over the word "mean" in line 5, Robinson retaliating irritably by quoting Webster's dictionary at the head of his June 10 letter: "Mean — that which is intermediate between two extremes." Next day he expressed himself bewildered by her interpretation of "mean" as an adjective. "In the light of this I feel that the thing must be changed, though I am not yet reconciled to the idea. The possibility of taking 'mean' as an adjective had never occurred to me." Later he deplored the fact that he had "ever passed my stuff around for individual criticism" and more than half thought it would be the last time. "I discover too many things — and yet it paid in the sonnets on the woman." (Cary, pp. 115, 116, 117, 122.)

He was heartened by some of his friends who could not imagine any intelligent person misconstruing the word, but he stewed uncomfortably over it for several months. On September 11 he summarized his dilemma to Mason: "Your remarks on 'Emerson' set me all askew again. The line you like has been so repeatedly damned for being unintelligible that I had come to the conclusion that it (or rather 'mean') would have to come out. When I wrote it, I thought I had done something large and I was quite puffed up; but when I began to be criticized for joining a noun with an irrelevant adjective, I began to wonder what the devil was the matter. Of course I meant 'mean' as the opposite of the extreme ('madness') but you are the only one out of six or seven who see it in that light. It is true that 'mean' has two meanings (I beg your pardon) but it seems to me that the obvious gets in somewhere. I don't know whether I shall keep the line or not." (Mason, *VQR* [Winter 1937], pp. 68-69.)

Despite all the annoyance and indecision evoked by this Lilliputian controversy, the questionable word remained unaltered in *Captain Craig* (1902), all subsequent editions of that title, the *Collected Poems*, and *Sonnets 1889-1927*.

[2] "Twilight Song," pp. 169-171. For the gestation of this poem, see note 8 to John A. Macy's review in the Chicago *Evening Post*, October 25, 1902, in this volume.

. . / / . .

Within four months of publication the original stock of some 500 copies of *Captain Craig* was virtually exhausted. On March 10, 1903 Houghton Mifflin issued another 270 copies which conformed in every respect — excepting insertion of the line "SECOND EDITION" on the title page — to the first trade edition in light green cloth at the same price of $1.00. The company mounted a modest advertising campaign for this book by "Edwin A. Robinson," notably a sextodecimo four-page flyer announcing: "With the appearance of a second edition of Mr. Robinson's little volume, *Captain Craig: A Book of Poems*, only a few months after its first publication, the publishers take pleasure in presenting a few of the notices which it has received, beginning with some personal opinions."

The notices quoted therein are from the *Dial*, Boston *Evening Transcript*, the New York *Evening Post's* reprint of Higginson's review in the *Nation*, Chicago *Evening Post*, *Argonaut*, Boston *Journal*, Chicago *Tribune*, and *Independent* (the complete text of each is included in this volume). The "personal opinions" were garnered from William James, LeBaron R. Briggs (professor of English at Harvard), and Josephine Preston Peabody.

William James, whose *The Varieties of Religious Experience* Houghton Mifflin had recently published, wrote: "The author of *Captain Craig* is a genuine poet, for whom I cannot but predict an important future. One page read, I had to finish the entire book, so fascinating were the original sense of life and the verbal felicities." When solicited for a statement, he had written the editor in confidence: "The book is lent or I should refresh my memory a bit — but broad synthetic praise is best for a circular. I think that story of the 2 old men (I can't recall their names) is *fully* as good as anything of the kind in Wordsworth." (New York Public Library.)

LeBaron R. Briggs wrote: "Though the power that underlies Mr. Robinson's poems does not always express itself clearly, the reader cannot but feel its presence and its fascination. I believe that few books of contemporary verse are so imaginative or so interesting." Praise enough, but he could not resist the academic thrust toward regularity which was the staple of Clinton Scollard *et ce cercle*.

Josephine Preston Peabody wrote: "I consider Mr. Robinson distinctly the most original of our younger poets. And I find him striking for a curiously distinguished Americanism, a type of mentality — if it can be called a type — that combines certain of the finest and most significant traits of American thinking, the penetration without the superficiality of cleverness that is becoming our reproach."

To supplement this circular, Houghton Mifflin took an ad in several newspapers and periodicals, headed by the caption "A Genuine Poet" and playing up the full passage by James. Alas for Robinson, neither the extra expenditure nor the goodwill of James turned out to be materially helpful. The second printing sold lackadaisically, and it marked the last professional connection between Robinson and the house of Houghton Mifflin.

CAPTAIN CRAIG

A Book of Poems

BY

EDWIN ARLINGTON ROBINSON

SECOND EDITION.

Boston and New York
HOUGHTON, MIFFLIN & COMPANY
The Riverside Press, Cambridge
1903

Verse is not his medium

CAPTAIN CRAIG
H. W. Boynton

Probably no valid distinction between verse and poetry can be made on the score of humor in the pure sense. Poets are often most humorous when they are most serious, and it is particularly hard to be sure where the merit lies when, as so often happens in Browning, a serious vein of poetic discourse is accompanied by an obligato of ironical reservations and subtle compunctions. Even when the strains appear to be most clearly distinguished from one another, they may be so implicated as to be really inseparable. This is Mr. Robinson's method in the poem which gives the title to his recent book of verse. There is always the danger of fancying resemblances, even when one has escaped the danger of fancying imitations; but a rough notion of Mr. Robinson's method may be suggested by imagining a person with the mental ingenuity of Browning and the bare diction of Wordsworth.

> I doubt if ten men in all Tilbury Town
> Had ever shaken hands with Captain Craig. [p. 1]

So begins his narrative, and such is the quality of very much of his blank verse; plainly jog-trot, often not distinguishable from the baldest prose:

> We waited there
> Till each of us, I fancy, must have made
> The paper on the wall begin to squirm,
> And then got up to leave. [p. 77]

This baldness is varied mainly by way of extraordinary metrical exploits, and whimsical figures of speech, as in lines like these:

> As unproductive and as unconvinced
> Of the living bread and the soul's eternal drought
> As a frog on a Passover-cake in a streamless desert. [p. 34]

But everywhere the difficulty lies deeper than metre; the masters of blank verse have been those who employed it most flexibly; but always under that restraining instinct for rhythm without which poetry can hardly be written, — certainly not poetry in the form of blank verse. This instinct Mr. Robinson entirely lacks. Consequently, while his book seems to me vastly more original and interesting than most of the books of verse with which we have been dealing, I think it contains little or no poetry. One of the shortest pieces of verse is perhaps the best, "The Return of Morgan and Fingal." The restraint of the simple ballad measure appears to have had a wholesome effect upon an instinct for expression which elsewhere, though it finds a forcible and often imaginative utterance, is not poetic. There is much power, even genius, in the book, and it is extremely well worth reading on that account; but it is reasonably clear that verse is not the medium of expression through which this power, or genius, can hope to become fully articulate.

From "Books New and Old," *Atlantic Monthly*, XCI (April 1903), 566-567.

Henry Wolcott Boynton (1869-1947) contributed numerous essays and book reviews to the *Bookman, Nation, Putnam's,* and *Outlook.* He wrote biographies of Fenimore Cooper, Washington Irving, and Bret Harte, also collaborated with Thomas Wentworth Higginson on a history of American literature.

After John Hays Gardiner and Laura E. Richards guaranteed the costs of *Captain Craig,* they conspired to secure for it the widest and most sympathetic promulgation. They made lists of possibilities, conjecturing, "Perhaps Dr. [William Allan] Neilson or Miss Peabody would do a review for the *Atlantic?*" (Hagedorn, p. 189.) It was Robinson's misfortune that the book was assigned to a temperament far less empathetic.

. . / / . .

A poet, not a versifier

CAPTAIN CRAIG

J.B. Kerfoot

For some time English Poetry has been in a rather bad way, and there have even been those who have despaired of the patient. One of the most encouraging bulletins we have had lately is a little volume called *Captain Craig,* from the pen of Edwin Arlington Robinson. The author is a bit inclined to the obscure, and in places is deplorably harsh, but he is a poet, not a versifier,[1] and he may go far.

From "The Latest Books," *Life,* XLI (April 2, 1903), 289.

This note was picked up by Robinson's home town paper, the Gardiner *Daily Reporter-Journal,* in its regular column of "Local Gleanings" on April 6, 1903, [3], with a number of errors in the transmission. Most glaring was the seemingly perverse insistence on rebaptizing Edwin as Edward even though *Life* ran the name correctly.

John Barrett Kerfoot (1865-1927), literary critic of *Life* from 1900-1918, was also associate editor of *Camera Work* for more than twenty years and a noted antiquarian in Jersey glass and American pewter. He published numerous articles on art and antiquities, and three books on varied subjects.

1 Kerfoot here anticipates Theodore Roosevelt's often quoted phrase, "not verse but poetry," at the close of his review of *The Children of the Night* in the *Outlook* of August 12, 1905, reprinted in this volume. Kerfoot, however, is less timorous about Robinson's prospects than the President was to be.

. . / / . .

On April 20, 1903 the Gardiner (Me.) *Daily Reporter-Journal* renewed its practice of picking up good reports on Robinson's books. In "Local Gleanings" on p. [3] appeared this paragraph: "Edward [*sic*]Arilngton [*sic*] Robinson's new book of poems, *Captain Craig,* has reached a second edition, the first having been published only a few months. Mr. Robinson is a Gardiner boy, and his friends here naturally are proud of his success. His work has received the highest compliments from all the critics, and the following from the New York *Independent* is a sample of them." Then it presents a telescoped selection of sentences from the *Independent* review of February 19, 1903, reprinted in full in this volume. Not only did the *Reporter-Journal* persist in calling Edwin Edward, it piled insult upon indignity by committing a transposition in his middle name.

. . / / . .

Keen insight into human nature

SOME BOOKS OF VERSE

Distinctive among recent books of verse is *Captain Craig*, by Edwin Arlington Robinson, published by Houghton, Mifflin & Co. The volume takes its title from the largest poem it contains. In this the author shows a keen insight into human nature, and words are admirably chosen to convey his meaning. There is no poem in the collection without a central thought, and in the most instances the thoughts are well expressed. The price of the book is $1.

From "Literary Note and Comment," Newark *News* (July 18, 1903), 14.

. . / / . .

These people are all queer

CAPTAIN CRAIG

Trumbull Stickney

There are those at home and abroad who tell us that our nation, our age and generation are drowned in material pursuits and drunk with brutality. Our artists, we are told, sell their souls or, to save them, hurry away from a civilization that deafens thought and kills fancy. Our novelists boil over the fire of magazines; our essayists string off their chapters week by week. In short, we live in a sort of railway station, and have time for only those things and people who can catch the express with us. What a consolation it ought to be to these critics to find our poets still singing, still thinking, still alive enough to believe in the Muse; to find them still mixing with life and not yet disgusted with it.

There are many happy hours to be spent in the verses of our contemporaries, though few people, I dare say, allow themselves the luxury. For my part, I owe this new author much more than that. The honesty and simplicity of his mind, the pathos and kindness of his heart, and above all the humor with which his imagination is lighted up continually, have made me begin life over again and feel once more that poetry is part of it, perhaps the truth of it.

His poems are chiefly scenes, where his odd acquaintances talk to him or write to him. He gives a few of their gestures and attitudes. A line here and there lets you see the speaker, evading his own conscience or yielding to his desire for confession. Then the author rather shyly disappears; his hero talks himself out; and often a last note, between humor and sorrow, closes the song. Such, you might say, is life.

CAPTAIN CRAIG (1903)

These people are all queer. Captain Craig,[1] Carmichael, Aunt Imogen, Lorraine, George Annandale, Vanderberg[2]: they are among those who after experience curl up in a corner and under persuasion will talk to you.

> I keep a scant half-dozen words he said,
> And every now and then I lose his name;
> He may be living or he may be dead,
> But I must have him with me all the same.[3]

You have met such people and felt that way; if you have not, you care nothing for the various members of your race, you let the faces on the street go by without seeing them, you are putting on your gloves instead of shaking hands. How much you miss! And then

> "But there is this to be remembered always:
> Whatever be the attitude you reach,
> You do not rise alone; nor do you fall
> But you drag others down to more or less
> Than your preferred abasement. God forbid
> That ever I should preach, and in my zeal
> Forget that I was born an humorist;
> But now, for once, before I go away,
> I beg of you to be magnanimous . . ."[4]

If we meet them in this spirit, we are going to pass through a series of feasts of reason and flows of soul. The dramatist shows us men and women directly, in their action on each other, moving and lost in the stress of life. Our author is more descriptive and sees the world in a way too characteristic not to engage us in his view. His people are all very real, but he has pointed out and chosen their realities for us. His poems then are not dramatic lyrics in any sense, but introductions to his friends

> "Therefore I welcome what may come,
>   Glad for the days, the nights, the years." —
> An upward flash of ember-flame
>   Revealed the gladness in his tears.
>
> "You see them, but you know," said he,
>   "Too much to be incredulous:
> You know the day that makes us wise,
>   The moment that makes fools of us . . ."[5]

Which do you prefer, Vanderberg who is speaking, or Robinson who is quoting? They were intimate friends:

> Though not for common praise of him,
>   Nor yet for pride or charity,
> Still would I make to Vanderberg
>   One tribute for his memory:
>
> One honest warrant of a friend
>   Who found with him that flesh was grass —
> Who neither blamed him in defect
>   Nor marveled how it came to pass;
>
> Or why it ever was that he —
>   That Vanderberg, of all good men,
> Should lose himself to find himself,
>   Straightway to lose himself again.[6]

But, you say, this is not poetry. I can only answer, What is it, then? and would you give us, after the many praiseworthy attempts since Aristotle, a definition of the art? The test of all forms of expression lies not in their resembling other forms, but in their proving adequate to the thought. Otherwise literature would be a long commentary on the classics, whereas the commentary can be left to scholars, while the classics grow more varied and more numerous. The fact that so much poetry past and present is written in what professors of rhetoric call an elevated style, does not necessarily condemn authors who use plain Saxon. The metrics of Milton and Browning do not banish loose and smooth versification. The English sonnet is not bound to be serious, lyric and climactic, — let me prove it to you:

> Carmichael had a kind of joke-disease,
> And he had queer things fastened on his wall.
> There are three green china frogs that I recall
> More potently than anything, for these
> Three frogs have demonstrated, by degrees,
> What curse was on the man to make him fall:
> "They are not ordinary frogs at all,
> They are the Frogs of Aristophanes."
>
> God! how he laughed whenever he said that;
> And how we caught from one another's eyes
> The flash of what a tongue could never tell!
> We always laughed at him, no matter what
> The joke was worth. But when a man's brain dies,
> We are not always glad . . . Poor Carmichael! [7]

So we have one poet more, one more of those men like us but more than we; who make life richer and clearer, by bringing the smile and the tear nearer together, and in their mixture showing us the human face of men and women, as it looks, on the whole rather anxiously, before and upward.

From *Harvard Monthly*, XXXVII (December 1903), 99-102.

Joseph Trumbull Stickney (1874-1904), classical scholar and poet, was at Harvard at the same time as Robinson, his writings often appearing in the *Harvard Monthly* whereas Robinson's were consistently rejected. He was the first American to win the degree of *docteur ès lettres* from the University of Paris. He returned to teach Greek at Harvard but succumbed early to a brain tumor. His *Dramatic Verses* (1902) and *Poems* (1905) reveal him as one of the very few poets of his time to achieve an individual style. On learning of his sudden death, Robinson said to Miss Peabody: "We could not afford to lose him." He is one contemporary academic who championed Robinson's relaxed metrics and "plain Saxon" style.

1 Robinson to Edith Brower, August 17, 1899: "'The Pauper' is, I am afraid, just a little queer. I have no desire to be queer." (Cary, p. 102; see also p. 204, and Sutcliffe, p. 303.)

2 A character in "Sainte-Nitouche."

3 "The Corridor," p. 163.

4 "Captain Craig," p. 61.

5 "Sainte-Nitouche," p. 153.

6 *Ibid.*, p. 150.

7 "Captain Craig," p. 37.

. . / / . .

Rather than document separately each of the excessive number of factual errors and misleading assertions in the following essay, it seems wiser to collocate them here, by way of a cautionary preface:

Robinson did not "seek" employment in the subway. It was obtained for him on a suggestion by George Burnham, whose brother-in-law was a construction engineer on the project. As Hagedorn says (p. 202), Robinson "acquiesced."

Robinson did start writing "Captain Craig" in New York City during the spring of 1898 and he did complete it there in May 1900, but he wrote considerable portions of it in the return interim at Gardiner and while employed at Harvard in January-June 1899.

As a young man, Robinson's father did work for a time as a shipwright in Boston, which hardly qualifies calling him a shipbuilder. He dealt in lumber and ran a general store in Head Tide, Maine, until shortly after Edwin was born. The family moved to Gardiner, where Edward Robinson invested in western mortgages, became director of several banks, selectman, alderman, representative to the legislature in Augusta, and a leader in other civic affairs.

There is small likelihood that Laura E. Richards interceded with Edward Robinson to send Edwin to Harvard in 1891; she tells of meeting the poet for the first time after receipt of an inscribed copy of *The Torrent and The Night Before*, 1896. (Richards, *E.A.R.*, p. 49.) Hagedorn (p. 61) declares that Edwin's brother Herman tipped the balance in Edwin's favor.

Robinson did not "continue" at Harvard: his schooling there ended in June 1893; his employment started in January 1899. His position was not "private secretary of President Eliot"; his duties were strictly clerical. He told Harry Smith that he overhauled graduates' applications, describing himself as "a sort of assistant secretary and metaphorical bottle washer to the whole concern." (*Collamore*, p. 16.)

The Torrent and The Night Before contains forty-six poems, not two. French is counting only the two title poems.

The Children of the Night was published in December 1897. Like many others, French omits the initial *The* of the title, twice.

Laura Richards did advance Robinson's cause with Edmund Clarence Stedman, but Robinson had met him at the Authors' Club before she began her recommendations. See Robert J. Scholnick, "The Shadowed Years: Mrs. Richards, Mr. Stedman, and Robinson," *Colby Library Quarterly*, IX (June 1972), 510-531.

Richard Watson Gilder, editor of the *Century*, knew about Robinson through his submission of poems to that magazine (he accepted "Uncle Ananias") and the enthusiasm of President Roosevelt for Robinson's **work**.

The first edition of *Captain Craig* appeared in October 1902. French seems to know only the second edition of 1903. The book could not have been "the product of the poet's work in the subway," since he did not begin working there before November 1903.

A strange personality

A POET IN THE SUBWAY

Hailed as a Genius by Men of Letters, Edwin Arlington Robinson Has to Earn His Living as a Time-Keeper.

Joseph Lewis French

> To me the groaning of world-worshippers
> Rings like a lonely music played in hell
> By one with art enough to cleave the walls
> Of heaven with his cadence, but without
> The wisdom or the will to comprehend
> The strangeness of his own perversity,
> And all without the courage to deny
> The profit and the pride of his defeat.[1]

Thus sings the poet Edwin Arlington Robinson. Yet even a poet must have the means to live. If his genius, though winning applause, fails to provide the necessities, what then?

After a long battle with this question Edwin Arlington Robinson sought employment in the New York Subway.

And thus it was that the poet became a laborer and his days are passed in the dark and damp recesses of the unfinished tunnels of upper Broadway.

Emerging from the depths at close of day he can look out over the broad Hudson rolling majestically oceanward as always through the centuries. Combined with inflections upon the day's labors underground this spectacle of the mighty river could easily remind Mr. Robinson of his own words:

> With searching feet, through dark circuitous ways,
> I plunged and stumbled; round me, far and near,
> Quaint hordes of eyeless phantoms did appear,
> Twisting and turning in a bootless chase, —
> When, like an exile given by God's grace
> To feel once more a human atmosphere,
> I caught the world's first murmur, large and clear,
> Flung from a singing river's endless race.[2]

Edwin Arlington Robinson has been a resident of this city four years. *Captain Craig: A Book of Poems*, the work that has contributed most to his renown, was written here. It reflects the author as a man of liberal culture, a philosopher and a humorist.

There is much that is genial and broadly sympathetic in the story of Captain Craig. But the writer of it is a strange personality. Those who judge him by his poetry do not take measure of his temperament. He is a mystery even to his friends. Though many have sought his acquaintance and his friendship he has preferred the lonely life here in New York as elsewhere. Those who have tried to lionize him as a new star on the literary horizon have all encountered this insurmountable obstacle. Those who have sought to befriend him in his hard struggle with the material facts of life have fared but little better.

It was in the extremity of poverty, having refused the aid of those who would cheerfully have assisted him, that Edwin Arlington Robinson applied last fall for a position in the rapid-transit company's subway work. As he was skilled in no branch of it, but few positions were open to him. Last November he was assigned to duty as a time checker in the uncompleted tunnels and the excavations in progress at the northern end of the route under Broadway.

Edwin Arlington Robinson combines with his duties of checking the time of the laborers, who are mostly Italians, to a limited degree that of an inspector, for he takes account of the stone and other material delivered at the tunnels for construction work.[3]

It is an all-day task, this altered avocation of the poet, and a wearying one. The tall man in glasses, wearing a sombrero and a shaggy overcoat, is known to all the laborers as the time checker. They are all known to him by name, but there the acquaintance ends. The book that is the product of the poet's work in the subway is far removed from poetry.

Yet all that is most positive in the individuality of Edwin Arlington Robinson — that which accounts for the well-guarded seclusion of his life. Its aloofness from persons and affairs — so far as it is not temperamental, is due to the feeling that his mission is that of a poet.[4] In an early production he wrote:

> What does it mean, this barren age of ours?
> Here are the men, the women, and the flowers,
> The seasons, and the sunset, as before.
> What does it mean? Shall not one bard arise
> To wrench one banner from the western skies,
> And mark it with his name forevermore?[5]

Very early in life Mr. Robinson's exceptional talent was apparent to those who knew him well and were able to judge it. His home was in the little village of Gardiner, Maine, which is also the home of Mrs. Laura Elizabeth Richards,[6] the author, and daughter of Mrs. Julia Ward Howe.

In the silent, isolated youth, Edwin Robinson, the son of a shipbuilder, Mrs. Richards recognized the elements of genius. It was through her influence that, in 1891, when Edwin was twenty-two years old, he was sent to Harvard, where he took a two years' special literary course. He continued for a time at Cambridge as the private secretary of President Eliot, but the college life and this work were not congenial: Robinson was poor, proud and ambitious. He had already decided to "consecrate his life to poetry."[7] In the university President Eliot, Prof. James and especially Prof. Lewis E. Gates recognized him as a dawning literary genius.[8]

In 1896 Mr. Robinson's first book, consisting of two poems, was published. It was entitled *The Torrent and The Night Before.* The latter recites in blank verse the reveries of a young man on the eve of his execution for the murder of his wife.

In 1898 his second book of verse, under the title *The Children of the Night,* was published, and soon afterward Mr. Robinson came to this city.

It was through Mrs. Richards, whose interest in his fortunes led her to seek him out, that Edmund Clarence Stedman,[9] Richard Wilson Gilder[10] and others of literary note were made acquainted with his presence here. His works were favorably known to them, and Mr. Stedman, Mr. Gilder, Edward Eggleston, R.H. Stoddard[11] and many of the younger literary folk showed themselves cordially desirous of furthering the young poet's interests.

Through Mr. Stedman, who had already published some of the poems in *Anthology,*[12] Robinson was afforded the opportunity to try daily journalism as a means of livelihood on the *Tribune* and the *Evening Post.* He made one contribution to the editorial columns of each paper. One of these was a satirical criticism of the poetry of a certain popular writer of verse under the title "Peaches and Ether."[13]

Mr. Robinson spent several days' work over his two newspaper articles and then abandoned the effort to enter daily journalism. He locked himself up with his poetry, and those who would reproach him for not choosing a more "practical" work could find the answer in his *The Children of the Night*:

> Dear friends, reproach me not for what I do,
> Nor counsel me, nor pity me; nor say
> That I am wearing half my life away
> For bubble-work that only fools pursue.
> And if my bubbles be too small for you,
> Blow bigger then your own: the games we play
> To fill the frittered minutes of a day,
> Good glasses are to read the spirit through.[14]

His *Captain Craig* was published in 1903. After the appearance of this volume many efforts were made to introduce Mr. Robinson to the literary circles of this city and of Boston, but these efforts only served to withdraw him more and more into his hermit life.

From New York *World Magazine* (May 15, 1904), 10.

Joseph Lewis French (1858-1936), novelist, poet, anthologist, and journalistic hack, listed in *Who's Who* as author of twenty-seven books, was a salesman for Richard G. Badger, who had published Robinson's second book. A Dickensian figure — flamboyant, garrulous, crapulous, unpredictable, short-fused this side of madness — French borrowed money and clothes indiscriminately with not the slightest intention of returning them. Once he tried to wheedle the very suit off Robinson's back, cadged $5.00 from him on his deathbed. One day Morris Raphael Cohen, the philosopher, "found Robinson almost shaking with agitation and fear." French "had descended on him suddenly at Peterborough. 'I helped him once,' Robinson said, 'and as a result he thinks I owe him more and more.'" (Leonora Cohen Rosenfield, "The Philosopher and the Poet," *Palinurus*, I [April 1959], 32.) It must be said, however, that French was genuinely fond of Robinson, and attempted to secure the Nobel Prize in poetry for him. French thought he recognized hmself as Count Pretzel von Wurzburger, the Obscene, in "Captain Craig," and was both flattered and angered. (See Hagedorn, p. 149 *passim*.) French is one of that strange quintet of Robinson's early critics (Thorne, Peck, Thompson, Ranck) who might well have sat for one of his portrait-poems.

French proposed the idea of a feature article to the editor of the *World* Sunday magazine section. The latter solicited a statement from Stedman who, in turn, informed Robinson of the plan. Appalled by the thought of such publicity, Robinson insisted that it be dropped. French promised, again with no intention of keeping his word. To Robinson's dismay and humiliation, the essay appeared in six-column spread embellished in the center by his photograph from the shoulders up, as on a medallion, flanked on his right by a facsimile of the 1903 edition title page of *Captain Craig*, and on his left by a drawing of himself in sombrero and mackintosh, dangling a lantern, as he watches laborers digging in the subway tunnel.

At the upper, far-right column of the article, boxed in rippling lines, the following words: "By Edmund Clarence Stedman": "Edwin Arlington Robinson is a true poet, and a man of fine talent. He has good blood in his veins. In some respects he is a typical representative of the old New England family, with but few left in its latest generation, and estate a thing of the past. Some of Mr. Robinson's earlier lyrics and sonnets were beautiful and original. His 'Captain Craig' is a striking bit of realism; the poet comes right down to the soil. Such a poet gains at first a select audience if any."

Robinson had little recourse but to accept French's insistence that it was all for his own good. "French isn't a man you can get rid of," he said to a friend. "There are times when I think he would shoot me without a moment's hesitation. It's quite possible — sometimes I think it is quite probable — that I shall meet my death at French's hands." (Hagedorn, p. 291.)

1 "Octaves" V, *The Children of the Night*, p. 95.

2 "For a Book by Thomas Hardy," *Ibid.*, p. 56.

3 Robinson worked at the subway excavation from November 1903 to August 1904, earning $2.00 per day for a ten-hour shift. His chief task was to check off each laborer as he arrived in the morning and departed at night. Since he also did keep records of the truckloads of materials dumped at the mouth of the tunnel, he said he was "dignified by the name of Inspector." This he shrugged off with typical detraction. "I carried a lantern in the dark," he explained. (Evans, p. 676.) The long hours left him exhausted and unfit for writing; he spoke of their "paralyzing effect" on his mind. Later, he took a ride over that section of the subway and remarked, "On the whole, I'm rather glad that I built it." (Hagedorn, p. 208.)

4 "It must have been about the year 1889 when I realized finally, and not without a justifiable uncertainty as to how the thing was to be done, that I was doomed, or elected, or sentenced for life, to the writing of poetry," Robinson wrote in "The First Seven Years," *Colophon*, Part IV (December 1930), n.p.

5 "Sonnet" (Oh for a poet), *The Children of the Night*, p. 63.

6 Laura E. Richards (1850-1943), Pulitzer Prize-winning author of many juvenile verses and stories, notably *Captain January*, came to live in Gardiner, Maine, in 1876 after marrying Henry Richards. On pages 48-50 of her short biography of Robinson, she describes him around the time of the appearance of *The Torrent and The Night Before* as "a slender figure, erect, distinguished, breeding and race in every line of it; dark, glowing eyes; brilliant color." She invited him to her home and he accepted, with the proviso that she not allude to him as "a Hermit Thrush." They "talked of books in general, and of *the* book in particular." He formed "the habit of dropping in once a week," and their friendship prevailed until his death. She and her husband's cousin, John Hays Gardiner, helped him over numerous financial humps.

7   Robinson wrote to Richard Watson Gilder that he was "cursed with the poetical microbe." (Hagedorn, p. 215.)

8   When Robinson came to work in the Harvard administration offices, Charles William Eliot, inaugurator of the elective curriculum, asked him if he was married and decreed it "A great mistake" that he was not. "Robinson took an intense dislike to the distinguished inquisitor," says Hagedorn (p. 148). In later years Robinson remarked "that he had at one time thought Charles W. Eliot possessed of the elements of greatness, but that he had changed his mind about him when he revealed no more wisdom than to establish a school of business in a university devoted to liberal ideas." (Brown, p. 28.)

William James wrote a bright testimonial to the second edition of *Captain Craig* at his publisher's behest (see above), not knowing, of course, that Robinson had found one of his books "entertaining and full of good things." On the larger scale, however, Robnson's estimation of James was minimal. He found James's style "forever prostituting itself to contemporary slang and slipshod affectations, by which he hopes, I suppose, to strike the popular chord and conceal its arrogance." And he burst out impatiently once: "Professor William James doesn't know anything about Herbert Spencer." (Torrence, pp. 15-17; Sutcliffe, p. 297.)

Of the three Harvard mentors cited here, only Professor Gates comes off without blemish. James L. Tryon, who took the courses with Robinson, wrote: "What appealed most in his study of English were the courses given by Professor Lewis E. Gates in eighteenth and nineteenth century prose writers, and of these he liked best and reacted most to the nineteenth century course which came in the first year of his admission." (Tryon, p. 9.) At the outset Robinson discovered that the course "means work," and he began to wish he had not taken it. Before a month was out he proclaimed English 9 "a splendid course." He did not cut a single lecture. (Sutcliffe, pp. 30, 37; Hagedorn, p. 71.)

Hagedorn (p. 81) professes that "Robinson made no impression at Harvard as a coming figure in literature," attributing this to the presence then of William Vaughn Moody and other more aggressive spirits than Robinson. Looking backward more than three decades, Robinson stated flatly that "he was uninfluenced by any of the faculty." (Evans, p. 679.)

9   Edmund Clarence Stedman (1833-1908), Wall Street broker, genteel poet, literary critic and historian, anthologist, received a copy of *The Torrent and The Night Before* but seems not to have responded. He was nonetheless impressed by Robinson's accomplishment and, with some prodding by Mrs. Richards, decided to include five of his poems in *An American Anthology, 1787-1900* (Boston, 1900). Temperamentally at opposite poles, they managed to hit it off satisfactorily, if desultorily. Robinson described Stedman to Miss Peabody as "a rather small and very courteous old gentleman with white hair who may say all sorts of complimentary things — rather too many, you may think at first — and tell you that you are a Rare Spirit. He will say no end of things, in fact, and he will mean all that he says." (Torrence, pp. 40-41.) Robinson told Mason that he and Stedman would sit on anthills on the back lot of his house and discuss farming and Art, Robinson's "chief recreation" being the consumption of Stedman's tobacco. "He likes me because I wrote a thing called 'The Clerks' and because I represent so many distinct varieties of imperturbable asininity." (Mason, *VQR* [Winter 1937], 67-68.) Stedman encouraged Robinson to write editorials for newspapers, promoted him among editors, and aided him financially from time to time. (See Hagedorn, pp. 163-164 *passim*.)

Stedman was one of those whom Robinson asked to read "Captain Craig" in manuscript. On July 11, 1900 Stedman's granddaughter wrote to Mrs. Richards: "Grandpa read 'Captain Craig,' and found it a very original production in choice and treatment of subject — if Browningesque in method. . . . Grandpa did what he could to secure it careful attention, . . . still he shared Mr. Robinson's fear that there was not much chance for it at Scribner's." (Scholnick, p. 525.) Robinson to Josephine Preston Peabody, September 14, 1900: "it is very amusing and sometimes hilarious; and, as a whole, it is elevating — so Mr. Stedman says, though he doesn't care for it"; and to

Edith Brower, July 12, 1901: "Tell me if you find *C.C.* tedious in the opening. Stedman did; and if he did I suppose others will." (Anderson, p. 84; Cary, p. 144.)

10   Richard Watson Gilder (1844-1909), leader in New York City artistic, social, and civic life, was editor of the *Century* from 1881 till his death, author of sixteen volumes of poems and presidential biographies, and a prime mover in Robinson's association wth Theodore Roosevelt. In 1905 he invited Robinson to lunch and to submit verse to the magazine. He published "Uncle Ananias" in the "In Lighter Vein" department, Robinson receiving the first payment for a poem since *Lippincott's* had accepted his sonnet on Poe ten years earlier.

11   Richard Henry Stoddard (1825-1903), like Stedman and Gilder a force in New York City literary circles, wrote many literary reviews, and mostly genteel romantic poetry immensely popular in the past half century. Robinson and Miss Peabody went together to visit him in his last years. "The old man appeared glad to see these young people who were carrying on the torch. 'E.A.R.'s light comes out and shines when he is with the aged or the afflicted,' Miss Peabody wrote in her diary. 'So it shone doubly, that night.'" (Hagedorn, p. 182.)

12   In his *An American Anthology, 1787-1900* (Boston, 1900), pp. 727-729, Stedman included Robinson's "Luke Havergal," "The Ballade of Dead Friends," "The Clerks," "The Pity of the Leaves," and "The House on the Hill," the most prestigious attention paid Robinson up to this time. With unremitting self-deflation he said to Mason in May 1900: "I believe my uncomfortable abstraction called 'Luke Havergal' is also to be soused in anthological pickle — along with two or three others of the forlornly joyous breed." (Torrence, p. 30.)

13   In "Edwin Arlington Robinson, Journalist," *New England Quarterly*, XV (December 1942), 715-724, Alice Meacham Williams asserts on the evidence of letters between Robinson and Stedman that only one of the several pieces Robinson submitted was published — an editorial on William Jennings Bryan entitled "The Balm of Custom" in the New York *Daily Tribune* (October 7, 1900), 8, for which he was paid $4.25. She states unequivocally that "Peaches and Ether" was never accepted for publication.

14   "Dear Friends," p. 39.

.. / / ..

At this crucial juncture — Robinson's most daring deflection from poetic modes acceptable to public and critics — the estranged, displaced poet listened voraciously at every quarter for some word of vindication. He heard nothing, and the cumbrous echoes of silence desolated him. In a veritable *cri de coeur*, years and years after, he released the torment ingrowing since the appearance of *Captain Craig*. "If only they had said something about me! It would not have mattered what. They could have called me stupid or crazy if they liked. But they said nothing. Nobody devoted as much as an inch to me. I did not exist." (Brown, p. 66.)

This was of course hyperbolic, as the assemblage of some two dozen notices here testifies, though Robinson may not have seen any number of them. No matter. He stood at that point of self-knowledge where he could apprehend the enormous step he had taken — he had veered off the sanctioned highway into tangled, propitious country — and "nobody" seemed to have noticed, or cared. There is a persuasion among some literary historians, one of them Malcolm Cowley, that "Captain Craig" is a determining turn in American poetry from the desiccate foppery of the nineties toward the provocative vigor of the succeeding era. Be that as it may, the interminable decade of defeatism which Robinson endured between completion of *Captain Craig* and the publication of his next new book, *The Town Down the River* (1910), unquestionably affected his innovative spark. Did the imagined conspiracy of neglect derail his exploratory genius? Or did a failure of nerve, or stamina, unconsciously curb it? Robinson never again wrote with such freewheeling élan, from so liberated and liberating a posture. He would get his "hearing" later, though not quite as he had desperately craved.

THE CHILDREN OF THE NIGHT (1905)

The score and more reviews allotted *Captain Craig* by upper-drawer newspapers and magazines across the country did not affect Robinson's standing with poetry editors, who remained consistently unresponsive to his offerings. Predisposed to confections by the Frank Dempster Sherman-Clinton Scollard school of genteel metrists, they effectively barricaded the experimental route Robinson had hacked out for himself, and thus postponed onset of the new American style successfully promoted by Edgar Lee Masters in *Spoon River Anthology* a decade later. In the arid interval from August 1897 to August 1905 Robinson sold exactly one poem, and that possibly less on intrinsic merit than through a guileless conjugation of influence.

The three years 1902-1904 represent a crevasse in Robinson's experience which, except for impregnable faith in his essential role, would have consumed him entire as man and poet. Spent by the interminable wrangles over his several typescripts which finally metamorphosed into *Captain Craig*, depressed by its failure to raise him to prime poetic rank, reduced to living in a bare room and eating in shabby restaurants or by friends' largesse, he took such consolation in liquor as to endanger his survival in the brutal, heedless environment of New York. A providential job as timekeeper in the city subway system (described in the preceding article and notes) allayed his most pressing financial needs for ten months but did nothing to restore his spirit. On the contrary, he complained to Josephine Preston Peabody that the "subway business keeps my brain, or what used to be a brain, too tired" to read, write letters, or indeed to make poems.[1] Freed of this drudgery in August 1904, he fell back into the tides of circumstance, listlessly contemplating suicide as one way out of his idealistic-materialistic dilemma. When Willie Butler offered him a part-time job devising ads for his father's department store in Boston, Robinson weighed it against the drearier alternative of starvation, and accepted.

Shortly before this, at Groton School, Kermit Roosevelt was reading a book of poems he had borrowed from his dormitory master, a son of Laura Richards. Taken by the taste and power of the contents, he obtained from the publisher, Badger & Company, a copy of the 1897 edition of *The Children of the Night* and mailed it to the White House.² What followed is limned dramatically by M.K. Wisehart. Coming in late one afternoon "from a horseback ride in Potomac Park, the President, still wearing his riding clothes and brown leather puttees, dropped into a chair and picked up the book. Turning the pages, he read a little here and there. He became absorbed. He had thought to glance through it in a couple of minutes; but he didn't lay it down till an hour later, when he had read it all through. There were things in it that struck him hard. 'By Jove!' he exclaimed on one occasion. 'It's something I'd missed. It reads like the real thing.' "³

In the waning days of March 1905 Richard Watson Gilder, editor of *Century* magazine, called on Theodore Roosevelt in connection with an article he was writing on "The President as a Reader." Roosevelt announced that he had discovered a poet, Edwin Arlington Robinson. Did Gilder know anything about him? Gilder knew a little and promised to find out more. With typical impatience, Roosevelt rattled off his note to Robinson's old New York address on March 27: "Dear Mr. Robinson: I have enjoyed your poems especially The Children of the Night so much that I must write to tell you so. Will you permit me to ask what you are doing and how you are getting along. I wish I could see you. Sincerely yours."⁴ While the letter was being rerouted to Boston, Roosevelt wrote Gilder thanking him for his information and inquiring anxiously "how Robinson is getting along. Perhaps I could give him some position in the Government service, just as Walt Whitman and John Burroughs were given Government positions."⁵

On the same day, March 31, William Vaughn Moody apprised Robinson that he had "been discovered by the national administration. Roosevelt is said to stop cabinet discussion to ask Hay, 'Do you know Robinson?' and upon receiving a negative reply, to spend the rest of the session reading *Captain Craig* aloud." Through Gilder, Moody suggested "a nice lazy berth in the consular service in England."⁶ Roosevelt, who had a theory about American genius withering on foreign soil, thought this "inadvisable," as did Robinson, emphatically, for his own reasons. On April 11 he told Gilder he was content in his current situation, having two-thirds of his time to himself, and that he had made clear to the President he was not interested in "employment in strange lands — to wit, in Montreal and Mexico," and would switch only for "more congenial work, with more pay and the same amount of leisure."⁷ He held out specifically for New York City. After some slight additional legerdemain, Roosevelt obliged with a post in the Custom House and the admonition, "I want you to understand that I expect you to think poetry first and Treasury second."⁸

For Robinson the whole episode blossomed like a miracle, "one of those pleasant and unexpected things that come about as frequently as the Phoenix. . . . once every five hundred years."⁹ To John Gardiner he exulted: "I don't know a special agent of the Treasury from the mother of Samson. All I know is that it means two thousand a year, with plenty of time for my own work."¹⁰ Perhaps now the long creative drought might dissolve. Much of the substance for "a book of something like fifty poems" which he had started working on in January 1902 had been absorbed in the *Captain Craig* volume, and the poems he had expected to complete over the next "two or three years" had simply not materialized. In March he wrote hopefully to Mrs. Richards that "If I am spared another half a decade I expect to do a book of mixed short things." Still projecting for 1905 a new work "nearly all in rhyme," he told Gardiner in September 1904 that he was "feeling very well nowadays and I hope to bring something to pass before another winter is over."[11] A trio of ineluctable factors recast this plan: his protracted depression, the inimical editors, and Theodore Roosevelt.

Not one poem of Robinson's appeared in a magazine or newspaper during the grim stretch of 1901-1904. The single piece accepted in 1905 surfaced in the *Century*, edited by Richard Watson Gilder, who at this point may have been motivated more by sympathy than by strict judgment. In any case, he relegated "Uncle Ananias" to the department earmarked for prose and verse "In Lighter Vein," an anomaly Robinson's ironic eye did not fail to note.[12] It remained for a sturdier Samaritan to lead him out of the woods. Determined that his fellow citizens reap the benefits of his new-found protégé, President Roosevelt made some strategic inquiries of the executives at Scribner's, who thereupon agreed to issue a new edition of *The Children of the Night*. As a third propellant, the President broadcast his appreciation of Robinson's art from the national forum of the *Outlook* in August 1905. It was a performance unique in the history of American letters.

Hagedorn maintains that Scribner's "meekly accepted the presidential hint," suggesting unsubtle flourish of 'the big stick.' Roger Burlingame absolves Roosevelt of this tactic, citing his soft approach in an instance involving some verses written by Theodore junior.[13] Whether Scribner's buckled under the invisible weight of the Capitol or decided to gamble on Robinson's future product, the firm acquired the original plates of the 1897 *Children* from Richard Badger and put them through another run.[14]

Viewing the languid pace of sales one year after issuance of *The Children* in 1897, Robinson had prophesied glumly: "It is hardly probable that a second edition will be called for." However, before two more years elapsed he was planning not only to resuscitate the book but also to insert massive revisions: "I am sorry now for about one half of *The Children*, and I hope to be still sorrier before I republish any of it." In February 1901 he reviewed for Edith Brower his current designs to demolish and reconstruct.

I find that if I am [to] please everybody I shall have to throw away everything in the book but 'The Clerks,' 'John Evereldown,' and 'Cliff Klingenhagen'; and even two of these have been questioned — one for its immorality and one for its prose. . . . I shall have to go back to my original idea of throwing out a dozen or fifteen things which are such utter rubbish that they make me sick when I think of them, and of letting the rest stand — partly for filling, I must confess, and partly because now and then a mortal finds something in them to like.[15]

All bravely and, without doubt, truly spoken. But when the long-desiderated opportunity came in 1905, the only textual change Robinson made was to eliminate the sestet from the sonnet "Boston" on page 51. Even the typographical error in "The Night Before" (When loves goes — page 78, line 23) made the transfer untouched.

Burlingame's contention that Roosevelt followed a median course in his advocacy of Robinson with Scribner's is further borne out by the President's behavior upon seeing an excerpt from his review displayed on the dust jacket of the 1905 *Children*. One day before its release to the public, Roosevelt's secretary, William Loeb, Jr., sent acknowledgement and this request to Scribner's: "The President is in receipt of the volume of Edwin Arlington Robinson's poems, *The Children of the Night*. On the paper wrapper of the cover is printed a quotation from the President. This is rather embarrassing because the President is continually asked for permission to be quoted in the advertisement of books, and the requests are invariably declined. Will you therefor discontinue the use of the President's name in any way in connection with the book, for the reason stated above?"[16] Thus ever does compassion yield to pragmatism in the higher reaches of politics.

. . / / . .

THE CHILDREN OF THE NIGHT. Published October 14, 1905 by Charles Scribner's Sons. Bound in green cloth, title and author's name stamped in gold on front cover and spine; all edges trimmed. Title page contains no colophon (present in the Badger edition). Leaves measure 17.5 by 10.8 centimeters. Edition of 500 copies at $1.25.

. . / / . .

CONTENTS

Except for the elimination of the sestet from the sonnet "Boston" on page 51, the text of this edition is identical with that of 1897.

The Children of the Night

A Book of Poems

BY

EDWIN ARLINGTON ROBINSON

NEW YORK
CHARLES SCRIBNER'S SONS
1905

Not verse but poetry

THE CHILDREN OF THE NIGHT

Theodore Roosevelt

The "twilight of the poets" has been especially gray in America; for poetry is of course one of those arts in which the smallest amount of work of the very highest class is worth an infinity of good work that is not of the highest class. The touch of the purple makes a poem out of verse, and if it is not there, there is no substitute. It is hard to account for the failure to produce in America of recent years a poet who in the world of letters will rank as high as certain American sculptors and painters rank in the world of art.

But individual poems appear from time to time, by Mr. Madison Cawein,[1] by Mr. Clinton Scollard, by Dr. Maurice Egan,[2] and others; and more rarely a little volume of poetry appears, like Bliss Carman's *Ballads of Lost Haven*.[3] Such a book is Edward[4] Arlington Robinson's *The Children of the Night*.

It is rather curious that Mr. Robinson's volume should not have attracted more attention. There is an undoubted touch of genius in the poems collected in this volume, and a curious simplicity and good faith, all of which qualities differentiate them sharply from ordinary collections of the kind. There is in them just a little of the light that never was on land or sea, and in such light the objects described often have nebulous outlines; but it is not always necessary in order to enjoy a poem that one should be able to translate it into terms of mathematical accuracy.[5] Indeed, those who admire the coloring of Turner, those who like to read how — and to wonder why — Childe Roland to the Dark Tower came,[6] do not wish always to have the ideas presented to them with cold, hard, definite outlines; and to a man with the poetic temperament it is inevitable that life should often appear clothed with a certain sad mysticism. In the present volume I am not sure that I understand "Luke Havergal"; but I am entirely sure that I like it.[7]

Whoever has lived in country America knows the gray, empty houses from which life has gone. It is of one of these that "The House on the Hill" was written. [The poem follows.]

The next poem, "Richard Cory," illustrates a very ancient but very profound philosophy of life with a curiously local touch which points its keen insight. Those who feel poetry in their marrow and fiber are the spiritual heirs of the ages; and so it is natural that this man from Maine, many of whose poems could have been written only by one to whom the most real of lives is the life of the American small town, should write his "Ballade of Broken Flutes" — where "A lonely surge of ancient spray / Told of an unforgetful sea"; — should write the poem beginning:

> Since Persia fell at Marathon,
>   The yellow years have gathered fast:
> Long centuries have come and gone.[8]

and the very original sonnet on Amaryllis, the last three lines of which are:

> But though the trumpets of the world were glad,
> It made me lonely and it made me sad
> To think that Amaryllis had grown old.

Some of his images stay fixed in one's mind, as in "The Pity of the Leaves," the lines running:

> The brown, thin leaves that on the stones outside
> Skipped with a freezing whisper.

Sometimes, he writes, as in "The Tavern," of what most of us feel we have seen; and then again of what we have seen only with the soul's eyes.[9]

I shall close by quoting entire his poem on "The Wilderness," which could have been written only by a man into whose heart there had entered deep the very spirit of the vast and melancholy northern forests: [The poem follows.]

Mr. Robinson has written in this little volume not verse but poetry. Whether he has the power of sustained flight remains to be seen.

From *Outlook*, LXXX (August 12, 1905), 913-914.

According to Hermann Hagedorn, biographer of both Robinson and Roosevelt, the President dictated this review "with the boy [his son Kermit] at his side to make suggestions." (*Edwin Arlington Robinson: A Biography* [New York, 1938], p. 218.) As Kermit remembered it, "he made me think that I was helping him write the review, and insisted on giving me half of the fifty dollars which he was paid." (William Lyon Phelps, "As I Like It," *Scribner's*, LXXXIX [January 1931], 95.)

Robinson's immediate response to Roosevelt's redoubtable puffery is described at second hand by Jessie B. Rittenhouse in a letter to her mother, November 1905: "A friend tells me he never saw a more distracted man than Robinson when the President exploited him. He walked the floor of his room exclaiming, 'I shall never live it down! I shall never live it down!' This may seem strange to you, but he is a serious worker, a rarely gifted poet who was being discovered everywhere by the natural course of events and he felt that the President's article would put him in the limelight and then react against him. There is something in this standpoint. The staying reputations are those slow in coming, and it would be a pity to make as talented a man as Robinson the victim of a premature popularity." (*My House of Life* [Boston, 1934], p. 212.)

Twenty-two years afterward, looking back more calmly on the effects of Roosevelt's interest in him, Robinson expressed sober obligation. On the solicitation of Frederick S. Wood he wrote: "And for that attention to a total stranger — an attention that was rewarded, I fear, with varying degrees of diligence and efficiency — I am happy too, owing to Colonel Roosevelt an increasing indebtedness of gratitude for which there is unhappily no tangible return. The best and only acknowledgment I can make of a most unusual act on the part of a most unusual man must apparently be told only in my gratefulness and in a few inadequate words." (Wood, *Roosevelt As We Knew Him* [Philadelphia, 1927], p. 393.)

To Florence Peltier, who was preparing a talk on Roosevelt in the spring of 1929, Robinson released his lingering distaste over the episode: "I don't like to appear ungracious, but that T.R. incident has been literally done to death. . . . Of course I appreciate all that the President did for me, but even the best things can be run finally into the ground. . . . Perhaps I can see you before long and explain a little better my attitude toward modern publicity methods." ("Edwin Arlington Robinson, Himself," *Mark Twain Quarterly*, I [Summer 1937], 13.)

1   Madison J. Cawein (1865-1914), a Kentucky poet who produced close to twoscore volumes of mediocre verse about his native scene and people. *Vale of Tempe*, published in 1905, may have caught Roosevelt's eye. In November of that year he reported to Kermit: "One day we had a rather forlorn little poet, Madison Cawein and his nice wife in at lunch. They made me feel quite badly by being so grateful at my having mentioned him in what I fear was a very patronizing, and indeed almost supercilious way, as having written an occasional good poem — that was in my review of Robinson." (Elting E. Morison, editor, *The Letters of Theodore Roosevelt* [Cambridge, Mass., 1952], V, 69.)

2   Maurice Francis Egan (1852-1924), professor of English at Notre Dame and Catholic universities, was another prolific author of books (some 35) and magazine pieces, taking into his province poems, stories, literary and drama criticism, and novels for juveniles. Versed in European affairs, he became a frequent guest at White House luncheons and "unofficial diplomatic adviser" to three presidents. Roosevelt appointed him minister to Denmark.

3   This volume, published in 1897 and subtitled "A Book of the Sea," is one of Carman's lesser regarded efforts.
    If one wonders about the standard that led Roosevelt to cite this odd quartet of poets as exemplars, this statement by him may enlighten: "The equation of personal taste is as powerful in reading as in eating; and within certain broad limits the matter is merely one of individual preference, having nothing to do with the quality either of the book or of the reader's mind." (*A Book-Lover's Holidays in the Open* [New York, 1916], p. 260.)

4   It is an irony of enormous proportion that Robinson's most solicitous benefactor should have misrepresented his name so. And it was not just a careless slip. The error was duplicated in the book listing at the bottom of the first column.

5   Roosevelt to his son Kermit, November 6, 1905: "I am much struck by Robinson's two poems which you sent Mother. What a queer, mystical creature he is! I did not understand one of them — that about the gardens — and I do not know that I like either of them quite as much as some of those in *The Children of the Night*. But he certainly has the real spirit in him. Whether he can make it come out, I am not quite sure." (Morison, V, 69.) Robinson's "Two Gardens in Linndale" was not published until *The Town Down the River* (1910).

6   Roosevelt ties Robinson to Browning by implication here. Browning's poem of this name is one of his "Dramatic Romances" included in *Men and Women* (1855).

7   Robinson to Edith Brower, April 21, 1897: "In a thing like 'Luke Havergal,' of course the meaning is all suggested, and is not capable of a definite working-out by anyone who doesn't happen to sympathize with the writer's fancy." (Richard Cary, editor, *Edwin Arlington Robinson's Letters to Edith Brower* [Cambridge, Mass., 1968], p. 39.)
    In 1927 Robinson wrote: "There were some strange and reprehensible derelicts in that book of mine; and the stranger and more reprehensible they were, the better the President seemed to like them — probably because they were not fundamentally vicious. The somewhat prevalent and wholly foolish notion that Colonel Roosevelt was tolerant only, or mainly, of biceps and sunshine are clearly disproved in his disinterested and business-like pursuit of the person who was responsible for this book just mentioned — a book in which the characters, taken together, are of a certainty neither strenuous nor sunny. They may be interesting, and I hope they are, but I am pretty certain that their combined example would lead one sooner to the devil than to the White House." (Wood, p. 392.)

8   "Villanelle of Change," p. 29.

9 To Lewis N. Chase, Robinson characterized "The Tavern" as one of his "purely fanciful sketches, without ethical or symbolical significance." (Ridgely Torrence, editor, *Selected Letters of Edwin Arlington Robinson* [New York, 1940], p. 104.)

"It was reported to Harry Bacon Collamore that about 1910 Robinson told someone that he thought 'The Tavern' was his best poem." (Chard Powers Smith, *Where the Light Falls: A Portrait of Edwin Arlington Robinson* [New York, 1965], p. 340.)

. . / / . .

It must be remembered that Roosevelt's review was based on the 1897 edition of *The Children* which his son Kermit had sent him. The *Outlook* published the critique two months before the second edition was available for distribution, with the dour result of premature publicity foreseen by Robinson. At least four journals of national prominence rushed into print while the 1905 edition was still in the reprint process. They greeted Robinson with mixed temper but inevitably turned up professional critical noses at Roosevelt, as much concerned with his amateur status as with Robinson's esthetic worth. This tempest in a teacup inspired the attention of a wider reading public to a poet previously scanted, though Robinson assessed it more notoriety than honest acclaim.

. . / / . .

With zeal both predictable and excessive, the first publication to deal with this unprecedented presidential blurb was a daily newspaper in Robinson's native Pine Tree State. Clearly overcome with emotion by the phenomenon, it fell into semi-coherent repetition and into the tradition of Maine reporters to call Robinson by his father's name Edward.

Remarkable, remarkable

THE PRESIDENT AS A LITERARY CRITIC

It is indeed remarkable that President Roosevelt finds time amid the multitude of cares and responsibilities[1] which, after all, seem to rest upon him lightly and which he throws off with so much apparent ease, for a wide reading of standard and current literature as was attributed to him in a late number of the *Century* magazine.[2] More remarkable still is the fact that he has found time for the work of a literary critic; but readers of the *Outlook* of Aug. 12, cannot fail to have noticed on page 913, a literary review "By Theodore Roosevelt."[3] This is a two-page article being a review of a little volume of verse, by Edward [sic] Arlington Robinson, entitled, *The Children of the Night*.

How many people in Maine know that this is a Maine book and that its author is a resident of Gardiner?[4] This is what gives the book and its author additional interest and to Maine readers the remarkable thing about it is that President Roosevelt in these most strenuous days finds time to critically read and review a book of poems by a Maine author.

President Roosevelt gives most generous praise to our Maine poet. His work has "the touch of the purple [which] makes a poem out of verse, and if it is not there, there is no substitute." It is true President Roosevelt, our new literary critic, says he is not sure that he understands Mr. Robinson's poem "Luke Havergal," "but I am entirely sure that I like it...."[5]

Bangor *Daily Commercial* (August 12, 1905), 4.

    This paean, published as an editorial, was immediately reprinted by the *Daily Kennebec Journal* of Augusta, Maine, on August 15, p. 6, under the title "The President and a Maine Poet."

1 In addition to the usual frenzies of office, President Roosevelt had arranged a conference of the warring Russian and Japanese nations at the Portsmouth Naval Base in New Hampshire, currently in progress. The peace treaty was signed on August 25.

2 "Remarks on Reading Suggested by a Distinguished Example," in "Topics of the Time," *Century*, LXX (May 1905), 154-155.

3 See preceding review in this volume.

4 Robinson left Gardiner permanently in 1899.

5 Following this statement, the editorialist reprints Roosevelt's aperçus on each of the individual poems, and sums up by quoting all of Roosevelt's third paragraph except the final sentence, which he had already utilized.

    . . / / . .

One of Badger's Boston Bards

CRITICISM BY UKASE

    Under his sign-manual as "President of the United States," Mr. Roosevelt issued through the last *Outlook*[1] a literary ukase bestowing honors on a poet, Mr. E.A. Robinson, who, as he thinks, has never received the attention he merits. Of the quality of this neglected volume, "not verse but poetry," as it is officially described, some notion may be gained by one of the President's quotations.

> *Come away! come away! there is nothing now to cheer us —*
> *Nothing now to comfort us, but love's road home: —*
> *Over there beyond the darkness there's a window gleams to greet us,*
> *And a warm hearth waits for us within.*[2]

    Just why these lines should be denied the status of verse does not appear, unless, indeed, verse is synonymous with rhyme or incompatible with poetry. But there are other mysteries in the critique. Where and what is that "certain sad mysticism" to be found? Is it in "The House on the Hill"? —

> There is ruin and decay
>   In the House on the Hill:
> They are all gone away,
> There is nothing more to say.

No doubt there is sadness in the words, "They are all gone away"; perhaps, too, when you come to think of it, that closing refrain, "There is nothing more to say," carries the mind to the ultimate abyss supposed to lie beyond the beginnings of creation.

But this is trifling with the particular when a question of large and general significance demands consideration. What will be the consequence if our Presidents usurp the authority of critics? These have been a race of pariahs from the beginning, a kind of parasite fattening on the feast of genius. A quaint writer has summed up their infamous reputation: "Ben Jonson spoke of critics as tinkers, who make more faults than they mend; Samuel Butler, as the fierce inquisitors of wit, and as butchers who have no right to sit on a jury; Sir Richard Steele, as of all mortals the silliest; Swift, as dogs, rats, wasps, or, at best, the drones of the learned world; Shenstone, as asses, which, by gnawing vines, first taught the advantage of pruning them; Burns, as cut-throat bandits in the path of fame; Walter Scott, humorously reflecting the general sentiment, as caterpillars." No doubt there is a body of critics in the world to-day, honest enough gentlemen many of them, despite their trade, who will welcome the comfort of such an accession to their ranks as an actual Chief of State. Shall we be called caterpillars any longer? they will exclaim, and fall to at the feast with redoubled vigor. But consider, on the other hand, the great army of original geniuses to whom the very thought of critic is an offence. Mr. Roosevelt has lauded one of Badger's Boston bards[3]; he has thereby given a grievance to the thousands unnamed. And if he praises now, he or his successor may at another time take to the invidious trade of picking flaws. "No," we can hear the hosts of genius cry out, "let us have no caterpillars in the White House!" And, besides the self-interested makers and despoilers of literature, there are a few lovers of fair play who honestly regret to see a person in high authority turn from his course to puff a book mediocre in character and little distinguished from scores of similar volumes put out by a busy press.

This union of political and literary authority in a single man is a dangerous business. An Augustus might foster good taste through his almoners, or a Louis XIV might give his sanction to the wholesome judgments of a Boileau, and evoke thereby a classic method of writing, but the efforts of statemen in recent years have been anything but encouraging. There is, for example, the living Admirable Crichton of the Teutons, whose imperial will would set the genius of Germany to writing plays and painting pictures to celebrate the deeds of the Hohenzollerns.[4] In England, the last century had its Gladstone, whose influence with the masses was far more effective in guiding the whims of popularity than any hereditary throne. A word from him, and *Robert Elsmere*[5] sold by the tens of thousands. It was he who made Amiel almost an English classic, and the sickly vapors of Marie Bashkirtseff were accepted as genius at his say-so.[6] Mr. Roosevelt's position is not unlike Gladstone's in this respect; he shows the same contrast between his practical and literary taste. From preaching the strenuous life in politics he finds it easy to pause long enough to boom the "Simple Life" of another preacher, with the result that the latter's book is hawked about city streets like a yellow journal.⁷ Hence it is not surprising to find him extolling a volume of verse in which he finds "a certain sad mysticism."

Perhaps the most curious thing in the whole affair is that Mr. Roosevelt should have selected a book of verse published as far back as 1897, and which, in the natural course of events (these butterflies of the trade are pathetically short-lived), has been forgotten. He might at least have chosen for our edification a later volume by the same author, which bore the name of *Captain Craig* — writing of a certain piquancy and amorphous originality, at least, and not without significance as an example of what the thoroughly self-satisfied modern taste can accomplish.

From New York *Evening Post* (August 14, 1905), 6.

The *Post*, politically opposed to Roosevelt, offered this carping article unsigned as a regular editorial.

1   See this essay, first in this chapter in this volume.

2   From "The Wilderness," p. 89.

3   Richard G. Badger (1878-1937), born in Roxbury, Massachusetts, founded the Gorham Press in 1894 and conducted it for forty years. He published the magazines *Poet-Lore* and the *Journal of Abnormal Psychology*; Eugene O'Neill's *Thirst and Other One-Act Plays* and of course the first edition of Robinson's *Children*. Badger fed on the vanity of poeticules, issuing their works at their own expense. Some of his "Boston bards," alluded to with undisguised New York City condescension to Boston's pretensions as the Athens of America: Edith M. Thomas, Harriet Prescott Spofford, Clifford Lanier, Mary Ainge deVere, Ethelwyn Wethereld, Madeline Bridges, Roy Farrell Greene, Herman Montague Donner, James Edward Routh, Jr., H. Talbot Kummer, Ellen Brainerd Peck, Hattie Horner Louthan. It should also be added to his credit that he did publish Robinson, Willa Cather, and Edgar Lee Masters.

4   Bernhard von Bulow (1849-1929), a cool, acute diplomat, was currently imperial chancellor to Kaiser William II, last of the Hohenzollerns. Vain, autocratic, hypersensitive of his withered arm, William dreamed of himself as a Crusader. Bulow, "perpetually humbugging him," saw to it that heroic paintings and statues of William in medieval armor were erected, and flattering literary portraits of him published.

5   This novel by Mrs. Humphry Ward questions miracles and other Christian dogmas. William E. Gladstone, four times prime minister, was greatly troubled by the book, expostulated personally to Mrs. Ward, then wrote out his misgivings in "*Robert Elsmere* and the Battle of Belief," *Nineteenth Century*, XXIII (May 1888), 766-788. It had the ironical effect of giving the book extensive publicity.

On this score Roosevelt wrote to Lawrence F. Abbott, July 8, 1907: "a President ought not to do as Gladstone did and take an interest in outside studies of any kind. But it is rather a hard proposition to live up to. For instance, in the *Outlook* I reviewed Robinson's poems because I felt that he merited more consideration than he had received and that my position as President gave the chance to call attention to him." Sententiously, he added: "the by-products of the Presidency are important." (Morison, V, 707.)

6   Henri François Amiel's *Fragments d'un Journal Intime* was published posthumously in 1883, translated two years later with an introduction by Mrs. Ward. Gladstone does not seem to have reviewed this book; his praise may have been recorded from a speech or interview. He did notice "Journal de Marie Bashkirtseff," *Nineteenth Century*, XXVI (October 1889), 602-607, averring that this diary by a sentimental Russian "opens a

new chapter in the experience of human nature. . . . It may even be pronounced a book without a parallel."
  Robinson read Bashkirtseff's *Journal* "but failed to be impressed. Of course it is a wonderful book, considering the age of its author, but there are too many 'O God!s' and 'I love hims.'" (Denham Sutcliffe, editor, *Untriangulated Stars: Letters of Edwin Arlington Robinson to Harry DeForest Smith 1890-1905* [Cambridge, Mass., 1947], p. 5.)

7 Possibly the naturalist John Burroughs (1837-1921), whom Roosevelt included in the party which accompanied him on a trip to Yellowstone Park in April 1903, and which Burroughs chronicled in *Camping and Tramping With Roosevelt* (1906). His current books *Far and Near* and *Ways of Nature*, recounting his love of the adventures in the outdoors, were enjoying brisk sales despite humdrum reviews.

. . / / . .

Thus, the backfire Robinson had nervously envisioned took less than forty-eight hours to transpire. The *Post* editorialist's final laudatory paragraph (one of the brightest on *Captain Craig*) may have been merely a sinistral shot at Roosevelt's deficient taste. In the next notice Robinson is made to bear the brunt of the sarcasm for the President's presumption upon the realm of literary criticism. The writer continues with some rotund reflections on "the perennial discontent with professional critics of literature" brought about by invasion of their preserve by "men out of the craft of letters" — "like," he pounded on, "Mr. Roosevelt and Mr. Gladstone."

Officially accredited poet of the Theodorian era

THE CHILDREN OF THE NIGHT

The President of the United States, in spite of any provision to that effect in our Constitution, has as much right as any private citizen to exercise the function of the critic and commend books in prose and verse to the attention of his fellow-men. Mr. Roosevelt's impulses prompt him to quick action in matters of art and literature as well as in affairs of state. We remember well a letter full of generous appreciation he wrote to one of our poets in the very thick of a heated political campaign. To the lasting credit of the poet let it be said that he never made the letter (which might have been the means of selling many of his books) public property, but keeps it carefully guarded among his private papers. Years hence his literary executor will have it incorporated in his "authorized" biography.[1] The latest subject of the President's literary enthusiasm is Mr. Edwin Arlington Robinson, whose volume of poetry (Mr. Roosevelt objects to calling it "verse") *The Children of the Night*, (published in 1897) he has commended in the *Outlook*. We cheerfully pass along the good word and cordially congratulate Mr. Robinson on his good luck. He is still a young man (in his thirty-sixth year), and will doubtless be encouraged to write many more books of verse for the edification of a people enlightened as to their worth by a Chief Magistrate who is also a popular hero. As for the professional critics who have hitherto failed to recognize the gifts of Mr. Robinson, they have only themselves to blame if they do not now hurry to "get on the band wagon." By the way, for this dropping into the "United States language" in commenting on the commendation of an American poet by an American President, we have no apology to offer. The subject is not one to be dismissed in a few words of effete English.

Doubtless even those American magazines which, with overladen verse galleys, have lately been deliberately discouraging the poets, will be glad enough now to accept Mr. Robinson's poetry and to pay him for it at the highest market rates. It is something now to be a Roosevelt poet, and it will surely be a glory of the future to have been an acknowledged and officially accredited poet of the Theodorian era. We prophesy a fine anthology by some coming Stedman of "The Theodorian Poets."[2] Edwin Arlington Robinson, one of the first of them, was born at Head Tide, Me., in 1869, and is a Harvard man. He lives in this city. Besides *The Children of the Night* he has published *The Torrent and The Night Before* (1896) and *Captain Craig* (1902).

From "Topics Uppermost," New York *Times Saturday Review of Books* (August 19, 1905), VI, 537.

---

[1] Besides the American poets mentioned in his review of Robinson, Roosevelt at one time or another also befriended Charles Hanson Towne, Richard Watson Gilder, John Burroughs, Hermann Hagedorn, Edgar Lee Masters, and Robert Bridges (also an editor at Scribner's). A letter of August 12, 1904 by Roosevelt to Burroughs, saluting him as "Dear Oom John," is printed in Morison, IV, 890.

[2] A punning reference to Edmund Clarence Stedman's *Victorian Poets* (Boston, 1876; reissued 1903), but inaccurate inasmuch as it is a critical review, not an anthology. See note 3 to John A. Macy's review of *Captain Craig*, in this volume.

.. / / ..

Not in the category of popular poets

A MAINE POET

Edwin Arlington Robinson, whose poems have been mentioned in such high favor in the recent issue of one of the large magazines by Theodore Roosevelt, is a Gardiner man, and another to join the rapidly growing list of Gardiner celebrities along with Mrs. Laura E. Richards, John F. Stevens,[1] Miss Kate Vannah, and Dr. Schumann of Farmingdale.

Mr. Robinson was born in the little town of Alna, some 35 years ago, and was the son of Mary Elizabeth Palmer and Edward Robinson. His father was a wealthy man in the days close following the war of '61 — that is, as rich men went in those days. Edwin's parents and their three sons went to Gardiner in 1870 and the family lived in a fine house at the corner of Lincoln avenue and Danforth street in that city. The elder Mr.

Robinson died at Gardiner about 12 years ago, and his widow survived him about five years. Both are buried in the Oak Grove cemetery at Gardiner. Edwin had two brothers — one was Dr. H.D. Robinson, who practiced in Camden, and who died some years ago, and Herman E. Robinson, who up to a short time ago lived in Gardiner.

Mr. Robinson is a graduate of the Gardiner high school and he has always been a deep student of the higher literature. Among the more educated of readers, his poems are quite well known but they are not of a class to be in the category with the "popular poets." Far above these "popular" efforts do the work of Edwin Arlington Robinson soar and so deep, yet finely drawn are his poems that it is almost necessary to translate the thoughts expressed before the meaning is intelligible. The deep appreciation evinced for Robinson's works by President Roosevelt, himself an author of note, is surely a fitting tribute to the skill and talents of our newest, yet not so new, Gardiner genius.

In 1895, Mr. Robinson issued a pamphlet, *The Torrent and The Night Before*, and his collection of poems brought him into some prominence. Two years later, R.G. Badger of Boston published a volume of poems by Mr. Robinson and this book was called *The Children of the Night*. The last book to be issued was published by Houghton, Mifflin & Co., of New York, in 1902, and is called *Capt. Craig, and Other Poems*.

Mr. Robinson is now attached to the special agent's office in the New York department of the Treasury Department, he being appointed there about two months ago by the President.

From "The World of Books," Lewiston *Journal Illustrated Magazine Section* (August 19-23, 1905), 11.

Some of the biographical and bibliographical data here need correction or amendment:
   a) Robinson was not born in the town of Alna but in the adjacent Head Tide.
   b) Robinson's father died July 1892; his mother in November 1896; his brother Horace in September 1899.
   c) *The Torrent* was published in 1896; *The Children* one year later.
   d) The subtitle of *Captain Craig* is *A Book of Poems*.

1 John Frank Stevens (1853-1943), a civil engineer of international stature of whom West Gardiner was justly proud. He made his mark with a number of major railroads in the South, Middlewest, and Canada, executing the extension of the Great Northern to the Pacific coast *through* the Rocky Mountains. He became chief engineer then chairman of the commission to construct the Panama Canal. He was decorated for his foreign services by France, Japan, China, Czechoslovakia, and received the Distinguished Service Medal from the United States.

. . / / . .

Brightest optimism and deepest faith

TOUCH OF GENIUS
A.G. Chase

Edwin[1] Arlington Robinson, of whom President Roosevelt, in the August number of the *Outlook* complimented in highest terms as a poet, is a Gardiner boy.

The article from the pen of the President is entitled "The Children of the Night," and is a pleasant comment on a collection of poems published under that name.

The President is much interested in the book and has taken a great and active interest in the young author, whom he thinks capable of work of the highest class. In him he believes he has found one of the few who — as the President expresses it — understands the "touch of purple that makes a poem out of verse."

He says of the work: "There is an undoubted touch of genius in the poems collected in this volume, and a curious simplicity and good faith, all of which qualities differentiate them sharply from ordinary collections of the kind."

Edwin Arlington Robinson was reared in Gardiner, Me. He was born in Alna, a nearby country town, his parents removing to Gardiner shortly after his birth. He was educated in the public schools of the city, graduating from the high school as poet of his class.

From earliest childhood he was unusually fond of books, always preferring them to the games which attract the average boy. As he grew this passion grew with him until it became the one consuming element of his life.

As is not unfrequently true in the case of genius, his parents did not thoroughly understand the temperament of the boy. They were ambitious for his welfare and his dreamy ways disturbed them.

To please them he attempted to engage in practical lines of business, but each trial proved most unsatisfactory. It was finally decided to educate hm still further, and in the fall of 1891 he entered Harvard to take up a literary line of work.

While in Harvard, his first poem, "Ballade of a Ship," appeared in the *Harvard Lampoon*.

He finished his course in Harvard in the spring of 1894, and his father having died during his second year in the university, he returned to Gardiner, to remain with his mother. The next two years were spent among his books, writing and studying.

In the winter of 1896 the death of his mother occurred. At the time of her death he had already placed a collection of short poems in the hands of publishers, and in December, 1896, shortly after, they came out in pamphlet form under the title, *The Torrent and The Night Before*.

These pamphlets he distributed among his friends and people of prominence in the literary world.

The year following, in December, '97, he published *The Children of the*

Night. This volume, with some additions, is substantially the same as *The Torrent and The Night Before.*

In the year '98 he returned to Harvard to occupy a position in the publishing office. He remained there during the school year, leaving, at its close, for New York City. While in New York in October, 1902, he brought out his *Captain Craig.*

It was in the early summer of the present year that President Roosevelt became interested in him and offered him a position in the Treasury Department of the U.S. Customs Service, Port of New York, where he is at the present time.

Mr. Robinson is of a very retiring nature and dislikes notoriety of any sort. He is not one to make a large circle of friends; he is by nature too retiring, too wrapped up in his world of dreams. He has lived so largely among his books that they have become his friends and comrades.

There is not an element of morbidism in his *The Children of the Night,* and nothing but the brightest optimism and deepest faith breathes from these few lines taken from one of his sonnets:

> Oh, brother men, if you have eyes at all,
> Look at a branch, a bird, a child, a rose, —
> Or anything God ever made that grows, —
> Nor let the smallest vision of it slip,
> Till you can read, as on Belshazzar's wall,
> The glory of eternal partnership![2]

President Roosevelt says: "Mr. Robinson has written in his little volume not verse but poetry."

From Boston *Sunday Globe* (August 20, 1905), 32.

Ambrose G. Chase (1845-1927), of Boston, came to work in Gardiner, Maine, around the time of Robinson's birth as agent for the Eastern Ice Company to oversee the harvesting and distribution of ice from the Kennebec River. He became for a time the Associated Press reporter for Gardiner and vicinity, and city editor of the Gardiner *Reporter-Journal,* resigning in October 1902 to set up a loan, insurance, and investment agency which he maintained for the remainder of his working career.

The inflated subcaption of this pedestrian sketch reads: "President Roosevelt Praises the Poems by Edwin Arlington Robinson — 'He Has Written in His Little Volume Not Verse but Poetry' — Mr. Robinson was Born in Maine, Educated at Harvard, and is Now in New York, Employed in the Customs Service of the Treasury Department."

1 To Chase's credit it must be noted that he was one of the rare Maine newspapermen who gave Robinson his proper first name, despite Roosevelt's own solecism in that regard. Nevertheless, Chase committed a disproportionate number of factual errors inexcusable in the light of his local advantage and Robinson's new-gained prominence:
   a) Robinson was born in Head Tide, not Alna, which is a short way up the Sheepscot River.
   b) Robinson's first published poem was not "Ballade of a Ship"; it was his third. It did not appear in the *Harvard Lampoon* but in the *Harvard Advocate* as "Ballade of the White Ship."
   c) Robinson entered Harvard as a special, nonmatriculating student. He left in June 1893, not "the spring of 1894."
   d) Robinson's father, Edward, died July 15, 1892, before the second school year

started.
   e) Robinson's job at Harvard started in January 1899 and ended in June; he worked in the administrative, not publishing office.
   f) Theodore Roosevelt's interest in Robinson was aroused in November 1904, not the summer of 1905; he made inquiries and wrote to the poet on March 27, 1905.
   g) Chases's quotation from Roosevelt's last paragraph is not strictly accurate, substituting "his" for "this."

2 Sestet from "Sonnet" (When we can all), p. 69.

. . / / . .

Hewing to its function as weekly coordinator of news and views in the world of letters, the *Literary Digest* scanned what had been written and cast some sprightly remarks of its own into the expanding Roosevelt-Robinson polemic. What this popular magazine said is of small importance; that it accorded Robinson so much space and national exposure at this vital juncture is the point.

A certain factitious interest

THE PRESIDENT AS A REVIEWER OF VERSE

Our many-sided Chief Executive appears in a somewhat novel light in a recent book review bearing his signature. His readiness to commend whatever appears to him virile and significant in current literature is no new phase. But his review of Mr. Edward [*sic*] Arlington Robinson's *The Children of the Night,* in the New York *Outlook* (August 12) is probably his first public appearance as the discoverer and revealer of an unappreciated poet. Even the average reader, whose concern with poetry, if we are to heed a plaint which never quite dies into silence, and which proceeds, presumably, from the pens of negelcted versifiers, is of the slightest, may be forgiven at least a certain factitious interest in this little volume which the President describes as containing "not verse but poetry." *The Children of the Night* is one of that numerous company of little books of verse which emerge upon a too indifferent world under the auspices of Mr. Richard Badger of Boston. It was published as far back as 1897, but has not received, according to Mr. Roosevelt, the attention it merits. "The 'twilight of the poets,'" says the august critic, "has been especially gray in America";. . . . [The bulk of Roosevelt's criticism follows, as does most of "The Wilderness."][1]

Just why these lines should be denied the status of verse, remarks an editorial writer in the *Evening Post*,[2] does not appear, unless, indeed, verse is synonymous with rime or incompatible with poetry. The same writer goes on to consider the consequence if our Presidents should usurp the authority of critics. [The long third paragraph follows.]

He comes to the conclusion that this union of political and literary authority in a single man is a dangerous business: [The fourth paragraph follows, omitting only the second sentence.]

From "Letters and Art," *Literary Digest*, XXXI (August 26, 1905), 271-272.

1 See Roosevelt's essay, the first in this chapter in this volume.
2 See this essay, the third in this chapter in this volume.

. . / / . .

In like case, *Current Literature* devoted two pages (388-389) to "The President as a Critic of Poetry" in its October 1905 issue, quoting liberally not only from the *Outlook* and the *Post* but also from the New York Times *Saturday Review of Books* (all reprinted in this volume). Even less consequential than those in the *Literary Digest*, the comments here serve simply as bridges between quotations. As before, the gain for Robinson, though he looked at it askance, lay in the exponential circulation of his name. The irony, now grown mordant through mindless repetition, is that he was again presented as Edward.

In the sector devoted to "Recent Poetry" in this issue of *Current Literature*, the editors saw fit to add this note: "President Roosevelt has time for something else than affairs of State, and in the *Outlook* recently he had an article on the poetry of Edward [sic] Arlington Robinson, in whose work, he thinks 'there is an undoubted touch of genius.' There is something in the following poem certainly that lifts it above the commonplace." Peculiarly, they chose to excerpt in its entirety "Twilight Song" from *Captain Craig* (1902). Edward is repeated in the byline.

. . / / . .

Democratic as Whitman, but not absurd

THE PRESIDENT'S NEW POET

No one will accuse President Roosevelt of having a poetic temperament, and yet any one who has read his books will recall how apposite are the quotations which he prefixes to them, or which he uses in them. He is an omnivorous and acute reader, and is frank in his appreciation of what he likes, often sending for the authors to talk about their books with them. He does this because he likes it.

It is very natural, therefore, that he should say what he thinks of a volume of verse by Edwin Arlington Robinson, published eight years ago, and write a short article about it. Any one who reads the book will discover that the President has put his finger on the best things in it. He has found true poetry there, and has, with good judgment, pointed it out. That is straightforward and fine, but "real critics" would rather sneer at the poetry and poke fun at the President — such is their superior nature.

Mr. Robinson's more recent volume, *Captain Craig*, is more ambitious than *The Children of the Night* — but is not so well weeded out. The title poem has over two thousand lines in blank verse, which has a great deal of the colloquial and intimate quality of some of Browning's longer pieces. There are stretches of commonplace, and islands of didacticism. There is also shrewd philosophy, biting satire, a touch of weirdness, and bits of poetic fancy.

The whole poem reveals the honest philosophy of an intellectual vagabond — a sort of Villon of New England, without his vices; a Maine Socrates with a bit of the laughter of Aristophanes.

At its worst the poem descends to rather bald, uninteresting prose; at its best it has a melody and swing that are alluring even when the meaning is vague.

There is an original point of view in all the poems, a way of looking at life that is half cynical, but altogether earnest where things that count are involved. The poet is something of an Anarchist toward conventional things. He is Democratic as Whitman, but his sense of satire keeps him from being absurd.

This is a good specimen of the verse in "Captain Craig":

> Do you think the golden tone
> Of that far-singing call you all have heard
> Means any more for you than you should be
> Wise-heartedly, glad-heartedly yourselves?
> Do this, there is no more for you to do;
> And you have no dread left, no shame, no scorn.
> And while you have your wisdom and your gold,
> Songs calling, and the Princess in your arms,
> Remember, if you like, from time to time,
> Down yonder where the clouded millions go,
> Your bloody-knuckled scullions are not slaves,
> Your children of Alnaschar are not fools. [p. 68]

From unidentified periodical (n.d.)

.. / / ..

The *Argonaut* took up the refrain in far-off San Francsico. In a note bracketed under the caption "Poems That Roosevelt Praises" the editors observed: "The *Outlook* of August 12th contains an article by President Roosevelt on the poetry of Edward [sic] Arlington Robinson, in whose work, says Mr. Roosevelt, 'there is an undoubted touch of genius.' 'The House on the Hill' is quoted by the President; the other poems here printed he does not specifically mention, but they are characteristic of Mr. Robinson's work." Thereafter the complete text of "The House on the Hill," "Twilight Song," "Erasmus," and "The Sage" is offered. (LVII, August 28, 1905, 158.)

.. / / ..

If Mr. Robinson had been a Canadian

AN APOLOGY FOR OVERLOOKING MR. ROBINSON

If while foraging in the underbrush of current verse a man actually thinks he has discovered some genuine poetry, we cannot see why he should not proclaim the fact, whatever office he may be holding at the time. Hence we missed the fine point of the sarcasms occasioned by President Roosevelt's praise of Mr. Robinson's *The Children of the Night*. There are, of course, many poets of the Robinson degree, but the President is not to blame if he has encountered only one of them. It is well known that he has had a number of other matters on his hands of fully equal importance.[1] Probably he is not even aware of the present poetical situation. Our poetry-shelf, which is about four feet long, is alternately filled and emptied three times a year. Not all the volumes of verse are sent to the newspapers and magazines, but on the average it is safe to say that any literary editor summarises, or assigns for review, or in some way disposes of twelve feet of minor poetry annually. Three-fourths of this is tinged with the "certain, sad mysticism" detected by the President in Mr. Robinson's verse, and one-half of it is almost if not quite Robinsonian in merit. The more anxious one is lest a genius may escape him, the more he will read, and from much reading he will, in spite of himself, grow callous. Hence, cold and routine methods of dealing with the problem have developed in editorial offices.

There are what may be called the spring and fall house-cleanings, when bales containing the verse of several months are shipped to men who are thought to possess richly emotional temperaments. The consignee then reads, one after the other, seventy or eighty volumes of heart's ease and heart's desire, despairs, loves, cradle-songs, moonbeams on the water, and negro lullabies. Numb and bewildered, he picks out six or twelve, according to the length of the article, and for each one mentioned passes over a score with a formal expression of regret that there is no room for them. Hence those strangely chosen groups of poets you find despatched at intervals by reviewers in the *Atlantic Monthly* and elsewhere. Novelists may receive individual attention. Poets are always handled in bulk and reviewed in dozens and half-dozens. A reviewer would as soon think of going off with one minor poet as of buying one egg. From this may be inferred the difficulty of reading the lines quoted by the President with anything like the President's astonishment. Under present conditions that first first fine relish is not for any rhyme-worn veteran, but for the men who are the busiest in other things, for the chance half hours of overworked executives. It is they who make these discoveries. Try as we will to overtake all fugitive verse of fair quality, an occasional Robinson still gets away. With creditable poets arriving in each mail, the thing cannot be prevented.

If Mr. Robinson had been a Canadian, such an oversight could not have occurred. It is likely that a special treatise would be devoted to him by Professor James Cappon of Queens University, Kingston, who is at present engaged on a series of *Studies in Canadian Poetry*. . . .[2]

From "Chronicle and Comment," *Bookman*, XXII (October 1905), 104-105.

The 1905 edition of *The Children* was still not in hand when the cynical critic of the *Bookman* made this two-faced defense of Roosevelt's zeal. The acid of disdain oozing through the facade of tolerance is obviously meant for Roosevelt's foolhardiness, not Robinson's ineptitude. This article is nevertheless valuable for its invidious picture of the actual practice in contemporary magazines and newspapers of lumping together anywhere from six to twenty-six superficial briefings on the contents of the overladen "poetry-shelf." Small wonder that it might take a presidential pronunciamento to winnow out a genuine poet or two.

When the 1905 edition was delivered to the *Bookman*, it was squeezed indistinguishably into a double-column roster of some 300 other titles in "The Book Mart," a Reader's Guide to Books Received, each of which was favored with from one to twenty-three lines of inane description. Robinson's due: "A collection of ballades, sonnets, and other verse on various themes." (XXII, December 1905, 412). Thus the anonymous bookman maintained his professional hauteur. If he was seeking a kind of vengeance on Roosevelt, he clearly achieved it by proxy through Robinson.

1 Roosevelt had urged Japan and Russia to end their armed hostilities. Through his arrangement they came to a peace conference in Portsmouth, New Hampshire, where they concluded a peace treaty.

2 A consideration of Cappon's book on Charles G.D. Roberts follows.

. . / / . .

A clever novice?

THE PRESIDENT'S POETICAL PROTEGE
Robert V. Hardon

Augusta, Maine
October 28, 1905

To the Editor of the *Transcript*:

Much has been written for and against the new poet (yet not so new) whom President Roosevelt has chosen to take up as his especial protégé, for this must be the President's intention, since Edwin Arlington Robinson has a position in the Treasury Department, to which he was appointed by the President last summer. Much has been said, indeed, and possibly my letter is not timely, now that our literary journalists have all had their little fling, one way or another.

It seems to me that Edwin Arlington Robinson is being greatly overrated, and granting that he has shown some talent as a verse maker, is it not quite sufficient to give him the credit of being a clever novice? Why tell this young man that he is the "coming poet laureate of America?" Why not Madison Cawein? Or why not Bliss Carman, or Frank Dempster Sherman, or why not John Vance Cheney?[1]

When one inspects the monumental works thus far produced by Robinson one must wonder wherein lies the "subtle mysticism" or this "faint sweet craftiness" of which Robinson's admirers have spoken. It is possible for the average intelligent reader to distinguish the difference between "subtle mysticism" and incoherency? Mr. Robinson may possibly enjoy a perfect understanding of his own poems, but who can understand "Luke Havergal?"

With such a magnificent appreciation from President Roosevelt, we expect great things from Mr. Robinson — great things. He is now placed in a rather unenviable position. Upon his next effort depends his future, his popular future, at least. Should he "make good" with his next book, and I understand that he has one in preparation, possibly Mr. Robinson will stand elected to the truly great.

From "Letters to the Editor," Boston *Evening Transcript* (October 31, 1905), 8.

1 John Vance Cheney (1848-1922), a lawyer turned librarian, was a lyric poet, a dignified, candid essayist, and a literary critic who published half a dozen books of verse. Conservative in his tastes, he abhorred free verse, distrusted Browning and Whitman. Of *The Torrent and The Night Before* he wrote Robinson: "Although busy to the point of desperation I find . . . I have got to read it. Like Artemus Ward's Tiger, it is 'small but healthy.'" (Sutcliffe, p. 267.)

. . / / . .

After all the preliminary expressions of disapproval and resentment against Roosevelt as literary critic came this first known appraisal of Robinson's book on its own strength, albeit not without a flick at the President in passing.

Imaginative beauty, pulsing with life

THE CHILDREN OF THE NIGHT

A small volume of poems, *The Children of the Night*, by Edwin Arlington Robinson (Charles Scribner's Sons) has had unusual attention drawn to it by President Roosevelt. The latter said: "There is an undoubted touch of genius in the poems collected in this volume, and a curious simplicity and good faith, all of which qualities differentiate them sharply from ordinary collections of the kind. Mr. Robinson has written in this volume, not verse but poetry." This indorsement tends to differentiate them sharply from ordinary collections perhaps more than any qualities which they possess. All the poems, however, show genuine sympathy and keen poetic feeling and the reflection that the old faiths and hopes of man are the only sure consolations of his pilgrimage. Among so many poems enriched by imaginative beauty and pulsing with life, it is with much hesitation that we have chosen the poem, "Dear Friends," to stand for the entire group. [The poem follows.]

From "Books," Boston *Herald* (November 4, 1905), 10.

. . / / . .

Presidential lightning has struck in the right place

THE CHILDREN OF THE NIGHT

President Roosevelt has recently gone out of his way (if such a thing be possible) to recommend the poems of Mr. Edward [sic] Arlington Robinson, and a new edition of *The Children of the Night* (Scribners) is the natural consequence. Lovers of poetry have known the book well enough these many years, and it is now likely to reach the eyes of many of the merely curious whether they love poetry or not.[1] This time the presidential lightning has struck in the right place, for Mr. Robinson's work has never got half the attention it deserved. This volume includes

"The Torrent" and "The Night Before," which poems gave a title to the author's first public venture.

From "Briefer Mention," *Dial*, XXXIX (November 16, 1905), 314.

---

1 This prediction was modestly fulfilled. The reissue at this time was 500 copies, with reprints in 1910, 1914, 1919, and 1921.

.. / / ..

He believes in the now

THE CHILDREN OF THE NIGHT

This is the book of a man whose work President Roosevelt in the hurry of his life has found time to mention with words of hearty praise. Any into whose hands the volume shall come can afford at least to confess that its contents reveal the author's sincerity. We may go farther still, and speak of the beauty of the simplicity of most of the verses, which casts aside the bonds of a smug sedateness with which so many verses are so nicely defined by their poets, and in natural, flowing phrases utters its impressions, its hopes and aspirations. No one poem in the book could better reveal the beauty we speak of, than the following, which is simply called a ["Sonnet" (Oh for a poet) follows.]

Mr. Robinson is one of the few clear-sighted poets of the present hour, the "living present," who hopes for the long-expected singer of new and valiant songs in recognition of the valiant, progressive spirit of the age. Always he believes in the now and its opportunities. He sings:

> We lack the courage to be where we are: —
> We love too much to travel on old roads,
> To triumph on old fields; we love too much
> To consecrate the magic of dead things,
> And yieldingly to linger by long walls
> Of ruin, where the ruinous moonlight
> That sheds a lying glory on old stones
> Befriends us with a wizard's enmity.[1]

The strength and sincerity of his song are always apparent, for he sings naturally and without a thought of imitation, not even imitating any individual of a "new school."

> To get at the eternal strength of things
> And fearlessly to make strong songs of it,
> Is, to my mind, the mission of that man
> The world would call a poet. He may sing
> But roughly, and withal ungraciously;
> But if he touch to life the one right chord
> Wherein God's music slumbers, and awake
> To truth one drowsed ambition, he sings well.[2]

With deft fingers, guided by a keen comprehensive thought observation, he draws, in poems, many pictures of places and people that thrill us in our immediate and happy recognition of them as beloved familiars. Is not this a city we know, with its progress and its traditions? ["Boston" follows.][3]

Though most of the verses are written in sonnets and octaves, we easily forget the rhymer's bonds in the joy of the poet's free and inspiring interpretations.

From "Books of the Day," Boston *Evening Transcript* (November 25, 1905), III, 4.

1   "Octaves" XVII, p. 107.
2   "Octaves" I, p. 91.
3   Robinson converts this sonnet from *The Children of the Night* (1897) into a rhymed octave. On page 51 of the 1905 edition the sestet which followed these eight lines is omitted.
  "I was referred to the other evening, here in Cambridge, as a fellow who wrote 'a corking good thing on a man who shot himself ["Richard Cory"], and a rotten sonnet on Boston.'" (Cary, p. 89.)

. . / / . .

Little tendency to echo poets of a larger gift

THE CHILDREN OF THE NIGHT

It is not difficult in reading Mr. Robinson's poems[1] to understand their successful appeal to President Roosevelt. There is in them, as he has said, "a curious simplicity and good faith," mingled with a strong feeling that sometimes struggles unsuccessfully to find the right rhythmical channels through which to flow. They are nearly always individual, and show little tendency to echo poets of a larger gift which too often is the hallmark of the minor poet. The mood is usually serious, and quite removed from the too sweet and pensive sadness of one who invokes grief as a becoming adjunct to his verse. The melancholy that is present is essentially that of sturdy middle age inevitably connected with the reflective years, but not without the tonic suggestion of time left and strength for action. The numerous poems of religious feeling are the product of a wholesome faith, and are free from conventionalities of wording. "The Dead Village" is characteristic of its author's mental attitude and mode of expression: [The poem follows.]

From "Recent Poetry," New York *Times Saturday Review of Books* (November 25, 1905), VI, 798.

1   The *Times* joins the gallery of malefactors upon Robinson's first name, rendering him as Edward in the table of contents on page 793, at the foot of this review, and in the *Index* volume. Switching to error by omission, it truncates him to Arlington Robinson in the subhead of the review.

. . / / . .

Sympathy is the dominant element

THE CHILDREN OF THE NIGHT

Sympathy is the dominant element in *The Children of the Night* (Charles Scribner's Sons), a little volume of poems by Mr. Edwin Arlington Robinson. It appears, indeed, in rather unusual measure for the work of a writer as keenly interested as Mr. Robinson is in technical forms. Quatrains, ballades, sonnets, and even a villanelle, are printed in this volume, and they are all deftly turned. This is the more creditable to Mr. Robinson, inasmuch as verbal felicity, so apt to be the first aim of the assiduous technician, is not one of his salient merits. On the contrary, he can begin one of his verses with the astonishing line: "Tumultuously void of a clean scheme."[1] But more often he says what he has to say smoothly and agreeably, as thus: ["An Old Story" follows.]

Mr. Robinson is interested in books as well as in life, and several of his best verses are on literary themes. A point of view which ought to be shared by every one, but is, as a matter of fact, none too common, is well expressed in the following sonnet: ["Verlaine" follows.]

Without accepting Mr. Robinson's conception of Verlaine as a "star," we may nevertheless appreciate his fling at the "long-clawed scavengers."[2]

From "Literary News and Criticism," New York *Daily Tribune* (November 30, 1905), 5.

1 "Octaves" IV, p. 94.

2 The first line of "Verlaine": "Why do you dig like long-clawed scavengers"; the last: "Can blot the star that shines on Paris now."

. . / / . .

The *Book Buyer* for December 1905 (XXX, 105) displayed exceptional admiration for "Mr. Robinson's Poetry," but not enough ingenuity to present its own analysis. "Mr. Roosevelt," it observed briefly, "found time, in spite of the pressure of the great affairs in which he is engaged, not only to read a volume of modern poetry, but also to write an appreciation of it. That distinguished appreciation of it has helped attract attention to Edward [sic] Arlington Robinson's volume of poetry, *The Children of the Night*, which most thoroughly deserved to be read on its own account. What Mr. Roosevelt said about these poems in the *Outlook* is well worth repeating."

Hereupon it quotes the third and the final paragraphs of his review, concluding: "It is not often a book of poems receives so interesting an endorsement, or deserves it so entirely."

. . / / . .

Think twice before applying the word "genius"

THE CHILDREN OF THE NIGHT

President Roosevelt has praised this book of poems, finding in them an "undoubted touch of genius." To this fact, no doubt, is due the reprinting of a little book now eight years old. We do not dispute the President's dictum; but we suspect that he has not kept *au courant* with the flood of American minor verse. Had he done so, he would think twice before applying the word "genius" to Mr. Robinson, notwithstanding the author's "curious simplicity and good faith."

From "The Book-Buyers Guide," *Critic*, XLVII (December 1905), 584.

. . / / . .

Greek clarity and saneness of vision

THE YOUNGER POETS OF NEW ENGLAND
Joseph Lewis French

. . . Edwin Arlington Robinson of Gardiner, Maine, is a Greek, nurtured in the New England tradition, and because he was born and grew up away off in a little isolated, inconsequential town of Maine, where he was free to obey the heavenly vision, he is more nearly a Greek than any singer of note whom we have amongst us today. His best work has always the dignity, the calm, the stateliness, that is Greece in the echo. He could not have achieved it amidst the roar and bustle of the cities, — perhaps other men could, — but other men in his time have not been born to dispute his particular laurel. To the fortunate circumstance that a youth with a poetic vision lived in a primitive Maine town, we owe some of the most flawless verse of recent years in American poetry. The point of view is the New England tradition but the note is the note of the old Greek masters. The voice is Jacob's, though the hands be Esau's. The lyrics that make up *The Children of the Night*, the thin volume that President Roosevelt has lately praised so highly, few though they are and slight in quality though many of them be, are yet a quite sufficient capital to set up a new poet in these times. The note is original and striking, — the frank, naked, democratic view of life is the inheritance of the Puritan ideal. No man has struck it with quite the same union of simplicity and force, and we must again thank the Greek clarity and saneness of his vision. It is the fulfillment of the Christian ideal as nourished by generations of New England thinkers, the stern law of personal accountability, united to the large charity of the Golden Rule, the intimate precept that God is Love, that Mr. Robinson preaches to us. No man, not even the men of the morning, Bryant, and the great names who followed him, has done it any better. In several of the pieces in *The Children of the Night* the Maine bard puts in perhaps an equal bid for immortality. Sympathy and conscience are the twin lenses through which he views life and mankind, and either note is found continually recurrent.

For pure artistry, Mr. Robinson cares a very great deal. Some of his work, in the earliest volume, seems cast in the mold of flawless authority. But for life and his fellow-men he cares a good deal more, and this is the ichor that makes a poet of him.

In "Captain Craig," a poem of sixteen hundred lines[1] published several years later, he attempts to amplify and extend his philosophy of life. In the meantime, however, the dreamy Maine boy, surrounded by the simple elemental forces that molded the clarity of the vision that gave us *The Children of the Night,* has gone to the great city, — first to Boston and then to New York. The impact of a complex, hustling, changing civilization (we find a prophecy of its influence in the sonnet, "Boston," written when he first came to the city, some eight years ago)[2] of necessity has impaired his note. In "Captain Craig" he endeavors to construct an epic picture of current civilization and the result is but too sad in many passages. The characters will not for an instant bear comparison with the strong, not to be forgotten portraits he gave us in "Aaron Stark," Richard Cory," "The Clerks,"[3] and others in the earlier volumes. These were intimate, first-hand studies with the breath of life in them that came as a fresh surprise to current readers of poetry. The muse becomes amorphous in "Captain Craig"; the canvas is now blurred and mean; now overloaded with detail. Still the central figure breathes the strong spirit of much of his earlier work, and while we cannot accept him as wholly human, we somehow pity him, sympathize with, and admire him. The other poems that make the second book[4] are for the most part extensions of his early New England studies. What the future has in store for Mr. Robinson, one of the very few genuine poets that New England has produced within the generation, and in his stark affinity with the soil and tradition perhaps the most important of them all, we do not know. He is very much in earnest, and he has "the aloofness of genius" in full measure. His life is lived very much alone, and from a personal acquaintance with him of half a dozen years, we affirm that we have never known a man who held himself so consecrated to his mission. He seems to be a poet, first and last and literally, nothing else. Had he not early given assured utterance to his inspiration it would have indeed been very difficult to account for him. With the native frankness and simplicity of his first tradition, he still follows the poet's path and lives the poet's life, and it is therefore more than reasonable with his ripening years to expect a greater profundity of utterance than he has yet given us.

From *New England Magazine,* XXXIII (December 1905), 425-426.

This segment is extracted from French's overview, whose thesis, summarized just before and after this examination of Robinson, is: a) "In a day when the lack of poetical inspiration appears to be a certain cause of at least subsidiary clamor, it is well to call immediate attention to the work of certain of our New England singers, in whom youth seems to vie with genius for the continuance of the sacred tradition of song"; b) "We have now among us in America, a band of young singers, including those here noticed, who are quite capable of not only sustaining, but advancing the traditions of the bay . . . at least a dozen bards now living in America who are the present-day peers of song of the English-speaking race." (pp. 424, 428.) The other poets discussed at comparable length are Frederic Lawrence Knowles, Josephine Preston Peabody, and William Stanley Braithwaite.

1 In the 1902 edition "Captain Craig" runs 2026 lines.

2 Robinson first went to Boston in the fall of 1891 to attend Harvard College. "Boston" was published in the Boston *Evening Transcript* on October 8, 1896.

3 French wrote "Richard Corey" and "The Twin Clerks," corrected here to preclude perpetuation of error.

4 Although French speaks of "earlier volumes" in this paragraph, he does not make it clear that he remembers *The Torrent and The Night Before* (which he mentioned in his 1904 *World Magazine* article), and that *Captain Craig* is actually Robinson's third book.

. . / / . .

On page 11 of her *A Bibliography of the Writings and Criticisms of Edwin Arlington Robinson* (Boston, 1937), Lillian Lippincott quotes the following as from the *Bookman*: "The book is a series of small-town sketches of small-town people and small-town places." A search of the *Bookman* following all known reprints of *The Children of the Night* failed to turn up the source of this comment. *Bookman* acknowledged receiving a copy of *The Children* in February 1898 (VI, 572) and in December 1905 (XXII, 412) but no subsequent notice of either was found.

. . / / . .

Poetry of a high order

THE POEMS OF EDWIN ROBINSON
Mowry Saben

There appeared in 1896 a thin little volume of poems with a paper back, entitled, *The Torrent and The Night Before*. The little volume had been printed, at the author's expense, and its distribution was provocative of expense rather than financial returns. The next year saw a more dignified edition of the work with various additions and some omissions, which now took the name of *The Children of the Night*. Its author was a young man quite unknown to fame except among his friends by the name of Edwin Arlington Robinson. The little volume was highly praised by a few discerning critics, but fell flat so far as the general public was concerned. A recent word of significant praise from Mr. Roosevelt has called attention to the volume, and a new edition has been brought out by the Scribners.

It would be very difficult to analyze adequately the little volume in the short space of an editorial article, and the book is a difficult one to analyze, anyway. There is something very unique about these poems, they are far removed from the conventional verse of our time. During Mr. Robinson's student days at Harvard he was a great admirer of such poets as Swinburne and Rossetti,[1] but little trace of their influence may be found here except in a few of the earlier poems, two or three of which appeared originally in the *Harvard Advocate*.[2] There is also a fine spirit of humanitarianism in many of the poems which has come as a later endowment, for while Mr. Robinson was always a warm hearted friend, he was afflicted during his student days with a kind of aristocratic aloofness, which made him somewhat oblivious to the common virtues of people. The *odi profanum vulgus* of the Roman poet, Horace,[3] was distinctly felt if never uttered, and the gospel of culture as preached by Matthew Arnold found in him a strong disciple.

Nevertheless, Mr. Robinson has evolved into a democrat, and to-day, in reading his poems, one is fully convinced that there is no mode of thought or human emotion with which he is unable to sympathize. How much Mr. Robinson's democracy is due to the widening of his culture, how much is due to actual experience of life might be difficult to determine, but the main thing is that this spirit has come to him. In reading these poems one perceives at once a breadth of view which loses nothing of its force, but gains force rather, from the distinct individuality of it. A man may be a democrat without looking at things from the eyes of a mob, in fact, the greatest democrats without exception have been men of the largest individuality. To see men as they really are, it is always necessary to see them as they think they are not. Walt Whitman sang a democratic gospel such as the ages never heard before, but for the reason that it was democracy, the very life-giving principle for which democracy stands in America and abroad, people blinked and rubbed their eyes, and then turned to the poets of the more aristocratic temper.

In the poems of Edwin Robinson there is much absent which readers of verse usually expect to find in present day versifying. There is a wholesale love for men and women everywhere found in these poems, but the common Jack and Jill affection, which is the theme of so many writers who know apparently no other, is conspicuous only through its absence. Not that Mr. Robinson is oblivious of the affection of man for woman or woman for man, the reality of this affection is known to him, and how much meaning may dwell in it will be found in his little poem entitled, "Her Eyes," but he never makes the sentiment unduly prominent as so many of our writers do. The world of Mr. Robinson's little volume is a big world, in which everything is significant from the leaves of autumn to the inner light, that lighteth every man who cometh into the domain of flesh.

There is something Platonic[4] about *The Children of the Night*. One may begin to read a poem in which every object described is commonplace, and yet find after reading a few lines that he is in the world where shines "the light that never was on sea or land."[5] To many indeed Mr. Robinson's world will seem as unreal as the world of Spenser's *Faerie Queene*.[6] But the reality will slowly grow with successive readings of the poems and with experience. Mr. Robinson has seen much in everyday life and everyday things which escapes the eyes of most of us, that is all. Some of these poems which seemed to the writer entirely meaningless eight years ago are as clear as crystal to-day. Others are not, but that they have a profound meaning he cannot doubt.

The surest mark of genius that any book can have is found in the fact that in successive readings one always finds something new. A book which is not worth reading again and again is not worth reading at all. *The Children of the Night* will amply repay frequent perusal. The simplest piece therein is not so simple as it seems, and in many a line, or collection of lines, there is a depth of meaning that may not be evident for a long time. One may not read this volume on the run or with a mind perturbed with a hundred cares. The shallow and frivolous will quickly throw the book aside, for it is not for such, but the man or woman alive to the mystery which lies as a background behind every object, and dwells in all things, will linger long and tenderly over many a line which will be found to have a haunting persistency.

Two or three years ago Mr. Robinson brought out a somewhat larger volume called *Captain Craig; A Book of Poems*. In this later volume our poet has grown more mystical. Still, it will be found to possess a charm for all who have enjoyed the first, and to some it seems the deeper book of the two. Whatever Mr. Robinson writes is poetry, and though it may be impossible to translate this poetry into prose, that is no defect. No poetry can be translated into prose. Homer's *Iliad*[7] in the most literal translation is still poetry, only much of its poetry has been lost. Perhaps, as Carlyle thought, whatever can be written in prose should be.[8] Mr. Robinson's deepest thought could have been expressed in no other way than the one he has chosen to express it. His verse is poetry of a high order.

From Denver *Republican* (December 3, 1905), 14.

Mowry Saben (1870-1950), by inclination intellectual, by profession journalist, attended Harvard the same academic years as Robinson, 1891-1893. As flamboyant as Robinson was reticent, Saben's offbeat personality and learning nevertheless appealed to Robinson and they maintained correspondence until Robinson died. For details of their long relationship see Sutcliffe, *passim*, and Richard Cary, "Mowry Saben About Edwin Arlington Robinson," *Colby Library Quarterly*, IX (March 1972), 482-497.

This critique appeared on the editorial page, unsigned. Aside from the internal evidence of friendship at Harvard which establishes the author of the piece, Saben acknowledged it as his in three letters to Howard G. Schmitt, first on July 8, 1939: "[I] wrote a column article on Robinson's work for a newspaper in Denver with which I was connected in 1905-6"; and again on August 18, when he remarked that Robinson "was very much pleased with it at the time." Saben saw Robinson only once between 1893 and 1906, in the company of Lawrence Henderson who later became a professor of biological chemistry at Harvard. Saben tells this story of the meeting to Schmitt (October 13, 1940): "Robinson then showed me a column editorial on him that appeared in the Denver *Republican*, saying that it was one of the very best things that had been written of his work, and he was wondering if I could tell him who wrote it. He would like, he said, to write the author of it and thank him. I told him that I knew who wrote it, and that I was probably better acquainted with the man than anybody else. Robinson demanded to know his name at once, and 'Chug' Henderson began to chuckle. He wanted to know if Robinson was blind. Well, he was, and he could hardly speak when I told him that it was I who wrote it, and that I was still on the editorial staff of the paper."

1   Robinson expressed his admiration of Dante Gabriel Rossetti in a letter to Harry

Smith on April 15, 1894, after reading Thomas B. Mosher's edition of *Old World Lyrics*: "But how Rossetti does beat them [John Payne and Andrew Lang] in his 'Ballade of Dead Ladies.' He seems to keep up the old French spirit without Payne's archaisms." (Sutcliffe, pp. 142-143.) In the *Harvard Advocate* of October 16, 1891 Robinson published "Ballade of the White Ship," having the same plot as Rossetti's "The White Ship" — a king's son and daughter drowned in shipwreck. Rossetti's poem is contained in his *Ballades and Sonnets* (1882); Robinson's copy, signed and dated November 19, 1891, is in Colby College Library. By 1898 Robinson had tempered his regard of Rossetti, telling Edith Brower, "I have only to say that I cannot bring myself to call him really great, though some of his sonnets are marvels of technique." (Cary, p. 82.) In the same letter he admits that "The Night Before" was "partly suggested by Rossetti's "A Last Confession." Indeed, "The Ballade of Dead Friends," "Luke Havergal," and Killigrew's parodic ballad in "Captain Craig" all owe something to Rossetti. In "Captain Craig" (1902, p. 50) Robinson wrote: "But what is wrong with Mr. Killigrew? / Is he in love, or has he read Rossetti?"

2 During his two years at Harvard Robinson published five poems in the *Advocate*: "Ballade of the White Ship," "Villanelle of Change," "In Harvard 5," "Menoetes," "Supremacy."

3 The quotation is from *The Odes*, Book III, Ode I, "A Chorus of Virgins and Youths."

After graduation from Gardiner High School in 1888 Robinson returned for an additional year during which he studied Horace and Milton. One result was "Horace and Leuconoë," a sonnet translation of Ode XI in Book I. Among Robinson's books at Colby College is a copy of Horace's *Works*, signed and dated April 30, 1890, and a second set was also available to him in the Gardiner home. Even before his first book was published, Robinson became an advocate of "Horace's advice to 'keep your piece nine years.'" (Sutcliffe, pp. 170-171.)

4 Robinson reports sitting up "until midnight reading Plato's *Apologia*" and Kipling's *Barrack-Room Ballads* (Sutcliffe, p. 70) and he informs Harry Smith that he must look into the idealist point of view on Nirvana and Heaven "before you make anything out of Plato." (p. 274.) Not until *Talifer* (1933) did Robinson put Plato in one of his poems, and then as one of several "offensive and irrelevant" intellects.

5 From stanza 4 of Wordsworth's poem "Suggested by a Picture of Peele Castle in a Storm."

6 In an unpublished letter of July 14, 1932 Robinson tells Craven Langstroth Betts that he has been avoiding *The Faerie Queene* for sixty-two years, "and there is no reason to believe that he ever read it." (Edwin S. Fussell, *Edwin Arlington Robinson: The Literary Background of a Traditional Poet* [Berkeley, 1954], p. 55.) There is no allusion to Spenser in Robinson's poems.

7 Harry DeForest Smith presented Robinson with Homer's *Works* on April 1, 1894, but Alexander Pope's translation of the *Iliad* and the *Odyssey* was available in the Gardiner home before then. Robinson utilized Homeric legend in "Isaac and Archibald," and made frequent allusion to Achilles, Agamemnon, Ajax, Antinous, the Cyclops, Ilion, Troy, Ulysses, and others in his poems.

8 Evidently a paraphrase of this passage from "The Hero as Poet" in Thomas Carlyle's *Heroes and Hero-Worship*: "whatsoever is not sung is properly no Poem, but a piece of Prose cramped into jingling lines, . . . What we want to get at is the *thought* the man had, if he had any; why should he twist it into jingle, if he *could* speak it out plainly? . . . I would advise all men who *can* speak their thought, not to sing it."

. . / / . .

THE CHILDREN OF THE NIGHT (1905)

Unusually good, especially the quatrains

WITH THE POETS

These are poems which the President says contain an undoubted touch of genius, a curious simplicity and good faith. The verses are unusually good, especially the quatrains, as this:

> As long as Fame's imperious music rings
>   Will poets mock it with crowned words august;
> And haggard men will clamber to be kings
>   As long as Glory weighs itself in dust.[1]

From "Books and Their Writers," Louisville *Courier-Journal* (December 9, 1905), 5.

1 "Three Quatrains" I, p. 13.

. . / / . .

A thread of what is called genius

THE CHILDREN OF THE NIGHT

In a little book of poems, *The Children of the Night,* issued by Charles Scribner's Sons, New York, Edwin Arlington Robinson sings in a pessimistic strain for the most part, although here and there he voices the faith and hope which must sustain every man who fights the battle of life. The poems are not equal in merit, but through them all runs a thread of what is called genius, a thread which is especially bright in the sonnet on "The Garden," in another on "Love,"[1] and in a poem called "The Night Before." In the last a man expecting to suffer the death penalty on the morrow opens his soul to one who had endeavored to give him hope and comfort. Possibly the key to the contents of the little volume may best be found in the following octave:

> To get at the eternal strength of things,
> And fearlessly to make strong songs of it,
> Is, to my mind, the mission of that man
> The world would call a poet. He may sing
> But roughly, and withal ungraciously;
> But if he touch to life the one right chord
> Wherein God's music slumbers, and awake
> To truth one drowsed ambition, he sings well.[2]

From "New Books," Milwaukee *Evening Wisconsin* (December 16, 1905), 6.

1 Evidently "Sonnet," p. 69: "When we can all so excellently give / The measure of love's wisdom with a blow."

2 "Octaves" I, p. 91.

. . / / . .

True, ringing true, and terribly right

PRESIDENT ROOSEVELT'S DISCOVERY

Unadulterated enthusiasm, considerable strength, and rather impetuous disregard for the conventional beauties of form, distinguish Edwin Arlington Robinson's *The Children of the Night*. We would whole-heartedly applaud the said impetuous disregard for the conventional, if we could find that Mr. Robinson has substituted, successfully, a newer, higher beauty. We do applaud his idea, which is striking root in every individual, to the effect that not the old order of poetry, but, assuredly, what modern degeneration assumes to be the old order, changes, and must yield place to new.

It is unquestionably because Mr. Robinson shows himself to be a diligent seeker after truth, and tries to build up his poetry upon the real and inexhaustible humanities of life, that he has deservedly won favor with President Roosevelt.

To prove this, here is a quotation, taken at random, from *The Children of the Night*. It is the sextet of a sonnet on George Crabbe:

> Whether or not we read him, we can feel
> From time to time the vigor of his name
> Against us like a finger for the shame
> And emptiness of what our souls reveal
> In books that are as altars where we kneel
> To consecrate the flicker, not the flame.

That is true, ringing true, and terribly right.

From "Recent Volumes of Verse and Plays," *Argonaut*, LVII (December 18, 1905), 488.

. . / / . .

His way of coining musical and suggestive names

THE CHILDREN OF THE NIGHT

Ferris Greenslet

Though not escaping the calamities of injudicious praise, the new edition of Mr. Edwin Arlington Robinson's *The Children of the Night* (Scribner's) is a very pleasant little book. No minor poet of the day is less indebted to poetic conventionalisms than Mr. Robinson, or more securely himself. His literary obligations are for impulses not for patterns, and always in wholesome quarters — witness this fine sonnet on Crabbe: ["George Crabbe" follows.]

One of the most characteristic and striking of Mr. Robinson's gifts is his way of coining musical and suggestive names[1] for his poetic characters — Luke Havergal, John Evereldown, Richard Cory, Aaron Stark, Cliff Klingenhagen, Fleming Helphenstine, Reuben Bright — each is a perfect symbol and almost a poem in itself, and they cling potently to the memory. Something of the same haunting individuality pervades all of Mr. Robinson's work, and makes it even when least poetic, of a curious vividness.

From "Recent Poetry," *Nation*, LXXXI (December 21, 1905), 507.

Ferris Greenslet (1875-1959), biographer of Walter Pater, James Russell Lowell, and Thomas Bailey Aldrich, was an associate editor of the *Atlantic Monthly* from 1902 to 1907, thereafter literary adviser and editor in chief at Houghton Mifflin Company.

1 See the section *Nomen Est Omen* in the chapter "Preliminary Vistas" of this volume.

. . / / . .

The magic touch of the Muse

THE CHILDREN OF THE NIGHT

President Roosevelt's favorable comment on this small volume of verse has directed public notice to it and aided the undiscerning to discover its beauties. Mr. Robinson really seems to have felt the magic touch of the Muse, and some of these verses make direct appeal to the heart. There are many good lines, tender and sincere sentiment and earnest feeling, so that the lover of poetry should not pass them by.

From "Among the New Books," Detroit *Free Press* (December 23, 1905), 9.

. . / / . .

The potency of the Roosevelt name carried Robinson into "The New Books" department of the American monthly *Review of Reviews*, XXXIII (January 1906), 122. Troweled in among threescore other digest notices and elbowed to the left by a photograph of Ethna Carberry (Anna MacManus), whose book enjoys twice the space given Robinson's, are Roosevelt's now unavoidable endorsements — "an undoubted touch of genius" and "not verse but poetry." The *Review's* total original contribution: "*The Children of the Night* shows real poetic insight and a fine touch."

. . / / . .

We call renewed attention

THE CHILDREN OF THE NIGHT
John B. Henneman

Mr. Robinson's *Book of Poems* has received a new edition, seemingly due to President Roosevelt's recent discovery of this "new" poet. Most of the contents, here rearranged, was virtually published before in 1896 and 1897,[1] being privately printed by the Riverside Press for the author, who lived in Gardiner, Maine. *The Torrent and The Night Before*, as the volume was then called, from its first and last poems, was reviewed at some length in the *Sewanee Review* for April, 1897,[2] nearly nine years ago, where the merits of many of these poems were then pointed out, and the author praised for "a knowledge of the technique of his art and a love for it."[3] The poem which now gives the title to this present volume, "The Children of the Night," was expressly singled out in that review, and many of the sonnets were praised, especially those to Matthew Arnold, Crabbe, Hood, Thomas Hardy, Verlaine, and "Horace to Leuconoë." We call renewed attention to the reissue of these poems and to the discriminating review of them at the time.

From "Reviews: Poetry," *Sewanee Review*, XIV (January 1906), 111-112.

John Bell Henneman (1864-1908), Shakespearian scholar and commentator on the history and literature of the South, was a professor of English at the University of the South and successor to William Peterfield Trent as editor of the *Sewanee Review*, 1901-1908.

1 Henneman's statement here may mislead. The contents of the 1896 *Torrent* are rearranged (and supplemented) in the 1897 *Children*. The 1905 *Children* is identical to the 1897 edition except for the omission of the sestet from the sonnet "Boston."

2 William Peterfield Trent did review *The Torrent* in April 1897 but he also reviewed *The Children* in April 1898, a fact that escaped Henneman. See both reviews in this volume.

3 Trent wrote: "an obvious love for it."

. . / / . .

Among the virile poets of our time

THE CHILDREN OF THE NIGHT

Lillian Kendrick Byrn

An impetuous disregard for the limitations imposed by conventional beauties of form, boundless enthusiasm and considerable strength characterize Mr. Robinson's work in this volume of poems. He shows himself a diligent seeker after truth, and treats of the real and inexhaustible humanities of life.[1] The forceful quality of Mr. Robinson's work assures him of a high place among the virile poets of our time.

From "Books and Authors," *Bob Taylor's Magazine*, III (April 1906), 116.

1 Note the deadly parallel between the preceding two sentences and the *Argonaut* review of December 18, 1905.

. . / / . .

Shining paraphernalia of the inner life

THREE AMERICAN POETS OF TO-DAY
May Sinclair

... Mr. Robinson is a poet of another world and another spirit. His poems fall into three groups: lyrics, — including ballads and old ballade forms, — character sketches, and psychological dramas, poems dramatic in everything except form. It is, in fact, difficult to name these dramas that cannot be played, these songs that cannot possibly be sung. But the point of view is dramatic, the emotion lyric. In his songs (since songs they must be called) he has reduced simplicity to its last expression. Take this one, "The House on the Hill": [The poem follows.]

Or "Cortège": [The poem follows.]

He has given us characters drawn to the life in the fourteen lines of a sonnet: ["Aaron Stark" follows.]

He tells a story in four stanzas: ["Richard Cory" follows.]

In some of his shorter poems ("Sainte-Nitouche," and "As a World Would Have It") he has pressed allusiveness and simplicity to the verge of vagueness. In his longer psychological dramas — for they are dramas in all save form — he is a little too analytically diffuse. In all he has rendered human thought and human emotion with a force and delicacy which proves him a master of this form. For imaginative insight, subtlety, and emotional volume, "The Night Before" may stand beside Browning's *A Soul's Tragedy* and Meredith's *Modern Love*[1]; and "The Book of Annandale"[2] will stand alone, though in a lower place, in its burning analysis of the conflict between scruple and desire. Quotation would give no idea of the spirit of this poem. It is woven all of one piece, and its strength lies in its profound human quality rather than in the force of single passages. Mr. Robinson has few purple patches; he works solidly and sombrely, often in gray on gray.

He has the great gift of spiritual imagination, and an unerring skill in disentangling the slender threads of thought and motive and emotion. All these qualities are conspicuous in the long blank verse poem "Captain Craig," which gives its title to Mr. Robinson's first volume, published in 1903.[3] At a first glance there is little charm about this severely undecorated poem, written in unmusical and often monotonous blank verse, shot with darts of intellectual brilliance, but unrelieved by any sensuous coloring. The charm grows in the reading. "Captain Craig" is a philosophy of life, taught through the humorous lips of a social derelict, a beggared Socrates, disreputable as the world counts reputation. It is a drama of the Unapparent, revealing the divine soul hidden in the starved body of that "sequestered parasite"; a soul that had the courage to be itself, abiding in its dream, facing the world as a superb failure: —

> He had lived his life,
> And he had shared, with all of humankind,
> Inveterate leave to fashion of himself,

> By some resplendent metamorphosis,
> Whatever he was not. [p. 1]

He finds, at last, his audience: —

> The Captain had one chair;
> And on the bottom of it, like a king,
> For longer time than I dare chronicle,
> Sat with an ancient ease and eulogized
> His opportunity. My friends got out,
> Like brokers out of Arcady; but I —
> May be for fascination of the thing,
> Or may be for the larger humor if it —
> Stayed listening, unwearied and unstung. [p. 4]

The Captain's religion is a protest against the sin of "accidia." He, ragged, old, and starved, challenges his friends to have courage and to rejoice in the sun: —

> There is no servitude so fraudulent
> As of a sun-shut mind; [p. 80]

He tells a story of a man he once knew, his fellow in failure, who dreamed that he was Aeschylus, reborn

> To clutch, combine, compensate, and adjust
> The plunging and unfathomable chorus
> Wherein we catch, like a bacchanale through thunder,
> The chanting of the new Eumenides,
> Implacable, renascent, farcical,
> Triumphant, and American. He did it,
> But he did it in a dream. When he awoke
> One phrase of it remained; one verse of it
> Went singing through the remnant of his life
> Like a bag-pipe through a mad-house. — He died young,
> And the more I ponder the small history
> That I have gleaned of him by scattered roads,
> The more do I rejoice that he died young.
> That measure would have chased him all his days,
> Defeated him, deposed him, wasted him,
> And shrewdly ruined him — though in that ruin
> There would have lived, as always it has lived,
> In ruin as in failure, the supreme
> Fulfillment unexpressed, the rhythm of God
> That beats unheard through songs of shattered men
> Who dream but cannot sound it. — He declined,
> From all that I have ever learned of him,
> With absolute good-humor. No complaint,
> No groaning at the burden which is light,
> No brain-waste of impatience — 'Never mind,'
> He whispered, 'for I might have written Odes.' [pp. 45-46]

This poem is now a challenge to the fight of faith in the unseen, now a sequence of austere moralizings, now a blaze of epigrams, and again it drops into the plainest prose. Here and there are concrete touches that paint the man: —

> I stood before him and held out my hand,
> He took it, pressed it; and I felt again

> The sick soft closing on it. He would not
> Let go, but lay there, looking up to me
> With eyes that had a sheen of water on them
> And a faint wet spark within them. So he clung
> Tenaciously, with fingers icy warm,
> And eyes too full to keep the sheen unbroken
> I looked at him. The fingers closed hard once,
> And then fell down. — I should have left him then. [p. 54]

Captain Craig is portrayed in all the shining paraphernalia of the inner life. His sustained flight of philosophy is broken by scraps of literary reminiscence, scriptural and classic, fragments, as it were, of gold or marble, showing in what quarries his brilliant youth once dug. There is an immense pathos in the closing scene. The Captain, having made so good a fight, desired to be buried with military honors, and requested that trombones should be played at his funeral, as a tribute to the triumph and majesty of the inner life. The day comes, —

> A windy, dreary day with a cold white shine
> That only gummed the tumbled frozen ruts
> We tramped upon. The road was hard and long,
> But we had the large humor of the thing
> To make it advantageous; for men stopped
> And eyed us on the road from time to time,
> And on that road the children followed us;
> And all along that road the Tilbury Band
> Blared indiscreetly the Dead March in Saul. [p. 84]

The message of this poet is: Be true to the truth that lies nearest to you; true to God; true to yourself; true, if you know no better truth, to your primal instincts; but at any cost, be true. "Captain Craig" is one prolonged and glorious wantoning and wallowing in truth.

What Mr. Robinson's work will be in the future it is as yet impossible to say. What he has done speaks for itself. His genius has no sense of action, brutal and direct; but he has it in him to write a great human drama, a drama of the soul from which all action proceeds and to which its results return.

From *Atlantic Monthly*, XCVIII (September 1906), 330-333; also in *Fortnightly Review*, n.s. LXXX (September 1, 1906), 429-434.

May Sinclair (1865-1946), British novelist, short story writer, poet, and essayist, was an early user of Freudian psychology and the stream-of-consciousness technique in fiction. Her fourth novel, *The Divine Fire* (1904), raised a large audience in the United States, and with the rest of her books was more widely read here than in England.

She made several trips to America. During one of these she met William Vaughn Moody, Ridgely Torrence, and Robinson at the Hotel Judson in Greenwich Village. In December 1905 Moody described her as "a drab and angular little lady, . . . meek-spoken, naive, wholly unworldly and without guile. . . . She has taken tremendously to Robinson, who consents for her sake to sit in the drawing-rooms of Philistia. There is a story of their having been seen at 2 A.M. leaning over the railing in the middle of Brooklyn Bridge, entirely incommunicative and at one." (Percy MacKaye, editor, *Letters to Harriet by William Vaughn Moody* [New York, 1935], pp. 245-246.)

Miss Sinclair conveys the gist of her critique on page 326: "The young American poets of to-day are, as far as form goes, anything but revolutionary; they are the born aristocrats of literature, careful of form, and fastidious to a fault in their choice of language. . . . Three young poets stand out among them: William Vaughn Moody, Edwin Arlington Robinson, and Ridgely Torrence. They are all three rich in imagination, but Mr. Moody is distinguished by his mastery of technique; Mr. Robinson by his psychological vision, his powerful human quality . . ."

She opens by quoting from Robinson's "Walt Whitman" (a poem which, ironically, he disavowed and never admitted to his collected works): "Where are the spiritual descendants of Walt Whitman? A younger poet, Edwin Arlington Robinson, tells us that

> We do not hear him very much to-day: —
> His piercing and eternal cadence rings
> Too pure for us — too powerfully pure,
> Too lovingly triumphant, and too large;
> But there are some that hear him, and they know
> That he shall sing to-morrow for all men,
> And that all time shall listen."

Moody is analyzed first, Robinson second, then Torrence.

1 "The Night Before" is a long, melodramatic poem in blank verse; *A Soul's Tragedy* a drama in two acts, the first in blank verse, the second in prose; *Modern Love* a cycle of fifty sixteen-line sonnets. All deal with the stresses of unhappy love and jealousy, but Browning's and Meredith's are more complex and revelatory of character than Robinson's, an amateurish effort which he excluded from his collected poems. Browning too is said to have "despised" *A Soul's Tragedy*. For Robinson's opinions on Browning, see Robert Steed Dunn, *Harvard Monthly*, February 1897, note 1, in this volume; on Meredith, see Boston *Evening Transcript*, October 29, 1902, note 6.

2 To John Hays Gardiner, in December 1901, Robinson said wryly of this poem: "Six hundred lines of blank verse without any bumble-bees or sunsets is a pretty stiff dose." (Fussell, p. 200.)

3 *Captain Craig* is Robinson's third volume, published on October 4, 1902; a second edition issued March 10, 1903. Terming *Captain Craig* Robinson's first volume is particularly peculiar in the face of the fact that Miss Sinclair quotes "The House on the Hill," "Aaron Stark," and "Richard Cory" in full, and erects a prominent comparison with "The Night Before" — all four poems in both editions of *The Children of the Night*, three carried over from *The Torrent and The Night Before*, none contained in *Captain Craig*.

. . / / . .

Severe, yet sensitive art

A LITTLE-KNOWN AMERICAN POET
T. P. O'Connor

I referred in a note last week to an article in the *North American Review* by Miss May Sinclair[1] on three modern American poets. Concerning the work of one of these in particular, Mr. Edwin Arlington Robinson, I think my readers may care to hear something further. Mr. Robinson's verse is fashioned with the utmost simplicity; it depends for its effect upon emotion unadorned by the usual elaborate ritual of poetry. Miss Sinclair says: "His poems fall into three groups: lyrics, — including ballade forms, — character sketches, and psychological dramas, poems dramatic in everything except form. It is, in fact, difficult to name these dramas that cannot be played, these songs that cannot possibly be sung. But the point of view is dramatic, the emotion lyric."

Emotion unadorned.

A good example of Mr. Robinson's severe and yet sensitive art is "The House on the Hill" [the poem follows]. Nothing could be simpler than that, yet it has the thrill of real feeling. Mr. Robinson is better, however, when he forsakes these too mechanical forms of verse.

A story in four verses.

It is not an easy thing to tell a story in four verses, but Mr. Robinson has done it: ["Richard Cory" follows]. Not great poetry — not, indeed, poetry at all — but an admirably effective piece of verse.

"Captain Craig."

Mr. Robinson's first volume, published in 1903, consisted of a long poem in blank verse called "Captain Craig."[2] Miss Sinclair writes: "At first glance there is little charm about this severely undecorated poem, written in unmusical and often monotonous blank verse, shot with darts of intellectual brilliance, but unrelieved by any sensuous coloring. The charm grows in the reading. 'Captain Craig' is a philosophy of life, taught through the humorous lips of a social derelict, a beggared Socrates, disreputable as the world counts reputation. It is a drama of the Unapparent, revealing the divine soul hidden in the starved body of that 'sequestered parasite'; a soul that had the courage to be itself, abiding in its dream, facing the world as a superb failure." Certainly the conception of "Captain Craig" is admirable, though he is more an idea than a character; it is usually the comfortable man who makes philosophy talk in rags, and one rather feels that Mr. Robinson is doing this. However, the poem has unquestionable force. When the Captain died he wished to be buried with military honours, and requested that trombones be played at his funeral: [the last ten lines of the poem follow].

This poet's message is, says Miss Sinclair, "Be true to the truth that lies nearest to you; true to God; true to yourself; true, if you know no better truth, to your primal instincts; but at any cost, be true." It is not a new message, but it is one always worth reiterating.

From *T. P.'s Weekly*, VIII (October 5, 1906), 419.

Thomas Power O'Connor (1848-1929), journalist and editor widely known as "Tay Pay" during his forty-nine years in the House of Commons, consistent champion of the Irish Nationalist cause. Author of books on Napoleon, Disraeli, Beaconsfield, Gladstone, and the Parnell movement, he founded several journals in London besides this "penny literary paper of more than ordinary merit" in 1902.

1 This article actually appeared in the *Atlantic Monthly* and the *Fortnightly Review* in September. See it above.

2 *Captain Craig* was published in 1902, reprinted in 1903. It was Robinson's third book, consisting of the title poem and fifteen shorter selections.

. . / / . .

Orphic stride, condor flight, dolphin-dive

ROBINSON, MY HAND TO YOU
Edwin Markham

"It is hard to have the awkward squad firing over your grave like this," said the late Edmund Clarence Stedman to me once in speaking of the leaden verses ejected by the inadequately inspired in honor of great men. In the same spirit, Lincoln might well consider it an insupportable weight of glory to have to endure the many wreaths of verse laid in heaps upon his tomb.

Still, at least two of the centenary tributes are noble remembrances of the great President.[1] Edwin Arlington Robinson (whom I knew as a poet before he was laurelled and heralded by President Roosevelt) has in *Scribner's Magazine* a tribute which he calls "The Man Who Came."[2] Only Emily Dickinson, among our poets, has the surprising Orphic stride, the sudden condor-flight and dolphin-dive of Mr. Robinson. Here is one fine stanza celebrating Lincoln, who, the poet says, had "the smouldering, and the flame / Of awful patience":

> For he, to whom we had applied
> Our shopman's test of age and worth,
> Was elemental when he died,
> As he was ancient at his birth:
> The saddest among kings of earth,
> Bowed with a galling crown, this man
> Met rancor with a cryptic mirth,
> Laconic — and Olympian.

From "Bookland," New York *American* (February 13, 1909), 13.

Edwin Markham (1852-1940) is remembered for "The Man With the Hoe," inspired by Jean Millet's painting, and his Lincoln poems. "The appearance of Robinson's *Children of the Night* in 1897 was the authentic announcement that a poet had arrived," he wrote. "No other poet, since Browning, has projected on his pages so long an array of sharply accentuated characters. Robinson, like Browning, is chiefly concerned with the inner adventures of his characters; but he finds most of his heroes among the defeated and the discredited. While Robinson, like Browning, has an optimistic attitude toward human follies and failings, yet his attitude is less flamboyantly hopeful." (Edwin Markham, editor, *The Book of Poetry* [New York, 1927], I, 393.) In this anthology Markham included Robinson's "The Master," "Richard Cory," "Miniver Cheevy," "The House on the Hill," "Flammonde," and "Many Are Called."

Markham also mentions Robinson in *The Younger Choir* as one of the "poetic witnesses." See Richard LeGallienne, *Forum*, January 1911, note 2, in this volume.

Robinson contributed this "Quatrain" to *A Wreath for Edwin Markham* (Chicago, 1922), p. 20, on the occasion of his 70th birthday:

> Time, always writing, sees no trace
> Of all he writes on Markham's face.
> On Markham's face he writes in vain
> Apollo rubs it out again.

After Robinson died Markham said, "He was a great poet, and his death is an incurable disaster to American letters. No one can take his place . . . let us sing his praises!" ("Dean of American Poets Pays Tribute," *Mark Twain Quarterly*, II [Spring 1938], 17.)

1 Markham reprints Percy MacKaye's "Lincoln Centenary Ode" following this acclamation of Robinson's poem. Markham was himself roundly praised for *Lincoln, and Other Poems*, published in 1901.

2 This poem, first published in *Scribner's* XLV (February 1909), 150-151, was renamed "The Master" and collected in *The Town Down the River* (1910), pp. 3-7, with one textual change. In quoting, Markham deviated from Robinson's line arrangement, here reinstated.

Regarding this change of title, Robinson wrote to Kermit Roosevelt in 1909: "Rather a foolish thing to undertake, I suppose, — but I have discovered that folly and wisdom occupy the same hut on Parnassus, and that wisdom is not always at home." (Louis Untermeyer, *Edwin Arlington Robinson: A Reappraisal* [Washington, D.C., 1963], p. 33.)

THE TOWN DOWN THE RIVER (1910)

Cushioned in a sinecure paying him a life-saving wage, subject of a kinetic review by the President of the United States, and assured of book publication by the eminent house of Scribner's, Robinson, one expects, would be in a mood of relative euphoria during the latter days of August 1905. On the contrary, he wrote to Edith Brower at this time: "I seem to be pumped dry. Now and then I do a small thing, but it is always something that I had in mind some years ago. . . . I shall keep writing and sooner or later bring out my new book — out of habit, apparently . . . no doubt I shall believe in it in my blind way. . . . It is something that keeps me going and knocks pessimism on the head."[1]

This lassitude of spirit may be laid to the unconscionable trials and ultimate disappointment attending *Captain Craig*, an experience which permanently blocked Robinson's trajectory as a vanward poet. Then there was the matter of his Puritan conscience. Although he could be flippant concerning the position Roosevelt had arranged for him — "Good salary. Little work. Soft snap!"[2] — he remained profoundly uneasy about accepting this money without having to render commensurate service. He clung to the job as basic to survival, but it kept his creativity in a state of unproductive ferment. "The strenuous man has given me some of the most powerful loafing that has ever come my way," he told Laura Richards, describing his duties as chiefly "drawing semi-long breaths and looking around." "Sometime there is going to be something to do. . . . It is a sad life. If my next book turns out pessimistically you are to attribute the fact to T.R., not to me."[3] This sense of decelerated drive he expounded repeatedly, to Mrs. Richards: "The stuff I have been writing of late has been so bad that I have been ashamed of it and of myself. I shall do better pretty soon. At any rate I am not likely to do worse"; and to Craven Langstroth Betts: "I have many things on the ways, but they don't seem to move."[4]

However, move he did physically to the Hotel Judson, an intimate rendezvous in Washington Square for rising writers, artists, and musicians this side *la vie Bohème*. Here Robinson consorted with Ridgely Torrence, Lyman Beecher Stowe, Olivia Howard Dunbar, Daniel Gregory Mason, William Vaughn Moody, Percy MacKaye, Louis Ledoux, the ineludible

Joseph Lewis French; and here he had one memorable skirmish with the dazzling Isadora Duncan. Robinson enjoyed the distilled esoteric ambience of the Judson after his own reticent fashion, and founded several lifelong friendships there. Kindred in aim and touched by his evident needs, they nonetheless invoked no immediate release for his congested energies. Ungregarious as ever, he slept mornings, turned up afternoons at the Custom House, read a newspaper through, left it conspicuously on his rolltop desk as a token of his attendance, took supper at an inexpensive restaurant, and nights — like his own Miniver Cheevy — he "kept on drinking." For days on end, sometimes for full weeks, he did not even bother to go to the Custom House. It was a sterile, self-immolating program, and no one recognized this more smartly than himself.

Months before his appointment, Robinson had begun sketching out a prose comedy. Driven by indigence at the time, he conjured up images of instant acclamation on Broadway and a salvational flow of money. After his rescue by Roosevelt, Robinson's thoughts slanted more than ever toward the plight of his brother's family in Maine. His pay about covered his own requirements, leaving little to stretch over his sister-in-law and three small nieces. To further pique his eagerness, the American theatre in 1906 resounded to the success of lyric dramas by Moody, MacKaye, Torrence, and Josephine Preston Peabody. If these companions of his could do it, he reasoned, why couldn't he? So commenced a decade during which he never stopped reaching for the gold ring, devoting to this hapless quest hours and efforts he might better have utilized developing his given genre. In a letter to Kermit Roosevelt on April 4, 1907 he confessed to total abdication: "[Some months earlier] a tall and uncompromising being called Modern American drama . . . got the best of me; and I have been in his power ever since."[5]

For three years he applied himself by compulsion to dramas and at random to poetry. Between January 1906 and October 1908 *Scribner's* magazine — with one eye on Roosevelt's shadow — printed six of Robinson's poems; *Lippincott's*, seemingly startled by his abrupt emergence under such brilliant auspice, ran his sonnet on Poe, which it had bought and held for eleven years; the *Atlantic Monthly* brought out "Calverly's." Though no great outpouring by any standard, this exceeded by two his periodical appearances in the preceding nine years. Here was at least a quantum of proof that he was indubitably a poet, however ruinous his daily schedule. In July 1908 his occupational complacency suffered an unnerving jolt. A change of officials at the Custom House bred demands that Robinson be on hand during regular working hours. "'This is particularly rotten just now, as I am in a mood for work (work with me means studying the ceiling and my navel for four hours and then writing down perhaps four lines — sometimes as many as seven and again none at all)." He dubbed himself moodily "a prisoner in Room 408," slumped in "a state of semi-agitated punk."[6]

His principal irritant these days was "a fear that I may turn out a disappointment to my friends and to T.R. — who must be wondering . . .

how long it takes a man to write a hundred pages of verse." He knew the President expected another book from him, and he fretted over the insensitive clamor for quantity: "a fellow has to be dead before the public understands that a dozen titles are quite enough to string wires on that will reach through ten times as many centuries — perhaps." He consoled himself with the observation that "there is only a visual resemblance between verse and the other thing."[7]

In March 1909 a severer concern than Roosevelt's impatience assailed Robinson. With the advent of Taft to the White House, the new regime at the Custom House imposed fixed duties on Robinson and insinuated the necessity of a uniform. This last touch he viewed as a "death-warrant," took the hint and resigned. No longer cumbered by extraneous employment, in July he turned full attention to his next volume of poems. In September he returned to Gardiner, helping his sister-in-law and nieces as he might, his brother Herman having died early that year. There was nothing left now in Tilbury Town to distract him. He settled down abstemiously to revising and rearranging the prospective contents of *The Town Down the River*. Back again in New York City, by the end of December he was living alone in a studio built expressly for him by Mrs. Clara Davidge in the backyard of her Washington Place home. Within this unimaginably ideal aura he completed his book, adopting the title from a chorus for his "Tavern Songs," which he had proposed to Harry Smith back in October 1894.

It "is going to make a big difference in my life," Robinson said to Torrence when Scribner's took on *The Town*. "The President has been expecting work of me, and here it is."[8] He promptly wrote Roosevelt and on June 25, 1910 had this return confirmation: "Indeed it will give me particular pleasure to have you dedicate your volume to me." Then, mindful of the unauthorized use of his name by Scribner's in advertising the 1905 *Children of the Night*, Roosevelt prudently apposed, "Of course you will not put this letter in the book — I suppose that is needless advice on my part!"[9]

The long, long trek had started when Robinson's job at the subway excavation terminated in August 1904. Unleashed from this numbing lockstep, he had envisioned a new assembly of poems within six months. By some exquisite quirk of numerology, it materialized six years later. "The good Gawd knows that I have been long enough at it," he exclaimed to Edith Brower when finally it loomed on the verge of reality.[10]

1910 was not a scintillating year in American literature. No outstanding or enduring novel made its debut. The prize-winning drama was Josephine Preston Peabody's *The Piper*; the most formidable biography, Gustavus Myers' *The History of the Great American Fortunes*; Robinson's strongest contender in the field of verse, John Lomax's compilation of *Cowboy Songs*. LeGallienne, Kilmer, Braithwaite, the metropolitan newspapers and the national magazines came forward with reviews of *The Town Down the River* more receptive in trend than those accorded his earlier, less conventional books. His retreat from experiment — the concession he made to public acceptance — availed him no whit. His reputation did spread somewhat, slightly. There was no general annunciation of another true poet newly arrived. Self-defensively, Robinson insisted that the book would raise no "immediate noise."[11]

On the 19th of October Robinson's perennial partisan, Roosevelt, wrote with galvanic assurance: "There are few things I could appreciate more than having your volume of poems dedicated to me. I read them through last night and with the utmost delight of course. I believe in you more than ever."[12] Pity the recipient's faith in himself was not coated in such impregnable steel. For three decades now Robinson had conceived his role as unalterably the poet. But there were moments during that long sahara when high resolve sagged under heat of adverse criticism, forthright ridicule, or outright neglect. His recurring syndrome of determination and detraction in these early years is demonstrated in this self-evaluation sent to Miss Brower less than a month after *The Town* appeared. Comparing it with *The Torrent and The Night Before*, he said: "If my poetry is really good for anything, the same quality should be found in both books. I like to believe that the last one is a little better done and, as a whole, rather more worth doing — but my opinion may not be of much value."[13]

Two of his friends, poets both, uttered in this hour more sturdy and discerning judgments of his ability. During one of Robinson's self-abrading moments, Ridgely Torrence interrupted with, "Just shut up. You know what they say: It takes seventeen years for the public to understand a poet. That gives you still some years to go." And Torrence reports William Vaughn Moody proclaiming, "When we're all dead and buried, EA will go thundering down the ages."[14] Counting Roosevelt, here was a trio who called the turn on Robinson before he saw it himself clearly. He did have the afflatus. It took twenty (not seventeen) years for the public to catch up. And he has proved more durable than his brighter contemporaries, Moody included.

.. / / ..

THE TOWN DOWN THE RIVER. Published October 8, 1910 by Charles Scribner's Sons, New York. Bound in dark green cloth, title and author's name stamped in gold on front cover and spine, gold rule along front cover edges; top edge gilt, front and bottom edges untrimmed; leaves measure 17.1 by 11.5 centimeters; 790 copies at $1.25.

THE TOWN DOWN THE RIVER

A BOOK OF POEMS

BY
EDWIN ARLINGTON ROBINSON

NEW YORK
CHARLES SCRIBNER'S SONS
1910

THE TOWN DOWN THE RIVER

Contents

The Master (Lincoln)	1
The Town Down the River	9
An Island (Saint Helena, 1821)	23
Calverly's	41
Leffingwell	
I The Lure	44
II The Quickstep	46
III Requiescat	48
Clavering	50
Lingard and the Stars	54
Pasa Thalassa Thalassa	59
Momus	64
Uncle Ananias	66
The Whip	68
The White Lights (Broadway, 1906)	71
Exit	73
Normandy (From the French of Bérat)	74
Leonora	76
The Wise Brothers	78
But for the Grace of God	80
Au Revoir (March 23, 1909)	83
For Arvia, On Her Fifth Birthday	85
The Sunken Crown	87
Doctor of Billiards	89
Shadrach O'Leary	91
How Annandale Went Out	93
Alma Mater	95
Miniver Cheevy	97
The Pilot	100
Vickery's Mountain	102
Bon Voyage	106
The Companion	109
Atherton's Gambit	111
For a Dead Lady	114
Two Gardens in Linndale	116
The Revealer (Roosevelt)	123

A distinct advance in poetic insight

NOTES ABOUT BOOKS AND AUTHORS

A book of poems — *The Town Down the River*, by Edwin Arlington Robinson — will come out this month.

This volume is made up of new poems now first collected, by the author of that remarkable volume *The Children of the Night*,[1] published a few years ago. It shows a distinct advance in poetic insight and in that unusual ironic view, based on a deep philosophy, which has not appeared in modern verse since Browning. Some of these poems have been published in periodicals, and "Miniver Cheevy" gained a very wide popularity. Among the younger poets Mr. Robinson stands conspicuous for originality of thought and terseness of expression. Many of his lines are epigrams.

From *Book Buyer*, XXXV (September 1910), 123.

[1] The *Book Buyer* was published by Charles Scribner's Sons, which explains the amplitude of this advance notice and the ardor over his preceding volume, also brought out by Scribner's. Coyly, it neglects to state that "Miniver Cheevy" first appeared in *Scribner's Magazine.*

. . / / . .

Uneven, cryptic, humanitarian

POEMS BY EDWIN ROBINSON

Mr. Edwin Robinson,[1] who is one of the writers honored with the seal of Rooseveltian approval, has brought out another volume of poems. It is entitled *The Town Down the River*. In its unevenness, occasionally cryptic quality, and humanitarian appeal, Mr. Robinson's verse shows the influence of Browning. It is a pronounced suggestion in "How Annandale Went Out": [The poem follows.]

"Miniver Cheevy," which first appeared in *Scribner's Magazine* and was widely quoted, is a very effective preachment: [The poem follows.]

From "Books and Authors," Boston *Daily Advertiser* (October 12, 1910), 8.

[1] For reasons privy to itself, the *Advertiser* omits Robinson's middle name here, as also in its review of *Captain Craig* on October 25, 1902.

. . / / . .

On October 15, 1910 the Boston *Herald* listed *The Town Down the River* in the section "Books on Reviewer's Table," with the appended comment: "A small collection of verses, more or less wilful in construction and expression. The author dedicates this book to Theodore Roosevelt" (p. 7). A notice at the end reads, "All books listed here are subject to further review in future issues." On December 10 and again on the 24th, longer critiques were granted several volumes of "recent verse," but not to *The Town Down the River*.

In its overview of "The Scribner October Books" one week later the New York *Sun* summarized and paraphrased the *Book Buyer* aptly while managing to distort Robinson's name in a manner he had grown accustomed to: "while for poetry there will be *The Town Down the River*, by Edward [*sic*] Arlington Robinson, who wrote *The Children of the Night*, a volume compared to Browning because of its poetic insight based on a philosophy of somewhat ironic view" (p. 10).

. . / / . .

Distinctly original note in modern American poetry

DOWN THE RIVER
William Stanley Braithwaite

Mr. Robinson's new book of poems (seven years have elapsed since the last) has all those qualities, grown perhaps, a little more subtle in execution, by which he is distinguished from all contemporary American poets. It is not difficult to account for an art whose results are so obvious and definite in its plasticity; but there seems to be no accounting, none convincingly, of the secret by which spiritual perception and vision weaves its significance throughout and symbolizes realities and circumstances. Mr. Robinson's poems are for the most part delineations of the soul etched into portraits of psychology and with each line eaten by the acid experience upon the plate of life. The process is the direct labor of fate working in the poet's imagination without sentiment or equivocation, but with a relentless regard to truth grim and absolute, which often transfigures the instinct into a strange and curious aspect of beauty. The puritanism, however, goes no further than simplicity of motive, for in the end Mr. Robinson's art achieves a pagan magic of irresponsibility which becomes almost riotous in response to the instincts of the individual. It may seem hard to reconcile these attributes with the spiritualizing qualities we discern in Mr. Robinson's poetry; it is not this that makes his influence difficult to disengage from his method, but the achievement is undeniable and stands as one of the very few and distinctively original notes in modern American poetry. In accomplishing this result his art on the verbal side is wrought with all the patience and reticence which seems instinctive and temperamental in the poet's conscious attitude toward the drama of man's soul. Words may be used and misused as symbols interpreting the spirit. Mr. Robinson never misuses them, never betrays their confidence, but by respecting their commonest value and constant employment, endows them with impressive and significant, and often unrealized meanings. He makes simple words and simple phrases accomplish spiritual reticence and psychological suggestion. They are so woven into the very composition of feeling and thought that speech becomes presence and presence motion through language.

Mr. Robinson's art may have the appearance of being ascetic; rather it is restraint, an altogether different matter than poverty of resource of which it may be charged. This fact as well implies harmonic rather than melodic rhythms which may easily lead carelessness to assume his versification to be wilful.[1] We dwell upon this point because it is essential to a wholly sympathetic approach to the peculiar and attractive lyricism that the poet has evolved to embody and express spiritual motives struggling through sombre and complex realities in human nature. Often the threads are very slender but withal vital, the symbolism vague and allusive, but of characteristic significance. Compressing in the narrow limits of a sonnet the portrait of a complete character, and in a short lyric a complete story of human fate and circumstance, artistic necessity has compelled him to this form of which practice has made him master.

Mr. Robinson's concern is wholly with the soul, either as a portrait in psychology, or as the medium through which experience works to the climax of a story that reveals the effect of circumstance upon human fate. He translates what many take to be mystery in human nature into nothing more than the assumption of will; but then the peculiar richness of his imagination, the extraordinary keenness of his psychological vision, lies in his ability to penetrate the mysterious and subtle motives of the will, and justify its associations through deed and temperament with the ideals of society. To us the most wonderful part of this poet's work is those portraits in which the character of the soul is drawn with such remarkable clearness of feature, and every feature harmonized so as to emphasize a single quality of temperament. These characters sketched into large and tremendous results upon the limited canvas of the sonnet are as distinct and valuable an achievement in poetic art as Browning's invention of the monologue as a medium of spiritual psychology. We recall the wonder with which these strange and curious inhabitants of Mr. Robinson's imagination first took our acquaintance in *The Children of the Night*; and how he showed us there that even in the sordid environment of such lives as "Aaron Stark" and "Reuben Bright" there could break through the hard realities of their natures a spiritual reflection of traits and ideals undiscovered by the world. To these the poet has added another fascinating gallery of characters in this new volume, but he has softened his sketches by an indefinable air of mysticism which has added something deeper and more haunting to his art. "Calverly's," "Leffingwell," "Clavering," "Lingard,"[2] "Uncle Ananias,"[3] "Shadrach O'Leary," "Miniver Cheevy"[4] and "Vickery"; all are here, each with his interesting psychology, and also with his very human susceptibility. These make up the poet's "book of scattered lives,"[5] a book indeed unlike any other company of beings who are as incapable of dreaming as they are capable of making action a dream and silence a reality. These two stanzas from "Calverly's" will give the reader some idea of what this company is like; it will also hint that each in fulfilling himself became anointed with destiny, which however obscure in each man's life, makes him splendid by virtue of it:

> There'll be a page for Leffingwell,
> And one for Lingard, the Moon-calf;
> And who knows what for Clavering,
> Who died because he couldn't laugh?
> Who knows or cares? No sign is here,
> No face, no voice, no memory;
> No Lingard with his eerie joy,
> No Clavering, no Calverly.
>
> We cannot have them here with us
> To say where their light lives are gone,
> Or if they be of other stuff
> Than are the moons of Ilion.
> So, be their place of one estate
> With ashes, echoes, and old wars, —
> Or ever we be of the night,
> Or we be lost among the stars.

The other fine things in this new book of Mr. Robinson's we can do no more here than to recommend most heartily and urgently to the reader who wants the representative best in contemporary poetry. We have tried to indicate some of those qualities in his poetry which we believe give him a unique and serious bid for remembrance. We have dealt, perhaps, a little long upon these qualities to the exclusion of a more specific examination of the book in hand, but if Mr. Robinson's two previous books, *The Children of the Night* and *Captain Craig*,[6] are of the essential spiritual tenor of the present volume, and unlike any other quality in American verse, and being somewhat drowned in the mellifluous chorus of contemporary praise, we wished to emphasize the presence and quality of this voice sounding after a long silence. But there is in this book such masterly and haunting symbolism as "The Town Down the River,"[7] after which the volume is named; "Pasa Thalassa Thalassa,"[8] "Vickery's Mountain,"[9] "The White Lights,"[10] "Bon Voyage," "For a Dead Lady,"[11] and "Two Gardens in Linndale,"[12] all achievements that could not be possible without Mr. Robinson.

From "Books of the Day," Boston *Evening Transcript* (October 29, 1910), III, 6.

William Stanley Braithwaite (1878-1962) was the grandson of a British admiral who retired to the Barbados and married a Negro. Literary editor of the *Transcript* and of the Brimmer Press, Braithwaite also compiled the impressive *Anthology of Magazine Verse and Year Book of American Poetry* from 1913 to 1929, wherein he frequently commended Robinson and reprinted his poems as among the best of the current year. Poet, novelist, and short story writer of solid ability, Braithwaite wound up his career as a professor of literature in the Atlanta University.

Braithwaite subtitled this perceptive essay-review "The Spiritual Qualities of an American Poet." After reading it, Robinson sought out the author. They met for the first time in the Boston Public Library, remained friends to Robinson's last days. Across the years Braithwaite became his strongest and most eloquent partisan, a fact Robinson acknowledged after his *Merlin* review with typical Down East declination: "I am naturally grateful to W.S.B. for all he says though I wish . . . he wouldn't write such formidable long sentences." (Esther Willard Bates, *Edwin Arlington Robinson and His Manuscripts* [Waterville, Maine, 1944], p. 6.)

On the flyleaf of Truman H. Bartlett's heavily annotated presentation copy of *The*

Town Down the River (now in Colby College Library) Bartlett noted below an attached clipping of Braithwaite's review: "Chocorua Oct. 31, 1910 — 'The best thing ever written about my work,' says R."

1 Braithwaite doubtlessly read the Boston *Herald* note two weeks previously (see above).

2 In these four poems, under the corporate title of "Calverly's," Robinson "enshrined the romance of the fellowship of his early years in New York with Burnham and Betts and Coan and Louis." Of "Lingard and the Stars" in particular: "he set a monument to evenings in Olivia Dunbar's tower-room [in the Hotel Judson] when the table danced until the boarder below complained of the noise." (Hermann Hagedorn, *Edwin Arlington Robinson: A Biography* [New York, 1938], p. 238.)

Theodore Roosevelt to his son, April 11, 1907: "Robinson's letter and poem have come and I send them back. I like the poem, even tho I do not understand every word of it. Leffingwell, Lingard and Clavering are not real characters at all. They are simply like the various individuals mentioned in *The Children of the Night*." (Will Irwin, editor, *Letters to Kermit from Theodore Roosevelt 1902-1908* [New York, 1946], pp. 187-188. Robinson rather badly miscalculated the President's estimate of his characters. See note 7 to Roosevelt's review of *The Children*, August 12, 1905, in this volume.

3 This poem originally appeared in *Century* magazine, edited by Richard Watson Gilder, in a department reserved for prose and verse "In Lighter Vein." Robinson bridled, then shrugged. "When I found that 'U.A.' was to be tucked away in small type I felt that I was placed in a false [position]. After that I felt rather silly for taking a small matter so seriously. But it is still a question in my mind just why R.W.G. should pay twenty dollars for a few lines to go along with J.K. Bangs & Co. No, dear child, I am not puffed up, but puzzled, and peradventure a bit punctured, as to my amazing dignity." (Richard Cary, editor, *Edwin Arlington Robinson's Letters to Edith Brower* [Cambridge, Mass., 1968], p. 151.)

Behind the scenes Gilder had informed his poetry editor that Roosevelt was interested in Robinson, that the latter deserved help. "Most of this is unuseful to us but 'Uncle Ananias' might do for 'In Lighter Vein' — don't you think? & if so accept, send him the much needed check." The sympathetic subordinate is said to have paid five dollars in excess of the usual rate, the first remuneration received for a poem by Robinson in a decade. (Emery Neff, *Edwin Arlington Robinson* [New York, 1948], pp. 136, 142.)

4 Hagedorn (p. 238) is of the opinion that Robinson "'spoofed' himself in 'Miniver Cheevy.'"

5 This phrase is from stanza 2 of "Calverly's" (p. 42). Robinson also used "scattered lives" in "The Night Before" (*The Torrent and The Night Before*, p. 40), and as a tentative title for a group of short stories he was writing around 1895 (see Denham Sutcliffe, editor, *Untriangulated Stars: Letters of Edwin Arlington Robinson to Harry DeForest Smith 1890-1905* [Cambridge, Mass., 1947], pp. 202, 219; and Wallace L. Anderson, "E.A. Robinson's 'Scattered Lives,'" *American Literature*, XXXVIII [January 1967], 498-507, where Sutcliffe's misreading of the word "lives" is corrected.)

6 Braithwaite's ignorance of *The Torrent and The Night Before* is also apparent in his reviews of May 28, 1913 and August 11, 1915.

7 Robinson to William Vaughn Moody, October 13, 1908: "I enclose 'The Town Down, etc.' at your request, hoping that you will not feel compelled to read into it the history of heaven and hell and Head Tide — after the manner of certain others whom I might name." (Edwin S. Fussell, "Robinson to Moody: Ten Unpublished Letters," *American Literature*, XXIII [May 1951], 187.) See also note 1 to the New York *Tribune* review, November 2, 1902, in this volume.

8 Robinson "packed . . . all that Israel Jordan had meant to him in his boyhood into 'Pasa Thalassa Thalassa.'" Jordan was a sea captain who lived diagonally opposite the Robinsons in Gardiner. "The mariner, himself, 'with his hard red face that only

his laughter could wrinkle,' came and went; came, bringing nuts and oranges to the children of the neighborhood; went, carrying their imagination." (Hagedorn, pp. 237, 14-15.)

9 Robinson to Louis V. Ledoux, July 20, 1910: "Also, it comes over me that Vickery's psychology is sound — a point upon which one or two have differed." (Ridgely Torrence, editor, *Selected Letters of Edwin Arlington Robinson* [New York, 1940], pp. 66-67.)

To Edith Brower, March 15, 1914: "Others have had similar trouble with 'Vickery,' trying to read into it all manner of stuff, when I merely meant that the gold was waiting for him, but that the Fates and devils wouldn't allow him to accumulate sufficient sense and energy to go and get it. Maybe there is so much Vickery in all of us that we don't recognize him when he is set before us." (Cary, p. 155.)

To Lewis N. Chase, July 11, 1917: " 'Vickery's Mountain' . . . is after all merely a study of human inertia, which is in Vickery's case something stronger than he is." (Torrence, p. 104.)

10 Written after seeing the first performance of Moody's *A Sabine Woman*, later retitled *The Great Divide*. Robinson heralds the advent in America of a classic popular drama on native themes parallel to that of Greece and Elizabethan England.

11 Robinson to Edith Brower, March 15, 1914: "As for the obscure line in the 'Dead Lady,' I never thought of meaning or indicating anything more than her way of presuming on her attractions and 'guying' those who admired her. Perhaps you looked for something deeper." (Cary, p. 155.)

12 Robinson "felt that 'Two Gardens in Linndale' deserved a place in anthologies as much as the inevitable 'Miniver Cheevy.' " (Bates, p. 23.)

. . / / . .

In its weekly section on "Books Authors," the Portland (Me.) *Evening Express & Advertiser*, October 31, 1910, p. 18, did take a quick glimpse at Robinson's new book, managing to mistitle it *A Town Down the River* and misname him Edward in the caption. The reviewer apparently never got past the table of contents. "*A Town Down the River*, written by Edwin [correctly this time] Arlington Robinson, and published by Charles Scribner's Sons, is dedicated to Theodore Roosevelt, and is a collection of poems, the following being the titles:" ["The Town Down the River" (correctly this time) and the other poems are mechanically listed, with no commentary.]

. . / / . .

Charity for the half-realized dream

EDWIN ARLINGTON ROBINSON'S NEW POEMS

Although this is Mr. Robinson's fourth volume of verse he was known to comparatively few readers until the republication of *The Children of the Night*, in 1905 — a volume which Mr. Roosevelt wrote about when President in terms of keen appreciation. The present volume contains the best of the poems that Mr. Robinson has written in the past five years. He is a most conscientious worker who has the highest conception of the poet's duty to write only the best that is in him. What he especially puts into his poetry is a philosophy of life, particularly the philosophy of failure. He has the facility which Browning had of creating a character in a few words and attaching to it a characteristic name, so that he dramatizes and, to a certain extent, visualizes his philosophy. Instead of generalizations he gives us the tragedy, or comedy with its tragic side, in the careers of Calverly, Leffingwell, Lingard, Miniver Cheevy, and the rest. In all of these it is the high dream and the imperfect achievement that is celebrated; the ironic misinterpretation which the world gives to incomplete or distorted lives, the lack of vision which we all have in judgment upon our fellow men:

> I say no more for Clavering
> Than I should say of him who fails
> To bring his wounded vessel home
> When reft of rudder and of sails[1]

For another, whom the world brands "parasite and sycophant," the plea is made that he had been lured by "high promises"[2]; of another that he "died because he could not laugh."[3] Indeed, each one of these striking poems suggests a whole life-story with strange dramatic insight.

There is also the other side to this philosophy of life — a sincere admiration for a great character such as Lincoln,[4] and a perception of the tragedy that also accompanies his success as well as failure. Charity for the broken statue, the incomplete design, the half-realized dream is the prevailing tone of his comment.

Any sympathetic reader will miss the best of Mr. Robinson's verse if he does not grasp the originality of the rhythm and the singing quality of such poems as "Pasa Thalassa Thalassa" or "Leonora" or "Miniver Cheevy." He is not lyric but his rhythms have a lilt that is original and sticks to the memory. "The Town Down the River," for instance, has the swing of rushing waters in it as well as a pictorial allegory.

Poetry of this kind is surely worth while. It has an individual quality — sincerity, directness, and comprehension; it is not made up of the gaspings and complainings of weak and inefficient people. Moreover, there is workmanship in every line — the marks of the patient artisan who polishes the work and returns again to give it added finish.[5]

From *Book Buyer*, XXXV (November 1910), 181.

1 "Clavering," p. 50.
2 "Leffingwell," pp. 44-45.
3 The character Clavering in "Calverly's," p. 42.
4 "The Master (Lincoln)," pp. 3-7. On March 15, 1909 Roosevelt wrote Robinson: "As for the Lincoln poem, I saw it in manuscript, for Kermit showed it to me, and Senator Lodge read it aloud to us when it came out, bringing it over to say that he regarded it as a *very* notable poem — in which we all agreed with him!" (Colby College Library.) See John W. Crowley, "E. A. Robinson and Henry Cabot Lodge," *New England Quarterly*, XLIII (March 1970), 115-124.
   In Bartlett's copy of the book, this note is penciled among others at the end of the poem: "It cost me over a year's work to write this poem,' says R."

5 "For two weeks I've gone to my studio every morning after breakfast, and stayed there till five o'clock. For two weeks I've searched for one word — and I haven't found it yet," Robinson told the young interviewer Frederika Beatty. Asked if he had had a good productive day, he responded, "Today, I removed the hyphen from hellhound." ("Edwin Arlington Robinson as I Knew Him," *South Atlantic Quarterly*, XLIII [October 1944], 379.) For other comments by Robinson on the meticulosity of his revisions, see note 2 to Sherman's review in the *Book Buyer*, December 1902, in this volume.

. . / / . .

On page 203 of its December issue the *Book Buyer* (XXXV) cogently capitalized on Braithwaite's strong endorsement. "Of Edwin Arlington Robinson's new volume of poems — *The Town Down the River* — the Boston *Transcript* sets forth comprehensively the more salient characteristics." It thereafter quoted several sentences from Braithwaite's third and final paragraphs. It has already been pointed out that these repeated notices were not entirely altruistic. The *Book Buyer* was Charles Scribner's Sons' house organ.

. . / / . .

Art full of reticence and haunting melody

THE TOWN DOWN THE RIVER

Among these seven books of verse[1] at least three stand out with distinction among the poetry of the year. Mr. Robinson is one of the three or four foremost American poets, while in England Mr. Phillips holds a like position. *The Town Down the River* is full of that ironic philosophy, that psychological portraiture in human nature, of which he is master, and of an art full of reticence and haunting melody.

From "Book Notes," *Poet-Lore*, XXI (November-December 1910), 491.

This note was probably written by Helen Archibald Clarke, a consistent booster of Robinson and still editor of *Poet-Lore*.

1 Stephen Phillips' *Pietro of Siena*, and volumes by Martin Schultze, Samuel L. Simpson, Eben E. Rexford, Emily Sargent Lewis, Mrs. Schuyler van Rensselaer.

. . / / . .

Some lines to remember

THE TOWN DOWN THE RIVER

A small book of poems which takes its title from one of them. The verses have merit. There are some lines to remember:

> Few are alive who report, and few are alive who remember,
> More of him now than a name carved somewhere on the sea.[1]

From "Gossip of New Books and Their Writers," Denver *Republican* (November 13, 1910), II, 3.

In length and tone a distinct retrenchment from Mowry Saben's expansive purview of Robinson's work in this paper in 1905. Saben had moved on to other pursuits and other journals but enough of his spirit seems to have clung to the Republican to admit even this ambivalent curt-dismissal, open-applausive notice.

1 "Pasa Thalassa Thalassa," p. 63.

. . / / . .

A month after Robinson's poem "The Man who Came" appeared in *Scribner's*, it was reprinted in full by *Current Literature* (XLVI, March 1909, 333-334) under this observation: "It is a great year for centenary celebrations and the poets are doing their part. Mr. Robinson gives us in *Scribner's* a poem on Lincoln, stating in a foot-note that the lines are to be supposed to have been written not long after the Civil War." In *The Town Down the River* he renamed the poem "The Master (Lincoln)."

In April (p. 448) *Current Literature* again singled Robinson out: "The Lincoln centenary has come and gone, and any number of Lincoln poems have been given to the world. None that we have seen — with, perhaps, one exception, that of Mr. Robinson's, printed in this department last month — has the note of real inspiration." The editor then cites Hermann Hagedorn's ode as "one of the best-builded of them all" and quotes an extract from it.

For still another encore, the magazine commented upon the book's publication:

A haunting charm, hard to isolate, easy to feel

THE TOWN DOWN THE RIVER

There is a haunting charm about Edwin Arlington Robinson's poetry that we find it hard to isolate, but easy to feel. It is not so much in his phrasing or his melody as in the homely subjects he chooses and, still more, his quaint outlook upon life. We select two poems from this new volume (*The Town Down the River* — Scribner's), the best poem in the book — "The Master" — having already been printed by us: ["Calverly's" and "Uncle Ananias" follow.]

From "Recent Poetry," *Current Literature*, XLIX (December 1910), 685-686.

. . / / . .

Dedicated to Theodore Roosevelt

SONGS OF THE MINOR CHOIR

The Town Down the River, by Edwin Arlington Robinson, is published by Scribner's Sons and dedicated to Theodore Roosevelt. After a poem on Lincoln,[1] the Town Down the River has a place in the book, and the watcher discourses interestingly, on and with the people who pass by him:

the boy and maiden, the fiery folk, the weak and world-humbled, and the aged ones. This imaginative poem is followed by "An Island (Saint Helena, 1821)," and a section called "Calverly's." "Miscellaneous" includes "Pasa Thalassa Thalassa" and "Leonora," each having death as the subject. The latter is a crisp little fragment, which has good work in it, perhaps the best of its kind in the book. "Normandy," and other poems of varying types are also in this volume by Mr. Robinson, and a final one to Mr. Roosevelt, called "The Revealer."[2]

From Brooklyn *Daily Eagle* (December 17, 1910), 6.

The title of this review derives from a prefatorial note concerning poems by Julia Ward Howe, Helen Keller, "and a Chirping Chorus of Singers, Some With One Tune, Some With Many." Following reviews of the two named poets is a subtitle, "Other Piping Notes," comprising a reprint of Oscar Wilde, Emily Sargent Lewis, Burgess Johnson, Cale Young Rice, the Robinson notice, and six more of comparable length.

In the department "Authors and Their Ways," the *Eagle* on November 19, 1910, p. 5, had included among two columns of brief notes on "What the Writers Are Doing and Planning" the following: "Did you ever guess that Broadway was poetic? Read this from *The Town Down the River*, by Edwin A. Robinson, and mend your thinking." The last stanza of "The White Lights" is then quoted.

1 "The Master" subtitled (Lincoln).

2 This poem is also subtitled, (Roosevelt). After Lyman Abbott of the *Outlook* — a magazine which Roosevelt served as contributing editor from 1909 to 1914 — rejected Robinson's poem, he wrote to Louis V. Ledoux: "By the way, did Abbott seem to know what I am driving at in T.R. or did he disagree with it with some degree of intelligence? I have encountered so much rotten imbecility in the way of failure to get my meaning that I am beginning to wonder myself if it may not be vague. But I won't have it anything worse than obscure, which I meant it to be — to a certain extent." (Torrence, p. 67.)

On page 125 in his copy of the book, Truman Bartlett placed an asterisk after (Roosevelt) and wrote in the bottom margin: "To whom this book is mostly due — its existence, and many of the best things, says E.A.R." And at the end of the poem: " 'The most difficult thing I ever did' — said R."

Two other poems in *The Town Down the River* have Roosevelt as the innominate central character: "Au Revoir," subtitled (March 23, 1909), the day of his departure to hunt big game in Africa, and "The Pilot," an oblique reference to the culmination of his presidency.

. . / / . .

A realistic psychologue with debatable meanings

THE TOWN DOWN THE RIVER

Edwin Arlington Robinson is the poet whom Mr. Roosevelt praised, thereby drawing the attention to him of many people who otherwise, no doubt, would have been blissfully unaware of his existence. Those who know and follow current verse, on the other hand, are familiar with the original work of this young writer, whose earlier volume was hailed by the critics as something quite out of the ordinary. His present book, *The Town Down the River*, is dedicated to the Colonel and the final poem, a very suggestive one, called "The Revealer," refers to the doughty slayer of lions and (Tammany) tigers.

Mr. Robinson might be described as a realistic psychologue; that is, his interest, like Browning's, to whom he bears a certain resemblance, is in the subtle depths of character, and his manner of studying the same involves a plainness of speech which will probably repel those bred, as to poetry, upon the more conventional, pretty verbiage of the past. It is daring modern work in this sense and full of an odd kind of beauty, as well as being eminently thought-provoking. Its faults, so far as it has them, are the faults of obscurity and of cynicism. "Uncle Ananias" is a clever poem, but hardly a pleasing one, because of its implications. The lyric sequence, "Calverly's," attracts me strongly, but I cannot forbear asking myself if it would not be better if its steps were clear and it led somewhere. I am glad it is balanced by that fine piece of allegorical idealism which gives the book its name.

After closing the little volume, a feeling is left that you wish to read it again, both to clear up debatable meanings and for general enjoyment.

From unidentified periodical (December 19, 1910).

. . / / . .

Among the highest praised books

POEMS BY MAINE AUTHORS

Maine readers who love the finest verse and especially that written by Maine authors should not forget that new volumes of poetry by two natives of our state are among the most popular and highest praised books of the present season. One of these is entitled, *The Town Down the River*, by Edwin Arlington Robinson; . . .[1] The authors are not, we think, as well known as they should be, by our best cultivated people, although each book is the second volume[2] which the author has published.

Mr. Robinson is a native of Gardiner,[3] where he lived when his first volume, *The Children of the Night*, was published. That volume won the recommendation and the friendship of President Roosevelt, by whom Mr. Robinson was aided in his government aspirations. The Boston *Evening Transcript* says his latest volume "represents the best in contemporary poetry."[4]

From "An Evening With Books," Bangor *Daily Commercial* (December 31, 1910), 16.

[1] The second book, discussed in a final paragraph, is *The Seer*, a Longfellow memorial poem by Professor Henry Johnson of Bowdoin College.

[2] This reviewer is unaware of *The Torrent and The Night Before*, ironic in that it was zestfully noticed in the *Daily Commercial* of February 13, 1897, reprinted in this volume.

[3] Robinson was born in Head Tide. His family moved to Gardiner in September

1870, when he was not quite one year old.

4 Quoted imprecisely from William Stanley Braithwaite's review of October 29, 1910, reprinted in this volume.

. . / / . .

A poet of steel and grit

THREE AMERICAN POETS
Richard LeGallienne

Three volumes of new-born American poetry,¹ published within a week or two of each other, just come into my hands, force upon me the reiteration of a protest and an affirmation, which I — and not I only — have made so often of late that it already seems a form of indignant platitude. Reviewing in this same magazine, a short time ago, *The Younger Choir* — a selection from the writings of one small group of younger American poets² — and reviewing elsewhere Mr. Charles Hanson Towne's notable *Manhattan*, I could not but exclaim upon the strange and unutterably stupid superstition that poetry in America is dead, and that, generally speaking, "there are no poets nowadays."

The three poets whom I propose to appreciate once more victoriously remind one of the opacity of a public that asks, or pretends to ask, for poetry, yet cannot see it when it is there shining and singing, so to say, under its very nose, or, if it sees it, churlishly refuses to buy. "If there were dreams to sell . . . who then would buy!"³

There are dreams to sell to-day as of old, more dreams, perhaps, than ever; but Beddoes was right — where are the buyers?

Yes! the fault is with the public — not with the poets. There are, perhaps, more good poets — I say good, not, of course, great — in the world at this moment than there have ever been before in its history, and America is entitled to a proud percentage of them. It would, indeed, be almost safe to say that there are more poets in the world to-day than there are readers, or at all events, buyers, of poetry; and that, under the conditions, poets manage to get published at all is a circumstance which shows the modern publisher in an unaccustomed light, as a quixotic lover of literature: for not one volume of poetry in a hundred can possibly pay its expenses, and even poets with well-established names, to whom important reviews devote columns of appreciation, know to their cost, or rather the cost of their publishers, that fame is more cry than wool, and that, unless a poet can contrive to feed, clothe and house himself on his laurels, it is likely to go hard with him in a world, which, as Villon sang, will

> . . . grind him to the dust with poverty,
> And build him statues when he comes to die.⁴

The public only cares for poetry that has some national or moral or mawkishly sentimental theme — or, may be, makes some momentarily sensational appeal. The best in its great "popular" poets it knows nothing of. It knows Tennyson by "The Charge of the Light Brigade," and "The May Queen," but probably never heard of "The Lotus Eaters," or "Lucretius." Similarly it knows Longfellow by his grotesque "Excelsior," and knows nothing of his

>   Spanish sailors with bearded lips
>   And the magic of the sea, —[5]

all that finer gift of his which has been obscured for even true lovers of poetry by what one can only describe as his horrible popularity.

The three poets who are the occasion of all this righteous indignation have, I fear, little factitious popularity to hope for from the nature of their themes. They are just — poets. They have no special "message," nor are they "prophets" of anything in particular. One of them, indeed, Mr. Robinson, has been brought as nearly in touch with "the great heart of the public" as the appreciation of Mr. Roosevelt could bring him.[6] How near that is I have no means of knowing. Mr. Roosevelt would seem to occupy the same position of general *arbiter librorum* which Mr. Gladstone — sharing the honors with Queen Victoria — held in England. A word from Mr. Gladstone made the fame of Mrs. Humphry Ward, and, perhaps to his greater credit, it made the — Anglo-Saxon — fame of Marie Bashkertseff.[7] I hope, for Mr. Robinson's sake, that Mr. Roosevelt's fiat on literary matters has a like potency in America. But, unaided by some such reverberating advocate, I fear that Mr. Robinson's muse, alike with the muses of Miss Beall and Miss Murray, will not "put money in" his "purse," or in that of his publishers — for the very good (and discouraging) reason that all three volumes are too good poetry to appeal to the bad taste and general ignorance of the so-called "reading public" — God-a-mercy!

If this prognostication should prove unduly pessimistic, I shall thank their publishers for letting me know; for, indeed, it would be cheering news, faith for cloudy days, to hear that such good, even fine, and, in some instances, remarkable, poetry, had actually — sold.[8]

. . . .

(I don't think, by the way, that there is a single love-song in Mr Robinson's volume!)[9]

. . . .

Mr. Robinson, also, as I have hinted, has passed the period of his *sturm und drang*. He, too, has gone through the mill — in a man's way; and his book is not a book of love-songs. It is occupied almost exclusively with men who have gone through the mill also: Lincoln, Napoleon, Theodore Roosevelt (the particular god of his idolatry), and certain sad, cynical, good-hearted men, comrades in the misfortunes of existence, with whom he has been accustomed to foregather at "Calverly's" —

>   We go no more to Calverly's,
>   For there the lights are few and low;

And who are there to see by them,
Or what they see, we do not know.

Leffingwell, Clavering, and Lingard are the names of these friends — of whose individualities and fates Mr. Robinson gives us somewhat too cryptic glimpses — in a literary medium compounded of Browning and Mr. A.E. Housman — of The [sic] Shropshire Lad.[10] I don't mean that Mr. Robinson is a mere imitator of either of these two poets — for he has a very marked individuality of his own — he is a poet of steel and grit, refreshingly bracing after the too much honeycomb provided us by some of our younger poets; but he has none the less been markedly influenced by Browning and Housman, and their influence has resulted in somewhat too stringent and tight-packed a style, in too many dark sayings and drastic abbreviations of his meaning. So far, he is a poet of vividly etched lines rather than complete poems, flashes of insight, and lightning glimpses of character. His characterizations of Lincoln in "The Master" are particularly searching:

> Shrewd, hallowed,[11] harassed, and among
> The mysteries that are untold,
> The face we see was never young
> Nor could it ever have been old.
>
> For he, to whom we had applied
> Our shopman's test of age and worth,
> Was elemental when he died,
> As he was ancient at his birth:
> The saddest among kings of earth,
> Bowed with a galling crown, this man
> Met rancor with a cryptic mirth,
> Laconic — and Olympian.

"Cryptic mirth" would be no bad description of a certain persimmon humor which pervades Mr. Robinson's volume, in such delightful characterizations as this of "Miniver Cheevy":

> Miniver cursed the commonplace
>   And eyed a khaki suit with loathing;
> He missed the mediaeval grace
>   Of iron clothing.
>
> Miniver scorned the gold he sought,
>   But sore annoyed was he without it;
> Miniver thought, and thought, and thought,
>   And thought about it.
>
> Miniver Cheevy, born too late,
>   Scratched his head and kept on thinking;
> Miniver coughed, and called it fate,
>   And kept on drinking.

Or this tender *vale* for Clavering:

> He clung to phantoms and to friends,
>   And never came to anything.
> He left a wreath on Cubit's grave.
>   I say no more for Clavering.

Perhaps what I have been trying to say of Mr. Robinson's point of view is best expressed in this whimsical sketch of Shadrach O'Leary: ["Shadrach O'Leary" follows.]

Whatever the value of Mr. Robinson's muse, it is assuredly not that of a "small, ink-fed Eros."[12] As I said before, there is not one love-poem in his volume, though he has a very beautiful dirge "For a Dead Lady" —

> The forehead and the little ears
> Have gone where Saturn keeps the years;
> The breast[13] where roses could not live
> Has done with rising and with falling —

and he has a charming poem to a baby.[14]

From *Forum*, LXV (January 1911), 80-82, 88-90.

Richard LeGallienne (1866-1947), English journalist, essayist, poet, and novelist, lent himself to the influence of *fin de siècle* esthetes, notably Oscar Wilde. None of his work is entirely free of the touch.

1 After his florid introduction, LeGallienne reviews Dorothy Landers Beall's *Poems*, Ada Foster Murray's *Flower o' the Grass*, and Robinson's current volume.

2 This collection of fifty-five poems, with an introduction by Edwin Markham (New York, 1910), presents thirty-six poets now largely forgotten, but with Zona Gale, Joyce Kilmer, Ridgely Torrence, Ellery Leonard, Ludwig Lewisohn, George Sterling, Charles Hanson Towne, and Louis Untermeyer. Markham refers to Robinson (with Moody, Cawein, MacKaye, Carman, Reese, "and half a dozen others") as "Of course on the chronological slope below," and "our older clients of Apollo." The anthological group he considers "a still young band of singers" who are "reinforcing the actives."

3 LeGallienne distorts Thomas Lovell Beddoes' "Dream-Pedlary" in order to make his own point. The first two lines of the poem read: "If there were dreams to sell, / What would you buy?"

4 This translation of stanza 1, lines 4-5, of "Ballade au nom de la Fortune" from "Poésies Diverses" seems to be LeGallienne's own. This too is at variance with Villon's point of view and intent, serving LeGallienne's immediate purpose.

5 Here too LeGallienne misrepresents without fair warning. He omits the word "And" before "Spanish" as well as the line which comes between these two: "And the beauty and mystery of the ships" in Longfellow's "My Lost Youth."

6 See Theodore Roosevelt's review of *The Children of the Night* in *Outlook* for August 12, 1905, reprinted in this volume, and for numerous comments made in the press on succeeding pages.

7 See notes 5 and 6 to the New York *Evening Post* review of *The Children of the Night*, August 14, 1905, in this volume.

8 Not until the popularity of *Tristram* in 1927, with its adoption by the Literary Guild and its numerous reissues, was Robinson able to live solely on the royalties from his writings.

9 To clarify retroactive statements made by LeGallienne in respect to Robinson, these remarks about the two female versifiers are excerpted from the omitted material: "Love! love! love! . . . rings from end to end of Miss Beall's volume"; and, Miss Murray "is no *sturm und drang* singer such as Miss Beall."

10 For Browning see the section *Browning, Browning, Browning* in the chapter

"Preliminary Vistas" of this volume; also note 1 to Robert Steed Dunn's review in the *Harvard Monthly*, February 1897, reprinted in this volume.

With only cautious reservations about Housman's range and tone, Robinson extolled his work consistently from the time he picked up a first edition of *A Shropshire Lad* for a quarter in a Boston bookstall until the year before he died.

Robinson told Joyce Kilmer: "Within his limits, I believe that A.E. Housman is the most authentic poet now writing in England. But, of course, his limits are very sharply drawn. I don't think that any one who knows anything about poetry will ever think of questioning the inspiration of *A Shropshire Lad*. ("Edwin Arlington Robinson Defines Poetry," New York *Times Magazine Section* [April 9, 1916], 12.)

On May 2, 1923 he wrote to Laura E. Richards: "I don't believe there is any need for worrying over cheerful Mr. Housman. When I read three pages of his first book, years ago, I knew that he had come to stay. . . . His kingdom is a small and not very jolly one, but he is the boss of it, and that's enough." (Torrence, p. 130.)

To Lucius Beebe: "The name of A.E. Housman, for instance, is as secure to fame as that of any poet of the last seventy-five years. He is a king in a small kingdom, despite the fact that he published his *Shropshire Lad* at the time when the name of Rudyard Kipling filled almost the whole poetic horizon." ("Robinson Sees Romantic Strain in Future Verse," New York *Herald Tribune* [December 22, 1929], I, 19.)

"A.E. Housman — his work, don't you agree, is pretty nearly perfect," he said soberly to Karl Schriftgiesser ("An American Poet Speaks His Mind," Boston *Evening Transcript Book Section* [November 4, 1933], 1.)

And to Houston Martin on January 12, 1934: "there seems to me to be no question as to the enduring quality of A.E. Housman's poetry. I do not think of any living writer whose work is likely to live longer — if as long." (Torrence, p. 174.)

On his part, Housman scarcely returned the compliments. Cyril Clemens reports his saying, "I got more enjoyment . . . from Edna St. Vincent Millay than from either Robinson or Frost." (Grant Richards, *Housman, 1897-1936* [Oxford, 1941], p. 340.)

11 Truman Bartlett asterisked this word in his copy of the book (p. 5) and noted below: "'ragged' written until proofs came to Chocorua in Aug. '10 — disliked by Hunt, & changed in Chocorua." At this time Robinson was staying with Bartlett — a gifted, eccentric sculptor and natural philosopher — in his New Hampshire hideaway.

Hunt is probably Edward Eyre Hunt (1885-1953), a Harvard graduate of 1910 who worked as secretary of appointments and assistant in the English Department for the next two years. Thereafter he held a series of high Federal posts, including the State Department, was a war correspondent, and an official in Red Cross relief in Europe. He wrote several books on national economics, unemployment, and rehabilitation. He was decorated for his services by Italy, France, and Belgium.

12 Line 12 of "Shadrach O'Leary": "And the small, ink-fed Eros of his dream."

13 For "breast" LeGallienne substituted "heart," with true turn-of-the-century delicacy.

14 "For Arvia, On Her Fifth Birthday." She was Percy MacKaye's daughter.

.. / / ..

Vain regret for the impermanence of the individual

THE TOWN DOWN THE RIVER

What is particularly baffling to the habitual reader of current verse is the difficulty of detecting any larger spirit blowing through it all and ordering it to one common issue in the end. Much of it is merely inadvertent; the writers never repeat their initial indiscretion. Even that which shows some sort of conviction moves to as many motives as there are poets. All that can be said of it in a general way is that, on the whole, it seems inclining to develop a kind of racial consciousness as contrasted with the individual temper of the past. There are, of course, the usual humanitarian themes. . . . [Examples follow.]

But this is not all. While this sort of thing is fairly familiar by this time, there is also a disposition to stretch the elementary sympathy for humanity in such a way as to include the vital experiences of nature and the generations of animal life as a whole. It is in this direction, if anywhere, that the modern epic is to be looked for — in the strange adventure of evolution. In fact, wherever a voice is heard to speak with assurance, you shall find that the singer is inspired by this new sense of kinship with things that grow and change. . . . [Examples follow.]

Or again, as in Mr. Robinson's "Calverly's," it may consist with a vain regret for the impermanence and fleetingness of the individual, the creature of hapless and haunting memory: [Stanzas 1, 2, 4 follow.]

From "Recent Verse," *Nation*, XCII (January 5, 1911), 11.

This review is typical of the running practice of the day: to take an overview stance, establish a controlling thesis, and support it with illustrations from the fistful of poets under consideration — a practice conducive to grievous Procrustean travesties. This flick at Robinson's work is of a piece with the one-comment, one-quotation coverage of twelve volumes of verse occupying two pages (Robinson is third in order). Other poets of contemporary prominence similarly treated are William Watson, Stephen Phillips, Cale Young Rice. The rest have gone with the snows.

Drawing bead on each of the other volumes in this gallimaufry, the anonymous critic decrees the following as salient aspects in the indifferent flux of current poetry:

1) "this sense of mutability may combine with a vision of succession equally fugitive and tantalizing."

2) "the humanitarian and the racial are inextricably mingled and the whole melancholy procession of mortality parades its wrongs and misery."

3) "dreams of instability and revolution [and] participation in the common shifty human heritage."

4) "Without confidence in his own fixity [the individual] is able to find no stay, no principle of support outside of himself — only a flux and ceaseless agitation."

5) "poets . . . avoid contemporary problems altogether and take refuge in some quiet chamber of the fancy aloof from all such vexatious concerns."

6) others present "the least possible surface to the blows of circumstance by immersing [themselves] in the study of Greek."

A veritable compendium of thematic blemishes, self-neutralizing in that it could be leveled at almost any moment in the rise — or decline — of any emerging, diverse culture.

. . / / . .

Conscious of a sublime answer somewhere

THREE POETS OF THE PRESENT

Three volumes of verse have lately been added to the singing brooks that flow forever to the brimming river of poetry, chattering or chanting, according to the power at their well-spring, but never ceasing to flow during all the centuries since man invented words.

These three books[1] are by men who have already attracted many settlers to their banks, being known for their tuneful numbers, and they need but little introduction. They are not deep or wonderful, but they reflect the sun and shade and have a musical voice; often, too, they sing with a note of passion and sincerity that thrills upon the hearer and brings him back to listen again.

First, as by far the more original and intense in spirit, is Mr. Robinson's *The Town Down the River*. This collection of poems possesses an esoteric quality, addressing itself rather to a special than an average experience or understanding of life. That is to say, the book reveals a distinctly individual point of view and manner of feeling — something expressive of a small group more than of humanity at large. The volume is such a one as might have been recited, evening after evening, to a coterie of young people, who, drifted together from the four corners of the world on the same quest, seeking an answer to the same secret, met, after the day's artistic endeavor, in some quiet café unknown to the rest of the town to listen and discuss and criticise. The group falls apart and vanishes; but there survives, among much not worth remembering, this handful of poems too good to disappear with the rest. Fantasy, an odd, shy, self-confidence, a bitter tenderness, are contained in these verses. At times a rare beauty shines through the words. The poem that gives the book its title seems to us particularly characteristic of Mr. Robinson's art. There is an elusive imagination in it, an apparent simplicity veiling a subtle and curious wisdom, a wisdom content to question, ponder, doubt, yet conscious of a sublime answer somewhere. "Calverly's" is also a remarkable poem, with its sharply etched though shadowy portraits — each, as it were, suppressing a cry of pain and hiding its face as it dies. Then there is the delicate and lovely "Leonora," grim as lovely. Mr. Robinson may be said to put what appeals to him into words, just before it escapes into the region beyond words, to be master of a genre of the spirit. We quote, among many worth quoting, this: ["For a Dead Lady" follows.]

From New York *Times Review of Books* (February 12, 1911), VI, 79.

---

1 Robinson, *The Town Down the River*; Cale Young Rice, *Song-Surf*; Irving Bacheller, *In Various Moods*.

.. / / ..

A parsimonious poet

THE TOWN DOWN THE RIVER
William Morton Payne

Mr. Edwin Arlington Robinson, the author of *The Town Down the*

River, is a parsimonious poet, but when he gives us dole of his riches, we know that the coin is no counterfeit. He is a reticent poet, but a few of his words will outweigh the fluent utterance of the more voluble. Witness these lines about Lincoln:

> For he, to whom we had applied
> Our shopman's test of age and worth,
> Was elemental when he died,
> As he was ancient at his birth:
> The saddest among kings of earth,
> Bowed with a galling crown, this man
> Met rancor with a cryptic mirth,
> Laconic — and Olympian.
>
> The love, the grandeur, and the fame
> Are bounded by the world alone;
> The calm, the smouldering, and the flame
> Of awful patience were his own:
> With him they are forever flown
> Past all our fond self-shadowings,
> Wherewith we cumber the Unknown
> As with inept, Icarian wings.[1]

Witness also these words of Napoleon, half-delirious upon his death-bed at St. Helena:

> What ruinous tavern-shine
> Is this that lights me far from worlds and wars
> And women that were mine?
> Where do I say it is
> That Time has made my bed?
> What lowering outland hostelry is this
> For one the stars have disinherited?
>
> An island, I have said:
> A peak, where fiery dreams and far desires
> Are rained on, like old fires:
> A vermin region by the stars abhorred,
> Where falls the flaming word
> By which I consecrate with unsuccess
> An acreage of God's forgetfulness,
> Left here above the foam and long ago
> Made right for my duress;
> Where soon the sea,
> My foaming and long-clamoring enemy,
> Will have within the cryptic, old embrace
> Of her triumphant arms — a memory.[2]

Mr. Robinson's attitude toward life in its conventional manifestations is bitter or contemptuous, his expression almost acrid, and yet his vision is transfigured with gleams of idealism. The City of God may be as yet unbuilded, but somewhere — possibly in this land of ours — foundations are being laid. Even so godless a spot as Broadway may prove to be its site. ["The White Lights (Broadway, 1906)," follows.]

We may not chide for his too infrequent stage entrances the poet who has grave and measured discourse like this. There is hardly another

American singer now left us who has equal right to say, *"Mon verre n'est pas grand, mais je bois dans mon verre,"*³ and whose thought has such quintessential purity of distillation.

From "Recent Poetry," *Dial*, L (March 1, 1911), 164-165.

---

1 "The Master (Lincoln)," p. 6.

2 "An Island (Saint Helena, 1821)," pp. 27-28.

3 Alfred de Musset, "La Coupe et les Lèvres," *Premières Poésies, 1829-1835* (Paris, 1899), p. 226. In the "Dédicace to M. Alfred T[atet], Musset writes:

> On m'a dit l'an passé que j'imitais Byron:
> Vous qui me connaissez, vous savez bien que non.
> Je hais comme la mort l'état de plagiaire;
> Mon verre n'est pas grand, mais je bois dans mon verre.
>
> [Last year they said that I imitated Byron:
> But you who know me, know well it is not so.
> I hate plagiarism as I hate death;
> My glass is small, but I drink from my glass.]

. . / / . .

Pipes not a lullaby

THE TOWN DOWN THE RIVER

... Nor is Clinton Scollard the only surviving poet of the active generation who gives us pleasure. ... There is excellent verse to be found in Alida Chanler Emmet's *Psyche Sleeps*. Truth to tell, Psyche sleeps not alone. But Edwin Arlngton Robinson, tho he has Momus for interlocutor, pipes not a lullaby: ["Momus" follows.]¹

Yes, as Mr. Richard LeGallienne tells us, "there are, perhaps, more good poets ... in the world at this moment than there have ever been before in its history," and America has a proud percentage of them, ...²

From "Good American Poets," *Independent*, LXX (March 2, 1911), 470.

Another of those provoking minimal-mention cluster reviews, in this case eleven books of verse, Robinson's the last.

1 "Momus," pp. 64-65, as rendered by the *Independent* here is one of the ghastlier examples of careless transcription, containing some dozen solecisms. Robinson and his editors at Scribner's seem to be at fault themselves in not inserting quotation marks at end of line 7, stanza 2, perpetuated in the *Collected Poems*.

2 See LeGallienne's critique for the *Forum*, January 1911, reprinted in this volume.

. . / / . .

Always a hidden something in the lines

THE TOWN DOWN THE RIVER

Andrew Marvell, in the poem "To His Coy Mistress," starts from his secure revery, and flashes this disconcerting fear:

> But at my back I always hear
> Time's wingèd chariot hurrying near,
> And yonder all before us lie
> Deserts of vast eternity.

This intruding thought of universal transcience haunts the verse of Edward[1] Arlington Robinson (*The Town Down the River*, Charles Scribner's Sons). The tone of this poet is regret. His heritage has been scattered and trodden under foot, his sad, kind-hearted, cynical friends are memories, and his old haunts have been given over to a strange generation.

> We go no more to Calverly's,
> For there the lights are few and low;
> And who are there to see by them,
> Or what they see, we do not know.[2]

But from these regrets the poet has distilled verses of the rarest imaginable beauty. The shapes he calls up are scarcely visualized. There is always a hidden something in the lines — each poem has a lyric secret. We may add that at times his style is too cryptic and occasionally the meaning dives into complete obscurity and does not reappear again for several stanzas.

Mr. Robinson uses all the arts of this type of poetry — a type that is accurately described in one of the essays of Paul Elmer More. Mr. More has been speaking of the poetry of Thomas Bailey Aldrich: "The essence of this poetry lies in irony — not the grim sort we know from the tragedians and satirists, but a self-deprecating irony that is half a confession of weakness and half a deliberate veiling of strength in gentleness. Reticence, suggestion, and accepted littleness are its indispensable qualities. The regret of an idealized past will linger in it. . . . It is touched by the tragic brevity and insufficiency of life, but has no grief more clamorous than a sigh. It sees the incongruity of human pretensions, but indulges in no mirth more boisterous than a smile."[3]

These lines were not written concerning Mr. Robinson's poetry, but they will be found to apply very directly to the following selections from his book. ["Clavering," "For a Dead Lady," "Uncle Ananias" follow.]

From "Current Poetry," *Literary Digest*, XLII (March 4, 1911), 424-425.

---

1 "He was caustic, too, about the many printed variants of his name. People persisted in calling him Edward — or Edgar. . . . At the sight of all such errors he was mildly beside himself. 'No name in the language . . . has so many wrong connotations as Edward. . . . You'd think some of them would be getting it right by this time.'" (Rollo Walter Brown, *Next Door to a Poet* [New York, 1937], pp. 77-79.)

2 "Calverly's," p. 41.

3 Paul Elmer More, *Shelburne Essays: Seventh Series* (Boston, 1910), p. 148. Two sentences in this context quite applicable also to Robinson's work but not included by this reviewer: "It must have its roots in deep emotion, but its manner is rather of one who sees passion in another than of one who himself feels"; "It knows the deception of the world, but harbours pity and not cynicism." More is discussing good *vers de société* and his passage begins, "Its essence lies in irony . . ."

.. / / ..

Neither a reactionary nor a rebel

THREE BOOKS OF VERSE

To be pessimistic about the present practice and future prospects of poetry has become so much a matter of habit, so automatic, that it is not easy to consider the verse of the hour with an open mind. The bodies of the critics are piled high around the cradle of almost every poetic reputation, to recall Mr. Huxley and the theologians.[1] The well-worn reference to the damning of Keats has served long and well to point a moral, not because it was exceptional, but because the idea went abroad that the poet was murdered by the *Quarterly*, an impression which enormously underrates the vitality of the author of *Hyperion*, a piece of astonishing vigor and promise, and enormously overrates the destructive power of the *Quarterly*.[2] As a rule, correct verse of academic quality gets prompt recognition; its merits are so obvious, often so admirable, that a trained mind familiar with the standards promptly recognizes and generously applauds them. And verse at the other extreme, which startles and shocks, attracts immediate attention, and is either "viewed with alarm" or hailed as the song of a new age. The verse that often meets a disheartening silence is the sincere, genuine, promising work which lacks the academic precision but stirs with life either in imagination or phrase; or the verse which avoids violence of invective and betrays originality in clear conviction and compressed vigor of style; the verse, in a word, which is neither academic nor journalistic, but fresh, human, and alive. Of great poetry there is obvious lack, but so far as good, sound verse is concerned the situation is by no means so desperate as the professional alarmists would lead us to believe.

Mr. Robinson, for example, has published work of a very reassuring quality, and his latest book of verse, *The Town Down the River*, will comfort those who have been led to expect that new poetry must be as polished and lifeless as the statue of the "Greek Slave,"[3] or as noisy, violent, and profane as a far Western bar-room on a festive night. Mr. Robinson is quietly himself; he is neither a reactionary nor a rebel; he steers clear of the commonplace and escapes the strain of a deliberate and painful effort to be original. His quiet speech, his fresh perception, his penetration are shown in these lines on Lincoln:

> For he, to whom we had applied
> Our shopman's test of age and worth,
> Was elemental when he died,

> As he was ancient at his birth:
> The saddest among kings of earth,
> Bowed with a galling crown, this man
> Met rancor with a cryptic mirth,
> Laconic — and Olympian.[4]

The poem which gives its title to this volume has that elusive quality of imagination which haunts all memorable things in life; a sense of mystery which does not impair the sense of reality, but conveys the parable without weakening the force of the fact; and the style is full of the strength of plain words and compressed experience. There are songs in this book which lack enchantment, but have the vibration of life.

From *Outlook*, XCVIII (June 3, 1911), 245.

The two other books reviewed after Robinson's are *Poems* by Mrs. Schuyler van Rensselaer and *The Poems of Sophie Jewett*.

1 "Extinguished theologians lie about the cradle of every science as the strangled snakes beside that of Hercules." From "The Origin of Species [1860]," in *Darwiniana, Essays* by Thomas H. Huxley (New York, 1896), p. 52.

2 Upon publication of *Endymion* in 1818, John Keats was virulently attacked in the *Quarterly Review* and *Blackwood's Magazine* as a disciple of the radical Leigh Hunt and a member of the "Cockney School of Poetry," basis of the popular legend that the "Scotch reviewers" hastened his death.

3 A nude female marble figure in neoclassic style by Hiram Powers (1805-1873), Vermont sculptor who spent the last four decades of his life in Italy. Formal and idealized, it established a standard for American taste during the Victorian epoch.

4 "The Master (Lincoln)," p. 6.

. . / / . .

No justification save its own beauty

A CLASSIC POET

Joyce Kilmer

The motives of poets are, as a rule, not hard to find. Thus George Herbert wrote for the glory of God, Walt Whitman for the glory of Man, and Baudelaire for the glory of the Devil. There are few books of verse in which there is not evident a definite purpose to edify, to amuse, to corrupt, to shock, to influence in some way the prospective reader. The most enthusiastic disciples of "Art for Art's Sake" were all of them preachers, whole-heartedly intent on spreading their special gospel of Beauty. Even when the poet's aim is not directly to teach or to persuade, there is frequently a conscious effort at self-advertisement — self-revelation is perhaps a more courteous phrase. The poet is striving to tell the world about his love, or his hate, about his lady or his enemy, about his spiritual or physical emotions or sensations. So even the most personal lyric becomes didactic from his desire to teach the public to be interested in his affairs.

This statement is not made in a spirit of hostile criticism. From the vine-crowned scop chanting his saga of blood and fire among the warriors in the banquet hall to the modern versemaker typewriting his quatrain for the magazine, the poet has had in mind his audience. This is just; this is, in fact, inevitable. But it is, nevertheless, true that the reader of verse grows weary of the constant repetition of direct and obvious appeals, and seeks often in vain for the poem which shall not force its message upon him, for the poet who shall write neither to persuade nor to exhibit, but in response to the creative urge.

This phenomenon, poetry with no purpose, with no cause save its own demand to be, with no justification save its own beauty, distinguishes the work of Edwin Arlington Robinson[1] from that of most of its contemporaries. It is a fact that Miss May Sinclair, writing in the *Atlantic Monthly* six years ago, stated that this poet had a message, and that it was "Be true to the truth that lies nearest to you, true to God, if you have found him; true to man, true to yourself; true if you know no better truth to your primal instincts; but at any rate be true."[2] But this teaching is not definitely stated in any of Robinson's poems. If it can be derived from them as a whole, it must be by a reader of the philosophic type, who sees in every simple statement a premise of some large conclusion.

No, Robinson does not preach, nor does he argue. He states, he describes, he narrates, not, it seems, so much for the sake of his audience as for his own relief. Yet he is by no means remote or unworldly. There are few poets who are so invariably human. In fact, humanity is an obsession with him. He is a realist in the proper meaning of the word; not a nominalist, nor a morbid chronicler of sordid detail, but a student of life. He writes of the present, knowing that it is an aspect of eternity; of man, knowing that he is immortal and incomprehensible. There is in his verse a surprising lack of classical allusion and scholarly decoration.[3] His lyrics are austere expressions of simple emotions, his character sketches are impartial portrayals of subjects rich in actuality, his narratives are economical statements of tremendous and real events. Nothing is added, nothing taken away; the words set forth the fact in all its beautiful and terrible clarity.

One characteristic of his sternly simple method is evident in his treatment of the fixed forms of versification. Usually the poet who prides himself on his strength takes particular delight in breaking the laws of his craft, in showing contempt of rhyme and rhythm.[4] To such a writer the word "sonnet" smells of the prison. The suggestion that he should write a ballade or a rondeau would seem to him a wanton insult. But this is not Robinson's attitude. The forms of poetry exist; they are established; he accepts them. But the forms are made for the poet, not the poet for the forms. So, for example, in "The Growth of 'Lorraine'" he makes two sonnets, faultless in construction, tells a story of love and death which, expanded, might fill a volume.[5] This is not the use to which sonnets are generally put, but what does it matter? The sonnet form is a difficult instrument, and the player who has mastered it has won the right to play on it any time he wishes.

Equally typical in Robinson's treatment of that highly artificial form, the villanelle. What thoughts of delicate splendor that word calls up! Troubadours and lutes and laughter, painted fans and painted ladies. But Robinson does not think of this. There is something he wants to say, the villanelle seems to be a convenient method, so he uses it. The result is a poem of striking simplicity, of striking effectiveness, but so different in spirit from the traditional villanelle that its form is at first scarcely recognized. For Robinson uses the forms of poetry as boldly as though he had invented them: ["The House on the Hill" follows.]

Aside from "The Master" and "For a Dead Lady," Robinson is perhaps best known for his brief sketches in verse, labeled in most part with unusual proper names, such as Cliff Klingenhagen, Leffingwell, and Miniver Cheevy. Sometimes these are dramas in little, sometimes they are studies of character. It is natural that an isolated poem of this type, seen in the pages of a magazine, should repel rather than attract the casual reader. For, as has been said before, Robinson does not explain or elaborate or even suggest an emotion. The poem arises as the spontaneous expression of a strong impression — it is naked of intent. But when these poems are considered together they develop a congruity and interrelation which make clear the separate meaning of each. "How Annandale Went Out," for example, is mystifying to one who has not read "The Book of Annandale."[6] But when it is once seen that there is no lesson to be learned, no hidden meaning to be sought, when the poems are taken at their face value, their power is immediately felt. They are all studies of life. They are tragic, because life is tragic; humorous, because life is humorous; fantastic, because life is fantastic. The rustic amorist, John Evereldown, goes at night through the Maine woods to his assignation in Tilbury Town; Richard Cory, the pattern of wealth and respectability, goes home and puts a bullet through his head; the miser, Aaron Stark, laughs at the sound of unmerited pity; the butcher, Reuben Bright, tears down his slaughter house in grief at his wife's death; Shadrach O'Leary, the erstwhile poet of passion, grows sane and forgets the "small ink-fed Eros of his pen," and Miniver Cheevy keeps on drinking. In these poems men and women do wise, foolish, saintly, and damnable things. For these poems are life; not life as Robinson would wish it to be, or thinks that it was of old, but as it is now, seen clearly and seen whole. He is forced to portray life and to chronicle life. He does not explain, for he cannot understand.

While the thought in Robinson's poems is set down simply and without rhetorical elaboration, it is done with no disregard of technique. In fact, the almost Greek lucidity of his work comes from a scrupulous care for words, a precision which would have delighted Pater. Coleridge's test for a blameless style was its "untranslateableness in words of the same language without injury to the meaning."[7] Take from Robinson's poem on Lincoln this stanza and apply the test to it:

> For he, to whom we had applied
> Our shopman's test of age and worth,
> Was elemental when he died,
> As he was ancient at his birth:
> The saddest among kings of earth,
> Bowed with a galling crown, this man
> Met rancor with a cryptic mirth,
> Laconic — and Olympian.³

Can any part of this be translated into words of the same language without injury to the meaning? "Merchant" will not do for "shopman" nor "anger" for "rancor," nor "crown of thorns" for "galling crown." Try to paraphrase it, and the finality of the wording is at once apparent. This is the English of a master.

Not as a prophet, not as a teacher, but as a student of mankind does Robinson hold his place among poets. Always he looks at humanity, patiently, earnestly, searchingly. His poems spring from his contemplation of the fact of life, they are compounded of sympathy and wonder.

From New York *Times Review of Books* (September 8, 1912), VI, 487.

Alfred Joyce Kilmer (1886-1918), American poet and journalist still memorialized by the title piece of his *Trees and Other Poems*, was killed in the second battle of the Marne.

After reading Kilmer's critique Robinson wrote him, September 15, 1912: "Let me thank you for your friendly notice of my books in the Times *Review*. You say things in it that I have been waiting for someone to say, and I am very glad on general principles that you should care enough for the books to put yourself to the trouble of writing about them." (Louis Untermeyer, *Edwin Arlington Robinson: A Reappraisal* [Washington, D.C., 1963], p. 34.)

To Edith Brower, October 2, 3 or 4, 1912, he wrote: "I didn't know that Kilmer cared for my books until I saw him in the *Times*." (Cary, p. 154.)

1 This article is subtitled "Edwin A. Robinson — An essay in Appreciation." At the head of the text are listed *Captain Craig* (1902), *The Children of the Night* (1905), and *The Town Down the River* (1910).

2 This September 1906 essay, "Three American Poets of To-Day," is reproduced in this volume. Kilmer mangled both words and punctuation of Miss Sinclair's original, just as he took liberties with punctuation and capitalization in the short excerpt from "The Master," below.

3 This is a remarkable statement in view of the fact that of the 151 poems in the three volumes under review here six have titles derived from classical sources and twenty-eight have at least one classical allusion. As to scholarly decoration, thirteen titles contain the name of an author, artist, philosopher, biblical or legendary character; forty-seven poems have references to myths, persons, or places (twenty-two biblical, seven British, seven European, three Jewish, one Norse, six Oriental, one American); eight poems contain foreign words or phrases; three, quotations or paraphrases; four mention authors or their works; one, a painter; one, a ceramist; two, a sculptor or sculpture; one, a composer; five, a philosopher or philosophic system; three, a scientist or scientific principle. It must also be remembered that most of the poems contain multiple instances — clusters rather than single mentions — so that the numerical total outruns this bare categorical count. "Captain Craig" alone, a veritable granary of allusion and decoration, would constitute a repudiation of Kilmer's statement.

4 "I am essentially a classicist in poetic composition, and I believe that the accepted media for the masters of the past will continue to be used in the future. There is, of course, room for infinite variety, manipulation and invention within the limits of traditional forms and meters, but any violent deviation from the classic mean may be a confession of inability to do the real thing, poetically speaking." (Beebe, I, 19.)

5 See note on compression in the section *Olla Podrida* in the chapter "Preliminary Vistas" of this volume.

6 These poems and "Annandale Again" are examined in this light by David S. Nivison, *Colby Library Quarterly*, V (December 1960), 170-185. Robinson's brother Horace, a doctor who apparently administered himself a fatal overdose of morphine, is generally cited as the original of George Annandale.

7 *Biographia Literaria*, Chapter XXII.

8 "The Master (Lincoln)," p. 6.

. . / / . .

A sort of incurable optimism

A DISCUSSION OF THE EXACT VALUE OF ROBINSON'S POETRY

Louis V. Ledoux

New York City, N.Y.

The New York Times Review of Books:

It is pleasant to read so sympathetic a piece of criticism as that of Edwin Arlington Robinson's poetry in your issue of Sept. 8, but there is more to be said on the subject than Mr. Kilmer has taken space to say.[1] Mr. Robinson's *The Town Down the River* — and whatever is said of this book applies with certain modifications to his others — is perhaps the most distinctive, if not also the most distinguished, volume of American verse that has appeared in some years, but there must be positive qualities of excellence other than those pointed out by the critic to make it so.

The characteristics of Mr. Robinson's poems most conspicuous to me are kindliness, humor, sympathy, and a sort of incurable optimism that sometimes seems to be amused at its own pig-headedness.

He draws people not at all in the manner of Christy or Charles Dana Gibson[2]; they would do poor service on a fashion plate, and there is no Greek god among them — no young Apollo. In the main his characters are a sorry lot — "derelicts of all conditions"[3] but what could be more kindly than his attitude toward them:

> I say no more of Clavering
> Than I should say of him who fails
> To bring his wounded vessel home
> When reft of rudder and of sails;
> . . . .
> I think of him as I should think
> Of one who for scant wages played,
> And faintly, a flawed instrument
> That fell while it was being made;[4]

But let us take an instance better because more comprehensive of the same attitude. The title poem of *The Town Down the River* describes various companies of people, young and middle-aged, weak and strong, toiling blindly toward the goal of their illusions, and of each group the watcher by the way asks in kindly wisdom: "Do you really know where you are going? Are you sure the fruit you are after will not turn to ashes in your mouths, and that the town whose lights have lured you is really worth going to? Are you directing your lives sanely, and toward a worthy end?" But later, when the aged ones come to him still toiling on but a little doubtful at last, ready to be freed from their illusions and to escape the lure, he urges them forward on their way. It is kindly and it is wise, and most of it is not humorous.

The humor in Mr. Robinson's poetry is more difficult to point out by illustration, for it is a pervading essence seldom embodied in any concrete form, and then dancing away like an elfin sprite. Sometimes it is in a word or the turn of a phrase and sometimes it is so subtle that the reader who takes either the author or himself too solemnly misses it entirely; but from almost every page, when it is looked at long enough, the elf peers out, and his face when once seen is hard to forget, even though he seldom grants more than a glimpse of himself. Mr. Robinson's humor is like the deity of the Pantheists: it cannot be proved, but may be observed anywhere. He never has written a humorous poem, for life as he sees it is too pitiful for that, but nearly every one of his poems is filled with a humor that is based on sympathetic insight, and never descends to ridicule.

> Miniver coughed, and called it fate,
> And kept on drinking.[5]

Miniver's whole life is sketched in these two lines with the sureness of characterization and the direct simplicity of diction so characteristic of the author, but one feels that he would have been a good friend to Miniver, kindly in his attitude toward him, and though fully aware of his humorous aspects yet having a thoroughly sympathetic understanding of each crotchet and foible.

Mr. Robinson's presentation of his characters is as sympathetically understanding as, for example, Sterne's Uncle Toby[6]; but there is something more than this, something more positive; there is the quality of invincible optimism which is a distinct expression of a philosophy of life. As we look at the "derelicts of all conditions," our attention is called not to the fact that they are derelicts but to the somehow frustrate possibilities in them, to that helpless what-might-have-been which is at once the pathos and the hope of life. It is a philosophy like that of Rabbi Ben Ezra,[7] but the optimism is even more pronounced, for most of the people described by Mr. Robinson do not even try to be anything worth being. Some casual, undeveloped germ of good — and there is that much even in the worst of us — is enough to make Mr. Robinson treat a character with his wonted kindliness, sympathetic insight, and genial humor; and is enough to make him reclothe the sorry being in the garments of his own incurable optimism and send him out with a feeling of new self-respect to meet the eyes of an incredulous world. The good in apparent failure, the hope in apparent hopelessness, is the keynote of these books, and the optimism of them would be almost pathologic did not their author see the pity and tragedy of life so clearly.

By no means all of Mr. Robinson's poems are character studies of human derelicts. In his latest volume the fine poem on Lincoln, the Greek elegiacs, &c., are examples of a totally different though equally high order of attainment, but in all there is the characteristic style, the peculiar excellence of diction so clearly pointed out by Mr. Kilmer, and in all there is the same attitude toward life, the same philosophy.

These books do not yield themselves lightly to the casual reader; there is a cryptic quality about them which has made Mr. Robinson a peculiarly difficult nut for the critical teeth to crack; but very little poetry has succeeded in being good poetry without being unconsciously didactic, and the lesson to be derived from Mr. Robinson's work is this of Christian charity, kindliness, and the constant observation of whatever is good in the midst of evil.

In these days, when we are so prone to rush into the literary wilderness after some new thing, it is curious that work as strikingly original as Mr. Robinson's should not yet have become more widely known, but the very fact that it has not makes doubly pleasant the reading of so sympathetic a study of it as that by Mr. Kilmer in your issue of Sept. 8.

From New York *Times Review of Books* (September 29, 1912), VI, 533.

Louis Vernon Ledoux (1880-1948), valued friend, frequent patron, and literary executor of Robinson, wrote several essays, reviews, and celebratory notices on the poet principally in the *Times* and the *Saturday Review of Literature*. An executive in his father's assaying company, Ledoux was a poet in his own right, a connoisseur of Japanese art, and a crack tennis player. He dedicated his *The Story of Eleusis* to Robinson and Ridgely Torrence, and Robinson dedicated *The Porcupine* to Ledoux.

Robinson to Ledoux, October 1, 1912: "I wish to thank you all through for your *Times* letter, which is from its point of attack altogether the best thing that I have yet read about my *Town*. I make this qualification, not wishing to agree too eagerly with your praise, as such. The publication of such intelligent criticism of what my books are supposed at least to signify give me a great deal of pleasure at a time when I need a little cheering up." (Torrence, p. 76.) Robinson explains that he was undergoing "the woes of the wagon" — withdrawing from alcohol.

To Edith Brower, October 2, 3 or 4, 1912: "Ledoux's commentary seemed to me to be rather necessary, and it came all the better being unexpected." (Cary, p. 154.)

1 See the preceding review in this volume.

2 Both Howard Chandler Christy (1873-1952) and Charles Dana Gibson (1867-1945), American illustrators, created for fashionable magazine covers popular concepts of glorified American womanhood, cool, refined, and sentimental in keeping with upper-class tastes of the Gay Nineties.

3 "The Town Down the River," p. 19.

4 "Clavering," pp. 50-51.

5 "Miniver Cheevy," p. 99.

6 The invariably modest and amiable retired soldier whose hobby is military strategy, which he practices with miniature props on his bowling-green, in Laurence Sterne's *The Life and Opinions of Tristram Shandy.*

7 Robert Browning's learned holy man in the poem of this title summarizes his philosophy in the opening stanza with these phrases: "The best is yet to be"; "trust God: see all, nor be afraid!" Man, the work of God, is perfectible despite "what flaws may lurk."

. . / / . .

In this four-page overview of American poetry Miss Monroe assigns her loftiest encomiums to recently deceased William Vaughn Moody, "the most nobly impassioned and technically proficient of our poets." His name then suggests to her "three other poets, his friends" — Percy MacKaye, Ridgely Torrence, and Robinson.

A tense and stern simplicity

MODERN AMERICAN POETRY

Harriet Monroe

Edwin Arlington Robinson, the third of the trio, is our nearest equivalent to Mr. Gibson,[1] for his subjects are of common modern experience and his style is of a tense and stern simplicity, capable at times of austere dignity and beauty. "Captain Craig," a blank verse narrative of an old sailor's last years, reaches a climax of quiet strength, and "The Master" is a simple and noble expression of the average citizen's love, at once intimate and reverent, of Lincoln. Now and then also he has a strong satiric word for the poet who is "born too late," "who cursed the commonplace," and for "the small, ink-fed Eros of his dream."[2]

From *Poetry Review* (London), I (October 1912), 470.

Harriet Monroe (1860-1936), poet and lyrical dramatist, made her deepest impression on American literature by founding in 1912 and editing until her death *Poetry: A Magazine of Verse.* She was instrumental in the rise of many new poets in two generations. She published Robinson's "Eros Turannos" in 1914, "Bokardo" in 1915, and "Avenel Gray" (renamed "Mortmain") in 1922.

1 Wilfrid Wilson Gibson (1878-1962), English poet, quickly forsook his early models, Tennyson and Swinburne, for the forthright realism of George Crabbe, dealing with humble country folk and urban working poor in commonplace phrases and simple versification. By 1912 he had published a dozen slim volumes of mostly regional verse.

2 The first two quotations are from "Miniver Cheevy," pp. 99, 98; the third from "Shadrach O'Leary," p. 92.

. . / / . .

Familiarity breeds respect

EDWIN ARLINGTON ROBINSON
Louis V. Ledoux

In a recent poetry competition some ten thousand manuscripts, representing the selected output of about two thousand authors, were submitted. There is no dearth of verse in America — thousands are writing it — but only a few seem to have done work of much distinction or of an enduring value. Among these an unquestioned place is accorded today to Edwin Arlington Robinson. Ever since 1897, when his first book — *The Children of the Night*[1] — was published, this author has been growing steadily in reputation, while his two later volumes — *Captain Craig* (1902) and *The Town Down the River* (1910) — have more than fulfilled the promise of the first.

Taking these books as a representation, an interpretation of life as life appears to their author — and that is what all real poetry is — it at once becomes apparent that he sees life steadily and sees it whole, as the Greeks did — not shunning the evil in it and not blind to its good; neither so overcome by the tragedy of life that he fails to see its humorous aspects, nor so keenly sensitive to its humor that he disregards its pathos. In fact this blending of pathos and humor is one characteristic of Mr. Robinson's work, and it is a quality that should make him eminently successful in the drama, should he yield to the easy temptation of that form as his genius for characterization by swift, subtle touches would lead one to suppose that he might.[2] Many of his most distinctive poems are character studies done with a sureness of sympathetic insight, a deftness of characterization that discloses and explains completely the person described; showing him pathetic it may be, it may be humorous, but always thoroughly human. The fact that many of the characters Mr. Robinson has chosen to depict are derelicts — people who have been failures from the worldly point of view — has led several foolishly superficial critics into calling him a pessimist, whereas nothing is more certain than his invincible optimism. He directs the reader's attention not to the fact that the character he is drawing is a failure, but to the somehow frustrate possibilities that were in him. He may have a lame back, or a sick conscience, but Mr. Robinson wants us to know that he might have stood straight and been a reputable citizen if something hadn't happened. If something hadn't happened, what a fine man he might have been; but if any positive good appears in him, Mr. Robinson delightedly exhibits it with a half apologetic smile which seems to mean: You see he was not all bad and the rest of him might have been like this, if only something hadn't happened.

At first an artist can merely represent life; he cannot interpret it until later. In Mr. Robinson's first book he was content to represent, among others, realistically and with a whimsical sense of the humorous aspect of his particular obsession, "that skirt-crazed reprobate, John Evereldown." Very different is the kindly wisdom, the mature understanding and sympathy with which he interprets the lives of Clavering and the others who appear in *The Town Down the River*. The judgment is more mellow, and while there is the same humor, there is a sad tenderness that can come only from experience of life.

At the publication of *Captain Craig*, it seemed as though its author might be destined to carry on the New England tradition of a Whittier, as though he might produce some day a new "Snowbound" of infinitely subtle humor, and of immeasurably more profound psychology; Isaac and Archibald were distinctly New England types, but Aunt Imogen, the spinster, to whom came one day with the prattle of her sister's children the poignant realization that her lot in life was to be always only Aunt Imogen, was a character not of the east nor the west, but of universal experience, and it is toward the description of people who might be met anywhere that Mr. Robinson's art has tended to develop. Few of the characters in *The Town Down the River* have any local habitation, though it must be admitted that many of them have names. Take, for example, Miniver Cheevy; Miniver would be as much, or as little, at home in Minneapolis as in New York or Boston. ["Miniver Cheevy" follows.]

This is one of the most trivial poems in the book, but it will serve very well to illustrate some of the points we have been making. Is not the interpretation as well as the representation of Miniver's whole life in the last two lines?[3] We would not have known him or understood him any better if Mr. Robinson had written a two-volume novel about him.[4] The author's sympathetic insight and his humor are shown here as clearly as his deftness of characterization. The humanness of Miniver makes an irresistible appeal; and the kindly geniality of his presentation persuades us to like a person whom we might have scorned, or pitied or been bored by, if the essential humanity of his weakness, the side of him that is almost lovable had not been pointed out.

We must turn to other and more serious examples of Mr. Robinson's work to illustrate his other qualities, but that sad optimism which turns so wistfully to whatever may be good in ruined or futile lives is back of all his poems, and, as far as their content is concerned, is what more than anything else makes him distinctively his own.

Endowed as he is, with a peculiar excellence of diction that makes each word fit like a bit of mosaic into its context, Mr. Robinson finds his technique more than ample for his needs. He uses the old poetic forms, but his manner of writing is as much his own as is the characteristic attitude toward life of which poetry is the expression. He has done something new, and there are indications that his thoroughly original work may beget imitators — as is usually the case with work that is both original and good in any form of art. Mr. Robinson has been hailed by some as the prophet of a new humor, but it may be that in after years we shall look upon his as the first voice to give coherent poetic expression to that American democracy whose ideal is to see whatever is good in all men and to teach the doctrine of brotherhood through emphasis on our common humanity.

No good book yields itself lightly on first reading, and with Mr. Robinson's work it is especially true that familiarity breeds respect: his thought demands thought on the part of the reader. It would be unjust to give him only a casual reading, and it would be unjust to quote from his work nothing save one of his lighter pieces. The following poem shows him in a more serious mood: ["The Master (Lincoln)" follows.]

From "Some of the New Books," Minneapolis *Journal* (November 3, 1912), Woman's Section, 5.

In a letter to John G. Neihardt, dated November 20, 1912, Robinson confirms Ledoux's authorship of this unsigned critique.

1   Robinson's first book is *The Torrent and The Night Before* (1896), of which numerous critics in this compilation were unaware.
2   This prophecy was forlornly unfulfilled; Robinson was a flat failure as a dramatist. For more than a decade after 1905 he persisted in futile attempts to turn out a successful commercial play, only one (*Van Zorn*) achieving stage production for a week in a Brooklyn YMCA. Macmillan published *Van Zorn* (1914) and *The Porcupine* (1915) not for their inherent quality but to secure the rights to publish his poems. See Irving D. Suss, "The Plays of Edwin Arlington Robinson," *Colby Library Quarterly*, VIII (September 1969), 347-363.
3   "Miniver coughed, and called it fate, / And kept on drinking."
4   See note on compression in the section *Olla Podrida* in the chapter "Preliminary Vistas" of this volume.

. . / / . .

The most noteworthy living American poet

EDWIN ARLINGTON ROBINSON

Hermann Hagedorn

Fairfield, Conn.

The New York Times Review of Books:

Mr. Kilmer's article concerning Edwin Arlington Robinson and Mr. Ledoux's justly enthusiastic letter seem to point to the cheerful possibility that at last due recognition may come to the man who is by all odds the most noteworthy living American poet. This recognition has dawned slowly enough, to be sure. For decades critics here and abroad have been crying for American poets, successors to the New England group of the mid-century, lamenting that there were none comparable to the great dead. They have chased erotic will-o'-the-wisps and stammering disciples of Whitman, but the two really notable figures they have neglected. William Vaughn Moody is tragically dead at 40. For richness of imagination and passionate beauty of phrase he stands alone in American poetry with Poe. The other man is Robinson, utterly different from Moody, but worthy with Moody to a place among those few American poets who have looked at life, not through books, but squarely, directly, and told in splendid verse what they have seen. There is poignant humanity in Robinson's work, in "Captain Craig," "Uncle Ananias," "Richard Cory," "Leonora," "An Island," with the haunting line: "There are too many islands in this world."

The poems keep their freshness, as few poems do, because they have each the piercing interest of a personal touch with another life. Therein, indeed, they fulfill the function that only the truest art fulfills, for they open doors, they enlarge for us our cramped domain of spiritual experience. Robinson's people are all rounded figures; in the small space of a sonnet we are made to see them from a half dozen angles. We see the weakness, the badness, perhaps, but in each we see undeniably the streak of goodness. That, by a grace we cannot fathom, no man seems entirely without. Robinson's men are not heroes, any of them, and herein lies the greatness of his work — that he shows us that the most commonplace creature in the crowd, if we only look deeply enough at his being, is as interesting as Napoleon or the march of the constellations.[1]

Robinson is a very important figure in American literature. It might be excellent for Americans if they found it out.

From "Correspondence," New York *Times Review of Books* (December 1, 1912), VI, 747.

Hermann Hagedorn (1882-1964), ambitious writer of poems, plays, and pageants of idealistic trend, was Robinson's chief biographer and a rabid enthusiast of Theodore Roosevelt. Hagedorn met Robinson through Andrew Preston Peabody in Cambridge but came to know him well while they were summering in Chocorua, New Hampshire, in 1910. It was Hagedorn who suggested to Robinson that he go to the MacDowell Colony in 1911, a crucial turn in Robinson's creative life.

[1] "An Island (Saint Helena, 1821)" treats with Napoleon's last days there. There are several poems with astral metaphors in *The Town Down the River* but Hagedorn probably had "Lingard and the Stars," pp. 54-55, in mind.

. . / / . .

Second greatest living American poet

ALFRED NOYES SEES AMERICAN POETS LEADING WORLD MOVEMENT

Fred W. Thompson

Boston has for the past few days been entertaining a young Englishman of 32 years whom many men of letters throughout the world acclaim "the greatest living poet."

He is Alfred Noyes. In his own country they say he is the greatest poet since Tennyson. . . .

"I have the greatest admiration for the younger American poets," he said. "I think they are more frank and sincere than any other English or American poets of the past or the present. The work of these young men is having a great influence in the future. . . . [Tribute to Brian

Hooker as "the greatest living American poet" follows.]

"I think Arlington Robinson comes next to Hooker. In some ways I like him better," continued Mr. Noyes. "His style is sardonic, powerful; and his technic is almost perfect. He is surely the second greatest living American poet, if not the greatest. His 'Town Down the River' is one of his best things. I admire it tremendously. It is a masterpiece for which he will be remembered by coming generations."

[Brief biographical data on Robinson follow, including the misinformation that he lives in Gardiner.] . . . With his strong hands clasped between his knees, Mr. Noyes leaned forward in his chair and gazing reminiscently through the window into the rain-streaked twilight of the street repeated several verses from memory.

Here is the poem in full: ["The Town Down the River" follows.]

From Boston *Sunday Post* (March 2, 1913), 37.

Alfred Noyes (1880-1958) came to the United States in 1913 partly to lecture on poetry and anti-militarism, and partly to satisfy the desire of his American wife that "he should gather fresh experiences of her home land." From February to July he talked on Tennyson, Swinburne, the future of poetry, and of disarmament in Boston, Cambridge, New York, Philadelphia, Chicago, and elsewhere.

During Robinson's visit to England in 1923 he roamed about St. Albans with Noyes. " 'Noyes,' he said, 'is a man I like. He is a happy man — that is in so far as a poet can be really happy except when he is actually producing poetry.' " (Theodore Maynard, "Edwin Arlington Robinson," *Catholic World*, CXLI [June 1935], 268.)

Except for a couple of small advertisements, this interview — subtitled "Calls Brian Hooker Greatest American Bard With Arlington Robinson Next" — occupies six columns on the left of this page. The two columns on the right contain Noyes's "Greeting to America" and "the American poet Robinson whom he so much admired"; Robinson's "Richard Cory" and "Boston" reprinted with these respective comments: a) "This poem gives a good idea of the general style of the writer whom Mr. Noyes calls the second greatest American poet"; b) "Whom Alfred Noyes declares is, next to Brian Hooker, America's greatest poet."

Robinson to John Hays Gardiner, March 9, 1913: "Thank you for the *Post* article, which I had not seen. It is a bit sad that it should have come at just this time, for I have lately made up my mind to do as I told you one evening at the Harvard Club that I ought to do, and would do if I were a little bigger man. I don't know whether I am a bigger man or not, but I do know that I shall never make any money writing plays, and probably not in any other way." (Torrence, pp. 78-79.)

. . / / . .

Father confessor to all who have been through the mill

AN AMERICAN POET WITH A MESSAGE

Edwin Carty Ranck

An American whose work, it seems to me, should be universally known to all lovers of genuine poetry is Edwin Arlington Robinson. His three volumes, *The Children of the Night*, [*Captain Craig*, and *The Town Down the River*,][1] entitle their creator to rank with the most distinctive of American poets.

THE TOWN DOWN THE RIVER (1910)

When he was president, Theodore Roosevelt publicly proclaimed Mr. Robinson our greatest poet. Recently Mr. Hermann Hagedorn, himself a poet of rare distinction and charm, announced that, in his estimation, Mr. Robinson was "the most noteworthy living American poet." Still more recently, Alfred Noyes paid the highest tribute to Mr. Robinson's originality and power of characterization.[2] Despite this praise from three such eminent critics, I venture the assertion that the work of Mr. Robinson is known only to that small circle of men and women who are lovers of poetry for its own sake and who despise the trite and obvious forms of art. And yet Mr. Robinson is not an esoteric poet. His work is robust and vital and through it all there blows the very essence of Americanism. His understanding of human nature is so sympathetic and keen as to make him the kindly friend and father confessor to all who have been through the mill and suffered. Therefore, he seems to be a truly great poet.

Let me quote Mr. Hagedorn: "For decades critics here and abroad have been crying for American poets, successors to the New England group of the mid-century, lamenting that there were none comparable to the great dead. They have chased erotic will-o'-the-wisps and stammering disciples of Whitman, but the two really notable figures they have neglected. William Vaughn Moody is tragically dead at forty. For richness of imagination and passionate beauty of phrase he stands alone in American poetry with Poe. The other man is Robinson, utterly different from Moody, but worthy with Moody to a place among those few American poets who have looked at life, not through books, but squarely, directly, and told in splendid verse what they have seen."

It has been a mystery to me why Mr. Robinson's work is not universally known. His poetry is ruggedly individual. There is nothing else like it now written in this country. Behind each poem, however laconic it may be, we feel the presence of a whimsical personality who knows the bitterness and the sweetness of life; who sees the futility of the struggle and yet is not downcast, because he also sees the inherent good that glorifies every bit of human flotsam and jetsam that floats with the tide.

Edwin Arlington Robinson is an optimist. He is not the kind of optimist that opens his window and shouts to the passing throng that "God's in his heaven; all's right with the world."[3] But he is a real optimist in that he knows how hard life is and yet is not hard himself; he knows like the old lama in *Kim* that it is a great and terrible world and that every one has a burden to bear.[4] It is to these burden-bearers that he appeals. You may not see the optimism at first, but you will later. It is a subtle optimism, but it is there. It says to the man who thinks himself down and out: "You are human. You've got your good qualities. Get up, man, and look the world in the face. I am like you. We are all like you. It may be harder sometimes to live than to die, but if you play the game like a man your life has not been a failure."

That is the sort of optmism that Robinson's poetry teaches. It is not the mushy kind. It is a man's kind. You feel this spirit breathing from nearly every page in *The Town Down the River*. It is a peculiarly Robinsonian spirit. The reader feels that he has been given a mental slap on the back and is stimulated. There is something about it all that one cannot explain. It is just Robinson and therein lies the man's real genius. It is as if you stood on some eminence with the poet and watched the pitiful procession of life go by and listened to his tolerant comments. You know that he knows life and that he has a big heart. He may smile sometimes at the foibles of his fellow man, but it is always a kindly smile with a touch of sunshine and warm sympathy.

Mr. Robinson's ability to get all the meat of a subject in capsule form is truly remarkable. He can say more in a sonnet or in half a dozen lines than most poets can say in a volume. Take this little poem called "Boston," for instance, which is to be found in *The Children of the Night*: [The poem follows.]

How many writers in a hundred pages have given a clearer picture of the modern Boston striving with the old one of tradition?

And who can ever forget those lines in the poem on Lincoln, in the volume *The Town Down the River*:

> For he, to whom we had applied
> Our shopman's test of age and worth,
> Was elemental when he died,
> As he was ancient at his birth:
> The saddest among kings of earth,
> Bowed with a galling crown, this man
> Met rancor with a cryptic mirth,
> Laconic — and Olympian.[5]

Note the power of condensation in these four lines from "Miniver Cheevy":

> Miniver Cheevy, born too late,
>   Scratched his head and kept on thinking;
> Miniver coughed, and called it fate,
>   And kept on drinking.

The temptation to quote at length is always strong in referring to Mr. Robinson's poetry. Some of his notable poems are "John Evereldown," "Richard Cory," "Reuben Bright," "Uncle Ananias," "The White Lights," "Clavering," and "An Island." These are all remarkable for their high poetic quality and their wonderful understanding of the human soul. Mr. Robinson never judges the other man. But he looks far down into the depths of his being, and sees things there that we never see. And he picks up his pen and tells us what he saw, and our eyes are suddenly misty with tears and we feel a yearning sympathy for this other man that we never understood before. It is the real magic of genius. We have seen him through Robinson's eyes and we know that he is a human being who feels about life much as we do.

Edwin Arlington Robinson is not a dilettante. He does not write occasional verse. He only writes when he feels deeply and has something to say. He has written three volumes of poetry and there is nothing cheap or

unworthy of him in any one of them. He is real. He is sincere. He is vital.
___
From Boston *Evening Transcript* (May 12, 1913), 10.

Edwin Carty Ranck (1879-1957), Kentucky-born, was one of Robinson's most eccentric friends. He studied at Harvard for two years in George Pierce Baker's "47 Workshop," turned out numerous plays, several of which were published. Currently a freelance journalist, he worked earlier and later as dramatic critic for New York and Midwestern newspapers. Chard Powers Smith describes him as "a short, stocky, crude, ejaculatory, slobbering, popeyed, pugnacious misfit" (*Where the Light Falls: A Portrait of Edwin Arlington Robinson* [New York, 1965], p. 37), and he was not alone in his distaste for this feisty original. Yet, Robinson wrote, "In some strange way he has a stimulating effect on my sluggish creative faculties." (Hagedorn, p. 313.) Ranck was an unequivocal admirer of Robinson as poet from the time he met him at the MacDowell Colony in 1912, expressing his homage in an eponymous sonnet first published in the New York *Evening Sun* (June 14, 1919, p. 6), reprinted in Braithwaite's *Anthology of Magazine Verse for 1919* (Boston, p. 140), and in *Kentucky Poets*, foreword by Sarah Litsey (New York, 1936), p. 71, a summary of Robinson's philosophic attitudes rather than a eulogy of his person. For years Ranck let it be known that he was compiling a massive biography of Robinson but as yet none of his notes or manuscript have turned up.

1   Ranck says "three volumes" but actually only *The Children of the Night* is named in this paragraph. It is presumed that Ranck also seems not to know of the existence of *The Torrent and The Night Before*.

2   Roosevelt in the *Outlook*, August 12, 1905; Hagedorn in the New York *Times Review of Books*, December 1, 1912; Noyes in the Boston *Sunday Post*, March 2, 1913, all reprinted in this volume. Roosevelt was impressed but used no such superlative in his tribute.

3   Lines 7-8 of a song in part I (Morning) of Browning's poetic drama *Pippa Passes*.

4   In Kipling's novel the Tibetan lama with the "thousand-wrinkled face" sets out to find the holy River of the Arrow that would wash away all sin. On the road he and Kim encounter a varied cross-section of the populace, with sometimes distressing effects.

5   "The Master (Lincoln," p. 6.

.. / / ..

Mr. Robinson has waited

AMERICA'S FOREMOST POET
William Stanley Braithwaite

Theodore Roosevelt called him the foremost American poet of his day. He said so with the prestige of his position as President of the United States, and the poet's fame was heralded from coast to coast. That was eight years ago.[1] Edwin Arlington Robinson was a silent figure all through the din of this praise. His poetry became better known, and perhaps, the public stung to a more serious reading of it, it became a little better understood. The man hung back, as if to watch the effect: he took no personal part in what was a kind of triumph of his art. He had published two books up to that time: *The Children of the Night*, 1896, and *Captain Craig*, 1902.² May Sinclair, during her American visit in 1904, discovered three living American poets of the first rank: they were Edwin Arlington Robinson, William Vaughn Moody, and Ridgely Torrence. She wrote an article about them in which she clearly admitted they matched the best in England.³ Yet Robinson continued in the background of American literature. In 1910 Mr. Robinson's third [fourth] book, *The Town Down the River*, was published. A few people declared that, not since 1898, when Moody's *Poems* was published, had so significant a volume of American poetry appeared. Mr. Robinson was, if anything, still shrinking further from public recognition.

The poetry of the man was his only utterance. Behind his art was silence; as far as public acquaintance with him went he was an invisible figure. Lesser men went strutting across the stage of publicity; their exit was as swift as their entrance. Mr. Robinson was a kind of mystery. Yet his work was the kind that would arouse one's curiosity as to the man's personality. It was so plainly in the work itself, but it puzzled. Here was a poet considered by more than one competent authority the leading poet in a nation of ninety millions of people whom the public did not know. Here was a poet who had paid the finest tribute of any poet to the nation's idol, its greatest man, Lincoln, in a poem that contains among other magnificent stanzas, these:

> The face that in our vision feels
> Again the venom that we flung,
> Transfigured to the world reveals
> The vigilance to which we clung.
> Shrewd, hallowed, harassed, and among
> The mysteries that are untold,
> The face we see was never young
> Nor could it ever have been old.
>
> For he, to whom we had applied
> Our shopman's test of age and worth,
> Was elemental when he died,
> As he was ancient at his birth:
> The saddest among kings of earth,
> Bowed with a galling crown, this man
> Met rancor with a cryptic mirth,
> Laconic — and Olympian.⁴

and who was allowed for some inexplicable reason to remain personally obscure.

One must admit it has been somewhat of Mr. Robinson's own choice. But that does not explain the lack of general appreciation that the very high quality and individual character of his art has met with. There seems a change, however, in this. Like Browning and Meredith, men of the supremest genius, who had to wait for general recognition and understanding, Mr. Robinson has waited. It is seventeen years since Mr. Robinson published his first book. Within the present year more people really know and understand his poetry than in the year that Mr. Roosevelt brought the poet's name to the attention of the entire country. When Mr.

Alfred Noyes, the English poet, came over here a couple of months ago, he came declaring Mr. Robinson our foremost poet.[5] There has been a great deal talked and written about the poet since, but Mr. Robinson, as has been characteristic of his career, kept his silence — until now. He has allowed me to quote him. He is in Boston for a few days on his way to New Hampshire,[6] and during a visit I won his reluctant consent to publish a portion of his conversation regarding poetry, and especially about the message which is contained in his own extraordinarily individual art.

In the great forward movement of American life, in which today is preparing for the generation of tomorrow, the humanities are engaging the earnest consideration of the common mind as well as problems of an economic and scientific nature. Men sometimes forget this. Our economic structure would fall to pieces, our scientific attainments would advance very little the social welfare of mankind, if the humanities were neglected. That kinetic reorganization of society which H.G. Wells says is taking place,[7] would result in no vital advantage to the world if its hope were not based upon the humanities. And in the humanities poetry takes its place as the most insistent force, the ideal guidance of human endeavor. The industrial ascendency of the American people in the present generation, during which there has been an apparent disregard of the things of the spirit, has given us before the world the character of being a soulless nation. That is not so. The love of art that has been characterized by the purchase of great masterpieces of painting by our rich men, like Mr. Morgan and Mr. Frick,[8] represented deeper feeling and significance than mere competitive accumulation of baser values. The revival of interest in poetry was certain to accompany this influence of a sister art that was spreading over the country through the liberal patronage of American financiers. That signs of this revival of interest were everywhere to be seen was a fact that we accepted jubilantly. But what was to be the character and quality of the poetry shaping itself for this growing interest? I put the question to Mr. Robinson.

"I don't know anything about the poetry of the future," he said, "except that it must have, in order to be poetry, the same eternal and unchangeable quality of magic that it has always had. Of course, it must always be colored by the age and the individual, but the thing itself will always remain unmistakable and indefinable. It seems to me a great deal of time and effort is now wasted in trying to make poetry do what it was never intended to do."

Doing what it was never intended to do! What was it intended to do? It is given up as a hopeless and insoluble task, the attempt to answer inevitably the question "What is Poetry," which everybody was asking a hundred years ago and continued to ask in one form or another throughout the century. There were, beginning with Wordsworth and Coleridge and Keats and Shelley, so many different kinds of great poetry throughout the nineteenth century, even down to Francis Thompson and William Butler Yeats, that we all in our increasing wisdom saw the impossibility of coming to any terms in defining the matter. We couldn't do so adequately. Life itself being an eternal question we learned to ask another question about poetry: What does it intend to do? That is what is being asked today.

The question invites a good many considerations, and when you analyze these considerations you come pretty near being convinced that you are supposed to tell the secret of poetry which men have sought to understand for several hundred years. In the effort to determine what poetry is intended to do one confronts the old problems of the poet's message and his communication of that message through the symbols of speech shaped into certain fundamental forms of art. Mr. Robinson has said before that poetry "must always be colored by the age and the individual." Verse as a form of artistic expression is influenced by the age, poetry evoked by the individual. It acquires that magic which makes poetry "unmistakable and indefinable," through the peculiar spiritual message which the poet delivers. Every poet with a vital and significant message has been neglected and misunderstood. It has been Mr. Robinson's case. It is a sign of his genius, in his attainment in actual achievement to the front rank of contemporary American poetry. His art has been charged with a gloom that it does not possess if read intelligently. His message is as clear as daylight, as invigorating and inspiring as the sun. For the first time we have in Mr. Robinson's own words what that message is. I quote his answer to my question regarding the message so distinctive and originally contained in his poems.

"If I have a message," he said, "it ought to be pretty well revealed in the three books I've written.[9] If it is likely to be of any great value to the race, I suppose that a part of it might be described as a faint hope of making a few of us understand our fellow creatures a little better, and to realize what a small difference there is after all between ourselves as we are and ourselves not only as we might have been but would have been if our physical and temperamental make-up and our environment had been a little different.

"This may sound fatalistic, and if it does, I don't know what I can do about it. I've been called a fatalist, a pessimist and an optimist so many times that I am beginning to believe that I must be all three. I don't know what an optimist is exactly, but I have always liked the definition of one, as a man 'who doesn't care a damn what happens so long as it doesn't happen to him.'

"If a reader doesn't get from my books an impression that life is very much worth living, even though it may not seem always to be profitable or desirable, I can only say that he doesn't see what I am driving at. I am glad to be able to say that several people who did not see anything in them at first have come later to 'root' for them with considerable energy. I take this on the whole to be a good sign that I am not so silly as to suppose that any amount of praise and advertising can make poetry live unless the 'magic' quality to which I referred to before is in the poetry itself. If there is such a thing as the greatest single line in English poetry, I should be inclined to say that it is Wordsworth's 'The light that never was, on sea or land.'[10] I believe so firmly that poetry that is good for anything speaks for itself that I feel foolish when I try to talk about it."

That is more than the man has ever said before to the public. What he has said in the speech of his heart to the world, not to the world of today but to the world of later generations, let me quote this section from his poem, "The Town Down the River." [The four stanzas of section III follow.]

From Boston *Evening Transcript* (May 28, 1913), 21.

This interview is subtitled "Edwin Arlington Robinson, Crowned by Roosevelt and Alfred Noyes."

In his notable *Anthology of Magazine Verse for 1913*, first in the series that ran to 1929, Braithwaite wrote: "Another poet who has enriched the magazines this year, after a period of silence, is Mr. Edwin Arlington Robinson, and in 'The Field of Glory' we are under the spell once more of that characteristic magic with which he is endowed alone among American poets" (p. vii.) He reprinted the cited poem.

The 1914 issue of *AMV* is dedicated "To Louis V. Ledoux and Edwin Arlington Robinson / *Palmam qui meruit ferat*" and contains Robinson's "Eros Turannos" and "The Gift of God."

1 See Roosevelt's review of *The Children of the Night* in *Outlook*, August 12, 1905, reprinted in this volume.

2 The correct number of Robinson books is three; the correct listing, *The Torrent and The Night Before*, 1896; *The Children of the Night*, 1897; *Captain Craig*, 1902. In none of his three reviews between 1910 and 1915 did Braithwaite indicate the proper chronology.

3 See Sinclair's essay in the *Atlantic Monthly*, September 1906, reprinted in this volume.

4 "The Master (Lincoln)," pp. 5-6.

5 See Noyes's statement in the Boston *Sunday Post* of March 2, 1913, reprinted in this volume. In his "A Chat with Albert [*sic*] Noyes," Braithwaite describes his interview with Noyes in the study of the late Thomas Bailey Aldrich, whose widow was hostess to the English poet during his stay in the Boston area. Noyes admitted unfamiliarity with contemporary poets but was positive about Robinson. "[Noyes] spoke with enthusiasm of the remarkable poetry of Edwin Arlington Robinson." (Boston *Evening Transcript* [March 1, 1913], III, 3.)

6 Every summer from 1911 to 1934 Robinson lived at the MacDowell Colony in Peterborough, New Hampshire, where he did most of his writing for the year.

7 Wells in *The Discovery of the Future* (New York, 1913), p. 59: "Everything seems pointing to the belief that we are entering upon a progress that will go on, with an ever-widening and ever more confident stride, forever. The reorganization of society that is going on now beneath the traditional appearance of things is a kinetic reorganization."

Robinson was no proponent of Wellsian views. "Then I came home and read H.G. Wells's latest false prophecy, *The World Set Free*," he wrote to Mrs. Ledoux on April 23, 1914. (Torrence, p. 84.)

8 The acquisition of art objects by John Pierpont Morgan, the financier, and Henry Clay Frick, the steel magnet, were usually of spectacular scope. They had both been in the news recently: Morgan died on March 31; Frick had started building a lavish

home on Fifth Avenue in New York City, now a museum housing his art collection.

9 With his settled misconception on the number three, Braithwaite may have misquoted Robinson, or the latter may have considered *The Children of the Night* essentially an extension of *The Torrent and The Night Before*.

10 Line 3, stanza 4 of Wordsworth's poem "Suggested by a Picture of Peele Castle in a Storm."

.. / / ..

My poems speak for themselves

GREAT AMONG POETS HIDES IN MODESTY

Edwin Arlington Robinson, acclaimed by Theodore Roosevelt and Alfred Noyes the greatest living American poet,[1] has been living in Boston the past few days so quietly that Mr. Noyes and many others who long have been eager to meet him, did not know that he was here.

In a modest back bedroom at 93 St. Botolph Street a *Post* reporter found him, quietly seeking to avoid the honors and recognition such as have been showered upon the brilliant English poet, Alfred Noyes, since he came to Boston a few weeks ago.

Mr. Robinson's last book of poems, *The Town Down the River*, has won him quite a reputation abroad, but he is so unassuming that most Americans have never even heard of him.

In appearance Mr. Robinson is a medium sized man with a black moustache and black hair, parted in the middle and brushed close to his head. He has a high forehead and frank, friendly brown eyes. He looks, perhaps, a little more like an Englishman than an American and speaks with a slightly English accent, which makes his voice much pleasanter than the harsh, unmusical tones of most Americans.

When interviewed yesterday he wore spectacles and was clothed in a quiet brown suit and brown necktie. Although hailed by several competent critics as America's best poet, he turned out to be unassuming in manner and without any affectations.

About himself and his own poetry Mr. Robinson continually refused to talk in spite of repeated attempts to draw him into the subject. All through the interview he showed a great unwillingness to commit himself on any questions, and it was only with difficulty that a few scattered remarks were worked from him. What he did say he modestly insisted was of no real importance: "only a few haphazard thoughts."

When questioned about himself and his work Mr. Robinson simply said: "I have nothing to say about myself. My poems speak for themselves. It is foolish to take one's self too seriously."

"But surely some people need to have poetry interpreted for them. Many people misunderstand. What would you say to those who have accused you of being a pessimist and a fatalist?"

"When a man publishes books," quietly replied the poet, "he must take the consequences. A writer should not be his own interpreter. It is not the business of the writer himself to explain misunderstandings of his writings."

"Are you going to publish any new poems soon?"

"No. All that I have are merely in a fragmentary state. What is filling my horizon at the present is Constance Garnett's new complete unabridged translation of Dostoievsky's *The Brothers Karamazov*. You see," he added with a faint smile as he turned the subject to this work, "I'd rather not talk about myself."

When asked what was so absorbing about *The Brothers Karamazov*, he refused to say more than, "It explains itself, why it is great. I can't say anything more."[2]

On the big movements of today, such as socialism, woman suffrage, internationalism, political and religious developments, the natural reticence of Mr. Robinson was more pronounced than ever.

"All these questions," he said, as he pulled on his cigarette, "are too large for such a short talk. There is so much destiny in them," he added, revealing his inclination towards fatalism.

When asked about his feeling on the subject of international peace, the poet replied: "Universal peace has a pleasant sound, but I don't see it. I wish I did. I don't like to pose as an obstructionist, but I do not agree with Alfred Noyes on this subject. The idea seems to me impracticable."

In regard to woman suffrage he admitted he was strongly in favor of it, but said that militancy was setting the movement back in England just when it promised to be successful. "The English militancy," he continued, "is also detrimental to the progress of woman suffrage in this country. There have been too many metrical sermons and editorials on the subject, by the way," he added. "Poetry should not be propaganda, or if it is it ought to be well concealed. I suppose one might say it ought to be reprecipitated."

Asked whether the form of expression or the idea expressed was more important in judging of the artistic merit of a poem, Mr. Robinson answered with characteristic lack of commitment: "Good poetry must have good technique and also vision behind. Good technique is absolutely necessary. Of all the great poets the technique of Emerson comes nearest to being accidental. I agree with Noyes, by the way, that Emerson is the greatest American poet."[3]

"Speaking of the necessity of vision in poetry," ventured the reporter, "from what source do you get your chief inspirations?"

"I have had no inspiration lately," meekly replied the poet. "There is no use in talking of inspiration," he went on after a pause. "The less said about inspiration and 'the frenzy' the better. I've noticed that some of the fellows who have the finest frenzies are likely to write the worst stuff."

As to who was, in his opinion, the greatest living poet, Mr. Robinson again refused to commit himself. "Contemporary criticism," he said, "doesn't amount to much; it takes about 50 years before we can really judge a man's work. Before that time we don't get any perspective on his place in history. Kipling will take his place among the great ones. Kipling's reputation, however, among the public has been made by his jingo pieces. The majority do not know him by his best work. The poetry of Alfred Noyes is very good. I think his best things are "The Barrel Organ" and "The Seven Singing Seamen."

Speaking of American poets, he said, "I like Percy MacKaye[4] very much. His last book, *Uriel*, is his best work, by far — that is, of his poems; I do not speak of his plays. About present day writers, if I'm going to mention any of them, William Vaughn Moody was probably the best poet of his generation. A. T. Schumann[5] has a peculiar genius for writing ballads and rondeaus in the French form. Bliss Carman's earlier work was good, but later it has contained too many diffusions and repetitions. Other American poets whom I might mention with approval are Hermann Hagedorn, Josephine Preston Peabody[6] (now Mrs. Marks), Louis Ledoux, Ridgely Torrence,[7] Anna Branch[8] and Joyce Kilmer. There are two or three others whom I can't think of now and whom I'll be sorry tomorrow I did not mention. Some of the men not known at all put out the best work."

"Is there any striking difference between English and American poetry to today?"

"Yes. The English poets have a finish, a certain quality that most Americans don't have. It's a matter of tradition, I suppose. American poets have a definite advantage over the English, however, and that is their very freedom from tradition. But this has been said so much it's really not worth saying," he added with his usual apology.

About the future of poetry in America Mr. Robinson was quite optimistic. Although he agreed that the majority of Americans were absorbed in the business of accumulating money, he said: "It is the remnant that saves. Things don't stay as they are. The pendulum is going all the time, though it seems to go very slowly. I have great faith in the younger men. There is every indication of better work to come. I see many poems scattered about which make me think so."

To the question as to what he thought of the post impressionists in art he replied: "I like to keep an open mind even for the extremist experiments in any line, though I must confess that I'm rather stumped by the cubists. There is a suggestion of charlatanism there. There are always a few extremists, and, of course, experimenting is a good thing in art as well as in science."

Mr. Robinson was born at Head-of-the-Tide, Me., in 1869, and now lives at Gardiner, Me.[9] He has published three books of poems: *The Children of the Night*, 1896; *Captain Craig*, 1902, and *The Town Down the River* in 1910.[10] He declares himself to be fond of old songs, such as "My Old Kentucky Home." He is not, however, indifferent to the political upheavals of the moment, though he refused to comment himself on the subject.

His last book, for instance, which is dedicated to Roosevelt, contains a poem called "The Revealer (Roosevelt)," from which the following verses may be quoted:

> The lions, having time to wait,
> Perceive a small cloud in the skies,
> Whereon they look, disconsolate,
> With scared, reactionary eyes.
>
> A shadow falls upon the land, —
> They sniff, and they are like to roar;
> For they will never understand
> What they have never seen before.

The fatalistic tendency in Robinson's thought is suggested in this short stanza from "Au Revoir,"[11] which recalls, by the way, the shooting of Roosevelt in Milwaukee, though it was written in 1909.

> Though fever-demons may compound
>   Their most malefic brew,
> No fever can defeat the man
>   Who still has work to do.

One of the best poems is "The Master (Lincoln)" of which the following is a sample:

> He knew devoutly what he thought
> Of us and of our ridicule;
> He knew that we must all be taught
> Like little children in a school.

From Boston *Post* (May 30, 1913), 2.

---

1 See Roosevelt in *Outlook*, August 12, 1905, and Noyes in Boston *Sunday Post*, March 2, 1913, both reprinted in this volume.

2 Robinson "shared her [Mrs. Louis Ledoux's] interest in Dostoievsky" (Hagedorn, p. 275), and he once wrote to Ledoux "asking him to lend *The Possessed*" (Edwin S. Fussell, *Edwin Arlington Robinson: The Literary Background of a Traditional Poet* [Berkeley, 1954], p. 199.)

3 In his lecture at the Berkeley Lyceum Noyes said that "he reserved first place among American poets for Emerson. . . . 'You know, after all, the Englishmen were first,' he said, 'We gave integrity to the English language and Emerson wrote with a splendid integrity and a subtle sincerity and art that no other American poet has approached." (New York *Times* [March 6, 1913], 7.)

4 Percy MacKaye (1875-1956), American poetic dramatist known at this time for *The Canterbury Pilgrims, Jeanne d'Arc*, and *The Scarecrow*, came to know Robinson well at the Judson Hotel and the MacDowell Colony. Robinson dedicated *Roman Bartholow* (1923) "To Percy Mackaye," composed "For Arvia, On Her Fifth Birthday" for one of his daughters, and wrote an Introductory Letter for Christy MacKaye's *Wind in the Grass* (1931).

5 See notes, Boston *Evening Transcript*, March 29, 1916, in this volume.

6 Josephine Preston Peabody (1874-1922) was another of the poetic dramatist group (including Moody, MacKaye, and Torrence) with whom Robinson became intimately acquainted. He had praised her lyrics in *The Wayfarers* as displaying an imagination

"not of the pounding, pyrotechnic sort" (*Literary Review*, III [January-February 1899], 12-13, unsigned), had written to her while working in the Harvard office, and had called at her Dorchester home in March 1899 (see Hagedorn, pp. 151-152). Prior to publication of her next two volumes, she asked him to read and criticize them, and was not always happy with his intense strictures. "If Miss Peabody tells you that I am an untaught beast," he wrote Daniel Gregory Mason, "you will tell her that I am by nature as kind-hearted as a caterpillar, though I have a quaint way of smashing people's heads when I wish merely to call their attention to things of interest." (Mason, *Music in My Time* [New York, 1938], p. 84.) To John Hays Gardiner he said: "She has a great deal of talent and a good deal of confidence." (Torrence, p. 28.) And to Edith Brower: "As for Josephine Peabody, I agree with you in preferring her poems of childhood, though there are many beautiful things in her other books. She insisted on giving bread to people who wanted cake — as I told her once, and was nearly slain for my good intentions. Her place is safe enough in American literature." (Cary, p. 195.) She did go on to win the Stratford-on-Avon prize with her drama *The Piper* in 1910 but has faded out of the picture now.

Robinson sent her his manuscript of *Captain Craig*. Already established by her volume of verse, a play on Shakespeare, and her forthcoming five-act tragedy *Marlowe*, Miss Peabody prevailed on Small, Maynard to accept Robinson's book for publication — with the dolorous results already noted.

7   Ridgely Torrence (1875-1950), journalist, poet, dramatist, was working in the catalogue room of the New York Public Library when he ran across Robinson's *The Children of the Night* and was captivated by it. Although of quite antithetical temperaments, they formed a close friendship, solidified during Robinson's days at the Hotel Judson. When he and Robinson called on Edmund Clarence Stedman in his Bronxville home, it gave the latter his chance to perpetrate the oft-repeated pun, "Torrence — and The Night After." Torrence published several volumes of poems radiant with Transcendental faith, a lyric drama on Abelard and Héloïse, and a cluster of plays about Negroes. He edited *Selected Letters of Edwin Arlington Robinson* in 1940.

Robinson to Laura E. Richards, August 7, 1905: "I have been reading Torrence's monumental poem for the September *Atlantic*, by means of which he hopes to leap into immortal glory and leave Moody in the shadow, swearing. I don't think he will quite do it, but he will do enough to make some thousands of people rub their eyes." (Torrence, p. 62.) He was referring to "The Lesser Children," *Atlantic Monthly*, XCVI (September 1905), 326-330.

8   Anna Hempstead Branch (1875-1937), author of several volumes of poems and a poetical play, *Rose of the World*, lived for years at the Christodora House in New York City where she did volunteer social work, traces of which found their way into many of her verses. With the cooperation of Robinson, MacKaye, Margaret Widdemer, and William Rose Benet, she organized the Poets Guild. She also played a strong role in the establishment of the International Poetry Society. Dubbed by one critic "the Browning of American Poetry" (which must have caused Robinson one small smile), Miss Branch was more like Christina Rossetti in minor key, her metaphysical-moral lyrics giving off a Pre-Raphaelite glow.

Miss Branch, Hagedorn, Ledoux, MacKaye, Miss Peabody, and Torrence were among the leading American authors who paid tribute to Robinson on his fiftieth birthday in Bliss Perry's "Poets Celebrate E.A. Robinson's Birthday," New York *Times Review of Books* (December 21, 1919), 765-766.

9   Robinson had not lived in Gardiner since 1899.

10   *The Torrent and The Night Before* (1896) is not mentioned, and *The Children of the Night* was first published in 1897.

11   This poem, which Robinson subtitled (March 23, 1909), was in fact written on the occasion of Roosevelt's departure for a hunting expedition in Africa.

. . / / . .

Most individual of American poets

EDWIN ARLINGTON ROBINSON
Harold Trowbridge Pulsifer

Most of our impressions and opinions are transmitted to us, and expressed by us, through the medium of conventional symbols — symbols which are not single words, as we generally imagine, but rather groups of phrases, pendent upon some time-worn idea. Mention a familiar phrase, and its associate phrases troop through our minds with an alacrity which we flatter ourselves is due to our native intellectual alertness, but which, in fact, is no more to be counted to our credit than the act of falling down the stairs. The mental pigeonholes in which we keep these ready-to-wear and "just as good" substitutes for original thought are tightly locked against all freshness and innovation. They open willingly only to those thoughts which come swaddled in conventional garb, and are guaranteed neither to alarm nor annoy. For no form of human utterance is this more true than poetry. Those consummately commonplace and sentimental verses of Tennyson upon which so much of his popularity is based, and from which his real fame so justly suffers, furnish typical examples of the use of these thought-symbols as a pass-key to immediate acceptance.

Two other recourses there are for the poet who seeks an audience. He can batter down, as Browning did, the walls we have erected to preserve our self-sufficient complacency, or, as Francis Thompson is doing, with the help of time he can permeate our consciousness by a kind of spiritual or intellectual osmosis, that curious physical process by which two liquids of different densities interpenetrate through a common barrier.

It is by this latter process that Edwin Arlington Robinson will eventually receive the wider recognition he so richly deserves. The most individual of American poets, he combines intensity of thought and of feeling with a curious simplicity of actual expression which sometimes baffles even his most ardent admirers. In a dozen lines he can sum up the tragedy of a whole life and tell the story so directly and succinctly that the reader is hardly aware of the searching wisdom, the vision, and the understanding, which lie in every calmly chiseled phrase. Typical of his work are these brief verses from *The Children of the Night*, one of Mr. Robinson's earlier volumes: ["Richard Cory" follows.]

The words he used are the words of ordinary speech, put together sometimes in cadences that seem close to actual prose, yet so subtly combined that their half-hidden yet characteristic rhythm conveys to the attentive ear much of the story and most of the underlying emotion. He does not tear a passion to tatters. His method and manners are more that of Owen Wister's "Virginian" when he quietly drawled, "when you call me that, smile."[1] Mr. Robinson is an austere poet, austere in his attitude toward himself and towards his art, yet those who find his poetry cold and distant have little comprehension of his fundamental purpose.

Elsewhere in this number appears a poem by Mr. Robinson, one of the few which he has written in recent years,² and a photograph of a portrait of the poet painted by Mr. William Sherman Potts.³

From *Outlook*, CV (December 6, 1913), 736.

Harold Trowbridge Pulsifer (1886-1948), class poet and prize-winning writer at Harvard, joined the staff of *Outlook* upon graduation in 1911, becoming president and managing editor, 1923-1928. A prolific contributor of poems to periodicals and newspapers, he published half a dozen volumes between 1912 and 1947. Pulsifer was a firm friend of Theodore Roosevelt, for a time contributing editor to the *Outlook*, and he consorted with Robinson in New York City during the Twenties. The original typescript of this review is among Pulsifer's papers in Colby College Library.

1 In the second chapter of *The Virginian* (1902), the otherwise nameless title-character is involved in a card game. At one point Trampas, another player, prods him: "Your bet, you son-of-a————." With gentle intonation, "almost like a caress" yet "as if somewhere the bell of death was ringing," the Virginian utters this now classic rejoinder.

2 "The Field of Glory" appears on page 759, Robinson's first published poem since July 1910. Of Levi, the central character, Robinson wrote to Hagedorn, December 15, 1913: "If you tried to find any kind of hero in Levi, I don't wonder that you didn't succeed in caring much for him. He is just a poor devil, totally miscast, and with not much in his head anyhow. The world is peppered with his kind, and I simply drew his picture to let people see what they thought about it in the light of contemporary materialism." (Torrence, p. 80.) To Edith Brower, December 21, 1913: "I'm glad you liked Levi, and that you did not think that he was one of the Twelve Tribes, or an East Side Jew, as several of the doubtful-owlish have seemed to think. It *was* rather nasty of his old mother to look him up and down as she did, but even then I suppose he couldn't run away. And he wouldn't have done much if he had. I made him merely to let the Race-Optimist explain his optimism, and to justify it, if he can, from a materialistic point of view." (Cary, pp. 154-155.)

3 William Sherman Potts (1876-1930) studied at the Pennsylvania Academy of Fine Arts and in Paris under Jean Paul Laurens and Benjamin Constant. President of the American Society of Miniature Painters and a portraitist of note in his day, Potts is represented in the permanent collection at the Metropolitan Museum of Art. He painted Robinson, a reluctant subject, in 1910. The portrait is reproduced on a full page between pages 744-745; the original now hangs in the Edwin Arlington Robinson Memorial Room in Colby College Library.

. . / / . .

Poetry, poetry pure and simple

EDWIN ARLINGTON ROBINSON
Otto Frederick Theis

In the centre of Philadelphia, entirely surrounded by business, is a quiet library where there is an abundance of books. It is one of the old-fashioned libraries in which readers are allowed access to the shelves and where they may handle the books at their will. In it is an alcove of American poets with many hundreds of volumes. Many an hour have I spent in that alcove with some of the eagerness of a discoverer in thumbing over the volumes wondering when a page would turn to disclose a golden line.

It was not often that such came and usually the quest was wholly futile. Much verse there was that was merely pathetic or sadly ludicrous because of its ineffectiveness. Much there was that was more pretentious and facile in technique. It has been well said that the reading of mediocre poetry has its advantages in that it leaves the mind free and induces general reflections, and one impression that would imprint itself on the mind again and again in reading these volumes was that American poetry shows a greater gift of memory than imagination, that even the better of it is largely a mosaic of familiar phrases and ideas that have done service with greater poets and now have a shopworn air about them.

In reading genuine poetry such abstractions are impossible; the poet's words carry one along. A damp grey November afternoon when snow was in the air and dusk already falling has always remained distinct in my mind, for on it I came for the first time upon the following stanza:

> There is the western gate, Luke Havergal,
> There are the crimson leaves upon the wall.
> Go, — for the winds are tearing them away, —
> Nor think to riddle the dead words they say,
> Nor any more to feel them as they fall;
> But go! and if you trust her she will call.
> There is the western gate, Luke Havergal —
> Luke Havergal.[1]

Here was a poem which had music, in which the lyric accents were individual. It might have been one of those unaccountable accidents by which indifferent writers sometimes achieve happy effects, but it was not, for further reading of the volume disclosed the same fine qualities. The title was *The Children of the Night*, by Edwin Arlington Robinson, the author also of *Captain Craig* and *The Town Down the River*, a name then unknown to me, but one which has since come to stand for what to me is one of the most distinctive and original notes in American poetry.

Robinson is indifferent to what the current fashion in versification or mode of poetry may be. He has worked out his own way uncompromisingly. There are none of the pallid echoes heard in so many other poets. There is none of the clamor or noise of those who are, or think they are, creating new social or ethical standards. In the sweat of his brow he has labored to rid his verse of the non-essentials, or borrowed plumes, of the phraseology and diction of conventional poetry. The clichés, that have done service so many times that they leave only a blurred and irritating impression, are discarded. The meaty residue that is found in his pages is poetry, poetry pure and simple, and all the author's own.

As a consequence there is freshness and fullness in Robinson's art. The themes of his poetry are usually simple and consist of the common, concrete things of life. He often approaches these from unexpected angles and illumines odd corners of half-forgotten things so that they shine out with a light entirely their own. Because he is a poet and has the "sight within that never will deceive,"[2] they become endued with a wider significance; because in addition he has intelligence, they become "divinely shadowed on the walls of Thought."[3]

He is not unfamiliar with the windings and complexities of the human soul. On the contrary he is often even rather fond of what are called psychological states, as in the long narrative poem called "The Book of Annandale." But in the end there is always a beautiful clarification and the fundamentally important motive is touched. In this above all his true artist's vision appears, for, as he has said in one of his "Octaves," —

> To get at the eternal strength of things,
> And fearlessly to make strong songs of it,
> Is, to my mind, the mission of that man
> The world would call a poet. He may sing
> But roughly, and withal ungraciously;
> But if he touch to life the one right chord
> Wherein God's music slumbers, and awake
> To truth one drowsed ambition, he sings well.[4]

Taking his artistic ideal from this point of view, he has succeeded in introducing an admirable objectivity into his work, which has, however, nothing in common with the somewhat self-conscious *l'art pour l'art,* so often dragged in to justify dealing with erotic and neurasthenic miasmas. The morasses with their iridescences and corruptions may, indeed, be the subjects of art, as Baudelaire and others have adequately shown, but they are only relatively small spots on the face of the earth, and the poet who can enter there and return with treasures is rare. There is room for true *l'art pour l'art* in the highlands and lowlands as well. To wander through them among the emotions, the gestures, the things, that are a common heritage of man; to hold them up palpitating, stripped of inconsequentials, sincerely real, is also worthy of a poet's achievement.[5]

What theme, for instance, is more commonplace than that of the childless woman with unstilled mother instinct, and more likely to degenerate into mere rhetoric and false sentiment? Yet Robinson has taken it in his "Aunt Imogen," who has no love save borrowed love during four weeks in a year when she visits her sister's family, and made it eloquent with poignancy by the simplest effects. Through her little nephew's words, spoken with the unconscious cruelty of childhood, the realization is brought home to her that:

> They were not hers, not even one of them:
> She was not born to be so much as that,
> For she was born to be Aunt Imogen.

The hard sting of grief is told in splendidly simple lines, but she is not afraid to see the truth and she gains "the largess of a woman who could smile." When the little boy who had fallen asleep in her arms woke up again;

> She took hold of him and held him close,
> Close to herself, and crushed him till he laughed.

"Captain Craig," Robinson's longest poem, contains the same simple and great humanity. Captain Craig is a tramp, a waggles, a dead beat, but he is also a philosopher who has read Sophocles and made the thought of the wise men of this earth his own. So pretences have fallen away from him, and in the narrative pretences are shuffled off some half dozen characters and they become clearly outlined in their true stature. It is a poem somewhat intricate in structure and packed with thought so closely that the meaning is not always apparent at first glance; but surely this is a lesser fault than to have too many words and little thought. The rich kernel is always there, and it is that Captain Craig has "learned to laugh with God." In this phrase lies much of Robinson's attitude toward life, but his laughter is a mellow laughter that is often close to tears. It will be worth while to reproduce a longer excerpt from "Captain Craig" not only because this thought occurs in it, but to show what admirable blank verse Robinson can write.

> "I made a mild allusion to the Fates,
> Not knowing then that ever I should have
> Dream-visions of them, painted on the air, —
> Clotho, Lachesis, Atropos. Faint-hued
> They seem, but with a faintness never fading,
> Unblurred by gloom, unshattered by the sun,
> Still with eternal color, colorless,
> They move and they remain. The while I write
> These very words I see them, — Atropos,
> Lachesis, Clotho; and the last is laughing:
> When Clotho laughs, Atropos rattles her shears;
> But Clotho keeps on laughing just the same.
> Some time when I have dreamed that Atropos
> Has laughed, I'll tell you how the colors change —
> The colors that are changeless, colorless." [pp. 30-31]

Nowhere, perhaps, has Robinson's art found finer expression than in his shorter poems, especially certain sonnets that bear as titles oddish proper names like "Reuben Bright," "Aaron Stark," "Cliff Klingenhagen," that cling in the memory. In "Aaron Stark" it is a miser who has "eyes like little dollars in the dark"; in "Reuben Bright" it is a grief-stricken butcher who cries like a "great baby" and "made the women cry to see him cry." Similar verbal felicities can be found in nearly all his sonnets. They are marvellously complete portraits of types that on the surface seem utterly unadapted to poetic treatment. They appear almost haphazard and colloquial in expression, but this is only due to the fine art of concealing art. On each re-reading they grow on one and the appropriateness of the graphic epithets appears more perfect.

There is one sonnet in particular which, had I to make choice of a dozen English sonnets, I would include. It is called "The Clerks." [The poem follows.]

This is great as the paintings of Millet and certain of the works of Meunier[6] are great. If there must be a social function in art, as some insist, a single poem like this with its honesty and sincerity is of more value than thousands of versified tracts filled with bitterness and accusation.

There are other sides to Robinson's work. Often he is purely lyrical, and his lyricism is adequate in technique and individuality. He does not fashion "in a shrewd, mechanic way, /Songs without souls"[7]; he knows how to make haunting melody, as in his "Luke Havergal," a stanza from which has been quoted at the beginning of this article. It is a poem as unique as Dowson's "Cynara."[8] He knows how to suggest much in a few deft, unobtrusive lines, as in his "James Wetherell":

> We never half believed the stuff
> They told about James Wetherell;
> We always liked him well enough,
> And always tried to use him well;
> But now some things have come to light,
> And James has vanished from our view, —
> There isn't very much to write,
> There isn't very much to do.[9]

This is all we are told about James Wetherell. Probably he is one of the little great contemporaries, a governor, perhaps, or a congressman, or an alderman; but hasn't nearly all that is worth while saying about him poetically been said in these lines?

But Robinson is also adequate in more ambitious themes. "The Chorus of Old Men in 'Aegeus' "[10] is noble poetry and one of the finest expressions of the Greek spirit in English. It is sung after the king has leaped from the cliff into the sea. It is the Hellas of Sophocles that lies in choral lines like these —

> Better his end had been
> To die as an old man dies, —
> But the fates are ever the fates, and a crown
>   is ever a crown.

There is a progressive growth in Robinson's separate volumes and in the last one, *The Town Down the River*, slim though it is, there are passages that for sheer poetic inspiration surpass anything in the earlier books. Here is found the sonorous and magnificent "An Island." It is a monologue of the sick Napoleon on St. Helena in 1821. The emperor is agonizing under the pain of incurable disease, plagued with rats and a busying physician.

> There are too many islands in this world,
> There are too many rats, and there is too much rain.
> So three things are made plain
> Between the sea and sky:
> Three separate parts of one thing, which is Pain ...
> Bah, what a way to die! —

He is querulous and grim, a tragic, caged, sardonic figure, in the poem, but he is imperial withal, still the emperor for whom thousands were eager to rush into the mouth of death.

In the best sense of the word Robinson is an eclectic, and as the true eclectic tests all values himself, there must always be an undercurrent of sadness that there are so few. This wistfulness is found in much of Robinson's work, but there is no bitterness or complaint in it. Somewhere he says to his friends who reproach him for wearing half his life away for bubble work that only fools pursue:

> So, friends (dear friends), remember, if you will,
> The shame I win for singing is all mine,
> The gold I miss for dreaming is all yours.[11]

He has paid tribute to Erasmus in a sonnet and something of the spirit of that fine old humanist is in the warp and woof of Robinson's work. He is unafraid and uncompromising, he does not evade the hard facts of life, he never becomes flaccid with the radiant lies of romantic illusion, but he does not protest too solemnly. This is how the world looks to him.

> Some are the brothers of all humankind,
>   And own them, whatsoever their estate;
> And some, for sorrow and self-scorn, are blind
>   With enmity for man's unguarded fate.
>
> For some there is a music all day long
>   Like flutes in Paradise, they are so glad;
> And there is hell's eternal under-song
>   Of curses and the cries of men gone mad.
>
> Some say the Scheme with love stands luminous,
>   Some say 'twere better back to chaos hurled;
> And so 'tis what we are that makes for us
>   The measure and the meaning of the world.[12]

Those who burn flaringly and with a single idea and are fanatic dogmatizers are no doubt necessary. At close range they seem to loom large, but the distance of a little time shows that as artists there is little permanence in them.

When Tolstoy complains of Shakespeare that he is immoral and irreligious because he presents good and evil deeds, noble and ignoble passions, without ever taking personal position as to what he deems good or bad, he pays the finest compliment to true art.[13] When Robinson refuses to take position in regard to the so-called "burning questions" of the day, he is the greater artist for that. The poet has to do with unchanging moods and essentials, with the generic man; not with a mass of external phenomena, not with costume or dress.

Some one once said: "The Japanese paint a flowering twig and it is all of spring. Among us, painters paint all of spring and it is hardly a flowering twig." If the total volume of Robinson's poetry is not large, what there is of it has the qualities of real poetry. Even among the great voluminous poets much is only poor verse, and most of us must confess that what we would choose for ourselves would usually fill only a small space. The yard-stick is not the thing by which to measure poetry.

A better gauge is to be found in certain words of Leonardo da Vinci: "O artist, let your manifoldness be as infinite as the phenomena of nature. In that you continue what God has begun, do not strive to multiply the works of the hand of man, but the eternal creations of God. Imitate no one. Let each of your works be a new phenomenon of nature."[14]

Measured by this standard, Robinson's work is everywhere shown to be true poetry.

From *Forum*, LI (February 1914), 305-312.

Robinson to Edith Brower, April 15, 1914: "I am booked for Saturday evening with the man who wrote the *Forum* article. I had never heard of him at the time of its publication and have met him but once or twice since. He seems to be a very good sort." (Cary, p. 156.)

1   "Luke Havergal," *The Children of the Night* (1897), p. 32.

2   "Isaac and Archibald," *Captain Craig* (1902), p. 87.

3   "Unity," first of "Two Quatrains," *TCOTN* (1897), p. 116.

4   "Octaves" I, *ibid.*, p. 91.

5   This amoral doctrine of art for its own sake, with roots in Keats and the Pre-Raphaelites, reached its height in England with Wilde and Pater, had become decadent as Robinson matured. He did not hold with the theory that a work of art has obligation only to be beautiful of itself. He said to Edith Brower, March 14, 1897: "Art for art's sake is a confession of moral weakness. Art for the real *Art's* sake is the meaning and the truth of life. This is just beginning to be understood, and it is on this understanding that the greatness of future literature depends." (Cary, p. 28.) Despite his strong bias against materialism Robinson saw this particular refinement as a deterioration into mere polish and freakish interest in the unusual.

In his review of Josephine Preston Peabody's first book of poems, *The Wayfarers*, Robinson reiterated his distaste of "the rather distressing product of a school whose watchword is a self-confessed fallacy known as 'art for art's sake' — whatever that may be. Art is a means to an end." ("A Book of Verse That Is Poetry," *Literary Review*, III [January-February 1899], 12.)

6   Jean François Millet (1814-1875), French painter, and Constantin Meunier (1831-1905), one of his Belgian disciples, became distinguished for their treatments of social misery in the working classes.

7   "Sonnet" (Oh for a poet), *TCOTN* (1897), p. 63.

8   Ernest Dowson's "Non Sum Qualis Eram Bonae Sub Regno Cynarae" resembles "Luke Havergal" in that it has four iambic stanzas, each with the evocative refrain, "I have been faithful to thee, Cynara, in my fashion." Both are concerned with shadows and vegetation and desolate passion, but Robinson's tone is not cynical.

9   This is poem II under the title "Romance," *TCOTN* (1897), p. 119.

10 This poem is an outgrowth of Robinson's versification of Harry DeForest Smith's prose translation of *Antigone*. It is not a translation but an attempt to capture the Greek spirit in a choral ode such as Sophocles might have included in his lost play about Aegeus. Robinson wrote Smith on January 12, 1895: "have done the first chorus in 'Aegeus' — about fifty lines, which seem to me to have a little swing in them"; and on September 11, 1896: "I fancy [it] is pretty loud in places. As a whole it is unsatisfactory, but I am going to let it go, all the same" [into *The Torrent and The Night Before*]. (Sutcliffe, pp. 194, 253.)

11 "Dear Friends," *TCOTN* (1897), p. 39.

12 "The World," *ibid.*, p. 16.

13 Ironically, Robinson considered Tolstoy's *The Kreutzer Sonata* a "mixture of

truth and lie" and "a book that could never, it seems to me, do anything but damage in the world." (Fussell, *EAR*, p. 199.)

14 This appears to be a free and somewhat fanciful translation of Leonardo's text in *Leonardo Da Vinci On Painting, A Lost Book*, reassembled by Carlo Pedretti (Berkeley, 1964), p. 32: "Dico alli pittori mai nessuno debbe imitare la maniera dell'altro perchè sarà detto nipote e non figliolo della Natura, in quanto all'arte. Perchè, essendo le cose naturali di tanta larga abbondanza, più tosto si vuole e si debbe ricorrere a quella, che alli maestri chi da quella hanno imparato." The injection of God into this passage by the translator is either an unwarranted poetic paraphrase or an interpolation from another apparently not rediscovered *pensiero*.

.. / / ..

Of people rather than peoples

CASSANDRA

It is seldom that Edwin Arlington Robinson, who has received higher praise from discriminating critics than any other living American poet, writes on a national subject. There is, of course, his unforgettable "Lincoln,"[1] and the poems which Mr. Roosevelt inspired[2] might also be called national in their interest. But as a rule he prefers to write of people rather than of peoples. To a recent issue of the Boston *Transcript*,[3] however, he contributes a criticism of what he believes to be the American attitude toward life. It is characteristically filled with such bits of splendor as the "bivouac of the marching stars." Even those readers who disagree with Mr. Robinson cannot fail to feel the beauty and power of his poem. ["Cassandra" follows.]

From "Current Poetry," *Literary Digest*, L (February 20, 1915), 387-388.

1 "The Master (Lincoln)," first poem in *The Town Down the River*, pp. 3-7.

2 "Au Revoir (March 23, 1909)," "The Pilot," and "The Revealer (Roosevelt)," *ibid*, pp. 83-84, 100-101, 125-129.

3 "Cassandra," Boston *Evening Transcript* (December 21, 1914), 17; collected in *The Man Against the Sky* (1916) and *Collected Poems*.

CAPTAIN CRAIG (1915)

Despite five years of heightened public attention bestirred by Theodore Roosevelt's unprecedented endorsement of August 1905, publication of *The Town Down the River* failed to breach the opaque barrier between Robinson and the general sector of American readers. Exquisitely aware of Roosevelt's paternalistic regard, *Scribner's* magazine brought out twelve of Robinson's poems in the 1906-1910 period. Two other titans, *Century* and the *Atlantic Monthly*, also admitted him to their pages, the latter for the first time. And *Lippincott's* unveiled "For a Copy of Poe's Poems," which it had purchased and filed away eleven years earlier.

The reviews and notices between 1910 and 1915, although clogged with a residue of "the influence of Browning" and of Roosevelt's intervenience, were eminently on the high side. Robinson was cited for "distinct advance" in his art, for "conspicuous" originality, for "power of characterization," "directness," "strength in gentleness," and for his imagination, "pagan magic," and "thought-provoking" themes. Braithwaite's two reports were strongly approbative, as in varying degrees were those of Richard LeGallienne, Joyce Kilmer, Louis Ledoux, Harriet Monroe, Hermann Hagedorn, and Otto Frederick Theis — none without warrant in the current literary forum. Moreover, Carty Ranck proclaimed with relative restraint in the reputable Boston *Evening Transcript* that Robinson was "a truly great poet." Nevertheless, sales of *The Town Down the River* in an edition of less than 800 copies moved with galling slowness. Robinson's prediction to Ledoux that the book would make no "immediate noise" was bleakly realized. Never mind that this newer breed of critics hailed Robinson's light as a true beacon, for the public it was still a will-o'-the-wisp.

This obduracy and the need to eat regularly forced Robinson to face other expedients. He considered and declined a teaching post at three-four dollars an hour in the tutorial school directed by his boyhood friend James Barstow. "I can't do that. I've got my job, and I've got to do it, and I can't do anything else."[1] Prior to publication of *The Town* he had reverted to prose as a viable means of salvation. In July 1910 he spelled out his equivocal situation to Mrs. William Vaughn Moody: "I regret to report that I have written two chapters of the novel — if it may be called one, being a rehashing of an impossible play, with some added frills. . . . If the October book of verse should by any chance amount to anything, the novel will undoubtedly knock it on the head, and serve it right. I ought to be willing to be a freak forever, and not try to make money."[2] He was cannibalizing his failed play *Van Zorn* on the desperate gamble that if drama was beyond his métier perhaps the novel was not. His decade in the metropolis had honed rather than stilled the puritanic imperatives ingrained during his childhood and adolescence in smalltown Maine. "I am compelled to confess my conventional hankering for a little independence. It must be amusing to pay one's debts when most of one's friends have never dreamed of getting anything."[3] By November 1, in the congenial though sometimes pungent company of Truman H. Bartlett in Chocorua, New Hampshire, Robinson had got through two-thirds of his hackwork "at a fairly regular jog." When completed and typed, he dispatched it hopefully to one publisher after another. It was unanimously rejected.

In 1911 he made no change in objective though a crucial shift in locale. George Pierce Baker, with whom Hagedorn had collaborated on a pageant for the MacDowell Colony in Peterborough, New Hampshire, suggested that he get Robinson to spend a summer there. At first Robinson deflected all of Hagedorn's suasions, fearful of entangling himself in a matting of artistic temperaments. With July more than half gone, he abruptly decided to give it a try. After his initial suspicion wore off, he settled down to converting his second play, *The Porcupine*, into a novel. The woodsy quiet of the isolated Colony and the colonists' deference to each other's working hours enabled him to transcribe eight chapters in exceptionally short time. The finished product was destined for the same void as the novel he had fashioned out of *Van Zorn*. However, the tranquility of spirit and fresh volition gained over this late-summer of reappraisal more than repaid for days upon days of infertile writing. In New York in the fall Hagedorn offered Robinson a drink, which he refused. "I've had the kind of time this summer that I can't ever pay for, and the only way I can show my appreciation to Mrs. MacDowell is by doing the best work that's in me. And I can't work and drink at the same time."[4] This was not to be his final retreat from "the Dark House," as he called his penchant for alcohol, but it never again posed a serious threat to his creative impulse. With help at the worst times from the Ledouxs and his old friend Clara Davidge, he held his destructive inclination safely at bay.

In the first month of 1912 Robinson yielded utterly to "the playwriting devil" that was after him "with a red-hot iron."[5] With only *pro forma* vacillations toward poetry in May, he bound himself to a course of at least six plays to be accomplished in immediate succeeding years. His second summer at MacDowell he devoted to a play which he "packed off" to a typist in September and forthwith started on a new comedy. To Hagedorn he divulged that "having gone as far as I have into the playwriting game I can't stop now." Poetry was "so far in the future . . . that I can't reach it yet."[6] In October he supposed, but could not be certain, that "sooner or later" he would get back to his "proper business," admitting somewhat sheepishly that he was "still worshipping strange gods."[7]

By February 1913 Robinson had touched nadir. He wrote to Kermit Roosevelt out of a sustained weariness of failure. "Please don't ask me anything more about my novels, or too much about my plays. The novels are extinct; and when I have satisfied myself and all my friends that I cannot write a play, I shall probably have the good sense to go back to poetry." He preferred not to think of where he would be if Kermit's "astonishing father" had not "fished me out of hell by the hair of the head."[8] Not two weeks later, with the unquenchable buoyancy of native genius, he sprang back to a tonic position. On March 9 he exposed to John Hays Gardiner the undercurrent of introspection which had kept him awash for more years than he now cared to contemplate.

I do know that I shall never make any money writing plays, and probably not in any other way. It isn't that I can't write a play . . . but I cannot hit the popular chord, and for the simple reason that there is no immediately popular impulse in *me*. In poetry this is an advantage. . . . When I come down out of myself and try to write for the crowd, I perpetrate the damnedest rubbish that you ever heard of, . . . I see now that my past three years of floundering in prose have been due to nothing more serious than the fact that I had temporarily written myself out. At last I can see light again, and I am going to write another book of poems; . . . I feel that I have given the thing a fair trial and that it would be unfair to you as well as to myself to waste any more of my life in doing something for which I have come to see that I am not fitted.[9]

The staunch laudations of Noyes, Ranck, and Braithwaite in the Boston press at this time shored up his rededication. The bootless gyrations of his past three years came to a stop. In the summer of 1913 at MacDowell, Robinson occupied himself exclusively with the composition of new poems.

With sure instinct Scribner's balked at publishing *Van Zorn* and *The Porcupine* as either plays or novels, while advancing Robinson $100 for poems to be delivered. By June 7, 1913 Robinson's confidence was so thoroughly restored that he could exult, in his typical abstemious way, "I hope to leave enough behind me to leave a small dent."[10] In December he broke his silence of forty months with "The Field of Glory" in *Outlook* and followed up in a wide spectrum of magazines with seven poems in 1914 and an equal number in 1915.

Since his separation from the Custom House job Robinson had subsisted on loans and gifts from his Harvard crony Willie Butler, the sculptor James Earle Fraser, Hagedorn, Gardiner, Ledoux's father, Craven Langstroth Betts, and others. In the spring of 1914 this ignominy was relieved by a provision of $4000 in the will of John Gardiner, dead at 50. Louis Ledoux, striving in another quarter to improve Robinson's situation, pleaded with Scribner's to print Robinson's plays. When they remained adamant, Ledoux shifted his proposal to the friendlier ears of George P. Brett, president of Macmillan. "Brett recognized that his company would lose money and gain little *kudos* on Robinson's excursion into drama; but he had a shrewd suspicion that the poet had an economic as well as an aesthetic future. He agreed to accept a present loss for the prospect of a remote and larger gain."[11] Accordingly, he brought out *Van Zorn* in September 1914, a revised edition of *Captain Craig* in February 1915, and *The Porcupine* in September 1915. He thus secured for his company every subsequent book Robinson wrote, with the exception of *Lancelot* in 1920.

Braithwaite's inclusion of "The Field of Glory" and a note on Robinson's "characteristic magic" in the *Anthology of Magazine Verse for 1913*, followed by dedication to Robinson and two of his poems in the 1914 edition, kept Robinson's name visible among book readers while he labored on an enlarged version of *Captain Craig*. Reviewing Braithwaite's annual assessment of magazine poetry for the Boston *Evening Transcript*, Alice Corbin Henderson, associate editor of *Poetry*, elevated Robinson and Willa Cather above all the rest as "indeed poets of some distinction."[12] Shortly before publication of his first play Robinson announced gleefully to Mrs. Ledoux: "I'm pegging away on the new book [*The Man Against the Sky*] and admiring the cover of *Van Zorn* . . . C.C. is to be brought out in the same style."[13] For the first time after a painfully long remission the scattered shards of old, old hopes were beginning to fall back into place.

.. / / ..

CAPTAIN CRAIG, A Book of Poems. Published February 10, 1915 by The Macmillan Company, New York. Bound in maroon cloth, title and author's name stamped in gold on front cover and spine, gold rule along front cover edges; top edge gilt, fore edge untrimmed and bottom edge rough-trimmed; leaves measure 18.7 by 12.7 centimeters; unspecified number of copies at $1.25.

Alterations in this edition:

a) *Title page*: elimination of the Houghton, Mifflin & Company device; substitution of two lines, REVISED EDITION / WITH ADDITIONAL POEMS, and the current publisher's name, location, and year of publication.

b) *Dedication page*: inserted between title page and contents page — To / THE MEMORY OF / JOHN HAYS GARDINER.[14]

c) *Contents*: order of poems and pagination of the first sixteen poems, pages 1-171, follow precisely the 1902 edition; twelve "Variations of Greek Themes" and "The Field of Glory" are added to the 1915 edition.

d) *Text*: no verbal changes from the 1902 version.

CAPTAIN CRAIG

A Book of Poems

BY

EDWIN ARLINGTON ROBINSON

REVISED EDITION
WITH ADDITIONAL POEMS

New York
THE MACMILLAN COMPANY
1915
All rights reserved

CAPTAIN CRAIG (1915)

Contents

Captain Craig	1
Isaac and Archibald	85
The Return of Morgan and Fingal	103
Aunt Imogen	108
The Klondike	115
The Growth of "Lorraine"	121
The Sage	123
Erasmus	124
The Woman and the Wife	
I The Explanation	125
II The Anniversary	125
The Book of Annandale	127
Sainte-Nitouche	150
As a World Would Have It	159
The Corridor	163
Cortège	164
The Wife of Palissy	166
Twilight Song	169
Variations of Greek Themes	
I A Happy Man (Carphyllides)	172
II A Mighty Runner (Nicarchus)	173
III The Raven (Nicarchus)	173
IV Eutychides (Lucilius)	174
V With Sappho's Compliments	174
VI Doricha (Posidippus)	175
VII The Dust of Timas (Sappho)	176
VIII Aretemias (Antipater of Sidon)	176
IX The Old Story (Marcus Argentarius)	177
X To-Morrow (Macedonius)	177
XI Lais to Aphrodite (Plato)	178
XII An Inscription By the Sea (Glaucus)	179
The Field of Glory	180

Banners Unfurling

One sign of Robinson's growing impact as a poet on the larger public was raised in the Boston *Post* on February 12, 1915. For its observance of Abraham Lincoln's anniversary the *Post* ran on page 11 a two-column reprint of Robinson's celebratory poem, "The Master (Lincoln)" in boldface type within a decorative frame, under his full signature. Though the paper furnished no attribution, it had had to go back six years to the first appearance in *Scribner's* magazine or five years to *The Town Down the River* — a heartening mark of potential longevity in Robinson's work.

On receipt of the revised edition Theodore Roosevelt wrote: "Many of them [the poems] I am very fond of, perhaps fondest of all of 'Twilight.' " (Letter to Robinson, February 22, 1915, Colby College Library.)

.. / / ..

Nothing in all English literature quite like this

MR. ROBINSON'S *CAPTAIN CRAIG*

All lovers of poetry will be glad to learn of a new edition of Edwin Arlington Robinson's *Captain Craig*, a volume of poems which went through two editions, but which has been out of print for some time, for it is a work which seems destined to become a classic, and if our judgment be worth anything, it ought to become one. The new edition of Bartlett's *Familiar Quotations* gives four quotations from this book, and we should not be surprised if future editions gave even more.[1] One of the poems in the collection was regarded by the late Professor James to be almost as good as any of Wordsworth's.[2]

It will doubtless interest our readers to learn that the poem, "Captain Craig," which gives the book its title, had a rather peculiar inspiration. Captain Craig was a tramp or hobo, distinguished for his knowledge of Greek and for his enormous erudition generally, as well as for a certain quaint philosophy which comes out in all his conversation. Well, Captain Craig had a living prototype in a venerable Jew,[3] still living in England, who was the original of one of George Eliot's characters in *Daniel Deronda*,[4] a man of great learning and fine character, yet quite unable to earn a living. He spent a great deal of time in this country, was a friend of Longfellow and of many of the elder American writers, some of whom referred to him in their writings, but finally he became so poverty-stricken that he was forced to live in New York on the alms of a few young literary men, who were glad to make the old man's declining days as comfortable as possible.

Mr. Robinson's poem gives no slavish imitation of the man's characteristics; it is a highly original production, but if this man had never lived, it is hardly likely that Mr. Robinson ever would have written "Captain Craig."[5] There is nothing in all English literature quite like this poem, and it is a poem that no lover of poetry or of literature in general can afford to miss. It is full of shrewd philosophy and of exquisite humor. There is a fine spirit of humanitarianism in it, too, which ought to appeal to the sensibilities of all who read the poem. If Mr. Robinson had never written anything but "Captain Craig," he would have written enough to stamp him as a man of poetic genius, but he has several other volumes to his credit, and there are some other pieces in *Captain Craig* which are almost as good as the poem which gives the book its title. We predict that the new edition of the book will have the success that the two former editions had.

From Rochester *Herald* (March 4, 1915), 6.

1 This is the tenth edition, enlarged and revised by Nathan Haskell Dole (Boston, 1914). A total of eleven lines are quoted; the same number in the reprint editions of 1923 and 1930 by Dole. The prophecy came true under Christopher Morley, editor of the eleventh edition in 1937, in which thirty-four selections from numerous Robinson poems range over three pages, with an additional footnote to a quotation from Horace.

2 In a letter regarding his contribution to the publisher's advertisement of *Captain Craig* (2nd edition, 1903) William James said that "Isaac and Archibald" is "*fully* as good as anything of the kind in Wordsworth." See comments page 150, this volume.

3 Alfred Hyman Louis (1829-1915), a hyperbolic Cambridge-educated English Jew, is described at length by Hermann Hagedorn as bearded, bad-smelling, albeit dignified in frayed and stained clothes. (*Edwin Arlington Robinson: A Biography* [New York, 1938], pp. 132-136.) He claimed to be a protégé of the Rothschilds and Gladstone, repudiated because he turned Catholic, and counted among his intimates George Eliot, T.H. Huxley, Herbert Spencer, Browning, Longfellow, Howells, Trollope, Burne-Jones, Ruskin, Meredith, the Rossettis, Mill, Charles Kingsley, and Cardinal Manning. He had been a lawyer, poet, musician, politician, sculptor, journalist, editor of the *Spectator* and the *Fortnightly Review*, and author of several books. He was also a former inmate of a mental hospital, a drunk, a bum, and a pestiferous sponge.

In the winter of 1897 Robinson was introduced to him by Craven Langstroth Betts in the apartment of Titus Munson Coan. With William Henry Thorne as a fourth, they met frequently in second-rate restaurants to talk about life and letters. A man of phenomenal erudition, Louis arrogantly dominated these sessions — dogmatic, pontifical, garrulous, and fascinating — to a point. Although Coan put him down as "a brummagem Jesus," Robinson listened intently to his prolonged philosophizing on Greek, Roman, Jewish, and modern European cultures. However, Robinson could not indefinitely endure Louis' quenchless capacity for alcohol, his truculence, and continual demands for money. Not without reluctance, he cut off all contact with the old megalomaniac. Robinson dedicated *The Glory of the Nightingales* (1930) "To the memory of Alfred H. Louis."

" 'Old Mr. Louis knew of the use to which I put him,' observed Mr. Robinson. 'He read the manuscript. He laughed and was immensely pleased. He was tickled, as I have no doubt his ghost will be to-day by this association of him with the original Captain Craig. He never saw Tilbury Town, of course. The other characters in the poem, who also were taken somewhat from life, never saw him. It just pleased me to place him in that environment.' " (M.K. Wisehart, " 'By Jove!' Said Roosevelt 'It Reads Like the Real Thing!' " *American Magazine*, CV [April 1928], 80.) Hagedorn says that Robinson let Louis read the book with some trepidation, fearing he might resent the portrait. " 'Why should you have hesitated to let me read this?' he said, and his eyes filled with tears. 'This is the best justification I have of my existence. Now I seem to know why I am still in the world.' " (p. 162.)

4 Mordecai (Ezra Lapidoth), a young, consumptive, intellectual Jew, victim of poverty and hardship, who works in a bookshop, has extended conversations with

Daniel, who marries his sister. Louis often visited George Eliot until she too wearied of his aggressiveness and garrulity.

5 On most occasions Robinson accorded with this statement. To Nancy Evans he avowed "that only one of his characters was done from life; that one was Captain Craig, who was suggested by an elderly Jew." ("Edwin Arlington Robinson," *Bookman*, LXXV [November 1932] 677.) To Winfield Townley Scott: "The only model I ever used was an old English Jew for Captain Craig. I just transferred him to my mythical town [Tilbury], which is more or less Gardiner." (*Exiles and Fabrications* [Garden City, N.Y., 1961], pp. 163-164.) "Louis knew of course that he had suggested 'Captain Craig' to me." (*Edwin Arlington Robinson: A Collection of His Works From the Library of Bacon Collamore* [Hartford, 1936], p. 12.) And Wisehart quoted Robinson to this effect: "I came to know him well, and to feel that I wanted to perpetuate his personality." (p. 78.)

Two years later Carty Ranck elaborated on a remark Robinson had made during the Wisehart interview. "Last Summer I was talking with Robinson in his studio at the MacDowell Colony, of those tremendous trifles that change one's destiny, and he told me that he could never have written 'Captain Craig' if a friend had not forgotten his umbrella. This friend was a man named Blair, and the episode happened in Gardiner, Me. Robinson's slender but vital volume of poems, *The Torrent and The Night Before*, had just been published. At that time there were still a few copies left of this now priceless book, when Blair, who had gone out with the poet from wherever they were, suddenly remembered his fateful umbrella.

'So we went back,' said Robinson, 'and I happened to pick up an old copy of the *Century* magazine. In it was a short poem by Titus Munson Coan, and I thought I would send him a copy of *The Torrent and The Night Before*. Well, I did so, and in the course of time I received a very appreciative letter from him. He invited me to call on him if I came to New York. Later I did go to New York, and at the house of Dr. Coan I met Alfred H. Louis, who is the original of Captain Craig.' 'So you see,' said Robinson with a whimsical smile, 'if my friend Blair had not come back for his umbrella I should never have written "Captain Craig."'" ("Edwin Arlington Robinson," New York *Herald Tribune Magazine* [December 14, 1930], 8.)

And yet, to Edith Brower "he denied . . . that the prototype of Captain Craig was Alfred Louis, the remarkable English Jew who became a Roman Catholic, and was the most utterly perfect specimen of the raggedy Bohemian variety of high intellectual I've ever known. Yet every line of the Captain might be laid alongside of Louis and match without variance. Robinson said he didn't know he was painting Louis, and I believe him; I also believe that the pungently impressive personality of that strangely charming man was so embedded in his consciousness that, having selected the Captain's type, he worked it out subconsciously as we have seen, so that everyone who knew Louis is bound to find him in Captain Craig. And everybody except Robinson does!" ("Memories of Edwin Arlington Robinson" by Edith Brower in Richard Cary, editor, *Edwin Arlington Robinson's Letters to Edith Brower* [Cambridge, Mass., 1968], pp. 211-212.)

. . / / . .

The *Dial*, LVIII (March 18, 1915), 233, announced *Captain Craig* in its "List of New Books" but published no review thereafter.

. . / / . .

Almost imperceptibly coming into his own

A NEW POEM BY ROBINSON

A new volume of poems by Edwin Arlington Robinson is always an important event to lovers of literature, and those who enjoy meeting odd and original characters should make the acquaintance of *Captain Craig*. Here is a poet who writes with authority and distinction and whose fame is slowly but surely widening as the years go by. There are few poets writing in English today whose work is so permeated by individual charm as is Mr. Robinson's. Always one feels the presence of a man behind the poet — a man who knows life and people and things and writes of them clearly, with a subtle poetic insight that is not visible in the work of any other living American poet.

It is always interesting to watch the growth of a poet's fame, to see him gradually and almost imperceptibly coming into his own. Long admired by the initiated as the possessor of a singularly felicitous style and a power of condensation, granted to but few writers, Mr. Robinson, abhorring the tin pan methods of the modern household poet, has been quietly doing his own work in his own way. And now he is beginning to reap his reward in the constantly growing appreciation of readers in this country and abroad who admire the classic finish of his work and remember him as the author of that golden line: "By moonlit wharves in Avalon."[1]

In *Captain Craig*, Mr. Robinson reveals the sure touch of one whose art is ripe and mellow. The title poem is written in well-sustained blank verse that never halts or wobbles, and it tells the story of an eccentric old philosopher who has drunk deeply of life and whose shrewd comments to five or six young men[2] who have taken charge of the broken down old reprobate in Tilbury Town — an imaginary place that figures in many of Mr. Robinson's poems — and who get a certain sort of grim enjoyment from listening to the Captain's maunderings.

But Captain Craig has one good point. He is never a bore. While he may skip with goatlike nimbleness from one topic to another, there is always the stuff that makes life in his talk. The old captain has lived and sweated and suffered, and the reaction upon him is what the poet shows us most compellingly. In drawing Captain Craig, Mr. Robinson has created a portrait that sticks in the memory and will not be effaced. He meets the test of a real creation,[3] because when we have closed the book, we feel that we have parted with an old friend, a somewhat unmoral old friend, if you please, but one whose human failings endeared him the more to us.

Mr. Robinson makes us feel that we know his strange hero in the first half dozen lines of the poem. Here is the way it begins:

> I doubt if ten men in all Tilbury Town
> Had ever shaken hands with Captain Craig,
> Or called him by his name, or looked at him
> So curiously, or so concernedly,
> As they had looked at ashes; but a few —
> Say five or six of us — had found somehow
> The spark in him, and we had fanned it there,
> Choked under, like a jest in Holy Writ,
> By Tilbury prudence.

Then, for some eighty pages, we listen to Captain Craig discourse on life and its meanings. We follow him to his grave with the young men of Tilbury Town, and we smile ironically with the poet when he tells us that:

> ... all along that road the Tilbury Band
> Blared indiscreetly the Dead March in Saul. [p. 84]

"Captain Craig" is a poem that is worth reading again and again. This fantastic old philosopher with his refreshing views on life is a genuine addition to American literature.

There are other poems in this volume, some of which are almost as good as "Captain Craig" — notably "Aunt Imogen," "The Klondike" and "Isaac and Archibald." In the latter occurs this exquisite passage:

> Never shall I forget, long as I live,
> The quaint thin crack in Archibald's old voice,
> The lonely twinkle in his little eyes,
> Or the way it made me feel to be with him.
> I know I lay and looked for a long time
> Down through the orchard and across the road,
> Across the river and the sun-scorched hills
> That ceased in a blue forest, where the world
> Ceased with it. Now and then my fancy caught
> A flying glimpse of a good life beyond —
> Something of ships and sunlight, streets and singing,
> Troy falling, and the ages coming back,
> And ages coming forward: [p. 97]

Mr. Robinson has also tried his hand at giving us some variations of Greek themes, and, for each instance, the result has been happy. Take, for example, this fragment for Glaucus, which Mr. Robinson has called "An Inscription by the Sea":

> No dust have I to cover me,
>   My grave no man may show;
> My tomb is this unending sea,
>   And I lie far below.
> My fate, O stranger, was to drown;
>   And where it was the ship went down
>   Is what the sea-birds know.[4]

From Brooklyn *Daily Eagle* (April 3, 1915), II, 7.

In keeping with this ample appreciation of Robinson's achievement and potential, the title is printed in two-column capitals. The subcaption reads: *"Captain Craig, the Latest Creation by Edwin Arlington Robinson, Has a Touch of the Wisdom of the Ages — The Poet's Fame Growing."*

1 Line 4, stanza 3 of "The White Lights," in *The Town Down the River* p. 72.

2 Of these, four become identifiable: the narrator; Morgan, a fiddler; Killigrew, a rhymester; and Plunket, a scholar. They foregather at "The Chrysalis," a loose kind of club not unlike "The Quadruped" of Robinson's post high school days in Gardiner.

3 "The people in Mr. Robinson's poems are so real that even Amy Lowell supposed that the men from Tilbury Town were portraits," said Evans. (p. 677.) In common

with most poets growing old, Robinson hedged on imputed "influences" or completely repudiated them. In regard to "Rahel to Varnhagen" he told Esther Bates that "he did not take his character from [a] book, nor did he draw directly from life in any of his poems. He said he 'precipitated his own characters.'" (*Edwin Arlington Robinson and His Manuscripts* [Waterville, Maine, 1944], p. 5.) This conception he extended to locale. George Burnham reports Robinson saying to him "that neither Tilbury Town, nor any of the portrait-sketches, nor the 'Town Down the River' referred to any particular place. In no instance whatever in any of his writings did he refer to anyone or any place. Tilbury Town might be any small New England small town." (James S. Barstow, *My Tilbury Town* [New York, 1939], p. 7.)

4 "Variations of Greek Themes" XII, p. 179.

Robinson to Lilla Cabot Perry, December 2, 1913: "Of course you are right in your suggested improvement in the 'Inscription.' As a matter of fact, the line is hardly in the original at all, although it is suggested. In making the translations — if they may be called translations — I used Mackail's *Selections*, and used them most shamelessly — I mean the English part of them — for my knowledge of Greek was never more than Xenophontic, and now it isn't even that." (Colby College Library.)

.. / / ..

He reveals: he does not criticize

EDWIN ARLINGTON ROBINSON

Lincoln MacVeagh

As I write about Mr. Edwin Arlington Robinson, I seem for a moment carried back to a house I knew once, "Calverly's." There they all are, Calverly himself, Lingard, Leffingwell, Clavering, deep in the midst of one of their long silences filled with the blue smoke of pipes. Lingard nurses his knee and laughs softly to himself. Clavering dreams in the legendary past. The big, sombre, restless man is Leffingwell, And Calverly, leaning forward a little on the table, embraces them all with his quick glance, for his heart, like his house, is endlessly hospitable to these men. But I forget —

> We go no more to Calverly's.

I do not know whether the pictures I form of these men of Mr. Robinson's imagination would be recognizable to Mr. Robinson or not. But I do know that he would not care either way. Every one who knows the "Calverly" poems[1] knows each of the four friends better than if he had lived with them. And that is enough to satisfy Mr. Robinson. That is also why I shall venture to apply to the poet a much abused technical term and call him a "symbolist." It is because no other name will fit the process with which, given nothing more than five short poems and a poet's interpretative power, he has wrought the miracle of creating four characters and a house. The process is one which is repeated over and over again in Mr. Robinson's works. Briefly, it consists in suggestion, and the art lies in selecting the items best fitted to carry it. Here, for instance, is Mallarmé's famous definition of symbolism: "to choose an object and out of it to represent a state of soul."[2] But Charles Morice's is even better: "to give people a remembrance of something they have never seen."[3]

There could be no more exact description of the effect of Mr. Robinson's poetry.

But here his resemblance to the authentic symbolist ceases. It is a sufficient resemblance to make a reader of his poem, "The Town Down the River," think of such poems as Verhaeren's "Le Passeur d'Eau."[4] There is the same strong suggestion and the same near approach to allegory. But Mr. Robinson is more subtle than Verhaeren, and this excess of subtlety for a symbolist (whose method is already subtle enough) carries him over into what is indeed a method of his own. He symbolizes; that is true. But his symbolism is one degree refined over that of Mallarmé. It is no longer a progress from "object" to "state of soul," but from one state of soul to that soul's complete individuality. Mr. Robinson never leaves the psychological realm. He makes us know Leffingwell, Calverly, Lingard, in the most intimate way possible; that is, he makes us know what it would be like to be one of these men, even feel as if we had been each of them. But he does this not by describing well chosen actions or some physical feature, but simply and solely by expressing a significant feeling, emotion, or thought.

Take the poem of "Luke Havergal," for instance. There is no action, no story told, there is only the voice of the spirit telling a man, who has lost the woman he loves, to live out his life in patience for her sake.

> Go to the western gate, Luke Havergal!

And yet everything in the poem, the dignity of its rhythm, the stubborn repetitions, the idealism, the sound of the name "Luke Havergal" itself, incessantly returning, make the impression of an undefined but unmistakable personality. Thus, though after reading the poem you could not describe Luke Havergal's appearance, you must infallibly recognize him if you saw him. It is the same with many other poems, such as "Charles Carville's Eyes," or "Cliff Klingenhagen." Commonplace incidents are here for contrast gathered round the unique point, which in each case is what may be called a psychological gesture, expressive of a whole mind; the happiness of Cliff Klingenhagen who smiled over his wormwood, the revelations of Charles Carville's dead eyes, the tears of the butcher, Reuben Bright; all told not for what they are but for what they evoke. Each one of these short poems is a triumph of Mr. Robinson's individual method.

Mr. Robinson shows a fondness for the dramatic monologue ("An Island," "The Night Before," etc.). But here he is very much out of his true sphere. His way is to evoke the whole character from a single trait. This is wonderful when it is done once, but in a long poem or in a play the reader easily becomes surfeited by such a method, and too much power becomes a kind of impotence. In "An Island" the figure of Napoleon is blurred like an over-exposed photograph, and in the play of *Van Zorn* the principal character, for whose exposition the whole play exists, is photographed fifty times over on the same plate. This defect is even more evident in "Captain Craig." We recognize Mr. Robinson a hundred times along the weary road of this interminable poem, where he lies in wait to flash out with revelations of heaven or of the soul. But in the end we recognize nothing but the poet's inability to handle so large and sustained an expression.

Continued action, even psychical action such as is seen in the dramatic monologue, is not what interests Mr. Robinson. He prefers the sudden, unconscious gestures, finished almost as soon as begun, which reveal character in a flash. His genius is punctual and intense. Consequently in his work there is no exposition of contemporary thought, though the minds he portrays are contemporary; no controversy, no didacticism. He reveals; he does not criticize. And his revelation, at the same time that it is complete, is so indirect and oblique that we may say he really never expresses himself, but rather symbolizes himself. We imagine him an intensely human friend, gentle, glad to see us, but, no matter who we are or what we do, never surprised at us, and too really interested ever to be excited; a recluse, but a recluse who has drawn not away from the world, but into its heart; a stranger of few words in the presence of the noise and banality of the day, and a night-prowler, like Nietzsche's Zarathustra, "loving to look into the faces of all sleeping things."[5] It is said that he loves the New Hampshire hills and the faces of people from anywhere. He is always to be found — at Calverly's!

Let us go back, then, and find him there. Probably his limitations, his artistic conscience, his humanity, neither barbarous nor over-civilized but sanely contemporary, will save him from becoming popular. Ella Wheeler Wilcox and our own Hoosier poet[6] divide the field with the literary "freaks" and the little brothers of society. But between the two extremes of sentimentalism and idiocy there is still some ground left where the long labor and devotion such real artists as we have may train a small public to appreciate beauty. Mr. Robinson is one of these artists.

From *New Republic*, II (April 10, 1915), 267-268.

Lincoln MacVeagh (b. 1890), director of Holt & Company, president of Dial Press, was also a linguist and a diplomat, serving as minister and ambassador at various times in Greece, Ireland, Union of South Africa, Yugoslavia, Portugal, and Spain. This appears to be his sole critical effort on a major literary figure.

1 The "Calverly poems" in *The Town Down the River* (pp. 41-55) comprise "Calverly's," "Leffingwell," "Clavering," and "Lingard and the Stars," all grouped under the master heading "Calverly's."

2 From "Sur l'évolution littéraire": "C'est le parfait usage de ce mystère, qui constitute le symbole: évoquer petit à petit un objet pour montrer un état d'âme, ou, inversement, choisir un objet et en dégager un état d'âme, par une série de déchiffrements." (*Oeuvres complètes de Stéphane Mallarmé* [Paris, 1945], p. 869.)

3 Charles Victor Morice (1861-1919), poet, critic, editor, translator of Russian novels; friend of Verlaine, Mallarmé, and Coppée; he sometimes used the pen name of Karl Mohr. "Quant au symbole, c'est le mélange des objets qui ont éveillé nos sentiments et de notre âme, en une fiction. Le moyen c'est la suggestion: il s'agit de donner aux gens le souvenir de quelque close qu'ils n'ont jamais vu." He is quoted by Jules Huret in *Enquête sur l'évolution littéraire* (Paris, 1913), p. 85.

4 Emile Verhaeren (1855-1916), Belgian-French author of some forty volumes of

lyric poems and four plays. Considered Belgium's greatest poet, he deplored the overgrowth of the country by the cities, exalting humble people in an atmosphere of rural realism not unlike that of George Crabbe, one of Robinson's early exemplars. This is the first poem in Verhaeren's *Poèmes: IIIe Séries* (Paris, 1915), collected from his *Les Villages illusoires* (1895). It consists of fourteen stanzas of unequal length 3, 4, 5, 6 or 8 lines) in no discernible pattern, with an intermittent refrain, "vers la mer." Thematically, it does share Robinson's concern with the grip of the city and the death of illusions.

5 *Also sprach Zarathustra*, Section 8 of the Prologue, last paragraph: "denn er war ein gewohnter Nachtgänger und liebte es, allem Schlafenden in's Gesicht zu sehn."

6 James Whitcomb Riley (1849-1916), Indiana dialect poet of the simple, cheerful life marked with occasional pathos. On January 28, 1895 Robinson wrote: "I have been writing more music — this time to a little poem by J.W. Riley, . . . It begins and ends (every verse) with 'There! little girl; don't cry!' It is very pretty and simple and I could not resist the temptation." (Denham Sutcliffe, editor, *Untriangulated Stars: Letters of Edwin Arlington Robinson to Harry DeForest Smith 1890-1905* [Cambridge, Mass., 1947], p. 200.) Robinson composed "four or five pieces all told."

. . / / . .

Despite this trilogy of praise, Mr. Robinson has survived

CAPT. CRAIG

Edwin Arlington Robinson has been seriously handicapped by gaining recognition as a poet. First, Theodore Roosevelt, who was then President, acclaimed him the greatest living American poet.[1] He was trying hard to live this down when Alfred Noyes came to America two years ago and went up and down the country telling every one what a great poet Robinson was.[2] Robinson, who personally is as modest a poet as ever wore shoe leather, struggled manfully against this gratuitous praise. Recently a new prophet appeared in the person of John Cowper Powys, the English lecturer, who also discovered a wonderful corn-fed poet out West somewheres. Mr. Powys has solemnly declared with his best Cambridge accent that Mr. Robinson IS a poet.[3]

Despite this trilogy of praise, Mr. Robinson has survived, and in his latest volume (*Captain Craig: A Book of Poems*. The Macmillan Company) proves that he is writing as good poetry as is being written to-day on either side of the Atlantic. The title poem is a noteworthy achievement, and there are other poems in the book that are memorable for classic phrasing and for a certain odd twist that makes them distinctly different.

"Captain Craig" is an eighty-four [page] verse, but this fact should not frighten the reader, because Capt. Craig is a real human being, and when he talks he always says something worth while. Here, for instance, is what the old captain has to say about religion:

> I believe
> God's humor is the music of the spheres —
> But even as we draft omnipotence
> Itself to our own image, we pervert

CAPTAIN CRAIG (1915)   285

> The courage of an infinite ideal
> To finite resignation. You have made
> The cement of your churches out of tears
> And ashes, and the fabric will not stand:
> The shifted walls that you have coaxed and shored
> So long with unavailing compromise
> Will crumble down to dust and blow away,
> And younger dust will follow after them;
> Though not the faintest or the farthest whirled
> First atom of the least that ever flew
> Shall be by man defrauded of the touch
> God thrilled it with to make a dream for man
> When Science was unborn. And after time,
> When we have earned our spiritual ears,
> And art's commiseration of the truth
> No longer glorifies the singing beast,
> Or venerates the clinquant charlatan, —
> Then shall at last come ringing through the sun,
> Through time, through flesh, God's music of the soul. [pp. 8-9]

Capt. Craig is an old broken-down philosopher who has been knocked about and buffeted by life, but who still preserves a certain grim and mordant humor that permeates his sayings and gives them individuality. You may not agree with all that he says, but you will never be bored by him.

Some of the other notable poems in the collection are "The Book of Annandale," "The Klondike," "Aunt Imogen," and "Sainte-Nitouche" — all of which have a flavor all their own.

Mr. Robinson has also given us some variations of ancient Greek themes, and he has somehow managed to imbue them too with his own individuality. The verses from Lucilius, which Mr. Robinson has called "Eutychides," strike the modern Hermione clubs[4] just as strongly to-day as it probably did when Lucilius flung his rhymed sneer: ["Variations of Greek Themes" IV, follows.]

From New York *Evening Sun* (April 17, 1915), 7.

---

1 See Roosevelt's review of *The Children of the Night* in *Outlook*, August 12, 1905, reprinted in this volume.

2 See Fred W. Thompson in Boston *Sunday Post*, March 2, 1913, reprinted in this volume.

3 John Cowper Powys (1872-1963), individualistic British "aboriginal" novelist and poet, lectured through the United States for thirty winters, ten thousand times by his own estimate. On March 28, 1915 he told a group in the hall of St. Mark's Church on Second Avenue in New York City that "it was an awful shame that a second-rate critic from England should have to be called in to tell Americans who their poets are." (New York *Times* [March 29, 1915], 9.) Powys went on effulgently about *Spoon River Anthology* (1915), and it is Edgar Lee Masters, born in Kansas, who takes the brunt of this anonymous critic's sneer. Powys called Masters the third great American poet he had been able to discover. "He was the realist poet. Edwin A. Robinson was the poet of the metaphysical — the American Browning almost — and Arthur D. Ficke the poet's poet — the American Schiller." In his *Autobiography* (London 1934, p. 451) Powys said: "As for Edwin Arlington Robinson, I met *him* very early in my

American life and nothing could have exceeded his courtesy to me or my respect for him."

To a Robinson commemorative issue of the *Mark Twain Quarterly* (II [Spring 1938], 2), Powys contributed an amusing tribute called "The Big Bed," in which he said, "He was a character. . . . He was an original." "I praised a line of his: 'Come out, you laelaps, and inhale the night,' and told him how I had never seen the word laelaps since I saw a picture of a laelaps, a huge sea monster, in a book of prehistoric and imaginary and mythological monsters shown to me as a child at Dorchester, . . . Robinson said that he was more pleased at my liking that line about the laelaps than anything else I could have said. . . . in the later years our paths diverged, though once long after we met in the street and I felt passionately drawn to the man again! We met in Sixth Avenue under the elevated. That was the last, and that was long ago." "Laelaps" occurs in line 13 of "Lingard and the Stars" (*The Town Down the River*, p. 55).

4   Hermione is the subject of Don Marquis' *Hermione and Her Little Group of Serious Thinkers* (1916), which first ran piecemeal in his daily column in the New York *Sun*. She is devoted to a number of "causes" of the day which prove too much for her feeble intelligence, though she is unaware of the fact — an excellent vehicle for contemporary satire.

. . / / . .

For Truth, for intellectual and spiritual sincerity

TWO POETS OF THE DAY

Edwin Arlington Robinson's notable poem, "Captain Craig," has been issued in a revised form, accompanied by various new lyrics and poems of psychological insight.[1] "Captain Craig" is said to have had an original in a venerable Jew still living in New England.[2] Mr. Robinson makes him a lovable old scalawag, a combination of satyr and saint, much averse to earning a living, not a success as a beggar, but possessed of a tremendous philosophical intuition and an excellent knowledge of Greek. He exists on the charity of a few young literary men, entertaining them with Socratic dialectic and, whenever they are absent, with a voluminous correspondence mainly of analytical philosophy. Robinson has been called "The American Browning." His great passion is for Truth, for intellectual and spiritual sincerity. "The Book of Annandale," a splendid poem included in this collection, is one of the most moving emotional narratives found in modern poetry. *Van Zorn*, a drama published in 1914, illustrates the use of his interpretative method.

From *American Review of Reviews*, LI (May 1915), 632.

The other poet alluded to in the title is James Stephens, whose *Songs From the Clay* is reviewed in a first paragraph of equal length.

1   Robinson made no textual changes in "Captain Craig" for this reissue; only the twelve "Variations of Greek Themes" and "The Field of Glory" were appended to the text of the original edition.

2   See note 3 to the March 4, 1915 Rochester *Herald* review, above.

. . / / . .

The New York *Times Review of Books* of May 2, 1915 did not honor the book with a fresh review of its own, rather cribbed elements from the Rochester *Herald* (March 4, 1915), reprinted in this volume. Under "Books and Authors," page 176, appeared this item: "Captain Craig, the hero of Edwin Arlington Robinson's initial poem in the volume of verse of that title, had a prototype in a venerable Jew, said to be still living in England, who was the original of one of George Eliot's characters in *Daniel Deronda*. He spent much time in this country, was a friend of Longfellow and other writers of that time, and received sympathy and help from a number of young literary men in New York."

The *Times* did at least notice Robinson, and did not commit the error of the *American Review of Reviews* (above) in placing Alfred H. Louis in *New* England.

. . / / . .

Two grave faults: talkativeness and baldness

CAPTAIN CRAIG
Oscar W. Firkins

In "Captain Craig," the first and longest poem in Mr. Robinson's revised edition, a mendicant, who is likewise philosopher and optimist, preaches hopefulness, with tongue and pen, in expansive introspective discourses which I find myself quite unable to follow with any consecutive intelligence. I should not like to expose the reserves of my own waning faith in the kindness of the universe to the hazards of a second reading of these dismal incitements to cheerfulness. In "Isaac and Archibald," we are in quite another zone. Relieved of his optimism, Mr. Robinson becomes actually cheerful, and truth and vividness follow in the path of sunshine. In this homely, sauntering, half-blinking, rural idyl, a fresh reality has been firmly etched. There are two admirable old men who love each other without detriment to the gusto with which they see or foresee each other's increasing infirmities, and a thoroughly enjoyable boy in whom that alternation of eagerness and apathy, of wonder, and the calm taking of things for granted, which is so notable in childhood, is winningly portrayed.

In "The Book of Annandale" there are more psychological stagnancies, but power is again active in "The Woman and the Wife" and in the muffled drum-beats of two finely imaginative lyrics, "Cortège" and "Twilight Song." Readers of "Captain Craig" will be surprised at the nice frugality, the fine chariness, of treatment in the suggestive "Variations of Greek Themes."

Mr. Robinson has two grave faults: a talkativeness, not to say glibness, which seems in Shakespearean phrase to have borrowed Gargantua's mouth, and a frequent baldness — or even meanness — of rhythm and diction which is probably in his case half negligence and half insurgency. His evident wish to be a psychologist has received, I should surmise, but moderate encouragement from nature. What he can do and what is well worth doing is to sketch one class of realities vividly and to give clear lyrical embodiment to certain rare shades of universal feeling. The following is from "Twilight Song":

> But the road leads us all,
> For the King now is dead;
> And we know, stand or fall,
> We have shared the day's bread.
> We can laugh down the dream,
> For the dream breaks and flies;
> And we trust now the gleam,
> For the gleam never dies; —
> So it's off now the load,
> For we know the night's call,
> And we know now the road
> And the road leads us all.[1]

From "Recent Volumes of Verse," *Nation*, C (May 20, 1915), 562.

Oscar W. Ferkins (1864-1932), long a professor of English and of comparative literature at the University of Minnesota, playwright, essayist, and drama critic for the New York *Weekly Review*, wrote lives of Emerson, Austen, Howells, and Shelley.

[1] In this line Firkins created a distortion of meaning by transcribing "us" as "to."

. . / / . .

In her review of Edgar Lee Master's *Spoon River Anthology* Alice Corbin Henderson points out succinctly that Robinson "may be said to have been the pioneer in this particular field." (*Poetry*, VI [June 1915], 146.)

. . / / . .

Inimitable charm and skill

IN THE SHADOW OF PARNASSUS

Zoë Akins

Nothing in Edwin Arlington Robinson's recent book, *Captain Craig* (Macmillan's), pleases me as do the "Variations of Greek Themes." Mr. Robinson's gift for narrative verse is distinguished and his style clear and strong, but his handling of Greek themes reveals him as a lyrical poet of inimitable charm and skill. There is so little affected, so much that is done with ease and lightness of touch and sincerity in his work that the temptation to quote at length is strong; but the following "Variations" intimate forcefully and surely what is finest and most essentially poetic in Mr. Robinson's gift. ["A Happy Man" I, "The Dust of Timas" VII, "Lais to Aphrodite" XI, and "An Inscription by the Sea" XII, follow.]

From *Reedy's Mirror*, XXIV (June 11, 1915), 8.

This is the sixteenth article of a weekly series. Several lesser poets, Olive T. Dargan as an instance, received lengthier consideration.

Zoë Akins (1886-1958), a poet, playwright, and novelist, won the Pulitzer Prize in 1935 for *The Old Maid*, a dramatization of Edith Wharton's story.

. . / / . .

He has had to wait long

EDWIN ARLINGTON ROBINSON AND HIS DISTINCTIVE ART
William Stanley Braithwaite

When I heard again from the Gentle Poet,[1] she had flown from the seaside to the mountains. "I love the mountains," she wrote, "as you love the sea. The altitudes calm and inspire me; they do even more, they solidify my faiths which walk with me in disembodied yearnings on the lower planes of the world. Do not believe that I get away, because I never wish to, from the clamor of humanity; only up here it comes in echoes that I can distinguish. The mountains help me to distinguish the notes in that sad and wild music, and all the fortitude that I have to bear it and to consecrate my sympathy and strength in its service comes from these mountains, among whose massive shadows and eternal tranquility I realize the wonderful Presence of my faith.

"Passing through the city I thought, 'What poet should I take with me to the mountains?' I thought of the many poets you had praised, all of whose work I had not read. I wanted the poet who had a great sympathy with human nature, and who saw the humor in the varied experience of character. I thought afterwards why I had pondered so long in making my selection. For is there not one American poet you have praised in season and out as the greatest of all our poets? And when I thought about it a little more, didn't he seem the very poet for my mountains? I had read only one of his volumes, *The Town Down the River*, and that had left a magic upon me that I have never been able, nor do I wish, to escape. And I remember your writing that a new edition of an earlier book of his had been recently published, the volume called *Captain Craig*. I have been reading this remarkable book here, and it has made me ask the mountains many questions. Have they answered them all, you ask? I don't know. He packs his thought pretty tight. There is a line he has in 'Captain Craig' which warns 'what is a gift without a soul to guide it,'[2] and I interpreted its application to Mr. Robinson's own genius in this fashion. 'Without his soul of humor how can one be guided by the gift of his profound thought?' And I suspect his simplicity baffles a good many. Yet it is in his clean, severe, vibrant quality of speech which acts like a magnet upon the imagination. Take 'The Return of Morgan and Fingal,' 'The Book of Annandale,' 'Sainte-Nitouche,' and 'The Wife of Palissy,'[3] just to have a few, and what magic there is in the simplicity of expression, opening to the mind and emotions such a domain of human motives and character as no other poet in our country has ever accomplished. But I must not go on telling you about this master-poet; he awes me with his mysteries and silences, just as these mountains do; they reach so close to heaven, that it seems a profanation to bring one's human presence near their majestic solitude. I have very much the same feeling towards Mr. Robinson's poems; his muse is on the mountaintop of our humanity; there is a solitude about it, too rare to profane with misunderstandings and misconceptions. I cannot conceive of anyone not feeling the magic of it, the sympathy, the humor, above all the truth of human experience which he shows in his characterization of human personality. I must say, too, how much I enjoyed those delightful 'Variations of Greek Themes,' which I understand was not in the earlier editions of the volume. What a rich strain he would add to your lutanists, a noble figure to lead the orchestra, an inspiring and dominating singer to whom they all pay homage," concluded the Gentle Poet.

"And you, too," I answered, "so frankly acknowledge the greatness of this man. I will quote you a passage from 'Captain Craig,' that poem with more exalted wisdom, in spite of its rough verbal garments now and then, than any poem of our generation. Consider this:

> "Is it better to be blinded by the lights,
> Or by the shadows? By the lights, you say?
> The shadows are all devils, and the lights
> Gleam guiding and eternal? Very good;
> But while you say so do not quite forget
> That sunshine has a devil of its own,
> And one that we, for the great craft of him,
> But vaguely recognize. The marvel is
> That this persuasive and especial devil,
> By grace of his extreme transparency,
> Precludes all common vision of him; yet
> There is one way to glimpse him and a way,
> As I believe, to test him, — granted once
> That we have ousted prejudice, which means
> That we have made magnanimous advance
> Through self-acquaintance." [p. 27]

All great literature demands 'magnanimous advance through self-acquaintance,' and the great popular appreciation of the genius of Edwin Arlington Robinson has been retarded because the public for a long while refused him it. You will find poets read and quoted who hardly deserve the distinction. But this man is now coming into his own. He has had to wait long. But he knew how to wait, and knowing how to wait in art is the test of genius. Now wherever you hear people who know speak of American poets, they take the genius and place of Edwin Arlington Robinson as granted. They will say, we are in a wonderfully poetic period just now; we have poets on the crown of Parnassus, and they will name you Robert Frost,[4] Amy Lowell,[5] Edgar Lee Masters,[6] Anna Hempstead Branch, Ridgely Torrence, Olive Tilford Dargan,[7] and others, but on the topmost peak they assume that you know the place is occupied by the silent and lordly figure of this singer.

"The first edition of *Captain Craig* was published in 1902. It reached a second edition. Now thirteen years later is this new edition with the additions of the 'Variations of Greek Themes,' and the poem called, 'The Field of Glory.' 'Captain Craig,' as you know, tells the story of an old derelict picked up by a youth with an eye to character, to whom he discourses about the soul. It is very largely a portrait of character, character from almost every angle of human experience. But never was such philosophic wisdom salted with humor. Its pathos and tragic significance are all the more impressive for this soothing revelation of humor. Yet from the poem you can choose more aphoristic sayings than from any half dozen poems of the same length combined in American poetry. One calls to mind,

> The ways of unimaginative men
> Are singularly fierce . . . [p. 52]

and,

> a man may be as brave
> As Ajax in the fury of his arms,
> And in the midmost warfare of his thoughts
> Be frail as Paris . . . [p. 79]

"But I do not want to linger over 'Captain Craig' with its satire, its humor, its exorcism of human vanities, its compressed, sometimes strained, power of narration. For there's the story of 'Isaac and Archibald,' 'The Book of Annandale,' and the shorter poems, among which is the glorious ballad of 'The Return of Morgan and Fingal,' as elaborately wrought with a dim vision as Browning's 'Childe Roland to the Dark Tower Came.' And there is this poem 'Cortège' which still haunts with its grim procession: [The poem follows.]

The Greek quality in Mr. Robinson's art, the severity, the simplicity, the very balance and purity of his pathos and humor, his absolute recognition of fate and destiny in human circumstances, made it almost imperative that he should give us these paraphrases of the Greek poets that he has added to this edition of *Captain Craig*. From Carphyllides Mr. Robinson gives us these lines on "A Happy Man": ["Variations of Greek Themes" I, follows.]

From Marcus Argentarius is this "The Old Story": ["Variations of Greek Themes" VIII, follows.]

And I cannot resist from quoting, for the pleasure even that it gives of writing the words, this, "An Inscription by the Sea," from Glaucus, a perfect gem: ["Variations of Greek Themes" XI, follows.]

In almost twenty years, for it was in 1896, that Mr. Robinson published his first book of poems, he has only given us three books of verse.[8] Doesn't such patient and careful progress bring the great reward? I look forward confidently when his next book appears, which I understand is to be early next year, to a general and popular acclamation of this great poet.[9] To *Captain Craig* and *The Town Down the River*, I am sure you will now add the reading of *The Children of the Night,* and that these books, upon that treasury shelf of song which you keep for the masters, will have an honored place.

From "Books of the Day," Boston *Evening Transcript* (August 11, 1915), 18.

Braithwaite wrote a weekly series of seven articles for the *Transcript* from July 21 through September 1, 1915. Each had a specific subtitle under the continuing caption "The Lutanists of Midsummer." This installment is the fourth, the only one which surveys a single poet's work; the others at least two and as many as eight.

1 Braithwaite does not reveal the identity of his Gentle Poet beyond the facts that she is female, and that she was writing from the New Jersey coast before she fled to the mountains. Examination of Braithwaite's available correspondence has not yet turned up her name. It has been suggested that it could have been Sara Teasdale.

2 *Captain Craig* (1915), p. 23. The line reads, correctly: "What is a gift without the soul to guide it?"

3 Robinson changed this title to "Partnership" beginning with *Collected Poems*, 1921. To two editors he wrote: "In a misguided moment I changed it — with some notion, I suppose, of giving the poem a more general application. It is (or was) obviously one of Palissy's porcelains. Now it can be almost anything." (Gerald DeWitt Sanders and John Herbert Nelson, editors, *Chief Modern Poets of England and America* [New York, 1947], p. 495.) Palissy was a French potter of the 16th century.

4 Braithwaite brought Frost and Robinson together in 1915 but their friendship was at best wary (see Hagedorn, p. 339). Frost wrote an introduction to Robinson's posthumous *King Jasper*.

In 1917 Robinson praised Frost handsomely. "In 'Snow,' 'In the Home Stretch,' 'Birches,' 'The Hill Wife,' and 'The Road Not Taken' you seem undoubtedly to have added something permanent to the world." (Ridgely Torrence, editor, *Selected Letters of Edwin Arlington Robinson* [New York, 1940], p. 99.) Loath to discuss his contemporaries in print, Robinson nevertheless permitted Karl Schriftgiesser to quote him directly in the Book Section of the *Transcript* on November 4, 1933: "I think a lot of Robert Frost's work." In later days, however, he told Winfield Scott that the *North of Boston* poems "don't wear so well . . . Frost is a kind of professional farmer. He is a bit self-conscious, but harmlessly so. He's a good fellow — a good fellow." (Scott, p. 166.)

5 After reading Amy Lowell's *Men, Women, and Ghosts* Robinson wrote her on October 31, 1916: "The general effect of your new book is something, I fancy, like that of an avalanche. . . . Whether this kind of effect is the ultimate mission of art I am not prepared to say, but you may be interested to know that you have given me a pretty good shaking up; and I am not, I believe, very easily shaken." (Torrence, p. 99.)

This may be construed as guarded praise, or at least not uncomplimentary. In private, however, Robinson referred to her acridly as "She" — a species of formless, hovering monster. In a series of letters to Thomas Sergeant Perry and his wife Lilla Cabot between 1915-1922 (now in Colby College Library), Robinson rejected her free verse with this analogy: "When the pike isn't dozing, he might as well be for the most part. Otherwise he is likely to be opening and shutting his mouth without catching anything." He called her "a gifted lady" more or less satirically, cited her for industry and enthusiasm if not for style, and was relieved after reading her *Tendencies in Modern American Poetry*: "I have to say that she has let me down rather better than I expected. Where I looked for the stiletto and the bodkin, I encountered the meat-axe and the shillelah. . . . But I am glad that she wrote the article, and I can't yet be sure that she means murder." When she did not send him a copy of her *Can Grande's Castle* he concluded that "I was not lively enough in my appreciation of the last. . . . when it comes to 'polyphonic prose,' I find that the old order is changing so fast that I find nothing to do but let it change, and trust that it will readjust itself." And following her review of his *Collected Poems* (1921) he wrote: "I knew well enough that She would use the knife on me. . . . I should say some of her jabs were made with her eyes shut, though maybe I'm wrong."

He spoke with greater freedom in public after she died (1925). To Winfield Scott (p. 165) he said, "She was really quite medieval. . . . She should have lived in Renaissance Italy. She'd have enjoyed poisoning people. A grand talker. But always slaying six or eight people an evening. . . . Oh yes, she had a personality all right. But I'm afraid when her work is sifted there's not much there." And mordantly to Louis Untermeyer: "Amy Lowell might make real poetry out of her material, if she were a poet." ("E.A.R.: A Remembrance," *Saturday Review*, XLVIII [April 10, 1965], 33.)

In *A Critical Fable* (New York, 1922), pseudonymously signed "A Poker of Fun," Amy Lowell said among other things about Robinson: "excellent poet, / And excellent person"; "For a man of his stamp, / So conscious of people, it seems odd to scamp / Experience . . . live in a hollow"; "Robinson stays with his feet planted square / In the middle of nothing"; "He is cruel with dispassion, as though he most dreaded / Some shiver of feeling might yet be imbedded / Within him"; "The slightest conceivable hint of a thaw / Wounds his conscience as though he had broken a law"; "his quaint, artificial control / Is a bandage drawn tightly to hold down his soul"; "The heritage, left by those Puritan heirs. / His bogies and satyrs"; "his kind of *ad nauseam* metre"; "His books will be listed as 'reading required,'" (pp. 26-29.)

6   Robinson designated Masters "bitter — he's bitter as gall." (Scott, p. 166.)

7   Olive Tilford Dargan (1869-1968), Kentucky poet and lyric dramatist on the order of William Vaughn Moody, Ridgely Torrence, Percy MacKaye, and Josephine Preston Peabody, also wrote stories about mill and mine workers in the South.

8   Although he cites the year of its publication, the existence of *The Torrent and The Night Before* seems to have escaped Braithwaite's notice. He does not mention it in any of his reviews gathered in this volume nor in his biographical note on Robinson in *Anthology of Magazine Verse for 1919* (p. 310). He may have known about *The Torrent* but considered it to have been engrossed in *The Children of the Night*, overlooking essential differences between the two books. See the list of Robinson's modifications in the chapter headed "*The Children of the Night* (1897)" in this volume.

9   Braithwaite was solid in his prescience. *The Man Against the Sky*, Robinson's next book, made his name a household word in 1916.

.. / / ..

The week following his overview of Robinson, Braithwaite interjected this paragraph into his summer series of critiques. As has been observed, the Gentle Poet may well be Sara Teasdale.

To the manner born

AMERICAN NATURE CONTRASTED WITH CELTIC MYSTICISM
William Stanley Braithwaite

It is curious sometimes to realise how a simple word will astonish people. I don't think the Gentle Poet was astonished into an attitude of objection; but the fear we all have today of boldly paying the highest praise to a poet had made her wonder when I characterized Edwin Arlington Robinson as this "lordly poet." She wrote: "It was breathless admiration in realizing that his genius was fittingly and adequately described. The term we have learned to apply to Shakespeare, Milton[1] and Wordsworth, and I don't think I ever before thought very much why we did. It is because they probed the deepest into human nature and human experience, which gave them a certain nobility of sympathy and vision. Mr. Robinson has probed deeper into those mysterious depths of life than any American poet of today, and because he is of today is no reason why we should refuse him this true description of his poetic nature. Its guise he wears unconsciously, but comfortably. He is to the manner born of the great lineage. . . ."

From "Books of the Day," Boston *Evening Transcript* (August 18, 1915), 18.

---

1 Robinson spent an additional year at Gardiner High School after graduation in 1888, including a course on Milton in his schedule. He speaks of having read *Paradise Lost* and *Samson Agonistes* — "the work of Milton's to which he most frequently returned." (Edwin S. Fussell, *Edwin Arlington Robinson: The Literary Background of a Traditional Poet* [Berkeley, 1954], p. 67.) "I can't believe that I ever told you that whopper about reading *Paradise Lost* six times," he wrote Laura E. Richards. "In solemn truth I read it once when I was about sixteen and have never read it since — except in places." (*Ibid.*, p. 68; see also Sutcliffe, p. 143.) "I can read 'Lycidas' forever," he told Mrs. Louis Ledoux. (Fussell, p. 68.) And "he said he liked to read Milton's blank verse when he was writing it himself." (Bates, p. 30.) To Thomas Sergeant Perry, July 1, 1926: "I have just been reading over the fight between Adam and Eve in *Paradise Lost*, which ended, as you may remember, in a draw. Milton would not have made a good sporting editor." (Colby College Library.)

There are two editions of Milton's poetical works and a copy of *Paradise Lost* in Robinson's library, now in Colby College; also an unpublished letter to Laura E. Richards in which Robinson fancies a touch of Milton in "Captain Craig."

. . / / . .

For whatever esthetic or editorial reasons that moved him, William Dean Howells seems to have almost totally ignored Robinson's presence as a poet on the American scene. Just this once, while skittering through "sixteen or seventeen volumes of recent verse at hand," did he condescend to mention Robinson: "There is such fine, manly *go* in 'The Klondike' of Mr. Edwin Arlington Robinson's *Captain Craig: A Book of Poems* as makes you wish to read the whole book; . . ." ("Editor's Easy Chair," *Harper's*, CXXXI [September 1915], 637.)

. . / / . .

Braithwaite's *Anthology of Magazine Verse for 1915* was released on November 30. In his summary of "The Best Poetry of 1915" he allotted slightly more than a full page (pp. 246-247) to Robinson's *Captain Craig*. This notice is not repeated in full here because it is in every effect a condensation of Braithwaite's perceptions — which follow the remarks of the Gentle Poet — in his Boston *Evening Transcript* review of August 11, 1915, above. His innovations in *AMV* consist of: 1) appending the names of Louis Untermeyer, James Oppenheim, Amelia Josephine Burr, and Sara Teasdale to his roster of eminent contemporary poets; 2) adding to this list of preferred poems "the fine steel engraving of 'Aunt Imogen'"; 3) qualifying "The Book of Annandale" as "symbolic." In his introduction Braithwaite ranks Robinson with "the older and established names represented by some of the best work they have done in recent years," placing his name first on the rollcall (p. xviii). "Flammonde," "Old King Cole," and "Cassandra" are reproduced in the body of the volume.

. . / / . .

At last coming into his own

"—AND OTHER POEMS"

Louis Untermeyer

Almost as important as Claudel's book[1] is the new edition of Edwin Arlington Robinson's *Captain Craig* (The Macmillan Company). Important not only because of what it contains, but because its reissue is a sign that Robinson is at last coming into his own. Into his own — that is, in a popular sense; for Robinson has always had a following in the more restricted groups. The precursor of men like Robert Frost, Edgar Lee Masters[2] and the logical progenitor of half a dozen lesser poets, he sounded, long before they ever turned to their natural medium, that simple and direct speech which is almost our only poetic language today. So sharp, so clear-cut it was; so over-chiseled at times that many, missing the long-familiar decorations, accused him of indirection and obscurity. Before Robinson began our American critics used to complain that often they couldn't see a poem because of its "poeticisms." These were the same critics who later complained of Robinson's work that they couldn't recognize the poem because of the lack of them. . . . In *Captain Craig* can be found the best of Robinson: the flashing irony, the keen maker of sharp-edged phrase, the psychological play that led so many of the tribe of ticketers and pigeon-hole experts to name him the "Browning of America." There is also always present an undercurrent of lyricism as unconscious as it has been unappreciated. For good measure the new edition includes a dozen "Variations of Greek Themes," full of modernity and humor, and that splendid "war poem," "The Field of Glory."

From Chicago *Evening Post* (August 27, 1915), 9.

Louis Untermeyer (b. 1885), poet and translator, is further distinguished by his many excellent, abundant anthologies of modern British and American poetry. As early as 1919 he devoted some twenty-five pages to Robinson's work in his *The New Era in American Poetry* (pp. 111-135). In *Modern American Poetry* (1921) Untermeyer carried Robinson's "Vain Gratuities," greatly expanding his selection in subsequent editions. While Consultant on Poetry to the Library of Congress in 1963, Untermeyer arranged an extensive exhibit of Robinson books and manuscripts, and published a *Reappraisal* of his work.

In the early thirties Robinson made some of his rare comments on contemporary

English and American poets: Kipling, Housman, Sandburg ("should have stayed in the army; he's all blood and guts"), Amy Lowell, Vachel Lindsay ("shouts a good sermon, but poetry is not a revival meeting"). "Thank God I'm not one of them," sighed Robinson in conclusion. (Untermeyer, *Saturday Review*, p. 33.)

1 In "Spring and Summer Review, III," Untermeyer reviews Paul Claudel's *The East I Know* before coming to Robinson.

2 Robinson to Thomas Sergeant Perry, January 17, 1916: "Several people seem to have discussed my paternity in the case of Masters. I don't know that it makes any difference one way or the other, as he does his own thing in his own way. If the report were true, it would be another example of the son who attains to a prosperity the father never knew. Sometimes the son will kick the old man down stairs and out of the house." (Colby College Library.)

. . / / . .

By the end of 1915 Robinson seemed no great way nearer to attaining widespread recognition than heretofore. In his anthology for that year, published November 30, Braithwaite touted Frost and Masters as "the two great successes of the year." Robinson did lead his list of "older and established names," was well represented in his summary of 1915 publications, and *Captain Craig* did receive generous treatment, but the limelight fell elsewhere. On December 4 the *Literary Digest* reviewed Braithwaite's annual (pp. 1284-1285) and not anywhere in more than a page of text and four photographs (Frost, Masters, John G. Neihardt, Lincoln Colcord) was Robinson visible. It was the year that *North of Boston* and *Spoon River Anthology* broke upon the national consciousness as superb revelations of the American grain. With demoniacal irony-before-the-fact, Niehardt and Colcord were captioned as "two [who] are expected to impress us before another twelvemonth." For it was indeed the disregarded Robinson who was to do the impressing within two and a half months.

THE MAN AGAINST THE SKY

A Book of Poems

BY

EDWIN ARLINGTON ROBINSON

New York
THE MACMILLAN COMPANY
1916
All rights reserved

EPILOGUE

The poems which were to form the bulk of *The Man Against the Sky* (1916) began appearing in periodicals in February 1914. Fourteen of twenty-six in that volume got first airings in the *Atlantic Monthly, Poetry, Scribner's, Harper's Weekly, Cornhill Booklet,* Boston *Evening Transcript, Trend, Outlook,* and *Drama* between that date and November 1915. Robinson blocked out his new book in March 1915 and brought it to completion at the MacDowell Colony that summer. On July 29 he wrote Edith Brower, "I shall have another book of poems for you some time in February," adding murkily, "After that, the good Lord only knows."[1] "I carried a bundle of new poetry into the Macmillans the other day," he said to Daniel Gregory Mason on November 11, "and I expect in the course of time to see it come out in the form of another unprofitable slender volume. Who in hell invented the word slender?"[2] On November 16 he resorted to derisive oxymoron: "The whole immortal mush is now with the printer"[3]; on the 26th cloaked his joy in a pun: "The Macmillan printers are now at work on my latest intimations of mortality."[4] He had tentatively titled this collection *Flammonde*, after the opening poem, but the broader ring and reach of "The Man Against the Sky" prevailed.

One datum roundly accepted is that with publication of *The Man Against the Sky* Robinson arrived. Literary observers like Ben Ray Redman, Mark Van Doren, and Allen Tate concurred in retrospect that this book "awakened" the critics and reviewers, that it won "the wide attention" unaccountably withheld from Robinson till then, and that it thrust him into "the front rank" of American poetry. It was not necessary to wait on the verdict of history; the immediate tremor was unmistakable. Littérateurs at the highest level — Amy Lowell, Padraic Colum, Harriet Monroe, Louis Untermeyer, William Stanley Braithwaite, Edmund R. Brown, and Oscar W. Firkins — acclaimed the work vibrantly in the most influential newspapers and magazines, as did anonymous reviewers in the *North American Review,* New York *Times Review of Books, Outlook, Literary Digest,* and *American Review of Reviews.* The encomiums were lavish: "the most individual art of any in America," "enviable position in American letters," "a force in present-day literature," "one of the few moderns," and "at the head of our poetry to-day."

Braithwaite persisted in the role of Robinson's front-line advocate. Besides a commendatory review in the Boston *Evening Transcript*, he recapitulated in the *Bookman* and also made much of *The Man Against the Sky* in his *Anthology of Magazine Verse for 1916*, rating it among "the permanent additions to the art . . . that will have readers and admirers for a long time to come. . . . This volume contains the greatest poem ever written on Shakespeare, and numerous others which given the study that all profound and magical work demands, will satisfy the most exacting that in Mr. Robinson American poetry has to-day its deepest vision and most enduring speech" (pp. 249-250). At long last, the reading public began to listen, to read, and to believe.

Prophetically, Van Wyck Brooks had announced *America's Coming of Age* in 1915. Masters' *Spoon River Anthology* drew to him the appellative "Another Walt Whitman," and *Some Imagist Poets* loosed a fresh breeze over the American literary scene, depressed by the genocidal strife in Europe. Frost, Sandburg, Dreiser, and Ernest Poole propounded brands of realism more in tune with Robinson's unsentimental, sympathetic report of the world. The accession of such powerful allies unquestionably abetted his sudden elevation. No longer a lone maverick among the Victorian formalists, Robinson was borne forward on a swell of vigorous, new voices. Although he demonstrated greater depth and breadth in his latest volume, he had not materially altered his philosophic slant, his fundamental tone, techniques, or vocabulary. He had merely been caught up with. Of this he was intuitively aware.

> "You ask me if I think there is a new movement in poetry, and my reply is that there is always a new movement in poetry. There is always a new movement in everything, including each new inch of each new revolution of the earth around the sun. But if you mean to ask me if this new movement implies necessarily any radical change in the structure or in the general nature of what the world has agreed thus far to call poetry, I shall have to tell you that I do not think so. . . . Some of them [my friends] may call me a conservative, others a reactionary; and all this in spite of the fact that I have been accused in the past of being, if anything, too modern. But these accusations were made long ago; and I fancy that my limited public has come by this time to see that I was never so perilously modern, after all."[5]

From the outset Robinson "knew exactly what he wanted," enunciating with finality, "I'm going to be a poet."[6] "There's never been a time when I wasn't sure," he remarked to Ridgely Torrence[7] right after publication of *The Town Down the River*, though he never harbored "top-lofty notions as to the security of my alleged appointed seat" among the best of the western poets.[8] And he was willing to wait and sacrifice. "I starved twenty years, and in my opinion no one should write poetry unless he is willing to starve for it."[9] He was even reconciled to dying unrecognized, on the slim postulate that "fifty or sixty years after I am dead, someone may find something in [this stuff]."[10]

Two decades of disregard failed to faze Robinson's resolution. He had early gauged his prospects and acquiesced stoically with the realities. "I had read enough to know that writing poetry didn't mean a bed of roses.

Rather, I felt that I was 'in for it.' But I wasn't frightened. It seemed like a gigantic venture. I anticipated hardships. Looking back, I'm surprised that they weren't much greater than they proved to be."[11] He was sensible of his mundane shortcomings — "My total lack of commercial instinct and my indifference to the little whiff of newspaper notoriety that I might or might not get." He preferred his own way, shrinking from the assurance of "a man from the West" that " 'In four or five years, my dear fellow, I am confident that your name will be in the magazines.' What is there for a fellow to say?"[12] he inquired helplessly.

Robinson could jest, albeit somewhat grimly, about his relative anonymity as a poet up to this time. Herbert Gorman records his saying, "I had no public when I began. My public has accumulated, more or less under protest, very slowly,"[13] and Jay Hubbell quotes him indirectly in the same vein, "For some fifteen years, he once said, he had about fifteen readers."[14] He braced his perdurable expectancy against two standing pillars: 1) "always ... being able to do my work in my own way," and 2) "confidence that the end would take care of itself."[15] And so it came to pass that God's providence and Robinson's resolve fell into fortuitous conjunction. Or to view it in Trent's less theurgic terms: "The true poet sooner or later finds his public and his public finds him — often without the intervention of the critic, sometimes in spite of the latter's denunciations."[16]

Two tributes noteworthy for perception and concision must be allowed the last stroke on the profile of Robinson's courageous ascension. "No whim of public taste decreed his elevation," wrote Ben Ray Redman ten years after the fact, "no planned audacity won him sudden shocked attention; at no Byronic dawn did fame salute the opening of his eyelids. His has been the long, hard road; the copy-book road, so innocent of short-cuts."[17] And Malcolm Cowley in 1948:

Robinson was then [1920] the only American poet who had achieved not merely success but an integrated career and one that was marked by complete absorption in his art. For poetry he had sacrificed everything else: marriage, home, the respect of his neighbors and the hope of rising in the world. Poetry was his vocation, his avocation, for he lived without teaching or book-reviewing or reading from his books; he simply worked and expected to be fed like Elijah by the ravens.[18]

.. / / ..

Three poems pertaining to Robinson may be legitimately recorded here as the final "notices" he received before *The Man Against the Sky* dispersed the fog that had enveloped him for two benumbing decades. All were published shortly after the book but before Robinson's general accreditation. Thus they are acceptable as part of the precognizance, with elements of the surging appreciation, and of course contributory to its rising resonance. The first, written by a friend since Robinson's adolescence, was to be expected in the course of events. Still it required the cooperation of a large metropolitan newspaper to come to the public eye. Only three days before, the Boston *Evening Transcript* had run Braithwaite's opening salvo on the poet's extraordinary new volume. Robinson's name was now one to conjure with.

TO EDWIN ARLINGTON ROBINSON
(On reading his poem, "Calverly's")

Alanson Tucker Schumann

I always like your queer things,
   I always like your sad ones;
Your queer things are your near things,
   Your sad ones are your glad ones.

You write because you must write —
   It is your precious gift, friend.
My faith is that you just write
   To strengthen and uplift, friend.

So do the work you can do
   With purposeful essaying,
And let a smaller man do
   The lesser work of weighing.

From Boston *Evening Transcript* (February 29, 1916), 13.

Alanson Tucker Schumann (1846-1918), physician who preferred to practice on poems rather than patients, lived one street down from the Robinsons in Gardiner. Twenty-three years older, and voluble where Robinson was laconic, Schumann nevertheless consorted with the youth in whom he espied a special sensitivity. He led Robinson into the subtleties of French forms: villanelle ("The House on the Hill"), rondeau ("In Harvard 5"), rondel ("A Poem for Max Nordau"), ballade ("Ballade of Broken Flutes") which Robinson dedicated to his mentor. In "The First Seven Years," Robinson recalled: "I was chiefly occupied with the composition of short poems and sonnets, which I would read to my old friend and neighbor, Dr. A.T. Schumann, who was himself a prolific writer of sonnets, ballades and rondeaus, and a master of poetic technique. As I shall never know the extent of my indebtedness to his interest and belief in my work, or to my unconscious absorption of his technical enthusiasm, I am glad for this obvious opportunity to acknowledge a debt that I cannot even estimate." (*Colophon*, Part IV [1930], n.p.)

At the outset Schumann assured Robinson that he was the better poet. He introduced him into the home of Caroline Davenport Swan, former schoolteacher, where frequent sessions were held — with Henry Sewall Webster, a local judge of probate — "to go over each other's verse" and to discuss the poems in current magazines. They all published in William Henry Thorne's *Globe*.

Robinson and Schumann both wrote poems on Crabbe, Poe, Whitman, Arnold, and Hardy, but Robinson even then recognized the sharp difference in their approach and finish. On November 4, 1894 he remarked to Harry Smith: "Schumann has written some very warm blooded sonnets lately.... They are refreshing to one who has heard again and again some two hundred and fifty of the things written in the same style and the same vein. This monotony, more than anything else, I think, will stand in the way of their publication. They are too suggestive of papers 'of no particular value except to the owner' ... He runs Love a little too hard, it seems to me." (Sutcliffe, pp. 181-182.)

Upon Schumann's death Robinson composed an obituary tribute for the Boston *Evening Transcript*, saying in part: "though as patient and as careful in his work as a Chinese ivory carver, [he] was possessed at the same time of an extraordinary facility, which was often a source of wonder to his literary friends. He was at his best when manipulating the so-called 'set' forms of verse, producing on at least one occasion no fewer than three technically flawless ballades in a single day. . . . he wrote sonnets by the hundred, and always with his characteristic precision and general excellence." (March 30, 1918; III, 7.)

For detailed studies of Schumann's life and writings see Peter Dechert's doctoral dissertation, *Edwin Arlington Robinson and Alanson Tucker Schumann* (University of Michigan, 1955); also his "He Shouts to See Them Scamper So: E.A. Robinson and the French Forms," *Colby Library Quarterly*, VIII (September 1969), 386-398.

The jogtrot pace and humpbacked rhymes, better suited to *vers de société*, impart a misleading tone of triviality to Schumann's eulogy. Admittedly one of his lesser technical achievements, it nevertheless demonstrates his affective understanding of Robinson's strengths and weaknesses as a poet, of the governing paradox in Robinson's psyche, of Robinson's congenital preachiness, and his ineluctable drive to poetize. As Robinson gratefully avouched, Schumann's astuteness and his influence on the aborning poet were immense and incalculable.

. . / / . .

In 1907 Robinson wrote a sonnet for Percy MacKaye's daughter, "For Arvia, On Her Fifth Birthday," later published in *Scribner's*, *The Town Down the River*, and *Collected Poems*. In the same year he made at least one attempt at a sonnet for MacKaye's son Robert, and perhaps others for Christy of which less has been recorded. In 1909 MacKaye dedicated his *Poems* "To W.V.M. [Moody], E.A.R., & R.T. [Torrence], In Fellowship." Except to the initiate, this *entre nous* tribute to Robinson passed unnoticed. Not so the reciprocative poem MacKaye composed on the occasion of Robinson's forty-fifth birthday and published in full panoply two years thereafter (April 1916) in the impressive two-volume omnibus of his work, *Poems and Plays*. Coming from a poet-dramatist amply recognized and esteemed for the epic verve and catching language of his patriotic pageants, communal masques, blank verse tragedies, social and folk comedies,[1] this accreditation of Robinson as a peer spirit could not help but heighten his visibility in the public focus. Relatively few may have remarked MacKaye's slip in celebrating Robinson's anniversary one day in arrear of its actual occurrence.

TO "E.A."
[Edwin Arlington Robinson]
WITH CAKE AND CANDLES[1]

Percy MacKaye

E.A.—Of all the alphabet
That combination is the key
To unlock a door of memory
Into a quiet hall-room, set
With pen and pipe, where smoke of fancy
Swathes with a gentle necromancy

(Remote from Gotham's glare and racket)
One who reclines in crimson jacket
And smiles, in cryptic meditation,
To hold a friendly hand to me.—
E.A.!—Yes, there's the combination:
The door turns inward to the light
Of kind eyes through the dark.—To-night
Candles illumine there, like day,
The sign above the knocker: See!
Entra, Amice, Remane!—Thanks; your key
I turn, E.A.—
To friendship the true way.

                1 On his birthday: 23 December, 1914.

From *Poems and Plays of Percy MacKaye* (New York, 1916), I, 124.

1 By 1916 MacKaye's name was notable for productions of *The Canterbury Pilgrims, Jeanne d'Arc, Sappho and Phaon, The Scarecrow, Mater, Anti-Matrimony, Sanctuary, St. Louis, Sam Average, A Bird Masque, Caliban by the Yellow Sands,* and others.

.. / / ..

It is axiomatic of parody that its point is blunted if the subject is not substantially familiar. Sometime in 1915 then, Louis Untermeyer, our strongest poet-anthologist, must have judged Robinson to be as well-known as Masefield, Yeats, de la Mare, Chesterton, Pound, Teasdale, Amy Lowell, Kipling, Noyes, Dobson and sixteen others whom he included in "The Banquet of the Bards" section of his book of parodies on contemporary poetic styles. Only Masefield, in fact, preceded Robinson in the order of presentation.

In his testimonial to Robinson's centenary in the *Colby Library Quarterly* of December 1969 Untermeyer recalled: "Some years ago I wrote a series of parodies around a central idea. I conceived of a project which enlisted the modern poets in an effort to rewrite *Mother Goose*. Each poet was supposed to take a particular jingle and remold it nearer to his heart's desire. This is the way I thought E.A. Robinson would revise what we know of Simple Simon in one of his sonnet portraitures."

EDWIN ARLINGTON ROBINSON
Tells What He Knew of *Simple Simon*.

Louis Untermeyer

What does it matter — who are we to say
How much is clear and how much there must be
Behind his mystical directness — see,
He left us smiling, and a bit astray.

Yet there were times when Simon could convey
A cryptic sharpness, etched with something free;
For he was touched with fire and prophecy,
And we who scarcely knew him, mourn him. . . . Eh?

I'll say this much for Simon: If his ghost
Has half the life of many men, or most,
He will not rest in the ophidian night.
He will come back and storm the western gate,
Scorning such lesser things as Death and Fate. . . .
Well, there is that side, too. . . . You may be right.

From "————and Other Poets" (New York, 1916), p. 19.

Untermeyer's timing was peerless. Robinson was never again to taste the bitter fruit of nonentity. The man against the trend had truly become the man against the sky.

NOTES

PRELIMINARY VISTAS

1 For references to Robinson criticism not otherwise identified in this chapter, consult the CONTENTS pages of this volume.
2 Herbert S. Gorman, "Edwin Arlington Robinson, and a Talk With Him," New York *Sun* (January 4, 1920), 7.
3 Richard Cary, editor, *Edwin Arlington Robinson's Letters to Edith Brower* (Cambridge, Mass., 1968), pp. 101, 169.
4 *Ibid.*, p. 52.
5 Emery Neff, *Edwin Arlington Robinson* (New York, 1948), pp. 240-241.
6 Cary, p. 52.
7 Hermann Hagedorn, *Edwin Arlington Robinson: A Biography* (New York, 1938), p. 101.
8 Cary, p. 39.
9 Harry Salpeter, "E.A. Robinson, Poet," New York *World* (May 15, 1927), 8M.
10 Cary, p. 68.
11 Denham Sutcliffe, editor, *Untriangulated Stars: Letters of Edwin Arlington Robinson to Harry DeForest Smith 1890-1905* (Cambridge, Mass., 1947), p. 53. See also letter of May 13, 1896, "My religion seems to be a kind of optimistic desperation" (p. 246).
12 Cary, pp. 89, 140.
13 Letter to Hermann Hagedorn in Ridgely Torrence, editor, *Selected Letters of Edwin Arlington Robinson* (New York, 1940), pp. 80-81.
14 Florence Peltier, "Edwin Arlington Robinson, Himself," *Mark Twain Quarterly*, I (Summer 1937), 6.
15 Cary, p. 76.
16 " 'No name in the language,' he once declared to me, 'has so many wrong connotations as Edward.' " Rollo Walter Brown, *Next Door to a Poet* (New York, 1937), p. 78.
17 The correct version appears later in Thorne's text.

GENESIS OF A POET

1 Edwin Arlington Robinson, "The First Seven Years," *Colophon*, Part IV (1930), n.p.
2 Robinson himself subscribed to a mystico-biological theory of esthetic determination. "Heredity has a good deal to do with it — perhaps everything, when it comes to

the arts. In the great shuffle of transmitted characteristics, traits, abilities, and aptitudes, the man who fixes on something definite in life that he must do, at the expense of anything else, if necessary, has presumably got something that, for him, should be recognized as the Inner Fire. For *him*, that is the Gleam, the Vision and the Word! He'd better follow it." M.K. Wisehart, " 'By Jove!' Said Roosevelt 'It Reads Like the Real Thing!' " *American Magazine*, CV (April 1928), 84.

3 Laura E. Richards, *E.A.R.* (Cambridge, Mass., 1936), pp. 3, 6.

4 Gorman, p. 7. During the same interview he declared that "One of my earliest recollections" was of reading these poems by Thomas Campbell and Poe to his parents. Oddly, a bare seven years thereafter he wrote Emma S. Robinson, "By the way you will know from Van Doren's book that I used to read to my mother while sitting on the kitchen floor — an occupation that I don't remember." (Colby College Library; May 18, 1927.)

5 For listings of these books now in Colby College Library, see James Humphry, III, *The Library of Edwin Arlington Robinson* (Waterville, Maine, 1950); Richard Cary, "The Library of Edwin Arlington Robinson: Addenda," *Colby Library Quarterly*, VII (March 1967), 398-415; "Robinson Books and Periodicals, II," *CLQ*, VIII (June 1969), 334-343; "Robinson Books and Periodicals, III," *ibid.* (September 1969), 399-413; "Additions to the Robinson Collection," *CLQ*, IX (September 1971), 380-381; "Additions to the Robinson Collection, II," *CLQ*, X (June 1974), 386-387.

6 Gorman, p. 7.

7 Richards, p. 6.

8 *Ibid.*, p. 14.

9 Hagedorn, p. 31.

10 Richards, p. 7; Mark Van Doren, *Edwin Arlington Robinson* (New York, 1927), p. 14.

11 Richards, p. 25. Hagedorn, p. 32, proffers a variant account.

12 *Colophon*, n.p.

13 *Ibid.* This volume of Virgil, marked and dated by Robinson as he completed each section, is in Colby College Library.

14 Hagedorn, p. 46.

15 "Thalia," March 29, 1890, p. [3]; "The Galley Race," May 31, 1890, p. [3]; reprinted in Charles Beecher Hogan, *A Bibliography of Edwin Arlington Robinson* (New Haven, 1936), pp. 167-173.

16 Torrence, p. 7. At the end of his first year he wrote: "Sometimes I get rather blue in thinking over the fact that I should now be a much different person from what I am had I come to Harvard three years ago as a Freshman"; and when about to leave at the end of the second: "Sometimes I try to imagine the state my mind would be in had I never come here, but I cannot. I feel that I have got comparatively little from my two years, but still, more than I could get in Gardiner if I lived a century." Sutcliffe, pp. 66, 103.

17 Hogan, p. 99.

18 Sutcliffe, pp. 144-145.

THE TORRENT AND THE NIGHT BEFORE (1896)

1 Torrence, p. 9.

2 Sutcliffe, p. 219.

3 *Ibid.*, pp. 125-183 *passim*.

4 *Colophon*, n.p.

5 Sutcliffe, p. 165.

6 William Henry Thorne, "Wreck of the Mayflower," *Globe*, IV (July-September 1894), 801.

7   See Robinson's letter to Harry Smith in Sutcliffe, p. 234, and to Arthur Gledhill in Hagedorn, p. 105.
8   *Colophon*, n.p.
9   Sutcliffe, p. 236.
10 *Ibid.*, p. 170.
11 *Ibid.*, pp. 237, 238.
12 *Ibid.*, pp. 241, 242.
13 *Ibid.*, pp. 243-253 *passim*. To an interviewer three decades later Robinson gave still another version of his feelings. He said he knew it was "difficult to get poetry published in America, but I thought that a publisher would be glad to get them. They came back. I was surprised, and hurt a little, I suppose. I sent them out again. Again I was surprised, but not hurt this time. As the manuscript acquired the chronic habit of coming back, I got over being surprised and got mad. I felt that all that work shouldn't go for nothing." Wisehart, p. 76.
   Reading the script for Houghton, Mifflin & Company, Horace Elisha Scudder "recognized the individuality of the poems, but their publication, he was sure, would be unprofitable. Houghton, Mifflin's recent experience with volumes of verse had 'been so very discouraging,' he wrote, 'that we cannot think it advisable to attempt a wider circulation to Mr. Robinson's poetry than he is likely to secure through friendly means.'" Ellen B. Ballou, *The Building of the House: Houghton Mifflin's Formative Years* (Boston, 1970), p. 487.
   Upon receiving a copy of the book, Scudder wrote Robinson, "May I express my pleasure at poetry which has so much warm blood in its veins?" Sutcliffe, p. 271.
14 Sutcliffe, pp. 251, 257. In an unpublished letter (Columbia University Library) to Edmund Clarence Stedman, December 21, 1899, Robinson remarked, "*The Torrent and The Night Before* — a name that ought to destroy a thousand futures." When Ridgely Torrence introduced Robinson to Stedman, the latter spread out his arms and exclaimed impishly, "Torrence — and the Night After." Hagedorn, p. 164.
15 Torrence, pp. 12-13.
16 Hogan, pp. 100-101.
17 Sutcliffe, p. 261.
18 *Colophon*, n.p. It is worth noting that Robinson capitalized the second *The* in the title and made it clear why. With few exceptions, this distinction has not been observed by the long line of Robinson commentators and scholars, including his chief bibliographer.
19 Sutcliffe, p. 265.
20 *Colophon*, n.p.
21 Brown, p. 63.
22 Sutcliffe, p. 266.
23 See *Colby Library Quarterly*, II (February 1947), 3-12; (August 1947), 52; (February 1948), 82; (May 1948), 105-106; (August 1948), 122-123; (February 1949), 153; (May 1949), 161-162; III (February 1954), 220; IV (August 1955), 64; (February 1956), 95; VII (December 1967), 511-527, 548.
24 Laura E. Richards, "A Book and Its Author," *Yankee*, II (June 1936), 26.
25 Alice Frost Lord, "Gardiner Associations of Poet Recalled by Present Resident," Lewiston (Me.) *Journal Illustrated Magazine Section* (March 30, 1940), A-8.
26 Robinson letter to Leonard M. Barnard, *ibid.*
27 Hagedorn, p. 111.
28 *Colophon*, n.p.
29 Cary, pp. 15, 16.
30 Sutcliffe, p. 274.
31 Cary, p. 37.
32 *Colophon*, n.p.
33 Hagedorn, p. 108.

THE CHILDREN OF THE NIGHT (1897)

1 Sutcliffe, p. 279.
2 Hagedorn, p. 118.
3 Cary, p. 35.
4 Sutcliffe, p. 281.
5 Cary, p. 35.
6 *Ibid.*
7 Hagedorn, p. 129.
8 Letter to Edith Brower, October 7, 1897; Cary, pp. 60-61.
9 Sutcliffe, p. 289.
10 Letter to Miss Roedel, May 28, 1927 (Colby College Library).

CAPTAIN CRAIG (1902)

1 Cary, p. 70.
2 Sutcliffe, p. 294. After numerous interruptions and recastings it became "The Book of Annandale."
3 Cary, p. 72.
4 *Ibid.*, p. 75.
5 Sutcliffe, p. 296.
6 Cary, pp. 80, 82.
7 *Ibid.*, p. 83.
8 Letter to John Hays Gardiner, November 2, 1898; Torrence, p. 15.
9 Cary, p. 86.
10 Hagedorn, p. 148.
11 *Edwin Arlington Robinson: A Collection of His Works From the Library of Bacon Collamore* (Hartford, 1936), p. 16.
12 See Cary, pp. 89, 92, 95, 101, 103, 104; Daniel Gregory Mason, *Music in My Time* (New York, 1938), p. 82; Torrence, pp. 19, 20.
13 Sutcliffe, pp. 303, 305.
14 Letter to Daniel Gregory Mason, April 18, 1900; Torrence, p. 28.
15 Cary, p. 114; Torrence, p. 30. In this letter to Mason on May 18, 1900 Robinson indicated that *Captain Craig* was now his title for the poem. As its rounds among publishers became more and more protracted, Robinson referred to it wryly as the Old Man of the Sea, the Serpent, the Incubus.
16 Daniel Gregory Mason, "Early Letters of Edwin Arlington Robinson: First Series," *Virginia Quarterly Review*, XIII (Winter 1937), 65.
17 Daniel Gregory Mason, "Edwin Arlington Robinson to Daniel Gregory Mason: Second Series," *Virginia Quarterly Review*, XIII (Spring 1937), 225.
18 Cary, p. 133.
19 Mason, *VQR* (Spring 1937), 230-231.
20 Cary, p. 132.
21 *Ibid.*, pp. 134-135, 139-140.
22 Torrence, p. 50.
23 Hagedorn, p. 188.
24 For Gardiner's letters to Scribner's see Roger Burlingame, *Of Making Many Books* (New York, 1946), pp. 252-255.
25 Bliss Perry, *And Gladly Teach* (Boston, 1935), p. 177.
26 Ballou, pp. 487-488.

27 Percy MacKaye, editor, *Letters to Harriet by William Vaughn Moody* (Boston, 1935), p. 93.
28 Torrence, p. 156.
29 Hagedorn, pp. 187, 190.
30 Cary, p. 147.
31 Sutcliffe, p. 306. See Denham Sutcliffe, "The Original of Robinson's 'Captain Craig,'" *New England Quarterly*, XVI (September 1943), 407-431.
32 Letter to Brown, March 14, 1927; Torrence, p. 151.
33 *Ibid.*, p. 32.
34 *Ibid.*, p. 20; Cary, p. 104.
35 Edwin S. Fussell, "Robinson to Moody: Ten Unpublished Letters," *American Literature*, XXIII (May 1951), 178.
36 Wallace L. Anderson, "The Young Robinson as Critic and Self-Critic," in Ellsworth Barnard, editor, *Edwin Arlington Robinson: Centenary Essays* (Athens, Georgia, 1969), p. 84.
37 Sutcliffe, p. 303; Cary, pp. 102, 104; Anderson, p. 85.
38 Letter, October 15, 1901 (Colby College Library).
39 Fussell, p. 177.
40 Cary, p. 114.
41 Mason, *VQR* (Spring 1937), 225; Mason, *Music in My Time*, p. 82.
42 Cary, p. 89.
43 Anderson, p. 85.
44 *Music in My Time*, p. 125.
45 Sutcliffe, p. 306.

THE CHILDREN OF THE NIGHT (1905)

1 Hagedorn, pp. 202-203.
2 According to Kermit Roosevelt, in his letter of October 4, 1930 to Lucius Beebe, he came across the book in 1903, mailed a copy to his father on January 19, 1904, and one to his mother on August 29. (William Lyon Phelps, "As I Like It," *Scribner's*, LXXXIX [January 1931], 95.) The copy intended for the President must have eluded his eye, for he did not write to Kermit until November 3. "I have taken immense comfort out of the little volume of poems by Robinson, which you gave mother." (Will Irwin, editor, *Letters to Kermit from Theodore Roosevelt 1902-1908* [New York, 1946], p. 83.) Other letters in this collection leave no question that Kermit was Robinson's stoutest proponent in the matter of obtaining suitable employment. At one point Theodore called him "your poet."
3 Wisehart, p. 82.
4 Letter in Colby College Library. It was published with one misleading deviation in the text by Elting E. Morison, editor, *The Letters of Theodore Roosevelt* (Cambridge, Mass., 1951), IV, 1145.
5 Morison, IV, 1155.
6 MacKaye, p. 28.
7 Torrence, p. 59. He was working a one-third hour schedule for $10 a week.
8 Hagedorn, p. 217. Hagedorn adds: "'For once,' said Roosevelt a dozen years later, 'I went back on all my Civil Service principles, and played Maecenas.'" Even at the moment his conscience twitted. In a letter to James Hulme Canfield on August 16, 1905 he jested about his action — "tell it not in civil-service-reform Gath, nor whisper it in the streets of merit-system Askelon" — then turned serious. "I am free to say that he was put in less with a view to the good of the government service than with a view of helping American letters." (Morison, IV, 1303.)

9 Letter to Richard Watson Gilder, April 11, 1905; Torrence, p. 59.
10 Hagedorn, p. 216.
11 Torrence, pp. 49, 50, 54.
12 See his acerb letter to Edith Brower, Cary, p. 151.
13 Hagedorn, p. 217; Burlingame, pp. 255-257.
14 "Library Notes for E.A.R.'s Birthday," *Colby Mercury*, VI (November 1938), 209.
15 Cary, pp. 87, 135, 137.
16 Burlingame, pp. 280-281.

THE TOWN DOWN THE RIVER (1910)

1 Cary, p. 150.
2 Peltier, p. 6.
3 Torrence, p. 62; Hagedorn, p. 222.
4 Hagedorn, pp. 222-223.
5 Louis Untermeyer, *Edwin Arlington Robinson: A Reappraisal* (Washington, D.C., 1963), p. 32.
6 Letter to Daniel Gregory Mason, July 22, 1908; Torrence, p. 63.
7 *Ibid.*, pp. 63-64.
8 Hagedorn, p. 253.
9 Letter in Colby College Library.
10 Cary, p. 152.
11 Hagedorn, p. 259. To Louis Ledoux he griped on September 30, 1909: "I have been out of school for twenty-one years and am not yet of age with publishers." Neff, p. 152.
12 Letter in Colby College Library. Robinson responded on the 24th, highly satisfied "to know that you are pleased with the book and with the dedication" and observed that "whatever it may be worth, I don't see how it could have been in existence today if you had not taken such a friendly and substantial interest in my work." Untermeyer, p. 34.
13 Cary, p. 152.
14 Hagedorn, p. 250.

CAPTAIN CRAIG (1915)

1 Hagedorn, p. 254.
2 Torrence, pp. 67-68.
3 Hagedorn, p. 278.
4 *Ibid.*, p. 271.
5 *Ibid.*, p. 272.
6 Torrence, p. 74.
7 Cary, p. 154.
8 Torrence, p. 77. By inexplicable circumstance two years later Roosevelt converged upon the same metaphor, if only figuratively on the same locus, in a letter to Alexander S. Cochran. "When I was President, I cheerfully outraged the feelings of the ultra-Civil-Service reformers by fishing . . . Arlington Robinson, out of a Boston Millinery store, where he was writing metrical advertisements for spring hats, and put him in the Customs House. This got him a start; and he has done well ever since, although it is perhaps needless to say that Taft promptly turned him out." Morison, VIII, 887.

NOTES

9 Torrence, pp. 79-80.

10 Chard Powers Smith, *Where the Light Falls: A Portrait of Edwin Arlington Robinson* (New York, 1965), p. 238.

11 Hagedorn, p. 290.

12 *Poetry*, III (February 1914), 188.

13 Torrence, p. 85.

14 Of this innovation Robinson said to Lewis M. Isaacs: "I was wrong about the dedication in *C.C.* I remember now that Gardiner was so bewildered by the poem, which was pretty radical in those days, that I had not quite the heart to dedicate it to him as I had intended. But he came to think better of it before he died, and after his death I ventured to use his name. He was a good man, and I hope his ghost is not sorry for my well-meant acknowledgment." Letter, July 27, 1928; Torrence, p. 156.

EPILOGUE

1 Cary, p. 162.

2 Mason, *VQR* (Spring 1937), 239.

3 Letter to Edith Brower, Cary, p. 164. Robinson to Lilla Cabot Perry, November 10, 1915: "I am at last unburdened of my three years' burden of alleged poetry, and that the priceless mess is now in the hands of the publishers. It will all come out in a book sometime in February, and after that the world will go on pretty much the same." Colby College Library.

4 Letter to Amy Lowell, Torrence, p. 89.

5 Lloyd R. Morris, *The Young Idea* (New York, 1917), pp. 193-195.

6 George W. Latham, "Robinson at Harvard," *Mark Twain Quarterly*, II (Spring 1938), 19; James L. Tryon, *Harvard Days With Edwin Arlington Robinson* (Waterville, Maine, 1940), p. 16.

7 Hagedorn, p. 253.

8 Letter to Hagedorn, December 6, 1915; Torrence, pp. 89-90.

9 Smith, p. 22.

10 Hagedorn, p. 209.

11 Wisehart, p. 84.

12 Letter to Josephine Preston Peabody, June 25, 1901; Torrence, pp. 41-42.

13 Gorman, p. 7.

14 Jay B. Hubbell, editor, *American Life in Literature* (New York, 1949), II, 599.

15 Wisehart, p. 84.

16 William Peterfield Trent, "A New Poetic Venture," *Sewanee Review*, V (April 1897), 246.

17 Ben Ray Redman, *Edwin Arlington Robinson* (New York, 1926), p. 7.

18 Malcolm Cowley, "Edwin Arlington Robinson: Defeat and Triumph," *New Republic*, CXIX (December 6, 1948), 28-29.

INDEX: GENERAL

Abbott, Edward, 60-1, 105
Abbott, Lyman, 223
Academy, 102, 123
A. E. (George W. Russell), 36, 37
Akins, Zoë, 288-9
Aldrich, Thomas Bailey, 3, 5, 27, 44, 97, 99, 234, 255
Alger, Horatio, 20
Allen, James Lane, 74
Amateur, The, 21
American Review of Reviews, 199, 286, 287, 298
Amiel, Henri François, 176
Argonaut, 6, 8, 9, 14, 112, 143, 150, 184, 198, 200
Aristophanes, 141, 184
Aristotle, 156
Arnold, Matthew, 5, 20, 31, 32, 47, 57, 90, 194, 301
Atlantic Monthly, 24, 99, 110, 112, 152-3, 185, 201-3, 205, 209, 237, 270, 298
Austen, Jane, 148
Austin, Alfred, 45

B., R. H., 39-41
Bacon, Edwin Munroe (A Booktaster), 34
Badger, Richard G., 66, 67, 76, 92, 95, 175, 176, 182
Badger & Company, Richard G., 69, 70
Baker, George Pierce, 27, 64, 271
Bangor *Daily Commercial*, 12-3, 37, 53-4, 76, 149, 173-4, 224
Banville, Théodore de, 57
Barnard, Leonard M., 27
Barstow, James, 270

Bartlett, John, 276
Bartlett, Truman H., 217-8, 220, 223, 229, 271
Bashkirtseff, Marie, 176-7, 226
Bates, Esther Willard, 127, 145
Baudelaire, Charles, 37, 236, 264
Beddoes, Thomas L., 228
Betts, Craven Langstroth, 75, 107, 109, 218, 272, 277
Bible, 127
Bierce, Ambrose, 3
Blair, Arthur, 23, 65, 278
Blunt, Wilfred Scawen, 45
Boardman, S. J., 54
Bob Taylor's Magazine, 200
Bogan, Louise, 106
Book Buyer, 7, 15, 17, 131-2, 190, 214, 215, 219-21
Bookman, 10, 16, 49-50, 75, 184-6, 193, 299
Bookseller, Newsdealer and Stationer, 36, 76
Booktaster, A, (see Bacon, E. M.), 34
Boston *Courier*, 43
Boston *Daily Advertiser*, 118-9, 214
Boston *Evening Transcript*, 7, 10, 11, 12, 13, 14, 16-7, 17, 26, 31, 73-4, 75, 76, 87-90, 96, 125-6, 150, 186, 188-9, 215-7, 221, 224, 248-55, 269, 270, 273, 289-92, 293-4, 294, 298, 299, 300-1, 301, 302
Boston *Herald*, 187, 214-5
Boston *Journal*, 8, 11, 12, 13-4, 140, 150
Boston *Post*, 276
Boston *Sunday Globe*, 180-1
Boston *Sunday Post*, 247-8, 255, 256-9
Boynton, Henry W., 6, 7, 13, 14, 152-3
Bradstreet, Anne, 19

INDEX: GENERAL

Braithwaite, William Stanley, 6, 7-8, 11, 12, 14, 17, 193, 210, 215-8, 221, 225, 251-6, 270, 272, 273, 289-93, 293-4, 294-5, 296, 298, 299, 300-1
Branch, Anna Hempstead, 99, 128, 258, 260, 290
Brett, George P., 272-3
Bridges, Robert, 27, 178
Briggs, LeBaron R., 150
Brooklyn *Daily Eagle*, 7, 12, 222-3, 278-80
Brooks, Van Wyck, 299
Brower, Edith, 8, 9, 10, 15, 27, 27-8, 28, 44, 60, 65, 66, 75, 79-86, 107, 110, 120
Brown, Edmund R., 298
Brown, Rollo Walter, 27
Browning, Robert, 5-6, 14, 15, 20, 47, 48-9, 56, 90, 117, 118, 125, 139, 141, 143, 144, 152, 156, 162, 170, 183, 201, 204, 214, 215, 220, 224, 227, 228-9, 241, 243, 249, 251, 252, 261, 270, 286, 291, 295
Bryan, William Jennings, 163
Bryant, William Cullen, 5, 20, 37, 191
Bulwer-Lytton, Edward, 20
Bunner, Henry Cuyler, 3
Burlingame, Roger, 167, 168
Burnham, George, 67, 109, 129, 157, 218, 281
Burr, Amelia Josephine, 294
Burroughs, John, 44, 166, 177, 178
Butler, William E., 66, 106, 165, 272
Bynner, Witter, 27
Byrn, Lillian Kendrick, 200
Byron, George Lord, 20

Caine, Hall, 74
Campbell, Thomas, 306
Carleton, Will, 120, 121
Carlyle, Thomas, 99, 117, 141, 195, 196
Carman, Bliss, 3, 6, 11, 16, 27, 41, 43, 47, 112, 132-3, 134, 144, 148, 170, 186, 258
Carter, Nick, 20
Castlemon, Harry, 20
Cather, Willa, 273
Cawein, Madison, 3, 105, 128, 170, 172, 186
Century Magazine, 24, 163, 167, 218, 270, 278
Chamberlin, Joseph E., 7, 11, 31, 34, 131
Chap-Book, 11, 14-5, 18, 24, 93-4

Chase, Ambrose G., 10, 17, 180-2
Chatterton, Thomas, 36
Cheney, John Vance, 27, 64, 186, 187
Chicago *Evening Post*, 13, 119-20, 134-5, 150, 295
Chicago *Record*, 8, 44, 76
Chicago *Tribune*, 14, 144-5, 150
Christ, 97, 99
Christian Register, 9, 43, 76, 86-7
Christy, Howard Chandler, 240, 242
Cicero, 20
Clarke, Helen Archibald, 11, 18, 60, 104, 221
Claudel, Paul, 295
Cleveland *Leader*, 45-7, 60, 76
Clough, Arthur H., 66
Coan, Titus Munson, 44, 63, 75, 84, 107, 109, 218, 277, 278
Coismes, Lyonnet de, 57
Colcord, Lincoln, 296
Coleridge, Samuel T., 20, 238
Colophon, 64
Colum, Padraic, 298
Conservator, 59, 116
Coppée, François, 4, 28, 45, 48, 49, 52, 54
Cornhill Booklet, 298
Cosmopolitan, 24
Cowley, Malcolm, 163, 300
Cowper, William, 20
Crabbe, George, 5, 20, 31, 31-2, 243, 284, 301
Crane, Stephen, 3
Critic, 24, 26, 37, 75, 148-9, 191
Current Literature, 75, 183, 222

Daily Kennebec Journal, 38, 73, 174
Dana, Paul, 24
D'Annunzio, Gabriele, 5, 46, 47, 60
Dargan, Olive T., 290, 293
Davidge, Clara, 210, 271
DaVinci, Leonardo, 267-8, 269
Denver *Republican*, 92, 96, 193-5, 221-2
Denver *Times*, 11, 13, 39-41, 76
Detroit *Free Press*, 199
Dial, 16, 17, 24, 50-1, 76, 95, 141-2, 150, 187-8, 231-3, 278
Dickens, Charles, 19
Dickinson, Emily, 3, 5, 139, 206
Dobson, Austin, 45, 132
Dole, Nathan Haskell, 10, 12, 16, 36-7, 54, 277
Donne, John, 5

Dostoievsky, Feodor, 257
Dowson, Ernest, 266, 267
Drama, 298
Dreiser, Theodore, 299
Dryden, John 20
Dunbar, Olivia Howard, 208
Dunbar, Paul Laurence, 3
Duncan, Isadora, 209
Dunn, Robert Steed, 4-5, 6, 43, 47-8, 57

Eddy, Mary Baker, 99
Edwards, George Wharton, 27, 64
Egan, Maurice, 170, 172
Eggleston, Edward, 7, 16, 52-3, 53, 54, 64, 75, 160
Eliot, Charles W., 157, 159, 162
Eliot, George, 276, 287
Emerson, Ralph Waldo, 5, 20, 37, 62, 63, 91, 99, 140
Epictetus, 99
Erasmus, 5, 267

Fawcett, Edgar, 27, 64
Field, Eugene, 3
Firkins, Oscar W., 9, 10-1, 287-8, 298
Fortnightly Review, 201-3, 205
Forum, 225-8, 262-8
Foss, Sam Walter, 3, 96
Fox, Edward Proby, 26
Fraser, James Earle, 272
Freeman, Mary Wilkins, 74
French, Joseph Lewis, 7, 11, 12, 17, 103, 108, 113, 156-61, 191-3, 209
Frick, Henry Clay, 253, 255-6
Frost, Robert, 99, 229, 290, 292, 295, 296, 299

Gardiner *Daily Reporter-Journal*, 31, 38, 52, 53, 135-8, 153
Gardiner, John Hays, 5, 9, 10, 11, 13, 65, 87-90, 108, 110, 111, 153, 161, 166, 272, 273, 311
Gardiner *Reporter Monthly*, 21
Garland, Hamlin, 75
Garnett, Constance, 257
Gates, Lewis E., 159, 162
Gautier, Théophile, 131, 132
Gay, Will, 28
Gibson, Charles Dana, 240, 242
Gibson, Wilfrid W., 243

Gilder, Jeannette, 112
Gilder, Richard Watson, 3, 27, 75, 157, 160, 163, 166, 167, 178, 218
Gladstone, William E., 176, 177, 226
Gledhill, Arthur R., 22, 23, 26
Globe, 10, 17, 24, 26, 61-3, 76, 96-9, 301
Gorman, Herbert S., 300
Gosse, Edmund, 27, 37, 45, 64
Greenslet, Ferris, 15, 198-9
Guiney, Louise Imogen, 3

Hagedorn, Hermann, 12, 17, 20, 27, 62, 66, 74, 178, 222, 246-7, 249, 258, 270, 271, 272
Hake, Thomas Gordon, 5, 78
Hall, James Norman, 35
Hapgood, T. B., Jr., 69, 78
Hardon, Robert V., 186-7
Hardy, Thomas, 20, 27, 32, 77, 91, 148, 301
Harper's Magazine, 24, 99, 294
Harper's Weekly, 298
Hartford *Post*, 93
Harvard Advocate, 17, 38, 53, 54, 63, 194, 196
Harvard Crimson, 38, 53
Harvard Lampoon, 180
Harvard Monthly, 17, 43, 47-8, 75, 110, 154-6
Heine, Heinrich, 5, 20
Hemens, Felicia, 20
Henderson, Alice Corbin, 273, 288
Henley, William Ernest, 5, 45, 102, 104
Henneman, John B., 199-200
Herbert, George, 236
Higginson, Thomas Wentworth, 6, 9, 11, 17, 75, 92, 100-1, 102, 112, 139, 150
Homer, 195, 196
Hood, Thomas, 20
Hooker, Brian, 247-8
Horace, 21, 58, 194, 196
Houghton, Mifflin & Company, 110, 113, 114, 150, 151
Housman, A. E., 3, 5, 227, 229, 296
Hovey, Richard, 3, 43, 47, 133
Howe, Julia Ward, 159
Howells, William Dean, 3, 5, 75, 97, 99, 112, 294
Hubbell, Jay, 300
Hunt, Edward E., 229
Huxley, Thomas H., 235, 236

INDEX: GENERAL

Independent, 7, 10, 14, 16, 17, 32-3, 37, 76, 145-7, 150, 153, 233
Isaacs, Lewis M., 111

James, Henry, 74, 112, 136
James, William, 74, 150, 159, 162, 276, 277
Jefferies, Richard, 66
Jewett, Sarah Orne, 44
Johnson, Robert Underwood, 3
Jones, 23
Jordan, Alice, 90
Jordan, Augustus, 90

Kansas City *Star,* 108
Keats, John, 5, 20, 36, 97, 99, 120, 235
Kellogg, Elijah, 20
Kerfoot, John B., 153
Kilmer, Joyce, 15, 210, 236-9, 240, 242, 246, 258, 270
Kipling, Rudyard, 3, 5, 48, 66, 74, 75, 77, 127, 196, 249, 251, 258, 296
Knowles, Frederic Lawrence, 193

Landor, Walter Savage, 45
Lang, Andrew, 28, 45, 57, 196
Ledoux, Louis V., 6, 8, 9, 10, 12, 13, 14, 85, 208, 240-2, 244-6, 255, 258, 270, 271, 272
Ledoux, Mrs. Louis V., 259
LeGallienne, Richard, 4, 6, 17, 210, 225-9, 233, 270
Lewiston *Journal,* 8, 16, 129-31, 178-9
Lewiston *Saturday Journal,* 13, 31, 76-7, 78
Life, 153
Lincoln, Abraham, 204, 220, 226, 276
Lindsay, Vachel, 296
Lippincott, Lillian, 193
Lippincott's, 24, 34, 163, 209, 270
Literary Digest, 9, 123, 182, 234, 269, 296, 298
Literary Review, 78
Literary World, 16, 60, 76, 105, 123
Lodge, Henry Cabot, 220
London *Times Literary Supplement,* 123
Longfellow, Henry Wadsworth, 35, 37, 226, 228, 276
Louis, Alfred Hyman, 75, 107, 109, 111, 127, 128-9, 218, 277-8, 287
Louisville *Courier-Journal,* 197

Lounsbury, Thomas R., 27
Lowell, Amy, 99, 280, 290, 292-3, 296, 298
Lowell, James Russell, 83

McClure, Phillips & Company, 109
MacDowell, Mrs. Edward, 271
MacKaye, Arvia, 302
MacKaye, Percy, 207, 208, 209, 229, 243, 258, 259, 302-3
MacKaye, Robert, 302
Maclaren, Ian (John Watson), 62, 63-4
Macmillan Company, 272, 273, 274, 298
MacVeigh, Lincoln, 9, 281-3
Macy, John A., 8, 9, 12, 16, 119-20
Maeterlinck, Maurice, 5, 94, 95
Mallarmé, Stéphane, 5, 36, 281, 283
Markham, Edwin, 3, 206-7, 228
Marquis, Don, 286
Marryat, Frederick, 20
Martin, Edward S., 27, 133
Marvell, Andrew, 5, 234
Mason, Daniel Gregory, 108, 110, 208
Masters, Edgar Lee, 99, 165, 178, 288, 290, 293, 295, 296, 298
Matthews, William, 45
Meredith, George, 5, 125, 127, 201, 204, 252
Merimée, Prosper, 66
Meunier, Constantin, 265
Meynell, Alice, 112
Millay, Edna St. Vincent, 229
Miller, Joaquin, 100, 101, 102
Millet, Jean François, 265
Milton, John, 12, 20, 21, 145, 156, 196, 293-4, 294
Milwaukee *Evening Wisconsin,* 10, 197
Minneapolis *Journal,* 8, 10, 12, 13, 14, 16, 17, 244-6
Mitchell, S. Weir, 27, 64, 74
Monroe, Harriet, 243, 270, 298
Moody, William Vaughn, 3, 27, 85, 110, 120, 121, 162, 166, 203-4, 208, 209, 211, 219, 243, 246, 252, 258, 302
Moore, Thomas, 20
More, Paul Elmer, 234, 235
Morgan, J. Pierpont, 253, 255
Morice, Charles V., 281-2, 283
Morley, Christopher, 277
Morse, John T., 44
Mosher, Thomas B., 33, 36, 37, 57, 92, 95-6, 132, 196
Moulton, Louise Chandler, 3, 27

Musical Courier, 102-3
Musset, Alfred de, 233

Napoleon, 226, 246
Nation, 75, 92, 100-1, 102, 139, 150, 198-9, 229-30, 287-8
Neihardt, John G., 246, 296
Neilson, William Allan, 153
New England Magazine, 191-3
New Orleans *Daily Picayune,* 35, 76, 93, 96
New Republic, 281-3
New York *American,* 206
New York *Evening Post,* 7, 75, 101, 150, 160, 174-6, 182, 228
New York *Evening Sun,* 6, 117-8, 215, 284-5
New York *Mail and Express,* 122-3
New York *Sun,* 24, 75
New York *Times Review of Books,* 8, 230-1, 236-9, 240-2, 246-7, 287, 298
New York *Times Saturday Review of Books,* 7, 16, 177-8, 183, 189
New York *Tribune,* 14, 78-9, 128, 160, 163, 190
New York *World Magazine,* 158-61
Newark News, 154
Nietzsche, Frederick, 283, 284
Nordau, Max, 10
North American Review, 204, 298
North, Christopher (John Wilson), 51
Norton, Charles Eliot, 27, 38, 53, 64
Noyes, Alfred, 247-8, 249, 252-3, 255, 256, 257, 258, 259, 272, 284

O'Connor, Thomas P., 204-5
Oppenheim, James, 294
Optic, Oliver, 20
Outlook, 7, 11, 16, 52, 53, 76, 91-2, 96, 167, 170-1, 173, 223, 235-6, 261-2, 272, 298

Paine, Thomas, 5, 97, 98
Pater, Walter, 5, 66, 83, 85, 237
Payne, John, 57, 196
Payne, William Morton, 6, 10, 14, 15, 16, 17, 50-1, 95, 112, 141-3, 231-3
Peabody, Josephine Preston, 99, 108, 109, 110, 128, 150, 153, 193, 209, 210, 258, 259-60, 267

Peck, Harry Thurston, 10, 13, 16, 49-50, 103
Peltier, Florence, 171
Perry, Bliss, 110, 122
Philadelphia *Press,* 51-2
Phillips, Stephen, 120, 121, 221
Plato, 196
Poe, Edgar Allan, 13, 19, 20, 33, 34, 37, 54, 301, 306
Poet-Lore, 12, 16, 59, 76, 104, 221
Poetry, 298
Poetry Review, 243
Poole, Ernest, 299
Pope, Alexander, 196
Pope, Seth Ellis, 23, 65, 85, 111
Portland *Daily Press,* 129
Portland *Evening Express and Advertiser,* 219
Potts, William Sherman, 262
Powers, Hiram, 236
Powys, John Cowper, 284, 285-6
Procter, Edna Dean, 3
Publishers' Circular, 123
Pulsifer, Harold T., 6, 7, 9, 12, 17, 261-2

Quarterly Review, 235

Ranck, Edwin Carty, 6, 8, 12, 17, 103, 248-51, 270, 272, 278
Reader, 43, 132-3, 144
Redman, Ben Ray, 298, 300
Reedy's Mirror, 288-9
Reese, Lizette Woodworth, 3
Richards, Henry, 161
Richards, Henry Howe, 165
Richards, Laura E., 19, 20, 23, 27, 65, 66, 90, 94, 110, 112, 153, 157, 159, 160, 161, 162, 178
Riley, James Whitcomb, 3, 104, 283, 284
Rittenhouse, Jessie B., 171
Roberts, Charles G. D., 27, 64
Robbins, Linville, 23, 65
Robinson, Edward, 19-20, 22, 23, 67, 157, 178, 180
Robinson, Emma S., 35, 66, 67, 210
Robinson, Fanny M., 32
Robinson, Herman Edward, 21-2, 35, 65, 66-7, 179, 210
Robinson, Horace Dean, 23, 65, 108, 109, 179
Robinson, Mary Palmer, 19, 178, 180

INDEX: GENERAL

Rochester *Herald*, 12, 14, 276-7, 287
Ronsard, Pierre de, 32
Roosevelt, Kermit, 165, 172, 220, 272, 309
Roosevelt, Theodore, 6, 7, 9, 11, 14, 15, 75, 157, 166-206, 208, 209, 209-10, 211, 214, 218, 219, 220, 222, 223, 223-4, 224, 226, 228, 249, 251, 255, 256, 262, 269, 270, 276, 284, 309, 310
Rossetti, Dante Gabriel, 20, 57, 193-4, 195-6
Rostand, Edmond, 74
Russell, George William (see A. E.)

Saben, Mowry, 49, 57, 127, 193-5, 222
Saint Paul, 99
Sanborn, Franklin B., 112
Sandburg, Carl, 296, 299
Schumann, Alanson Tucker, 21, 23, 24, 32, 62, 68, 103, 178, 258, 301-2
Scollard, Clinton, 3, 15, 27, 64, 112, 148-9, 150, 165, 170, 233
Scott, Walter, 20
Scribner's Magazine, 24, 206, 209, 214, 222, 276, 298, 302
Scribner's Sons, Charles, 109, 110, 167, 168, 169, 208, 210, 211, 212, 214, 221, 233, 272
Scudder, Horace E., 27, 64, 307
Sewanee Review, 16, 54-6, 76, 86, 100, 199-200
Shakespeare, William, 12, 14, 19, 96, 127, 147-8, 267, 293-4
Sharp, William, 45
Shelley, Percy B., 5, 20, 97, 99
Sherman, Frank Dempster, 3, 9, 16, 131-2, 148, 165, 186
Sill, Edward Rowland, 66
Sinclair, May, 6, 11, 16, 17, 201-4, 204-5, 237, 239, 252
Small, Maynard & Company, 109
Smith, F. Hopkinson, 44
Smith, Harry DeForest, 8, 23, 26, 27, 35, 65, 75
Socrates, 99, 137, 140, 141, 184, 201
Sophocles, 265, 266
Spencer, Herbert, 162
Spenser, Edmund, 20, 120, 193, 196
Stedman, Edmund Clarence, 7, 27, 75, 109, 112, 119-20, 120, 156, 160, 161, 162-3, 163, 178, 206
Sterne, Laurence, 5, 241, 243
Stevens, John F., 178, 179

Stevenson, Robert Louis, 66
Stickney, Trumbull, 12, 14, 154-6
Stimson, Frederic J., 27
Stockton, Frank R., 75
Stoddard, Richard Henry, 3, 75, 160, 163
Stowe, Lyman Beecher, 208
Swan, Caroline Davenport, 21, 24, 27, 32, 42, 62, 301
Swinburne, Algernon C., 5, 20, 27, 37, 100, 102, 103-4, 120, 193-4, 243
Symons, Arthur, 45

Tabb, John Bannister, 3
Tate, Allen, 106, 298
Teasdale, Sara, 292, 293, 294
Tennyson, Alfred Lord, 5, 20, 77, 92, 97, 98, 100, 140, 144, 226, 243, 261
Thackeray, William M., 20, 148
Thaxter, Celia, 3
Theis, Otto Frederick, 7, 9, 12, 15, 16, 262-8, 270
Thomas, Edith M., 3
Thompson, Francis, 5, 261
Thompson, Fred W., 247-8
Thompson, Vance, 16, 50, 102-3, 104
Thoreau, Henry David, 44
Thorne, William Henry, 5, 10, 16, 18, 24, 50, 61-3, 75, 96-9, 103, 107, 116, 127, 128-9, 277, 301
Time and the Hour, 34, 76, 78
Tolstoy, Leo, 267-9
Torrence, Ridgely, 94, 109, 111, 203-4, 208, 209, 211, 243, 252, 258, 260, 290, 302
Towne, Charles Hanson, 178, 225
T. P.'s Weekly, 204-5
Traubel, Horace L., 12, 27, 59, 112, 116
Trend, 298
Trent, William Peterfield, 6, 7, 11, 16, 54-6, 58, 86, 100, 200
Tryon, James L., 44-5, 162
Turner, Joseph William, 170

Untermeyer, Louis, 6, 9, 12, 294, 295-6, 298, 303-4

Valéry, Paul, 37
Van Doren, Mark, 20, 298
Van Dyke, Henry, 3, 75
Vannah, Kate, 23, 58, 62, 178

Variell, Arthur Davis, 42
Verhaeren, Emile, 5, 282, 283-4
Verlaine, Paul, 20, 31, 32
Verne, Jules, 20
Villon, François, 5, 32, 42, 57, 184, 225, 228
Virgil, 20-1, 21

W., M. L. B., 129
Ward, Elizabeth S. P., 44
Ward, Mrs. Humphry, 176, 226
Webster, Henry Sewall, 21, 24, 32, 62, 94, 301
Wells, H. G. 253, 255
Wendell, Barrett, 27, 64, 66
White, Gleeson, 57
Whitman, Walt, 3, 4, 5, 12, 20, 44, 57-8, 97, 98, 116, 117, 119, 141, 166, 184, 194, 236, 246, 299, 301

Whittier, John Greenleaf, 5, 14, 20, 245
Wiggin, Kate Douglas, 44
Wilcox, Ella Wheeler, 120, 121, 283
Wilkes-Barre *Times*, 79-84
Williams, Talcott, 112
Wister, Owen, 5, 261
Wood, Frederick S., 171
Wordsworth, William, 5, 12, 20, 48, 50, 87, 90, 102, 103, 120, 150, 152, 196, 255, 276, 277, 293-4

Yeats, William Butler, 3, 5, 37, 74, 117, 118
Young, Edward, 20
Youth's Companion, 24

Zola, Emile, 31, 32, 66

INDEX: ROBINSON'S WRITINGS

Aaron Stark, 14, 31, 32, 36, 74, 79, 83, 94, 192, 198, 201, 204, 216, 265
Amaryllis, 67, 88, 171
Annandale Again, 240
Antigone (Sophocles), 23-4, 101
As a World Would Have It, 101, 201
Au Revoir, 223, 259, 269
Aunt Imogen, 110, 120, 121-2, 138, 155, 245, 264, 280, 284
Avenel Gray (Mortmain), 243

Ballade by the Fire, 68, 88, 93
Ballade of a Ship (Ballade of the White Ship), 38, 57, 59, 68, 79, 180, 196
Ballade of Broken Flutes, 57, 68, 74, 170, 301
Ballade of Dead Friends, 40, 68, 120, 163, 196
Ballade of the White Ship (see Ballade of a Ship)
Balm of Custom, 163
Ben Jonson Entertains a Man From Stratford, 127
Bokardo, 243
Bon Voyage, 217
Book of Annandale, The (see also George Annandale), 110, 124, 130, 155, 201, 204, 238, 240, 264, 284, 286, 287, 289, 291, 295
Bores, 21
Boston, 56, 168, 189, 192, 250

Calvary, 66, 67
Calverley's, 209, 216-7, 220, 222, 223, 224, 226-7, 230, 231, 234, 281, 282

Captain Craig, 1, 2, 7, 8, 13, 16, 17, 37, 43, 59, 90, 99, 107-64, 165, 167, 176, 177, 178, 179, 181, 183, 192, 195, 204, 205, 208, 217, 239, 244, 245, 248, 252, 255, 258, 263, 270-96, 311
Captain Craig (The Pauper), 6, 9, 11, 12 14, 32, 101, 107-63, 192, 196, 201-3, 205, 239, 243, 247, 264-5, 276-91
Cassandra, 269, 295
Charles Carville's Eyes, 67, 83, 282
Children of the Night, The, 2, 10, 13, 14, 16, 17, 18, 44, 57, 60, 63, 65-106, 107, 108, 118, 119, 120, 124, 131, 133, 138, 140, 160, 165-207, 210, 214, 215, 216, 217, 218, 219, 224, 228, 239, 244, 248, 250, 251, 252, 255, 256, 258, 260, 261, 263, 291, 293
Children of the Night, The, 41, 42-3, 48, 55-6, 58, 68, 69, 73, 76-7, 79, 81, 85, 89, 92, 95, 96-7, 149, 200
Chorus of Old Men in "Aegeus", The, 101, 266, 267
Clavering, 32, 216, 218, 220, 227, 234, 240, 244, 250
Clerks, The, 24, 93, 101, 102, 103, 120, 163, 167, 192, 265
Cliff Klingenhagen, 13, 14, 15, 67, 74, 83, 88, 167, 198, 238, 265, 282
Collected Poems, 2, 42-3, 44, 57, 58, 63, 75, 85, 86, 95, 111, 233, 302
Corridor, The, 155
Cortège, 201, 287, 291
Credo, 60, 62, 81, 85

Dead Village, The, 25, 68, 74, 118, 189
Dear Friends, 23, 93, 160, 187

Erasmus, 110, 143, 184, 267
Eros Turannos, 243, 255

Field of Glory, The, 255, 261-2, 262, 272, 273, 286, 291, 295
First Seven Years, The, 64, 145, 161, 301
Flammonde, 134, 206, 295, 298
Fleming Helphenstine, 14, 67, 79, 83, 94, 198
For a Book by Thomas Hardy, 37-8, 55, 66, 69, 89, 93, 158, 200
For a Copy of Poe's Poems, 24, 34, 209, 270
For a Dead Lady, 217, 219, 228, 231, 234
For Arvia, 229, 302
For Calderon, 41, 43, 66, 67, 94
For Some Poems by Matthew Arnold, 36, 55, 89, 200

Galley Race, The, 21
Garden, The (God's Garden), 63, 99, 197
George Annandale (see also The Book of Annandale), 107, 110
George Crabbe, 55, 74, 75, 78, 82, 83, 86, 89, 101, 198, 200
Gift of God, The, 255
Glory of the Nightingales, The, 277
God's Garden (see The Garden)
Growth of "Lorraine", The, 110, 135, 155, 237

Her Eyes, 55, 93, 193
Horace to Leuconoë, 56, 58, 68, 200
House on the Hill, The, 24, 39, 42, 55, 59-60, 63, 99, 118, 120, 163, 170, 174-5, 184, 201, 204, 205, 206, 238, 301
How Annandale Went Out, 214, 238, 240

I Make No Measure of the Words They Say, 63, 99
In Harvard 5, 38, 196, 301
Isaac and Archibald, 11, 13, 42, 63, 108, 110, 112, 124, 125, 126, 128, 130, 138, 140, 143, 144, 150, 196, 245, 267, 277, 280, 287, 291
Island, An, 223, 232, 247, 250, 266, 282

James Wetherell, 14, 95, 266
John Evereldown, 14, 32, 79, 94, 103, 134, 167, 198, 238, 244, 250

King Jasper, 1
Klondike, The, 110, 119, 120, 126, 138, 280, 284, 294
Kosmos, 42, 63, 99

Lancelot, 273
Leffingwell, 15, 32, 216, 218, 220, 238, 282
L'Envoi, 66, 67, 68, 84, 92, 93
Leonora, 220, 223, 231, 247
Lingard and the Stars, 216, 218, 220, 247, 282
Luke Havergal, 14, 39, 42, 48, 79, 83, 84, 86, 101, 103, 120, 163, 170, 172, 174, 186, 196, 198, 263, 266, 282

Man Against the Sky, The, 1, 12, 269, 273, 293, 297, 298, 299, 300
Man Against the Sky, The, 43, 58
Many Are Called, 206
Master (Lincoln), The, 206, 207, 220, 222, 227, 232, 235-6, 239, 243, 246, 250, 252, 259, 276
Menoetes, 38, 196
Miniver Cheevy, 15, 17, 32, 134, 206, 214, 216, 218, 220, 227, 238, 241, 243, 245, 250
Miracle, The, 24, 40, 42, 63, 93, 99
Momus, 48, 90, 233
Mortmain (see Avenel Gray)
Mulieria, 21

Neighbors, 16
Night Before, The, 6, 23, 35, 41, 43, 46-7, 56, 58, 60, 68-9, 84, 86, 87, 89, 93, 104, 168, 188, 196, 197, 201, 204, 218, 282
Normandy, 223

Octaves, 63, 66, 67, 74, 75, 80, 81, 82, 83, 85, 86, 86-7, 88, 90, 92, 95, 99, 102-3, 112, 158, 188, 190, 197, 264
Old King Cole, 295
Old Story, An, 36, 55, 190

Partnership (see also The Wife of Palissy), 292
Pasa Thalassa Thalassa, 217, 218-9, 220, 221, 223
Pilot, The, 223, 269
Pity of the Leaves, The, 67, 92, 120, 163, 171
Poem for Max Nordau, A, 13, 36, 37, 41, 43, 55, 57, 67, 88-9, 94, 301
Porcupine, The, 2, 13, 246, 271, 272

Rahel to Varnhagen, 281
Return of Morgan and Fingal, The, 6, 110, 128, 129, 144-5, 152, 289, 291
Reuben Bright, 14, 67, 78, 83, 86, 94, 198, 216, 238, 250, 265, 282
Revealer, The, 223, 258-9, 269
Richard Cory, 13, 14, 32, 66, 67, 73-4, 74, 75, 79, 170, 192, 198, 201, 204, 205, 206, 238, 247, 250, 261
Romance (see also James Wetherell), 66, 67, 94, 94-5

Sage, The, 110, 149, 184
Sainte-Nitouche, 110, 124, 130, 138, 155, 201, 284, 289
Scattered Lives, 23
Shadrach O'Leary, 216, 228, 238, 243
Shiras, 110
Shooting Stars, 63, 99
Sonnet (The master and the slave), 83
Sonnet (Oh for a poet), 24, 36, 37, 50, 51, 55, 60, 82, 86, 159, 188, 266
Sonnet (When we can all), 68, 86, 180, 197
Story of the Ashes and the Flame, The, 67
Supremacy, 22, 38, 61-2, 63, 103, 196

Tasker Norcross, 32
Tavern, The, 67, 171, 173
Tavern and The Night Before, The, 25
Tavern Songs, 25, 42, 210
Thalia, 21, 58
Thomas Hood, 22, 36, 55, 63, 68, 83, 89, 93, 99
Three Quatrains, 41, 197
Torrent and The Night Before, The, 1, 2, 4, 6, 8, 10, 11, 11-2, 12, 13, 16-7, 17, 18, 23-64, 65, 66, 67, 68, 69, 75, 76, 84, 85, 86, 91, 93, 95, 96, 97, 99, 104, 105, 107, 116, 119, 120, 131, 149, 157, 159-60, 161, 178, 179, 180-1, 193, 200, 204, 211, 218, 224, 246, 251, 255, 256, 260, 278, 293, 307
Torrent, The, 43, 44, 49, 69, 188
Town Down the River, The, 2, 8, 16, 17, 164, 207, 208-69, 270, 276, 289, 291, 299, 302
Town Down the River, The, 129, 217, 218, 220, 231, 241, 248, 251, 281, 282
Tristram, 228
Twilight Song, 110, 118, 120, 122, 126, 134-5, 138, 139, 149, 183, 184, 276, 287, 288
Two Gardens in Linndale, 217, 219
Two Men, 13, 67, 74, 88, 134
Two Quatrains, 67, 263-4
Two Sonnets, 41, 68, 83, 86

Uncle Ananias, 32, 157, 167, 216, 218, 222, 224, 234, 247, 250

Van Zorn, 2, 13, 246, 271, 272, 273, 282, 286
Variations of Greek Themes, 101, 280, 284, 286, 287, 288, 290, 291, 295
Verlaine, 25, 51, 55, 81, 83, 85, 89, 93, 101, 190, 200
Vickery's Mountain, 216, 217, 219
Villanelle of Change, 38, 170, 196

Walt Whitman, 59, 60, 83, 93, 101, 204
White Lights, The, 101, 217, 219, 222, 232, 250, 279
Wife of Palissy, The (see also Partnership), 110, 289
Wilderness, The, 39-40, 42, 56, 118, 138, 171, 174, 182
Woman and the Wife, The, 110, 123, 287
World, The, 93, 149, 267
Wreath for Edwin Markham, A, 206

Zola, 36, 59, 83, 89, 93